797,885 Books

are available to read at

www.ForgottenBooks.com

Forgotten Books' App
Available for mobile, tablet & eReader

ISBN 978-1-330-37477-1
PIBN 10043715

This book is a reproduction of an important historical work. Forgotten Books uses state-of-the-art technology to digitally reconstruct the work, preserving the original format whilst repairing imperfections present in the aged copy. In rare cases, an imperfection in the original, such as a blemish or missing page, may be replicated in our edition. We do, however, repair the vast majority of imperfections successfully; any imperfections that remain are intentionally left to preserve the state of such historical works.

Forgotten Books is a registered trademark of FB &c Ltd.
Copyright © 2017 FB &c Ltd.
FB &c Ltd, Dalton House, 60 Windsor Avenue, London, SW19 2RR.
Company number 08720141. Registered in England and Wales.

For support please visit www.forgottenbooks.com

1 MONTH OF
FREE
READING

at

www.ForgottenBooks.com

By purchasing this book you are eligible for one month membership to ForgottenBooks.com, giving you unlimited access to our entire collection of over 700,000 titles via our web site and mobile apps.

To claim your free month visit:

www.forgottenbooks.com/free43715

* Offer is valid for 45 days from date of purchase. Terms and conditions apply.

English
Français
Deutsche
Italiano
Español
Português

www.forgottenbooks.com

Mythology Photography **Fiction**
Fishing Christianity **Art** Cooking
Essays Buddhism Freemasonry
Medicine **Biology** Music **Ancient**
Egypt Evolution Carpentry Physics
Dance Geology **Mathematics** Fitness
Shakespeare **Folklore** Yoga Marketing
Confidence Immortality Biographies
Poetry **Psychology** Witchcraft
Electronics Chemistry History **Law**
Accounting **Philosophy** Anthropology
Alchemy Drama Quantum Mechanics
Atheism Sexual Health **Ancient History**
Entrepreneurship Languages Sport
Paleontology Needlework Islam
Metaphysics Investment Archaeology
Parenting Statistics Criminology
Motivational

SKETCHES IN HISTORY

CHIEFLY ECCLESIASTICAL

BY

L. C. CASARTELLI

BISHOP OF SALFORD

R. & T. WASHBOURNE

4 PATERNOSTER ROW, LONDON

BENZIGER BROS.: NEW YORK, CINCINNATI AND CHICAGO

1906

TO

THE RIGHT REV.

ADOLPHE HEBBELYNCK, D.D.,

RECTOR MAGNIFICUS OF MY ALMA MATER

THE UNIVERSITY OF LOUVAIN

BY KIND PERMISSION

DEDICATED.

PREFACE

THE sketches here reprinted, with few exceptions, appeared originally in the pages of the *Dublin Review.*

They do not pretend to be in any way original contributions, but merely amateur essays in a few of the more or less unfamiliar by-ways of history, chiefly ecclesiastical, based upon modern writers, whose books are indicated. The only excuse for their republication is in the hope that they may prove of some interest to Catholic readers, and especially that they may stimulate in some of our ecclesiastical students a taste for historical reading and study—so urgent a need at the present day. For this purpose I have added a list of the best books that may be consulted on each subject as an incentive to further research.

The article numbered IV. was originally published by the C.T.S.; No. IX. appeared in the *Rosary;* No. XIII. in the *Tablet;* whilst No. X. was first issued as a separate pamphlet. The rest appeared in the *Dublin.* To the Editors of the latter review and of the other periodicals just mentioned I return my thanks for permission to reprint.

I have in every case endeavoured, by suitable modifications, to bring the essays up to date by the aid of more recent publications, and have sometimes partly recast them.

For the excellent index I am deeply indebted to my former pupil, Mr. Joseph Lomax, of Oscott College.

✠ L. C. C.

ST. BEDE'S COLLEGE,
September 15, 1905.

CONTENTS

		PAGE
I.	THE ART OF BURIAL	1
II.	THE LOMBARDS	26
III.	THE ENGLISH POPE	52
IV.	THE CHURCH AND THE PRINTING-PRESS	90
V.	THE DUTCH POPE	104
VI.	THE ENGLISH UNIVERSITIES AND THE REFORMATION	154
VII.	TWO ENGLISH SCHOLARS AND THE BEGINNINGS OF ORIENTAL STUDIES IN LOUVAIN	186
VIII.	OXFORD AND LOUVAIN	197
IX.	THE LITANY OF LORETO AND ITS HISTORY	222
X.	A FORGOTTEN CHAPTER OF THE SECOND SPRING	238
XI.	THE MAKERS OF THE *DUBLIN*	269
XII.	THE CATHOLIC CHURCH IN JAPAN	300
XIII.	THE DANCING PROCESSION AT ECHTERNACH	344
	APPENDIX	354
	INDEX	355

SKETCHES IN HISTORY

I

THE ART OF BURIAL

If my illustrious townsman Thomas de Quincey was justified in entitling one of his most famous essays "On Murder as a Fine Art," perhaps I, too, may plead justification for the title I have ventured to give to the present essay.

Murder, indeed, may be fittingly described as a "fine art," in the sense that it is not a necessity of human life, but, as the cynic might say, rather a luxury—an unnecessary luxury—of civilization. Burial, on the other hand,—or, to put it more exactly, the disposal of the remains of our dead—is pre-eminently a "useful art"; nay, oftentimes one of the most necessary of all. The dead we have always with us. The most cultured nation of the twentieth century, as well as the most degraded savage horde of Africa or Australia; the men of the earliest dawn of human history at the beginning of the Stone Age, as well as those who shall be on earth long after our own time; of whatever race, tongue, religion, degree of civilization, epoch of history, or region of the habitable globe—all have been, are, and ever will be constantly face to face with the problem: what to do with the remains of their dead? To say nothing of the philosophical or religious beliefs or theories involved, the mere exigencies of sanitary needs are perpetually pressing this problem upon the attention of the survivors. And the more men prosper and multiply, the more great civilizations are built up, the more imperious becomes the necessity for a solution of the problem. And in this man is at once differentiated from the lower animals. Man, it will be remembered, has been ingeniously defined as "the only animal that cooks its food." We may venture to offer yet another definition: Man is the only animal that buries its dead.

So much for the importance of the subject, which has been dealt with in an exhaustive manner by a Belgian Catholic writer, a physician of distinction, Dr. Isidore Bauwens. His work, entitled "History and Description of Funeral and Mourning Customs among the Principal Nations," was published in Brussels in 1888. Unfortunately, this meritorious volume has attracted little if any notice, owing to the fact that it is written in Flemish, and so not generally accessible to the reading public. It deserves, however, to be more widely read, for, as far as I can judge, it not only contains a store of really interesting facts, but its able writer has gathered his materials with commendable diligence from the most recent and best authenticated sources, and hence may be relied upon as a trustworthy authority. The present paper is little else than a brief analysis of Dr. Bauwens' book, with a selection of some of his innumerable facts, and, following him, I shall attempt to lay before the reader, in historical form, a sketch of what is known of the various methods of disposing of the dead practised by the chief races of mankind in ancient as in modern times. The remarks or additions of my own are few and far between. As my task is purely expository, the reader will understand that I do not necessarily commit myself to all the theories or views enunciated by the author whom I have the pleasure of introducing to English readers.

I.

It may be useful to recall that, according to the conclusions of modern geologists, man made his first appearance on earth during the Quarternary period of geological history, and in that part of it which is known as the "Palæolithic," or Old Stone Age, from the fact that, in the absence of any knowledge of the metals, these prehistoric races made use of weapons and implements of roughly-hewn or split flint. Several races of man, distinguished by the physical characters of their remains, inhabited the greater part of Europe, portions of Asia and Africa, and of North America, during this period. It is customary to distinguish these races by the name of the localities where the most typical specimens of their remains have been found. Let us mention the three principal of these: (1) The "Canstadt," or "Neanderthal," or "Spy race," inhabiting especially the valleys of the Rhine and Seine, and probably extending to Italy and Bohemia—men of gigantic stature, dolichocephalous, with low receding brows, and skulls pointed behind, evidently savages of brutal appearance, and contemporaries of the great extinct quadrupeds which once roamed over Europe. (2) In strong contrast to these, the so-called "Crô-Magnon race," inhabiting South-West France, Italy, and the valley of the Meuse, gigantic in stature, and dolichocephalous like the former, but of handsome and intellectual appearance. These must have existed in Europe long after the Canstadt race, for, at least in the fourth of the progressive stages of their history which have been distinguished by archæologists, all the great mammalia, except the mammoth and the rhinoceros, had disappeared, while the reindeer browsed peacefully over the greater part of Europe. With these Crô-Magnon men appear, too, the earliest traces of human art, the curious outlines of mammoth or reindeer upon fragments of ivory or horn, which may be seen in some of our museums. (3) Contemporaneously with the race just described, portions of modern Belgium were inhabited by the small, squat, brachycephalic race, very like the modern Lapps, who are perhaps their descendants, known to science as the " Furfooz race."

Now, of *all* the above races of the Palæolithic period—the earliest human races of which Science has been able to find any trace—one broad statement may be made: that they all practised burial of the dead, in many cases with conspicuous care and the accompaniment of tokens of respect and veneration, and that no single trace of cremation in any form appears.

A great gap separates the period we have described from that known as the " Neolithic " or Polished Stone Age. Great changes of surface have by this time taken place. The sea, which had covered the modern Netherlands, has retired and left the flat country as it now exists. The race of men who occupy Europe has attained a very much higher level of culture. Together with the much finer, polished, or worked flint implements, has come in the practice of agriculture and other arts of life.

This is the period, too, of the " Lake Dwellers," who in the lakes of Switzerland, as well as those of Lombardy, Austria, and parts of Germany, built their curious villages, raised on piles above the surface of the water. But what particularly distinguishes the Neolithic period is that it was a time of the great stone buildings, the age of the well-known dolmens, cromlechs, menhirs, barrows, or mounds, scattered over England, Ireland, France, Scandinavia, and North America, and which, as Mr. E. B. Tyler writes, " may be traced in a remarkable line on the map from India across to North Africa, and up to the west side of Europe." I perhaps hardly need remind the reader of the wonderful monument of Stonehenge in this country. It is now pretty well established that nearly all, if not all, these curious stone erections, in their various forms and under their varied names, were nothing else than funeral monuments, vast graves, sometimes, as in the great burial mound of Karlby, in Gothland, still containing as many as eighty skeletons. It is remarkable that in the majority of these graves the bodies are found in the sitting or crouching position, which, as we shall see later on, is so common in many other parts of the world. The bodies of those buried in these structures are generally surrounded with a large number of weapons, ornaments, trinkets, and amulets.

Now, it is to be remarked that, though the great stone monuments of this age bear witness to the universality of inhumation, it is precisely in the same period that the first traces of the practice of cremation begin to appear, and this is also true with regard to the Lake Dwellings already referred to. But the practice was undoubtedly as yet only exceptional, and in some cases inhumated bodies and the ashes of those that have been cremated appear in one and the same grave.

Let me here add a remark with reference to both of the prehistoric periods with which we have already dealt. There are evidences in many sepultures of both the Palæolithic and Neolithic periods that some at least of the races practised that extraordinary custom which is still found among several widely scattered peoples of the present day—that, namely, of stripping the bodies of the dead of the flesh before the burial of the bones, which latter are occasionally found painted with a red colour. The meaning or object of this strange custom, whether ancient or modern, has not, as far as I know, been satisfactorily explained.

I must claim my reader's indulgence for a few moments whilst I refer in some detail to the remarkable and instructive discoveries of my distinguished friends MM. Henri and Louis Siret of Antwerp, two brilliant young students of the University of Louvain, whose explorations in the South of Spain a few years ago, as described by themselves before the British Association in Manchester in 1887, caused quite a sensation in scientific circles, so extensive were their discoveries, and so enormous the amount of objects, especially in silver, which rewarded their excavations. Suffice it to say briefly that these discoveries of innumerable traces of prehistoric man, his homes and workmanship, covered the Neolithic period, a period of transition, and a metal period. In the transition period MM. Siret discovered distinct traces of the influences of a foreign invasion, either hostile or mercantile and pacific, shown by the gradual admixture of bronze with stone implements. It is instructive to observe that together with this introduction of bronze appears also, for the first time, the practice of cremation, leading to the plausible conclusion that the metal and the new practice had one and the same source. It is also noticeable that ornaments are found only with the inhumated bodies, and probably only with females. Of the Third or Metal Age—so rich in silver that it might almost be called a Silver Age—MM. Siret discovered no less than fifteen entire villages, and in these villages they were able to explore with the greatest care as many as 1,300 burial-places. The remarkable thing is that during this period all traces of the practice of cremation *had disappeared*. The men of the period had returned to the primeval custom of inhumation; and, strangely enough, the graves as a general rule were beneath the floors of the houses themselves—a custom not unknown in other parts of the world. In four-fifths of the cases the bodies were found in the crouching, knee-to-chin attitude above referred to, packed in large earthen jars, sometimes with a hermetically-sealed cover, sometimes two such jars being joined mouth to mouth, and often two bodies, generally one of either sex, in the same jar. With the bodies, too, were found the remains of food, such as bones of oxen, also copper axes, and quantities of trinkets, especially in virgin silver.*

From all the facts, of which the above is a very meagre

* Mr. James McCarthy, of the Siamese Survey, informed MM. Siret and myself, at the British Association meeting referred to, that similar funeral jars are found in parts of Siam.

summary, Dr. Bauwens, whom I am still following, draws two general conclusions — namely — (1) To the earliest races the practice of cremation was unknown; (2) this practice came in with the race of the great stone-builders, who probably were also the introducers of the first of all known metals, bronze. The question at once occurs, Who were these people? Did they constitute one race or many? They must have been a people in whom the passion of wandering was strongly developed, for their structures are to be found in the Crimea, Southern Russia, Denmark, Sweden, Holland, England, Ireland, France, Spain, Germany, Africa, Palestine, India. Even their path may be traced. "It is evident," writes Felitzin, "that the dolmen builders travelled from the eastern to the northern shores of the Black Sea, where the Crimea offers a similar series of buildings." From Scandinavia, too, the dolmen followed the coast of Western Europe to Portugal, turned back by Marseilles, and along the valleys of the Rhône and Saône, eventually reached to near Berlin. Dr. Bauwens, following in this such authorities as Fergusson, Hamard, and d'Estienne, believes that this race was no other than that of the Kelts, or, at least, was an Aryan or Indo-Germanic people. And the same conclusion is pretty generally accepted for the contemporary Lake Dwellers, whom so eminent an authority as O. Schrader finds to be characteristically Aryan. (See his "Prehistoric Antiquities of the Aryan Peoples," part iv., chap. xi.) If the objection be made that these structures apparently belong to a period considerably before the great Aryan migration, our author answers that it is not at all impossible that detached tribes or hordes of Aryan wanderers, whether Keltic or otherwise, may, even during the earliest portions of the Neolithic period, have found their way into far distant parts of Europe, carrying with them the custom of cremation, as well as the knowledge of metal, to the less cultured or less gifted races among whom they established themselves.

II.

The thesis which underlies the whole of Dr. Bauwens' work is therefore this:

"The Aryans were the originators of cremation. All nations of Aryan origin made use of the funeral pyre. . . . On the other hand, cremation was unknown to the non-Aryan races, with the exception of a few peoples like the Japanese and Mexicans, among whom, however, the practice never attained such dimensions as it did with the Aryans."

It must not be thought that this theory is by any means new. Years ago Adolphe Pictet wrote in his "Origines Indo-Européennes":

"The most evident result of the researches of J. Grimm is that, without any exception, cremation from the remotest period had prevailed over inhumation among the Aryan peoples. The Indians, Greeks, Romans, Gauls, ancient Germans, Lithuanians, and the heathen Slavs, cremated their dead with certain ceremonies, which, in spite of their differences, offer unquestionable traits of agreement. The Eranians alone, on account of the great change which occurred in their religious beliefs, early on abandoned this ancient usage. For the nations of Europe it was Christianity that put a stop to cremation. This latter method of disposing of the dead was never practised by the Hebrews, Arabs, or Mohammedans in general. Such an agreement at once leads us to suspect a common origin dating from before the separation of the Aryans. Indeed, although the custom of burning the dead may be found here and there among other races of men (*e.g.*, Japanese and Mexicans), yet it never attained the same extension as in the Aryan family. The custom, as Grimm has pointed out, must have had its beginning in the earliest times of their pastoral life, before their departure from their nomadic home, for it enabled them to carry with them on their journeys the revered ashes of their dead."

It now becomes of importance and interest to inquire a little more fully into the funeral customs of the Aryans themselves. At this point I must beg to be allowed to decline entering into the fascinating discussion regarding the cradle-land of our Aryan ancestors, to which notable contributions were made in this country some years ago by Professor Sayce, Dr. Isaac Taylor, and Professor Rendal, of University College, Liverpool, on the one side, and by Professor Max Müller on the other.* The question, however, will not directly affect our present investigation.

To return: the evidence for the prevalence of cremation among the earliest Aryans before their separation is twofold—from language and from custom. On the philological side, it is curious that the first and strongest evidence is furnished by the language of that very branch of the Aryan family which we know to have abandoned both cremation and inhumation from religious motives—namely, the Eranians. For the very name of the repositories for their dead, which is to be found in their sacred book, the Avesta itself, and which has survived unaltered among their descendants up to the present day, is *dakhma*, clearly referable to the well-known Aryan root *dah*, to burn, and therefore originally signifying nothing else than "a burning place." A curious analogy is furnished by the Keltic, wherein we are told the word *adnacul*, or *adhnachd*, signifies burial-place, whilst a comparison with the negative adjective *neph-adhnachte*, "unburnable," shows that the original meaning of the word also involves the idea of cremation.

The Latin *funus*, again, seems clearly connected with the root *dhû*, appearing both in Sanskrit, and in the Latin *fumus*, "smoke." The connection, again, of *bustum*, signifying a tomb, with the old verb *buro* (still preserved in the compound *comburo*) is self-evident. It is sug-

* The best summary of the controversy and the most satisfactory refutation of the theories of European origin are to be found in several publications of the Rev. Père van den Gheyn, S.J., of Brussels.

gested, moreover, that the Greek *θύμβος* may be connected with the root *dhû* above referred to, and some writers have seen in *σῆμα* (a mound or barrow, grave, or gravestone, or also any mark or sign) the analogue of the Sanskrit *kshâma*, burning, from the root *kshâ*.

If we now turn to what literature and history have preserved us of the funeral customs of the ancient civilized Aryan nations, especially the Hindus, Greeks, and Romans, we shall find a superabundant amount of material, from which we can only afford time to glean a very few particulars.

The Rig Veda contains plentiful details of the funeral ritual in use among the early Aryan conquerors of India. From it we learn how the funeral pyre was built of carefully chosen and valuable woods, especially the *dêvadâru* (deodar, or divine tree). When the body, carefully prepared, had been reverently laid upon the pyre, the attendants thrice walked to the left around it—the so-called *prâsavya* rite, whose object was apparently to drive away evil spirits. When the fire had been set to the pile, a black cow or a black goat was brought forward and sacrificed, and the priest placed a kidney of the victim in each hand of the corpse, reciting meanwhile a verse from the Veda praying for the safe journey of the deceased in the nether world, and his protection from the two dread hounds of Yama. At this moment the widow stepped up to the pyre and laid herself down beside her husband. She was not, however, in Vedic times suffered to burn; for she was called away in the words of a Vedic hymn (R. V., x. 18, 8): "Rise up, O woman! come back to the world of the living! Thou art lying by one who is dead. Thy marriage with him is at an end." The cruel custom of "suttee," as it became called, or widow-burning, so prevalent for centuries all over India, and which our Government has had so much difficulty in repressing, is an abuse of later date, and utterly repugnant to the precepts and spirit of the most sacred of the Indian books. Strange to say, like an inverted pyramid, the whole vast structure of centuries of inhuman cruelty rests for its authority upon a single textual corruption—namely, the substitution of an *n* for an *r* in R. V., x. 18, 6 (ag*n*eh for ag*r*e). Finally, when, after the recital of many hymns, the body had been entirely reduced to ashes, these were carefully gathered together, and enclosed in an urn called *kumbha*.

I will not weary the reader with many details about the parallel descriptions to be found in the classical literature of Greece and Rome. The building of the funeral pyre as described by Homer and Virgil will occur to all, as also the triple running round the pile :

> Αὐτὰρ ἔπειτα
> τρὶς περὶ χαλκείοις σὺν τεύχεσι δινηθέντες
> τύμβῳ ἐνεκτερέϊξαν.*

Again, the slaughtering of black cattle occurs as an incident in the funeral rites of Greeks and Romans (*e.g.*, "Æneid," v. 97, vi. 243). Instead of the kidneys given by the Hindus, the Greeks put honey-cake in the hands of the deceased, wherewith to satisfy Pluto's three-headed hell-hound, Cerberus. The funeral-urns of Greeks and Romans are too well known to need further comment.

After speaking thus in detail of the crematory rites of the ancient Aryan peoples, it is curious to be reminded that in all probability, even among them, inhumation originally preceded cremation. Not only so, but it appears that the two rites existed side by side in Vedic times, and such is the conclusion of no less eminent authorities than Grimm, O. Schrader, and Zimmer. The last-named points out that in the Rig Veda the hymn R. V., x. 16, describes the disposal of the dead by cremation, whilst R. V., x. 18, describes the same by inhumation. Perhaps, as Pictet surmised, cremation was practised chiefly for the rich and noble, whilst the

* Apollodorus of Rhodes, "Argonauts," i. 1059 (compare "Iliad," xxiii. 13; "Odyssey," xxiv. 68; Virgil, "Æneid," xi. 188).

commoner folk had to be content with ordinary earth-burial.

If we may believe the testimony of Plutarch and Ælian, burial in the earth was the earliest method of disposing of the dead among the Greeks. During the Trojan War cremation seems to have become general, but, according to the legend, Herakles was the first to burn a body and preserve the ashes in an urn. In Homer the heroes are cremated with great pomp and ceremony, whilst the common warriors, as in Virgil, are merely buried. In 888 B.C. the practice of cremation was condemned by Lycurgus. Under Solon, in 600 B.C., burial in the earth appears to be the ordinary Athenian custom. According to Thucydides, the Pythagoreans committed the remains of their deceased to the earth, and the heroes who fell at Marathon (490 B.C.), as well as those slain at Platæa, were also reverently committed to the earth. In fact, the nearer we approach the Christian era, the more abundant become the evidences that inhumation was again steadily supplanting the practice of cremation.

With reference to the old Romans, we have the explicit tradition preserved by Pliny—"Ipsum cremare apud Romanos non fuit veteris instituti ; terra condebantur" (lib. vii., c. 54)—a testimony confirmed by Cicero ("De Legibus," ii. 22). In fact, the early Romans, like the silver-workers in prehistoric Spain, actually buried their dead beneath the hearths of their houses. It is evident, however, that from very early times both cremation and inhumation were practised side by side, for the Laws of the XII. Tables contain the express sanitary regulation : "Hominem mortuum in urbe ne sepelito neve urito." That burial was esteemed honourable, and, indeed, preferred by the noblest families during the palmy days of the Republic, appears from the magnificent graves along the Via Appia, wherein during our own times the entire bodies of many of the Scipios, notably of L. Cornelius Scipio Barbatus (Consul 298 B.C.), have been discovered (A.D. 1870). The custom of cremation appears to have been rendered popular by Sulla, who ordered the cremation of his own body, probably to prevent its being exhumed and dishonoured, after the manner in which he had treated the remains of his great rival Marius. From that time onward, and particularly under the Empire, cremation gained the upper hand, until, as in other parts of Europe, it was swept away by Christianity.

III.

I have above referred to the peculiar position taken up in this matter by one of the most celebrated branches of the Aryan family—I mean the Eranians. It is true that, as the word *dakhma*, already quoted, bears witness, cremation was in common vogue among them in the earliest times. It is also true that the Achaemenid Kings of ancient Persia, Cyrus and his successors, were buried in the earth. But it is likewise true that to that branch of the Eranian people which adopted the religious reform of Zarathushtra or Zoroaster both inhumation and cremation were entirely abhorrent. In their dualistic system earth and fire were sacred elements belonging to the realm of the good principle Ahura-Mazda. Death, on the other hand, caused the possession of the human body by the impure demon Naçus, one of the spirits belonging to the legions of the evil principle Angro-Mainyus. Hence the contact of a corpse was polluting in the highest degree, and to allow it to sully the elements of fire or earth or water was a sacrilege of the gravest kind. Strange indeed was the method excogitated by the Mazdean theologians for escaping from this dilemma—the same, indeed, as that practised by their lineal descendants, the Parsis of Bombay, at the present day. The bodies of the deceased were exposed in such a manner that the "four-footed or two-footed scavengers of Ahura-Mazda"—dogs, namely, and birds of prey—might consume all the soft portions of the human frame; and this stripping of the bones and leaving them clean and white was held to be a process of purification. It is not unlikely that the Eranians borrowed this strange custom from some of their Turanian neighbours, for there are still forms of it in use among some of the Mongolian peoples, notably in the Steppes of Tibet. The rite above described may be seen to the present day, scrupulously observed in all its fulness, in the so-called Towers of Silence, the *dakhmas* of the Parsis, outside of Bombay. In a paper contributed in 1890 to the *Babylonian and Oriental Record*, and since republished in a small pamphlet on "The Marriage and Funeral Customs of Ancient Persia," I venture to think that I have satisfactorily cleared up certain difficulties surrounding the passage in the Avesta (Vend., vi. 49-51), which contains the authoritative directions of the legislator for the disposal of the dead. I have there shown that, after the body had been thus stripped of its fleshy parts, the skeleton was to be carefully deposited in one of three kinds of receptacles—either in stone urns, or in concrete urns, or in cloth bags. Only in case of poverty, when the above *astodâns*, or bone receptacles, could not be procured, were the bleached bones to be left exposed on the bedding of the deceased in an elevated place.

Another of the great Aryan religions has played an important part in influencing funeral customs in the Eastern world. One of the most famous cremations on record is that of Buddha, and Buddhism has always adopted cremation as its special method of disposing of the dead. Hence it would appear that the spread of Buddhism has been the cause of the spread of cremation also in Ceylon, Siam, Burma, etc. In China, however, except in Buddhist monasteries, the custom has not succeeded in supplanting the old Chinese rite of committing the dead to Mother Earth. In fact, it may be said that the Chinese are pre-eminently a nation of earth-buriers, and it is well known what enormous importance even those who have emigrated to America attach to the privilege of having their mortal remains restored to their native soil.

A very interesting series of articles on "Ladak (or Little Tibet) and Ladaki Buddhism," by Father Henry Hanlon, of Leh (now Bishop Hanlon, of Uganda), published in *Illustrated Catholic Missions* (vol. ix., 1894-95), contains some exceedingly curious details of the funeral customs of that Tibetan country. The writer tells us that the *phos-spun*, or hereditary undertaker, ties up the corpse with ropes in the crouching knee-to-chin attitude already referred to, in as small a space as possible. After several days of elaborate religious rites, the corpse, shrouded in a cotton bag, is carried on the back of the chief mourner to the cemetery, where it is eventually burned in a kind of oven, amid ritual chanting.

"The reading and chanting continue until the first bone falls from the smouldering pyre; this bone is taken to the religious room in the house of the deceased, and pounded into dust, which is mixed with clay and moulded into a small image, called *thsathsa.* If the deceased was wealthy, a large cenotaph—*chorten*—is erected to receive the *thsathsa.* The poor deposit their image in old cenotaphs."

The following passage is also significant:

"In districts where wood is scarce the bodies are exposed to be devoured by eagles and ravens. According to General Cunningham, in Greater Tibet the dead are cut up and thrown to the dogs; this is called a 'terrestrial funeral.' But when the bones are bruised and mixed with parched corn, which is made into balls and thrown to the dogs, this is called a 'celestial funeral.'"

It will at once occur to the reader that, as we have hinted above, these details of the funeral rites of Central Asia probably serve to indicate whence the Eranians borrowed many of their strange and exceptional customs as recorded in the Avesta and subsequent literature.

But we are wandering somewhat from our subject. Let us return for a moment to the Aryans. Among the ancient Gauls, as with the more civilized of their sister races, both cremation and inhumation were practised. The same may be said of the Germans and the Scandinavians, but with all these, particularly with the last-named, yet a third method was employed—that of water-burial. Sometimes, as in the case of the Visigoths under Alaric, they buried their dead in the beds of rivers, in order to preserve them from exhumation and desecration by their enemies. In other cases water-burial was a result of the maritime predilections of the seafaring races. The corpse, bound round in woollen garments, and surrounded with all kinds of ornaments and implements, was laid out in a boat, and afterwards sunk out at sea. Sometimes, again, these sepulchral boats were buried in the earth itself. For English readers I can recommend on this interesting subject of Scandinavian burial the beautifully-illustrated work of Mr. Paul du Chaillu, entitled "The Viking Age" (London, 1889; see vol. i., chap. xix.). Boat-burial, however, is by no means confined to the Scandinavians, but is to be found up and down the world among the most different races.

IV.

As in so many other things, the Semitic races present a striking contrast to their Aryan neighbours in this question of the disposal of their dead. If the Aryans on the whole may be called a cremating race, and probably even the originators of cremation, the Semites are distinctively a non-cremating, an earth-burying race. This is emphatically true of their great empires in antiquity. Modern research has shown that the Assyrian and Babylonian Empires had their great burial-grounds in the ancient land of Lower Chaldæa, the plain that lies to the north of the Persian Gulf, especially at Warka and Mugheir. Indeed, the whole region may be called a vast cemetery, and every hill from Mugheir to the confluence of the Tigris and Euphrates is an accumulation of graves.

In all these Chaldean burial-places the bodies, like those of the prehistoric inhabitants of South-West Spain, are enclosed in great jars of earthenware—a custom, for the rest, which is also to be found in many parts of America, in Japan, and in Africa.

Peculiar interest, of course, attaches to the manners and customs of the people of Israel, and it has been maintained that cremation was not only in use, but also was held in honour, among them. This contention is not, however, borne out by an examination of Biblical history or antiquity. On the contrary, the Sacred Records show that from the time of the patriarchs onward the practice of burial was universal. It is maintained that the bodies of Saul and his sons were burnt (1 Kings xxxi. 12, 13). Jeremiah, too, says to Zedekiah, "Thou shalt die in peace, and according to the *burnings* of thy fathers the former kings that were before thee, so shall they burn thee" (Jer. xxxiv. 5). But even if we were to grant these cases of the cremation of some of the kings, it is evident from the overwhelming testimony of the other portions of Holy Scripture that in the vast majority of cases the deceased of the chosen people, especially their patriarchs, prophets, and kings, were buried, not burned. As a matter of fact, however, in spite of the agreement of the Vulgate with the Anglican A.V. and R.V., the above texts are merely instances of mistranslation. There is excellent lexicographical authority to show that the verb שָׂרַף translated above by "burn," really signifies here, not to cremate, but, constructed as it is with the preposition לְ—in other words, with the dative—to burn incense in honour of a person, a meaning strongly borne out by the parallel passages in Chronicles—*e.g.*, 2 Chron. xvi. 14, "And they buried (Asa) in his own sepulchres which he had hewn out for himself in the city of David, and laid him in the bed which was filled with sweet odours, and divers kinds of spices prepared by the apothecary's art, and they *made a very great burning* (שְׂרֵפָה) for (לְ) him." It is a very strong confirmation of this view that in all these passages the LXX. translates the verb in question by ἔκλαυσαν—they mourned or lamented. The testimony of written records is supported by the numberless ancient graves still to be seen in every part of the Holy Land, and especially about Jerusalem, to mention only Makpelah, the grave of the fathers, the well-known burying-place of the kings, and the graves of the prophets in the sides of the Mount of Olives. We are, therefore, justified in concluding that the Jews are no exception to the general rule that the Semites were essentially a burying, and not a cremating, race.

We cannot now make quite as broad a statement with reference to that other celebrated branch of the Semitic family—I mean the greatest mercantile nation of antiquity, the Phœnicians. It has hitherto been universally admitted that the Phœnicians never burnt, but always buried, their dead—generally, indeed, in curious coffins of human form. However, the year after the publication of Dr. Bauwens' work a curious discovery was made at Sûs, in Tunis, the site of the ancient city of Hadrumetum. It is that of a large Punic necropolis, in which the funeral chambers, instead of containing, like other Phœnician burial-places, entire skeletons, are filled with large earthenware jars containing bones of men, women, and children, all of which have been calcined, like those found in the burial-places of the Romans, who, as we know, practised cremation. Punic inscriptions on several of the jars leave no doubt as to their origin. At the same time, this discovery stands alone as a unique exception; and the fact that the date of the necropolis appears to be only just anterior to the Roman domination, or even contemporaneous with its commencement, renders it highly probable that the exceptional usage is due to Roman influence, and therefore deprives the case of some of its importance.

I think I shall not need to say much of the next great people of antiquity who now claim our attention. Of all ancient nations, the Egyptians are certainly those who devoted the most elaborate care to the burial of their dead. Need I remind my readers of the universal custom of the embalming of the bodies of both rich and poor, an operation in the case of the former of a most costly nature? or need I again enter into a description of those most gigantic of human structures, the Pyramids, which were nothing else but the burial-places of the Egyptian kings? But this is not all. Not only was embalming and burial the exclusive funeral rite of the empire of the Pharaohs during all the long series of their dynasties, but in the mind of the Egyptians cremation was regarded as the greatest of dishonours, as the cruellest of punishments that could be inflicted on a human being—a belief closely associated with the tenets of their religion, which taught that the destruction of the body would destroy the possibility of a future resurrection (Ebers, "Aegypten," p. 334).

Neither time nor space will allow us to follow our author in his minute and exhaustive study of the various other peoples, civilized and uncivilized, of ancient and modern times. We must content ourselves wth a few exceedingly summary remarks and a selection of one or two of the more striking or curious details.

V.

The most interesting section, I think, is that which treats of the New World. We have already remarked that, as in Europe, so in America, man made his appearance as early as the Quarternary epoch. Slight, indeed, are his traces during the Early or Palæolithic Age, but when we arrive at the period of polished stone and the introduction of metals (in America copper, not bronze), we find the whole of the New World covered with great structures, analogous to the great stone buildings of the Old World. In America these are called "mounds," and the race who built them are known as the "Mound-

Builders." They offer this peculiarity, that they are generally constructed in the form of men, quadrupeds, reptiles, or birds. They are more or less rare in South America, but extremely numerous in the North. They occur all along the valley of the Mississippi as far as the Gulf of Mexico, and stretch across from Texas to Florida and South Carolina. Their number diminishes as they approach the Atlantic; they are rare in the Rocky Mountains, and scarcely to be found in British North America. Great numbers of them were certainly burying-places, in some of which the corpses have evidently been flesh-stripped before inhumation. At the time, as in Europe, although in the majority of the mounds the bodies are found entire, yet there are occasional traces of the use of cremation, specially in the island of St. Catherine, on the coast of Georgia; but, as we have also seen to be the case in Europe, this cremation appears to have been introduced together with the use of metals. Passing now to historical times, we find at least five different methods of disposing of the dead, which are, and have been, in vogue among the different races of the continent. These are:

1. Inhumation, or earth-burial, by far the most common method in all parts of the continent. This burial is carried out either in graves or pits (the (commonest of all—*e.g.*, Mohawks, Crees, Seminoles, Comanches, etc.), or in towers (New Mexico, Sioux, Apaches, etc.), in stone coffins (Tennessee, Kentucky, Central America, etc.), in mounds (chiefly in Ohio, Illinois, North Carolina), in wigwams (some tribes of Carolina, Navajos of New Mexico, Arizona, etc.), or in grottos (particularly Utah, Colorado, Calaveras in California).

2. Embalming among some tribes of Virginia, Carolina, and Florida, but particularly, of course, among the Incas of ancient Peru, whose mummies have been discovered by thousands during the present century. These Peruvian mummies are generally found in the crouching knee-to-chin attitude.

3. A method which may be said to be characteristic of America is what we may call "tree-burial" and "platform-burial." Many of the Red Skin races place their dead in hollow trees; others, and especially the great Sioux race, expose them on a kind of platform fastened to the top of trees, where they are slowly dried up or decomposed by the sun and the elements.

4. Water-burial, though this is extremely rare, and found only in one or two tribes.

5. Cremation. Here and there in North America the practice of cremation is to be found among some tribes of British Columbia and California, the Tolkotins of Oregon, and others. Among the Tolkotins the usage was combined with an extremely peculiar custom, existing also among the Carriers: it is that, whilst the ashes of the cremated body were reverently buried, the larger bones were picked out, and placed in a bag, which the widow was obliged to carry on her back for some years!* But the race of cremators *par excellence* of the New World were the great Aztec nation and their kindred tribes of the mighty ancient Mexican Empire, though here, again, cremation was reserved for the royal family, and perhaps the nobles, inhumation being the lot of the common people. What distinguishes these Aztec cremation rites from all others is the almost incredible barbarity in which they were carried out. Innumerable human sacrifices accompanied the incineration of the kings. At that of Ahuïtzoll, in 1487, no less than 80,400 human beings were slaughtered round the funeral pyre, and their skulls employed for the decoration of the temple! But these terrible massacres were only in keeping with the other barbarous rites of the Aztec religion, which yearly demanded the slaughter, and even the eating, of tens of thousands of human victims.

Passing now from the New World to the Dark Con-

* This custom (which actually gave their name to the "Carriers") has now "long been abolished." See Father Morice, O.M.I., on "Carrier Sociology and Mythology," *Transactions Royal Society of Canada*, 1892, pp. 111, 112.

tinent, we must repeat what has already been stated for other parts of the world—namely, that the remains of prehistoric man in this continent show that inhumation was the primeval custom, and that the use of cremation made its appearance, as elsewhere, with the introduction of metals. But it has always remained an exceptional usage among the peoples of Africa, and so it is at the present day. Generally speaking, Negroes, Bantus, Kaffirs, Hottentots, Bushmen, commit the bodies of their dead to Mother Earth. It is unfortunately true that in some of the native kingdoms, especially of the West Coast, the funerals of the chieftains are accompanied with atrocities in the form of human slaughter which well-nigh approach those of the ancient Aztecs of Mexico. But it may be laid down as a general rule that through the length and breadth of the African continent inhumation as opposed to cremation is practically universal.

Among the Australian tribes almost every conceivable variety of method is employed in disposing of dead bodies, and similar diversities exist among other peoples of Oceania. Here, too, as in many regions of Africa, cannibalism prevails to a terrible extent, and may actually be reckoned as one of the current methods of the disposal of the dead.

With regard to the East Indian Archipelago and the adjoining regions of the Asiatic continent, it may be remarked that wherever Buddhism has spread cremation is in vogue; and as Buddhism is an essentially Aryan form of religion, we have here one more testimony to the Aryan origin of cremation.

VI.

It will perhaps occur to my readers that, in the foregoing hasty summary of the funeral rites of the principal peoples of the world, I have scarcely noticed many of the customs which almost universally accompany one or the other rites in both ancient and modern times. Some of these customs may be briefly mentioned here.

1. The well-nigh universal practice among both civilized and uncivilized peoples of burying with the bodies of the deceased all kinds of weapons, utensils, and ornaments, often those of a most valuable kind; similarly, the placing beside the corpse various supplies of both food and drink.

2. The extensively practised custom of burying with the deceased, either alive or slain, his favourite horse or hounds.

3. The analogous slaughter at the grave, or burying alive, of the wives or slaves of the deceased, in some instances, as we have already seen, assuming the proportions of a veritable massacre. It may be stated generally that the *raison d'être* of the above usages has been in all ages one and the same—namely, a belief that the disembodied spirit in the next world will require for its happiness all those objects, animals, and attendants to which the living man was accustomed in this world.

4. A custom found here and there among races most widely separated, in both time and space, of *eating* portions, or the whole, of their deceased relatives or friends. I will not here shock the reader with details of the disgusting practices to which this curious usage has given rise in certain parts of both the Old and New Worlds; suffice it to say that it seems to have had its origin, not in any natural cruelty or brutality, but in a widely-spread idea that by this means the good qualities of the deceased could be assimilated by the survivors who consumed them.

5. I have more than once referred to the strange custom of *flesh-stripping*, either by means of dogs and birds or by man himself. It may be added here that in Siam there is a strange combination of this repulsive rite with cremation itself. I have read few more disgusting descriptions than that by the Catholic missionary Abbé Chevillard, an eye-witness, in his interesting little book,

"Siam et les Siamois" (Paris, 1889, pp. 70-72) of the scene at the crematory, near Bangkok, where the *sapareu*, or professional corpse-butcher, is busily employed in slicing the fleshy parts from the corpse for the benefit of the dogs and vultures around. Here, however, as Siam is a Buddhist land, the fleshless bones are afterwards cremated.

One conclusion, indeed, may be drawn from all these strange, fantastic, repugnant, or even cruel rites: they each and all bear witness in their way to the universal belief of man, even when most degraded, in his own continued existence in a future life.

VII.

Let us conclude with the following brief statement of the general results of our investigation:

1. The primeval method of disposing of the bodies of the dead was, in all parts of the world, that of inhumation, or earth-burial.

2. The custom of cremation is, relatively speaking, of recent origin, and apparently contemporaneous with the introduction of the use of metals.

3. There is good reason for considering cremation to be characteristic of, if not originated by, the Aryan or Indo-European race, and its extension to other peoples has been chiefly due to Aryan migrations, and particularly to two great Aryan religions—viz., Brahmanism and Buddhism.

4. Although both language and comparative customs show that cremation was very extensively practised by the Aryans, even before their dispersion from their original home, yet their own traditions in most cases assert that inhumation was with them anterior to cremation; also that during the classical times of Hindus, Greeks, and Romans, even during the palmy days of cremation, earth-burial was in vogue at one and the same time, and held in equal honour, with cremation.

In Greece we have shown historically that cremation gradually died out, and the primitive use of burial once more prevailed.

5. With the great civilized non-Aryan peoples of antiquity, cremation was repugnant to both their national customs and their religious beliefs; and the same may, on the whole, be fairly asserted of nearly all the non-Aryan peoples, civilized or uncivilized, of the present day.

BOOKS TO BE CONSULTED.

Dr. Is. Bauwens. "Geschiedenis en Beschrijving der Lijkbehandeling en Rouwplechtigeden bij de meeste Volken." Brussels: Polleunis. 1888.

O. Schrader. "Prehistoric Antiquities of the Aryan Peoples." Translated by F. B. Jevons. London: Griffin. 1890.

O. Schrader. "Reallexicon der indogermanischen Altertumskunde." Strassburg: Trübner. 1901. (Especially *s.v. Bestattung*, pp. 76-84.)

Sophus Müller. "Urgeschichte Europas." Strassburg: Trübner. 1905.

(On the whole, these latest writers agree with Bauwens' views.)

II

THE LOMBARDS

I.

" FOUR invading nations . . . left no enduring memorial of their presence in Italy. The Visigoth, the Hun, the Vandal, the Ostrogoth failed to connect their names with even a single province or single city of the Imperial land. What these mighty nations had failed to effect, an obscure and savage horde from Pannonia successfully accomplished. Coming last of all across the ridges of the Alps, the Lombards found the venerable Mother of Empires exhausted by all her previous conflicts, and unable to offer any longer even the passive resistance of despair. Hence it came to pass that where others had but come in like a devouring flood and then vanished away, the Lombard remained. Hence it has arisen that he has written his name for ever on that marvel of the munificence of Nature :

" 'The waveless plain of Lombardy.'

" Strange indeed is the contrast between the earlier and the later fortunes of this people, between the misty marshes of the Elbe and the purple Apennines of Italy, between the rude and lightly abandoned hut of the nomadic Langobard and the unsurpassed loveliness of the towers of Verona. From the warriors ' fiercer than even the ordinary fierceness of the Germans,'* what a

* Velleius Paterculus.

change to the pale 'Master of Sentences,' Peter the Lombard, intent on the endless distinctions which made up his system of philosophy! Nay, we may go a step further, and by a kind of spiritual ancestry connect London itself with the descendants of this strange and savage people. There is a street in London bearing the Lombard's name, trodden daily by millions of hurrying footsteps—a street the borders of which are more precious than if it were a river with golden sands. From the solitary Elbe pastures, occasionally roamed over by some savage Langobardic herdsman, there reaches a distinct historic chain of causes and effects, which connects these desolate moorlands with the fulness and the whirl of London's Lombard Street."*

This eloquent passage of the distinguished historian of Italy and her invaders may serve as both a text and an apology for the present article. It indicates that the subject is one of very considerable interest in itself. But I shall hope to show, further, that it is, or ought to be, of more special interest to English readers, involving as it does questions of the "race philosophy"—I should be more inclined to style it "race chemistry"—so popular at the present day, and, in the present case, bring the Lombard race into close connection with the Anglo-Saxon. It may perhaps not be considered unbecoming if the present writer also pleads a personal interest in the theme, on account of the Lombard blood which he is proud to think flows in his own veins.

The term "Italian" is commonly used to signify all the inhabitants of the peninsula known to us geographically as Italy. As a matter of fact, it thereby includes several races which, in their origin at least, are ethnologically distinct. Even the casual tourist cannot fail to be aware of the wide difference in character, as in appearance, of the inhabitants of the North and of the South—a difference which has sometimes led, even in recent years, to feuds of no inconsiderable bitterness

* T. Hodgkin, "Italy and her Invaders," vol. v., pp. 1, 2.

between the two populations. Taking the great fertile plain watered by the river Po and its tributaries, the very names which it has borne in ancient and modern times witness to the ethnological difference of the populations which have occupied it. Under the Roman Republic and Empire it was known as Gallia Cisalpina, a name connecting it at once with the other Gaul across the Alps, and indicating its Gaulish or Keltic population. Its modern name is Lombardy, the land of the Lombards or Langobards, a purely Germanic name, indicative of the Germanic origin of its latest settlers.

Now, an exactly similar story is told by the names of the land in which we live. Anciently it was called Britain, or the land of the Britons, a Keltic name indicative of a primitive Keltic population. Nowadays it is known as England, the land of the Angles, the Germanic name of its Germanic invaders and settlers in the fifth century. These facts point to the conclusion that, broadly speaking, the constituent elements of the two races, the English and the Lombard, have been closely akin, while both have been, to a greater or lesser degree, welded together by a common element of Roman civilization. The analogy becomes all the more striking when we realize, as I shall show later on, that the original Langobardic and Anglo-Saxon tribes were, in all probability, the most closely connected of all the branches of the parent Teutonic stock.

The differences in the results of these ethnological admixtures are, of course, evident enough, especially in the domain of language and culture. In these islands, cut off *toto orbe* from the main body of the Roman Empire, the Roman language and civilization rapidly died out with the extinction of the Roman dominion, and the Teutonic speech of the invaders, in spite of all vicissitudes, has prevailed and subsists in the modern English. In the great plain of Northern Italy, on the other hand, the Roman civilization and language have in the long run prevailed in spite of all the successive waves of Northern invaders; and the modern inhabitants, with their mixed Kelto-Germanic blood and often strikingly Keltic or Germanic features, think and speak in a language which is purely Roman, whilst the language of the conquering Langobards has, to an extent almost unprecedented in history, disappeared.

After these general considerations, I purpose, following the lead of the able historians whose works are cited below, to summarise what history and legend have preserved to us of the romantic story of that interesting race, first cousins of the Angles, which has given its name to the modern Lombardy. For this purpose we possess two entirely different sources of evidence—the testimony of the classical Roman writers during the first six centuries of our era, and the native legends or sagas handed down from generation to generation of the old Langobard tribes themselves, and preserved to us in the (Latin) writings of their native historians or chroniclers. The earliest Latin historian who refers to the Langobards is Velleius Paterculus (A.D. 6). This writer, who accompanied Tiberius in his German expedition, characterizes the Langobards as "gens etiam Germana feritate ferior," and apparently locates them somewhere between the rivers Rhine and Elbe (ii. 106). The next to mention them is Strabo (about A.D. 20), who under the curiously corrupted form of Lankosargi places them beyond the Elbe (*πέραν τοῦ Ἄλβιος . . . καὶ Λαγκόσαργοι . . . νῦν δὲ . . . ἐκπεπτώκασι φεύγοντες*, vii., p. 42). The great historian Tacitus (A.D. 61-117) bears testimony to their extraordinary bravery in spite of the fewness of their numbers, and the courageous manner in which they were able to hold their own amidst powerful and numerous enemies ("Contra Langobardos paucitas nobilitat: plurimis ac valentissimis nationibus cincti, non per obsequium sed proeliis et periclitando tuti sunt," "Germania," xl.). The same writer, it is worth observing, locates the Langobards immediately south of the Angles, and bears testimony to their worship of the great Teutonic goddess Hertha, or Mother Earth.* The geographer Ptolemy (100-161) places the Langobards next to the Chauci, apparently between the Elbe and the Weser, though elsewhere he speaks of them as if they—or perhaps a branch of them—were near the north bank of the Rhine. After this last author there is a long and strange silence among the Roman writers concerning the Langobards of several centuries—a silence which is not broken until Peter the Patrician, under Justinian, in the sixth century, records the rout of the Langibards (*sic*), together with the Obii, on the Danube by Vindex—an event the account of which, however, it is considered he may very likely have borrowed from a contemporary, Dio Cassius (A.D. 165).

It will not have escaped notice that the above testimonies of classical writers bear witness to the gradual shifting of the habitat of the Langobards from the Baltic shores of North Germany, close by that of the kindred Angles, to the banks of the Danube. Such a migration is fully borne out by the native legends, to which we now must turn our attention.

We have the following authorities for these old Langobard sagas:

1. The *Origo gentis Langobardorum*, prefixed to the laws of King Rothari (668-669). 2. Abbot Secundus of Trent, *De Langobardorum gestis*. This writer died A.D. 612; as a young ecclesiastic, he had been an eyewitness of the Lombard invasion of Italy, and had stood sponsor to the son of King Agilulf at Monza. His work is unfortunately lost, but he is quoted by Paul the Deacon. 3. The *Codex Gothanus*, of much later date, probably A.D. 807-810, remarkable for its extraordinarily barbarous Latin.

* "Such were the rites with which the Angle and the Langobard of the first century after Christ, the ancestors of Bede and of Anselm, of Shakespeare and of Dante, jointly adored the Mother of Mankind."—HODGKIN, vol. v., p. 33.

But these authorities are insignificant by the side of the writer we have now to mention, PAUL THE DEACON, the native Lombard historian (725-795), who may be justly styled the Lombard Bede.

Paul, the son of Warnefrid and Theodelinda, was the fifth in descent from Leupicris, a Lombard who, at the invasion of 568, settled in Friuli, where—or at Aquileia—Paul was born about 725. He received an excellent education, and for some time was at the Court of the Lombard king Ratchis. The latter abdicated in the year 749, and became a monk at Monte Cassino. Hither Paul followed his royal master, and here he seems to have contracted a warm friendship with Arichis II., the Lombard Duke of Benevento, and his wife Adelperga, daughter of the last Lombard king, Desiderius. The fatal year 773 saw the invasion of Charlemagne, the overthrow of Desiderius, and the destruction of the Lombard kingdom. Among the captives carried off to Paris by Charles was Paul's brother Arichis, to the great distress of his wife and family. It was in order to obtain the freedom of this brother that the monk Paul in 732 ventured upon a visit to Charlemagne, at the Frankish Court. His great literary abilities and ready wit soon won him, not only the favour, but even the intimate and familiar friendship of the great Charles, who detained him during four years at his Court. It was during this stay that Paul came into constant intercourse with the great Anglo-Saxon scholar Alcuin. Alcuin, it will be remembered, the most illustrious product of the school of York, was intellectually, though not actually, the disciple of the great Anglo-Saxon doctor St. Bede. I cannot but think it very likely that Alcuin may have spoken much with Paul about Bede, the father of English learning, and of his great work, the "History of the English People." It seems to me more than likely that herein Paul found the inspiration for his own great and kindred work, the history of the sister nation of the Lombards. For in 736 the Lombard monk returned to

Italy, first to Rome and then to Monte Cassino, where he devoted the remaining nine or ten years of his life to various kinds of literary labour in both verse* and prose. Chief among the latter is his invaluable "Historia Langobardorum," as indispensable for the early history of the Lombards as is the corresponding history of Bede for that of their English cousins—or, rather, still more valuable as preserving the ancient sagas or legends of the race. This work, which ends abruptly with the death of the great king Liutprand, the Lombard Alfred, in 744, was in all probability cut short by its author's death in or about the year 795. Like the history of Bede, that of Paul the Deacon is distinguished by its extreme honesty, its absence of national bitterness, and its consequent trustworthy character.

II.

We may now leave for a time the solid ground of historical fact to follow the romantic legendary history of the early Lombards, as preserved to us in the pages of Paul and other native writers.

In the earliest times—so the Lombard saga goes—there dwelt a small but warlike race in the mighty island of *Scandanan*, whose name is interpreted "destruction,"† and whose shores were not only washed by the sea, but (owing doubtless to their flat character) were well-nigh washed away. The people were known as the *Winnili*, a name which there is little doubt signifies "warlike."‡ At last the land became too small for its inhabitants,

* It is interesting to note that Paul was the author of one of the best known hymns in the breviary, from the initials of which Guido d'Arezzo borrowed the names for the notes of the gamut :

> "*Ut* queant laxis *re*sonare fibris
> *Mi*ra gestorum *fa*muli tuorum
> *Sol*ve polluti *la*bii reatum,
> Sancte Joannes."
>
> *First Vespers of St. John Baptist*, June 24.

† *Cf.* Gothic *skathjan*, English *scathe*, German *schaden*.

‡ "Kampflustig," zu A.-S. *winnan*, Bruckner, p. 322.

whereupon the wise woman Gambara advised her two valiant young sons, Ibor* and Aio (or Agio), to lead forth one-third of the people, chosen by lot, to seek new homes. The gallant young chieftains and their tiny band of followers set forth, and came to the land called *Scoringa.*† Here they had to fight for life and liberty with the terrible Vandals, who, under their two chiefs Ambri and Assi, held all the countries round under the terror of their name. Summoned either to pay tribute or to fight, Ibor and Aio determined rather to die than to soil their name by paying tribute. The Vandals prayed for victory to Godan (or Wodan), the Winnili to his wife Freya, and the latter by a curious strategy succeeded in inducing her spouse to grant victory to the brave little army of the Winnili. It was in this battle, as the legend tells, that the Winnili obtained their new name, by which they were ever afterwards known. For, by Freya's advice, all the women of the Winnili, standing in the front rank at daybreak, let down their long hair and encircled their faces with it, as with beards, so that Wodan, looking upon them, exclaimed, "Who are all these long-bearded ones?" And ever after they were called *Langobardi*, or long-beards. After their victory over the Vandals, the Langobards moved southwards towards the land of *Mauringa.*‡ Here they had to contend with the Assipitti (perhaps the Usipetes of Cæsar and Tacitus); but, instead of a pitched battle between the two peoples, the issue was eventually decided by a single combat between two representatives, the Langobard champion being, strange to say, a slave. This latter, having been victorious, received freedom, not only for himself and his offspring, but also for a large number of his fellow-slaves. This curious circumstance would seem to denote

* Ibor is evidently the O.H.G. *ebur*, mod. German *Eber*, wild boar. *Cf.* the names of the two Angle leaders Hengist and Horsa.

† Shoreland, A.S. *score*; *Uferland*, Bruckner.

‡ Moorland, from *Maur*, "moor, swampy land" (Bruckner).

that, as with the Anglo-Saxons, the early Langobards had a serf population in addition to the freemen.

Having thus won their right to pass through the territory of the Mauringa, the Langobards pursued the course of their migration to *Golanda.** The succeeding stages of their migration are said to have been the three strangely named lands of *Anthaib*, *Bainab*, and *Burgundaib*, in all of which Bruckner supposes the word *aib*, meaning *gau*, valley or district. The last of the three names is clearly connected with the tribe of the Burgundians, but its position must be purely conjectural. About this time the two chieftains Ibor and Aio died, and the Langobards, "after the manner of the nations," chose for themselves as their first king Agelmund, the son of Aio, who reigned for thirty-three years.

With King Agelmund is connected the romantic legend of his successor, Lamissio (also called Lamicho). King Agelmund, riding out one day, came upon a pond in which seven new-born babes, all born at one birth, had been cast to drown by their inhuman mother. Halting his horse, the king turned over the bodies of the drowned children with his long spear, whereupon one of them who was still alive put forth his hand and seized the spear. The king, moved with pity, at once had the babe rescued, predicting a great future for it, and handed it over to a nurse to be carefully tended and brought up. And so the child was given the name of Lamissio, because drawn out of a pond, "which in their language is called *lama*." The youth grew up strong and apt in war, and on the death of his foster-father was elected by the people as the second king of the Langobards. This king fought and overthrew the Burgundians, by whom King Agelmund had been defeated and slain.

Under their fifth king, Gudeoc, the Langobards entered the fertile country of *Rugiland ;* and under the

* Bruckner writes this Gôlaida, but translates "herrliches Haideland." The meaning, however, appears to be "good land"

seventh king, Tato, they went forth once more into "the wide plains, which are called in barbarian language *Feld*." Here they came into contact with the Heruli, and at this point the old national saga of the Lombard migrations, as preserved by Paul the Deacon, coalesces with the stream of known history; for the war between Tato and the Heruli is recorded by Procopius, and occurred in A.D. 511 or 512.

It is worth while inquiring what amount of historical fact may be contained in the interesting legends summarised above. As Mr. Hodgkin points out, there are considerable chronological difficulties connected with the narrative as recorded by Paul; for, calculating backwards from the known date of the war with the Heruli, the earliest migration of the Winnili would not go farther back than about A.D. 320, whereas it is known from the Latin writers that they must have already been on the Baltic shores of Germany about the time of the birth of our Lord. But, in spite of all discrepancies as regards dates, there is every reason to believe that the legend, as a whole, preserves to us a fairly accurate record of the general trend of the Langobard migration. There can be no doubt that the original home of the Winnili, *Scandanan*, represents the Scandinavian peninsula,* and its description as lying low and being well-nigh washed away by the sea applies admirably to the low-lying portion of Southern Sweden, with its vast system of lakes. Again, the name *Scoringa*, the first home after leaving Scandanan, clearly meaning "shoreland," is most appropriate for the flat territory near the mouth of the Elbe in Northern Germany, and the existence in the Middle Ages of a tract of country on the left bank of the Elbe called Bardengau and of the city Bardowyk is generally admitted to point to the settlement here of

* Authorities hold that the name "Scandinavia," adopted from Pliny, is more correctly "Scadinavia," which Mr. Bradley refers to a Teutonic **skadino*, meaning "dark." See, however, note above, p. 32.

the Langobards, who were often known by the abbreviated name of Bardi. The next stage of the migration, *Mauringa*, evidently points to a land of moors, such as stretched along the Baltic eastward of the Elbe, perhaps in the neighbourhood of Holstein, or still further to the east.

It is almost impossible to suggest satisfactory positions for the remaining stages of the migration. In all probability they represent a gradual trend towards the south-east in the direction of the river Danube. *Rugiland*, no doubt, is the country to the south of Moravia and north of the Danube. The name of the "wide plains called *Feld*" is evidently the ordinary Germanic word for *field*, recalling that of the well-known flat district of the "Fylde" on the coast of Lancashire. It is taken, with great probability, to indicate some part of the great *pusztas* of Hungary, between the Danube and the Theiss. From this region, the scene of their war with the Heruli, the Langobards would seem to have turned westward, until they came to the north-east borders of Italy.

In the above account of the migration I have followed the views of Mr. Hodgkin, and, as far as I can see, the latest writer on the subject, L. M. Hartmann, is in substantial agreement with them. The very divergent and often fanciful theories of the migration advanced by other writers, notably Zeuss, Bluhme, Lud. Schmidt, Westrum, and von Stolzenberg-Luttmersen, seem to me very fairly summarised and justly criticised by Mr. Hodgkin. It seems not improbable that traces of the Lombards may be found in Western Germany, in Westphalia, near the Rhine, in Switzerland, and in other parts. But, then, we must remember that it is quite possible that detached wings of the Lombard horde may have made their way, or been forced, in directions different to the migration of the main body. However, it will be remembered that, according to the native legend itself, only one-third part of the Winnili left their original northern home to migrate southwards. What became of the remaining two-thirds? Were they absorbed into the neighbouring Germanic tribes, or did they preserve for any length of time a separate national existence, and perhaps migrate on their own account? Bruckner shows it to be probable—as Dr. Latham long ago said*—that some of the Langobards who had remained behind in Northern Germany may have accompanied their neighbours the Angles in their invasion of England, and have left traces of their presence in such place-names as Beardincgford, Bardenea, Beardeneu, etc., in the Saxon cartularies.

It will be observed that I have taken for granted that the national name "Langobard"—later on softened in Italy into "Lombard"†—really meant "long-beard." This is, of course, a disputed point. Koegel suggested that it meant rather "long axe," from the *barta*, which is still to be seen in our English words "hal*bert*" and "*part*izan." But it was the spear (*gar*, *gair*), and not the battle-axe, which was the characteristic national weapon. Others, again, like Leonhard Schmitt (in Smith's "Dictionary of Geography"), prefer "longshoreman," from *bord*, meaning "shore" (*border*). There seems absolutely no sufficient ground for doubting the obvious etymology embodied in the national saga, and taught long ago by Isidore of Seville; and all the three recent writers quoted at the end of this article agree in the opinion that the name means simply "long-beard." Bruckner most appropriately points out that the god Wodan himself is called in Old Norse "Langbarthr," "Long-beard"—a most significant fact when we remember the Langobard cult of Wodan, and which may explain why his royal favour was so easily won by the quaint trick of the Winnili women!‡

* "A Handbook of the English Language," London, 1873, pp. 75-80.

† Up to the year 1000 "Langobardi" is in use; from 1000 to 1200 is a period of transition; after 1200 "Lombardi" is in ordinary use.

‡ See p. 33.

III.

It is not my purpose to continue the history of the Lombard people in Italy after the close of this long migration. I shall therefore pass but briefly over the remainder of the story, which is familiar enough to the readers of European history. It was in the year 568* that, under their eleventh king, Alboin—whether at the invitation of Narses or not†—the Lombards poured over the Alps, and made their famous invasion of Italy. Alboin, the son of Audoin—which names correspond exactly with the Anglo-Saxon ones Ælfwyne and Edwin—is one of the most romantic figures in Lombard legend and history. His war with the Gepidæ, his slaying of their king Cunimund, and his wooing of the latter's daughter Rosamund, with the tragic story of the final catastrophe of that unhappy union, have formed favourite subjects for poet and artist. Four years after Alboin's successful invasion of Italy, the king, in a drunken bout, insisted upon his queen, Rosamund, drinking out of the goblet which, according to the barbarous usage of the times, he had had made out of the skull of her slaughtered father, the King of the Gepidæ.‡ To avenge this terrible insult, the outraged queen plotted with the King's *scild-por*, or shield-bearer, and foster-brother Helmechis to bring about the assassination of her cruel husband, her own hand to be the reward of the treachery. The plot was successful. Rosamund and Helmechis fled with the Lombard treasure on board a Byzantine vessel to Ravenna. Here Rosamund presented her paramour with a poisoned cup. Helmechis, after drinking half the

* The year also of the great defeat of the Kentish men by the West Saxons at the Battle of Wimbledon—"the first fight of Englishmen with Englishmen on British soil," says Green ("The Making of England," p. 117)—an interesting synchronism.

† Hodgkin entirely rejects the story (vol. v., pp. 60-65); Hartmann also.

‡ Paul the Deacon was shown the actual goblet by King Ratchis two centuries later.

draught and recognising that he was poisoned, forced the wretched woman to drink the remainder, and so the two accomplices died together, and the tragedy "which had begun with a cup of death at Verona, ended with a yet deadlier death cup at Ravenna." A few years ago Mr. Swinburne made this thrilling episode of Lombard history the theme of one of his most powerful dramatic creations.* And so deep an impression did the tragedy create upon the popular mind that traces of it are believed by some to remain in the folk-songs of the Lombard peasantry of the present day.†

It is desirable here to give two warnings that will tend to prevent some misconceptions on the subject of the Lombard influence in Italy. The one is that, as Bruckner most carefully and fully points out, not all traces of Germanic nomenclature, vocabulary, or custom to be found in medieval or modern Italy are to be attributed to the Lombards. Other Teutonic tribes had invaded Italy, especially Goths and Burgundians, and the Lombards themselves were doubtless accompanied by Teutonic allies, such as Gepidæ, Rugians, Saxons, Swabians, etc. Moreover, the Franks who overthrew the Lombard kingdom must have left some traces of their presence.‡ Hence, great discrimination must be exercised in sifting from the general mass of Germanic evidences those which are really Lombardic. This Bruckner most conscientiously does in his admirable essay and dictionary.

* "Rosamund, Queen of the Lombards." A Tragedy. London: Chatto and Windus, 1899.

† Thus in the popular ballad:

> "Sa ve digo, dona lumbarda,
> Spusème mi, spusème mi,
> Sa ve digo, sur cavalieru,
> Ajo zà marì, ajo zà marl,
> Vostru marì, dona lumbarda,
> Fèlu muri, fèlu murì."

(Comparetti e d'Ancona, "Conti e raconti del Popolo It.," vol. i., 1870.) The dialogue may be supposed to take place between Rosamund and Helmechis.

‡ Bruckner, pp. 1, 2.

A second warning is this: The fact that the great plain of Northern Italy bears the name of Lombardy must not lead us to imagine that the Lombard conquest and the Lombard influence were limited to that part of the peninsula. On the contrary, they overspread well-nigh the whole of Italy. The great Lombard dukedoms of Benevento and Spoleto occupied a considerable part of Southern and Central Italy. Tuscany and Umbria, too, were included in the Lombard conquest. So that the Lombard rule and the Lombard tongue held sway for a considerable time in every part of the country. Still, the true centre of Lombard power was always in the great northern plain, around its capitals of Pavia and Monza, and there probably settled the bulk of the women and children who accompanied the invading hordes on their great trek across the Predil Pass of the Julian Alps on that fateful Easter Monday of 568.

The history of the Lombard kingdom from Alboin (whose assassination took place in 572) to the defeat and deposition of the thirtieth and last king, Desiderius, by Charlemagne, in 774, will be found in every history of Italy. These two centuries of the Lombard supremacy in Italy form a record of turbulent and often savage times, though with here and there gleams of a brighter character. The seventeenth king, Rothari, is known for his famous code of laws, which is interesting, not only for its excellent legislation, so remarkably akin to the Saxon and Scandinavian legislations, but also because of the vast number of words and terms of the now lost Lombard speech which it preserves to us, as well as fragments of the old Lombard legends—notably a list of kings—which it also embodies. The most illustrious of all was, of course, the famous King Liutprand (712-744), also famous for his code of laws, as well as for his many kingly virtues.

It is frequently stated that Pope St. Gregory the Great brought about the conversion of the Lombards almost at the same time as he effected that of their Anglo-Saxon kinsfolk. The two cases, however, are not exactly parallel. The Lombards, before their invasion of Italy, had already embraced some form of Christianity, or, rather, of Arianism. Strange to say, of the time and place* of this conversion nothing is known, and it is clear enough that whatever Christianity they had was of a very superficial and skin-deep character, mixed with much of the pagan superstition of their forefathers. The earlier years of the Lombard dominion were therefore marked by continual hostility between the orthodox Italians and the rude Arian Lombards, who often cruelly persecuted and plundered the Catholic Church, so that we can understand Gregory the Great styling them "nefandissimi." King Authari, the second in succession after Alboin, however, married Theodolinda, daughter of the Catholic Duke of Bavaria, Garibald. This remarkable woman chose for her second husband Agilulf (590-615). It was through Queen Theodolinda, as in England through Queen Bertha, that the great Pope strove for many years to secure, not only peace with the Lombards, but also their conversion to the Catholic faith. He had the satisfaction at the end of his life, if not to bring about the conversion of Agilulf, at least to secure the baptism of his son Adelwald, and the gradual conversion of the Lombard people to the Catholic faith. In this sense, therefore, he is justly styled the "Apostle of the Lombards," as well as of the English.

Whenever a national poet shall arise for the Lombard race, he will have at his disposal an unrivalled treasury of romantic folk-legends to furnish forth the material of his epic. The sagas of the wise Gambara, priestess of the Earth, and her sons; the great trek from Scandinavia; the battle with the Vandals; the intervention of Wodan and Freya, and the strategy of the Winnili womenfolk; the slave's duel in Mauringa; King Agelmund and the finding of Lamissio; Lamissio's single combat with the Amazon; the story of Alboin and

* In all probability during the sojourn in Pannonia (Hungary).

Cunimund; the weird tragedy of Alboin and Rosamund; the romantic wooing of Theodolinda, daughter of Garibald, by Authari—here is a wealth of legend and legendary history such as few races can boast of, and which any nation might be proud to own.*

IV.

It is, of course, certain that the Langobards were a purely Germanic race; but the interesting ethnographical question now arises whether they belong to the Low German or High German division of the Teutonic family. Eminent authorities, like Grimm, Schmitt, Zeuss, Möller, and Much, have declared for the opinion that they belong to the High German race—an opinion which relies chiefly upon the powerful argument that the very numerous remnants of the Lombard vocabulary preserved nearly all show the phonetic alteration of consonants or *Lautverschiebung* characteristic of the High German.† But, in spite of this extremely weighty argument, the careful investigations of Hodgkin, and especially Bruckner, with whom the latest writer, L. M. Hartmann, unhesitatingly agrees, seem conclusive of the Low German origin of the Winnili or Langobards. The prevalence of the undoubted *Lautverschiebung* in their language is satisfactorily explained as a linguistic "contamination," the result of three centuries of residence in South Germany, and close

* Bruckner, in the most ingenious manner possible, shows that the Lombards possessed certain alliterative national ballads embodying many of these sagas, now known to us only by Paul the Deacon's Latin "History," and has very skilfully attempted partially to restore some fragments (see his work, pp. 19-21).

† For example: *por*, in *scild-por* (shield-bearer); *raub*, robbery (A.S. *reáf*); *pair*, boar; *pahis*, boy; *scuẓo*, shooter (*cf.* German *Schütze*); *tallis*, dale (*cf.* German *Thal*); *zân*, tooth (Mod. Ger. *Zahn*); *zôn*, garden (Dutch *tuin*, Mod. Ger. *Zaun*); *grap*, grave (A.S. *græf*, mod. Ger. *Grab*), etc. Also in proper names: Alboin, Ælfwyne; Aripert, Herbert; Hildeprand, Hildebrand; Claffo, A.S. Glappa.

contact with High German tribes. Even the second main argument which hitherto has borne great weight—viz., that the Langobards were reckoned by Tacitus and Ptolemy among the Suebi, and so must be generally classed as Suabians or High Germans—loses its value from the fact, already pointed out by Much, that undoubted Low Germans, like the Angles, were also sometimes included by the Latin writers under the same designation. The name, therefore, was either of merely political significance, or perhaps meant simply "freemen."

But there are convincing arguments for the thoroughly Low German character of the Langobards, and incidentally for their close connection with the Angles and Saxons, which I briefly summarise as follows, from the pages of Bruckner (pp. 24-32).

1. The extraordinary similarity between the Lombard *laws*, so fully preserved in the codes of Rothari and Liutprand, and the laws of the Angles, Saxons, and Frisians.

2. The striking analogy in both the technical and ordinary *vocabulary—e.g.*: (*a*) Legal terms: *fulc-free* (A.S. *folcfry*), folk-free; *fulboran* (A.S. *fulboren*); *selpmundius* (A.S. *selfmundich*), "sui juris"; *warigang* (*cf.* O.N. *skóggangr*, A.S. *waldgenga*), stranger; *vante-poro* (A.S. *vothbora*), spokesman; *aid*, oath; *aldius*, half-free man (A.S. *elde*, *ylde*, men). (*b*) Ordinary words differing from the High German: *fol* (A.S. *ful*), beaker, cup; *gaida* (A.S. *gâd*), goad; *traib* (A.S. *draf*), drove, drive; *drancus* (O.S. *dreng*, O.N. *drengr*), youth; *scaffardus* (O.S. *scapward*), steward; *bôn* (A.S. *bên*, O.N. *bôn*), boon, prayer.

3. The flexion in some points agrees with the Anglo-Saxon and Old Scandinavian as against the High German—*e.g.*, *aidos*, pl. of *aid* ("oath"), as against H.G. *Eid-e*.

4. An agreement in several *sagas and myths*, especially in the worship of Wodan and Freya. It is also

worthy of remark that the Anglo-Saxon hero Sceafa is actually designated in the "Traveller's Song" (v. 32) "King of the Langobards" (*Sceafa* [*weolde*] *Longbeardum*).

5. A decided parallelism in the royal *genealogies;* compare the Lombard Waccho and Claffo with the Anglo-Saxon Wehha and Glappa.

6. Paul the Deacon had already remarked upon the similarity of *dress* of the Lombards with that of the Anglo-Saxons—"qualia Anglisaxones" (H.L., iv. 22); which is said, by the way, to be the earliest use in literature of the name Anglo-Saxon.

7. Alboin, whilst in far-off Pannonia, appeals for help and support to the Saxons, as to old friends (*amici vetuli*, H.L., ii. 6).

The "Traveller's Song," attributed to Widsith, a well-known Saxon poem of the sixth century, has more than one reference to the Langobards. Besides the above mention of Sceafa, the poet tells us of his own visit to the Lombard King Alboin in Italy:

> "Ic waes . . .
> . . . mid Longbeardum . . ." (Line 159);

and more explicitly:

> "Swylce ic waes on *Eatule* (Italy)
> Mid *Aelfwine* . . . [Alboin].
> Bearn *Eadwines*" [Audoin]. (Lines 139-147.)

Almost in the style of the Vedic poets, he praises Alboin as having the "lightest hand of mankind to work love, most generous heart to deal out rings and bright bracelets." In line 194 he proclaims as his patroness "Ealhilda, Queen of Myrgingi, and daughter of Eadwin," who may perhaps be the Lombard Audoin.*

Bruckner thus concisely sums up the evidence for the ethnographical position of the Lombards:

"On the ground of the above-mentioned numerous facts we may unhesitatingly declare the Langobards to

* The ending *hilda, ilda,* is common in Lombard female names.

be Ingvaeones. Moreover, we seem justified in reckoning them in the Anglo-Frisian group, since they have the most points of agreement in laws, vocabulary, and legends with the Anglo-Saxons. But the fact that the languages of these people do not show the same phonetic changes must be explained by the migration southwards of the Langobards before the Anglo-Frisian phonetic laws had come into operation" (p. 32).

Many years ago Latham had come, by the same arguments, to the similar conclusion, that everything except the peculiar High German phonetic character of the Lombard glosses "points to their Angle affinity." He adds, however, "The great complication engendered by the High German character of the Lombard glosses cannot for an instant be ignored," and is driven to the expedient of supposing that these glosses are not Lombard at all, but Bavarian.* This explanation, however, is quite untenable in view of the great number of Lombard proper names preserved to us in documents.

The subject of the Lombard language is a fascinating one. On the one hand, the number of Lombard words and proper names which have been preserved is very great; on the other hand, the language itself has so utterly perished that nothing beyond a single sentence of three words—and that doubtful—has come down to us. Not an inscription, not a fragment of a folk-song, a charm, or a prayer has escaped the cataclysm. A single pronoun is known. A single imperative of a verb, a single preposition, are all that remain to complete our knowledge of the accidence. Yet, out of such unpromising materials has Bruckner, with characteristic German industry, succeeded in compiling his elaborate work of 338 pages on "The Language of the Lombards," of which over 150 pages are devoted to the "grammar"!

It is not easy to determine at what date the use of this

* Dr. R. G. Latham, "A Handbook of the English Language," *ut sup.*

Lombard language finally died out in Italy. Bruckner gives evidence to show that, although the Lombard kingdom came to an end in 774, the Lombard speech was still spoken by the majority of the people, even under the Franks, and that it cannot have died out entirely before A.D. 1000 at the earliest. It has left a very few traces in the Italian language itself, of which we may mention the words *strale*, arrow (*cf.* A.S. *strael*); *aggueffare*, to add to (*cf.* A.S. *wefan*, weave); *romire*, to make a noise (A.S. *hreám*, noise); and probably some endings such as *ingo*, *engo*, *asco*, *atto*, etc. It is not easy to explain the absolute loss of all literary monuments, of which some must surely have existed during the four or five centuries of the life of the Lombard language in Italy. We know that national songs or ballads certainly existed, and from the dialogues of Gregory the Great we learn of the existence among the Lombards of hymns and incantations, whilst Paul the Deacon tells us of songs about the valour and liberality of King Alboin, which reminded one of the above-quoted eulogy of the Saxon poet Widsith. This deplorable loss of an entire national literature is the more difficult to explain, as Bruckner tells us that the quantity of legal and other documents of the Lombard epoch, written in Latin, is so enormous that it is practically impossible to collect from them all the fragments in the language in the form of glosses, etc., which they contain. Space would not permit me to quote even a small percentage of the vast number of single Lombard words which have thus been preserved, like fossils, in these Latin documents. I merely append in a footnote,* in addition to those already quoted, a few of the more striking ones.

* *Adeling, Etheling* (A.S. *Athelinge*); *accar*, *field*, acre (A.S. *æcer*); *anagrip*, assault (Ger. *Angriff*); *berg*, hill (Ger. *Berg*); *braid*, broad; *braida*, level plain; *campio*, champion; *drancus*, youth (A.S. *dreng*); *faderfiu*, "father-fee," dowry (A.S. *fæder-feoh*); *flasgrá*, flax-gray; *gaida*, spear, goad; *gísel*, witness, bail (A.S. *gísel*, hostage, pledge); *guidus*, wide; *guidrigild*, wergild *haist*, hasty (A.S. *hæst*); *lagi*, leg; *land*, land; *lang*, long

It is interesting to remark that a single signature to a deed of the year 372 preserves to us the nominative singular of the first personal pronoun—viz., *ih*, I; whilst the solitary Lombard sentence above referred to is the juridical formula by which a testator proclaimed another person his heir—viz., "Lid in laib," meaning literally, "Go into (my) inheritance" (*i.e.*, Be my heir).*

It is not only in language, however, that the Lombards bore traces of their Germanic origin and their kinship with the Anglo-Saxon race. We have already noticed how their national historian Paul the Deacon, whose testimony is always valuable owing to its undoubted honesty, bore witness to the similarity in dress between his own people and the Anglo-Saxons. More than this, even physical features are eloquent in the same direction. To the present day, in spite of all historical vicissitudes, the Lombard race still bears strongly the evidences of its origin. The light, often ruddy, complexion and hair, which are still common in Lombard families (as in some of the writer's own family), and the general physical appearance, are strongly suggestive of kinship with the Angle and Saxon races.

The political institutions of the Lombard invaders of Italy tell a similar story, and remind one considerably of the state of things in the early Saxon history of this country. The kingship was not strictly hereditary, but rather elective, with a loosely hereditary character.

---

laubia, arbour (Ger. *Laube*); *laun*, reward (Ger. *Lohne*); *mar*, horse, mare; *marscalc*, marshall; *morgingâb*, dowry (Ger. *Morgengabe*); *nassa*, net; *plôvum*, plough; *pûl*, a boil or swelling; *scâla*, scale, skull; *skilla*, bell (Ger. *Schelle*); *smido*, smith; *stôlesazo*, lit. "stool-setter," master of ceremonies; *stupla*, stubble; *thinx*, "thing," assembly; *waida*, meadow (Ger. *Weide*); *waldus*, wood (Ger. *Wald*); *wifa*, whiff, whisp of straw, etc. Bruckner's dictionary occupies 136 pages of his book.

* *Lîd* is evidently the imperative of a verb equivalent to the A.S. *lethan*, to go, the causative meaning of which is preserved in our English "lead." *Laib* is the English noun "leave," in the sense of what is left or bequeathed. We still ask in this sense "How much did so-and-so *leave*?"

Hence its inherent weakness, and the "centrifugal" character of the political state, as Mr. Hodgkin points out. On the other hand, the line of kings presents great legislators in Rothari and Liutprand, who remind us of the Athelstan, Alfred, and Edward of Saxon England.

The love of liberty and the power of the public assembly, again, seems to connect the two races. The importance of the *Thinx* in Lombard public life, and its very name, of course recall emphatically the *Thing*, which all through history has been the distinguishing feature of political life among the Scandinavian peoples, and the name subsists to the present day as that of the Parliaments of Denmark, Sweden, and Norway.* Among the Lombards the *Thinx* was more a judicial than a political assembly, before which various public legal acts had to take place, especially all transactions regarding property. The Lombard codes have even preserved in their curious mixture of Latin and Teutonic forms the verb *thingare*, with the meaning of making away property by donation, and from this custom the word *thinx* came also to mean a donation of property itself. It was also called *gairethinx*, from *gar* or *gair*, spear, evidently the national weapon of the Lombards, which enters so continually into Lombard proper names, among which it may be interesting to note the ancient royal name Garibald, the modern surname Garibaldi, and probably the second part of the family surname of Dante, Ali*gherius*. Such legal terms already referred to as *guidrigild* (also *wirigild*), "weregild"; *faida*, blood-feud; *fio* or *fihu*, money; *morgincap*, the A.S. *morgengifa*, *faderfio*, and many others, show how extensive were the points of contact between the two legislations.

Finally, the Lombard temperament and character have preserved to the present day the clear traces of their

* So the Landsthing and Folkething of Denmark, the provincial Landsting of Sweden, and the Storthing (comprising Lagthing and Odelsthing) of Norway. So, too, the All-Thing of ancient Iceland, and the Tynwald (Thing-vallr) of the Isle of Man.

northern origin and kinship. The *dolce far niente* which characterizes the Southern Italian has never found place in the character of the steady and industrious Lombard peasant or artisan. During the Middle Ages the Lombard influence in arts and commerce was widespread throughout Europe. The "Magistri Comacini," the famous master-builders who went forth from the shores of the lake of Como, were the first creators of that powerful and solid Christian architecture which, from the eighth to the tenth century, was perfected in Lombardy itself, and from the close of the tenth began to spread throughout Europe under the names of Romanic and Norman. In another direction, the Lombard Street of London, as remarked by many historians, bears eloquent testimony to the part played by Lombard merchants and money-lenders in the early days of English trade.

The intellectual gifts of the Lombard race may be gathered from a few of the great names of the Middle Ages, whose etymology at once proclaims their origin, among which it may be sufficient to quote Lanfranc, Anselm, Peter "the Lombard," and perhaps, as already mentioned, Dante Alighieri.

In later times the talent and ingenuity, as well as the enterprise, of the people of Lombard blood have been shown in the important part they have played in adapting to practical use, and in popularizing throughout Europe, the discoveries of physical science which had their birth in Italy from the fifteenth to the nineteenth centuries. In this way the modern Lombards have played no inconsiderable part, not only in popularizing science, but also in advancing scientific research during the past few centuries. On this topic I may quote an interesting passage from a popular writer of the beginning of the last century. Speaking of the people of the province of Como, perhaps the most thoroughly Lombard of all parts of Italy, he says:

"The inhabitants of these places have devoted themselves principally to the manufacture of barometers, thermometers, and other useful instruments, which have at different periods originated in philosophical discoveries and improvements in the knowledge of physics. These simple mountaineers have shown a remarkable degree of intelligence in these matters, and an aptitude to comprehend and imitate machines and instruments used in the natural sciences as soon as they have been invented. With this branch of industry they not merely emigrate to all parts of Italy, but to France, England, Germany, Russia, to every part of Europe, whilst some have even crossed the Atlantic, both to North and South America. The emigrant Comaschi have served to familiarize even the poor and lowly with the discoveries of physics and useful inventions. Penetrating into one country after another, as they have long been doing, they may be considered as retailers and propagators of science."*

The modern Lombardy, again, is a land of textile industries. The province of Como alone contains 78·6 per cent. of the total number of spindles, and 50 per cent. of the weaving of the Italian silk trade. Biella, again, is the centre of the woollen and cotton textile trades, and Bergamo that of the finer manufactures. Indeed, the great development of the textile industries during the past few years, especially in Lombardy, has been of so remarkable a character, that an English observer in 1881, commenting upon the great growth of cotton manufacture, remarked upon the interesting fact that he found at Modrone a descendant of the illustrious and warlike Milanese family of the Visconti engaged in the peaceful occupation of cotton-spinning.

In spite, therefore, of the large admixture of other bloods, and the profound changes, political and social, which the race has undergone in the course of centuries; in spite, too, of the total and absolute loss, well-nigh nine centuries ago, of their national speech; and in spite of their linguistic and cultural absorption by the

* *Penny Magazine*, 1833, pp. 61, 62.

Italian elements of the land in which they finally settled, I feel justified in maintaining that the Lombards still form a real nation, and still preserve not merely their ancient name, but also a very large proportion of those physical, intellectual, and ethical qualities which characterize them as the real descendants of the brave little Teutonic tribe of the Winnili or Langobards, who in the early days of the Christian era set forth on their long migration from Southern Scandinavia towards their final home in the rich plain of Cisalpine Gaul. Nor do I think it too fanciful to hold, not only that the original Langobards were ethnologically the first cousins of the Angles, but also that their final settlement in a Keltic land, and their consequent absorption of Keltic elements, have ended in producing a type which has much in common with that resulting from the like conquest of Keltic Britain by the Germanic tribes of the Saxons and Angles.

BOOKS TO BE CONSULTED.

THOMAS HODGKIN. "Italy and her Invaders." Vols. v., vi.: The Lombard Invasion—The Lombard Kingdom. Oxford: The Clarendon Press, 1895.

LUDO MORITZ HARTMANN. "Geschichte Italiens im Mittelalter." II. Band, I. Heft: Römer und Langobarden. Leipzig: Wiegand's Verlag, 1900.

WILHELM BRUCKNER. "Die Sprache der Langobarden." Strassburg: Trübner, 1895.

III

THE ENGLISH POPE

" THE career of the only Englishman who has ever worn the triple crown* affords ample scope both for the picturesque and the scientific historian. There is no more striking illustration of the openings which the Medieval Church gave to humble worth and ability than the life of the poor Hertfordshire lad who, leaving England almost penniless, came to reorganize the Scandinavian Church, to beard the mightiest monarch of Western Europe since Charles the Great, and himself to dispose of kingdoms."†

These words of a non-Catholic writer seem to me worthily and fittingly to summarize the remarkable history of the only English Pope. The story of his life is one of which all English Catholics may well be proud, and it would seem but natural that it should be familiar to every Catholic child in this country. Strange to say, this does not seem to be the case. It may be doubted whether one out of a hundred of the children in our Catholic schools could tell, if asked, the name of the English Pope, and I suspect that but few of even our educated Catholics could give any adequate account of his career. It is at least curious that what interest has been taken in Pope Adrian IV. by Englishmen has been

* To be quite accurate, this is a misnomer. The tiara in Adrian IV.'s time had not yet assumed the three crowns, as his portraits show.

† *Manchester Guardian*, December, 1896.

chiefly on the part of non-Catholics. The largest and most elaborate biography of him is the sumptuous volume published within the last ten years by a High Church layman;* the article "Adrian IV." in the "Dictionary of National Biography" was from the pen of the late Bishop of London, Dr. Mandell Creighton. On our side, we have nothing to show but a small, popular, historical sketch of little over a hundred pages, by Richard Raby, published as far back as 1849. It is true that in Ireland much more attention has been devoted to Pope Adrian, but this is exclusively owing to the hot controversy concerning his much-disputed Bull to Henry II.; and, indeed, the interest in the doings of the English Pope has been strictly limited to this one phase of his policy. It is not easy to account for the comparative neglect into which the memory of this really great Englishman and great Pope has fallen amongst us. It is certainly not the fault of ecclesiastical historians, for all the great Continental writers on Church history, from Adrian's own time to our own, have done full justice to the greatness of this remarkable Pontiff—one of the most remarkable who has ever occupied the See of Peter. It does not, therefore, appear to me to be altogether superfluous, even though nothing new be left to write about him, at least to condense in popular form a summary of what is to be found in the various writers above referred to, and in some other historical sources.

There is another reason why it seems desirable to make an attempt at popularizing among our English Catholics a knowledge of the life of the English Pope. The story always appears to me one of the most essen-

* Mr. Tarleton's handsome quarto, with its fine illustrations and accumulation of material, is an indispensable book; but at the same time it must be admitted that its *inaccuracy* of detail (spelling, especially Latin, dates, figures, quotations, etc.) is simply phenomenal, and most irritating to the reader. The present article is based chiefly on the books mentioned at the end. There is also a "Memoir of the Life of Adrian IV.," by E. Trollope (London, 1857). A good bibliography is to be found at the end of Tarleton.

tially romantic and dramatic that has come down to us from the Middle Ages. It is well-nigh the most striking commentary which history has preserved of the words of the Psalmist : " The Lord is high above all nations, and His glory above the heavens. Who is the Lord our God, Who dwelleth on high, and looketh down on the low things in heaven and on earth ? Raising up the needy from the earth, and lifting up the poor from the dunghill, that He may place him with princes, with the princes of His people " (Ps. cxii. 4-8). More than this, it is a career which, as hinted in the quotation with which I began, contains a distinctly practical lesson for us to-day.

The life-story of Nicholas Breakspeare always presents itself to me in the form of a drama, whose successive acts rise on a scale of interest and grandeur worthy of the pen of a Shakespeare. For brevity's sake, as well as for the better order of the narrative, I will try and present the story in these successive acts.

I. The Poor Scholar.

The first act, then, opens in rural England in the very last year or years of the eleventh century.

" We find ourselves at the beginning of the reign of Henry I. Men just emerging from middle age were living who had fought in defence of Saxon England against the Conqueror, or who had helped in the Norman army to win for him this island kingdom. . . . The year 1100 may fairly be taken as marking the time when conquerors and conquered had commenced to settle down together. The rising generation could not remember the catastrophe of Hastings, and mixed unions were beginning to bear fruit in producing the ancestors of the (English) race of to-day. . . . Breakspeare, therefore, as a boy lived in a time of quietness between two stormy periods of history—the one before his time, the other after he had left the country."*

* Tarleton, " Nicholas Breakspeare," pp. 21-23.

The scene is laid in the rich and beautiful country around and under the sway of the great Benedictine abbey of St. Albans. Among the dependencies of the abbey was the village of Abbots Langley, just north of Watford. According to tradition, Nicholas Breakspeare was born in this village. Through the kindness of Mr. T. Mewburn Crook, of the Manchester Municipal School of Art, I have obtained two drawings of the old house in this parish, locally known as "Breakspeare's." In a letter dated June 17, 1898, Mr. T. Armstrong, a local resident, writes as follows:

"The building on the outskirts of the hamlet of Bedmond, in the parish of Abbots Langley, which is called 'Breakspeare's,' is held to be the place where Adrian IV. was born. It is known that he was born in the parish, and I think the tradition with regard to this particular spot may be accepted. The building is of brick, and is now divided into two or three cottage dwellings. It is not probable that any part of it is of the date of the Pope's birth, though portions of the interior seem to be older than the outside walls, which are comparatively modern. Parts of my own house in Abbots Langley are, no doubt, of great antiquity, but the oldest of them as reconstructed are not earlier than Tudor times. Houses, like everything else, decay and fall to pieces, and often the old material is partially used in the reconstruction. As I thought local tradition could be relied on, and that Nicholas Brakespeare was born in a house standing on the spot to which his name has been given, I had a very pretty water-colour made by a clever artist living in the neighbourhood, in which the group of houses and the surrounding landscape were represented, and this I sent to Rome, to be placed, with the consent of the Pope,* in that part of the Vatican where documents relating to the lives of his predecessors are preserved. It was presented by a friend of mine, a Monsignore, who told me that His Holiness was much

* Leo XIII.

pleased, and proposed to keep the drawing in his private apartment."

Although this house, on the spot where Nicholas, the son of Robert Breakspeare, was born, seems to be a somewhat substantial dwelling, and although there is evidence that down to the middle of the fifteenth century the Breakspeares were a decidedly respectable family, yet it is undoubted that Nicholas passed his boyhood in extreme poverty. His father, Robert, eventually became a lay-brother in the Monastery of St. Albans whilst Nicholas was still a boy—according to some, after the death of his wife, though another well-known account represents Adrian IV.'s mother as surviving that Pontiff, and being in great indigence at the time of his death. Be this as it may, it appears certain that the lad Nicholas was himself engaged for a time in servile work at the abbey, and that, in spite of his great talents, he was rejected by Abbot Richard, whether on account of his youth or of his poverty or of his father's position, when he tried to gain admittance into the monastery with the hope of eventually becoming a monk. Bitterly disappointed, and in a state of utter destitution, the high-spirited and indomitable Hertfordshire lad set out on foot to seek his fortunes in more congenial surroundings. Full of ardour for study, he turned his steps towards France.

" He worked his way probably through London and down the high road through Kent—that historic route which has been the main thoroughfare of so many travellers to and from the Metropolis—past Rochester and Canterbury, to Dover, from whence he obtained a passage over the narrow seas, possibly in the very same year when the *Blanche Nef* was wrecked on the treacherous rocks off Barfleur, and the brilliant company surrounding Prince William, together with that unfortunate son of King Henry, were drowned."*

On his safe arrival in France, young Nicholas devoted

* Tarleton, pp. 19, 20.

himself with great ardour to study—at first in Paris, then the most famous European seat of learning.* But after a few years he quitted Paris—about 1125—and gradually worked and begged his way southwards across the Rhône to Arles, where he again frequented, with great diligence and success, the celebrated schools of that city. An interesting question here arises as to the connection of Nicholas, during these *Wanderjahre* as a poor scholar, with the Order of the Norbertines or Premonstratensians. I am indebted to the Right Rev. Abbot Geudens, C.R.P., of Corpus Christi Priory, for a very full statement of the Norbertine tradition on this subject. He has forwarded me a copy of the note which Abbot Georg Lienhardt, of Roggenburg (Suabia), adds to his brief notice of Pope Adrian IV. in his "Auctarium Ephemeridum Præmonstratensium," under the date September 1. The following is a translation of the passage:

"That the blessed Hadrian was once, at least for a time, an *alumnus* of our Order he himself testifies in a Bull prefixed to our statutes, where he thus speaks in commendation of our white institute: 'Mindful how your institute and Order, *of which we were once an alumnus*, brilliant with abundant splendour of merits and fragrant with the grace of sanctity, hath extended its branches from sea to sea.' . . . Mention of this Bull is also made by Petrus Waghenare ('De Elogiis Sancti Norberti ejusque Ordinis,' p. 445), Ernestus Reubner, in his 'Chronicon Gradicense' (cap. iv., p. 23), and other historians of our Order, both ancient and modern. The authenticity of the Bull containing the above words was always held as quite certain and indisputable by the most illustrious annalist of our Order,† a most perspicacious

* A chronicle of the Irish monks at Ratisbon, quoted by Lanigan (vol. i., p. 155), contains a tradition that one of Breakspeare's teachers in Paris was an Irish monk named Marianus, of whom he afterwards spoke with great affection when he had become Pope.

† Abbot Charles Louis Hugo.

historian and skilled critic, in the third MS. volume of his Annals, p. 247. He quotes in the margin Chrysostom Van de Steere, Peter Waghenare, and Bernard a Sancto Leone, and draws the following conclusion as from certain premises: 'That blessed Hadrian was originally a professed member of the Premonstratensian Order, and that the above-mentioned Pontiff by the word *alumnus* meant exactly what is understood by the term *professus*.'"

The learned writer goes on to show that Nicholas passed some years in France before his entry (to be mentioned later on) into the Monastery of St. Rufus, and argues at some length that in the interval he studied in some Norbertine monastery, and "saltem aliquamdiu sub stipendiis Norbertinis militaverit." He further quotes again the annalist Hugo to the effect that the profession of Nicholas in the Order, and his quitting it after his profession, was an old tradition of the Order confirmed by "documents existing at Prague, Furnes, Antwerp, and in Spain."* The great authority of Abbot Hugo,† of course, makes his opinion of unusual weight; yet I must confess that so far as it is based upon the words of Pope Adrian's Bull prefixed to the statutes of the Order, it does not appear to me to be conclusive. The use of the word *alumnus*, even accepting the Bull as genuine, can surely mean little more than that Nicholas was for a time a pupil in one of the houses

* "Beatum Hadrianum vere apud nostros professum et post emissam professionem inde egressum fuisse atque a praedecessoribus veteris ævi acceptam esse traditionem quam exstantia Pragæ, Parci, Furnis, Antverpiæ, Hispaniæ monumenta confirmant."

† Charles Louis Hugo (who died August 2, 1739) was Abbot of Etwal, and afterwards Bishop of Ptolemais. He was historiographer to the Duke of Lorraine, and is considered as a most accurate and critical historian, well acquainted with his sources. "What he says," writes Abbot Geudens, "may be considered above criticism." By order of the General Chapter in 1717, held under Claudius Lucas, all the ancient documents from the monasteries of the whole Order were transmitted to him for the compilation of his annals.

in the Premonstratensians—probably, indeed, a poor scholar maintained by their hospitality or alms—a most likely supposition.* But if the tradition be really confirmed by other documents referred to by Abbot Hugo, and independent of the Bull, then the claim of the Norbertine writers would be substantiated. As far as I know, these documents have not been published; but Hugo, it must be admitted, writes as if he had seen them.

In any case, then, we are safe in concluding that during his wanderings as a *fahrender Schüler* in France Nicholas was in all probability under the influence and actual care of the White Canons of St. Norbert, and thus was very likely deeply indebted to them for his subsequent fame as a scholar and success as a Churchman.

After a short stay at Arles, we next find Nicholas wending his way northward to Avignon, where he sought and obtained admission, at first in a menial position, in the abbey of the Canons Regular of St. Rufus (Saint-Ruf), whose ruins are still visible near Avignon. These Canons Regular must not be confounded with the Canons Regular of St. Norbert, of whom we have been speaking; indeed, the Abbey of St. Rufus dates from a century before St. Norbert's own time. The Order took its rise early in the eleventh century in a secession from the cathedral church of Avignon, which was served by canons living in common, but who had become relaxed. Bonanni (in his "Ordinum Religiosorum Catalogus") gives A.D. 1000, and Hélyot (in his "Ordres Monastiques") 1039, as the date of this event. St. Rufus became the mother house of an independent congregation of Canons Regular, which had many houses in France and other countries, and even sent canons into Patras and other Eastern churches maintaining the Latin

* It is of some importance to note that St. Norbert founded his Order at Prémontré only in 1120, about the very year of Nicholas's arrival in France, and that it received Papal confirmation only in 1126.

rite.* These Canons Regular no doubt followed the rule of St. Augustine, which was, of course, the rule also adopted by St. Norbert in the foundation of his Order of Prémontré in 1120, almost in the very year when Nicholas Breakspeare passed into France.

It would appear that the poor English scholar waited for two or three years in his humble capacity of a lay-brother at the Abbey of St. Rufus, at the end of which time the canons, won by his docility, learning, and personal charms of character, finally admitted him to profession in their Order. Thus, the rejected postulant of St. Albans finally, by his steadfast perseverance, industry, and steady determination, reached the goal upon which his hopes had been fixed from boyhood. With this happy consummation the first act of his dramatic life—that of the poor scholar—fittingly closes.

II. The Abbot.†

The great talents and sterling merits of the young English monk were not very long in leading to the first step of promotion in his rapid career. In 1137, on the death of Abbot William II., Nicholas Breakspeare was unanimously elected as his successor. But with this new dignity trials very soon came. It would appear that some relaxation had crept into the house, and that the firmness of the new Abbot in correcting abuses very soon

* I am indebted for these facts about the Abbey of St. Rufus to Miss Speakman, M.A., of the Victoria University, who adds: "The dress, too, as given by these authors, is different from the Norbertine, although both are white. The canons of St. Rufus wear a sort of sash over one shoulder, and tied at the opposite side, Scotch fashion." The Abbey of St. Rufus was destroyed by the Calvinists in 1562.

† In an anonymous article of the *Dublin Review* for April, 1875, Nicholas Breakspeare is referred to as "O.S.B., Abbot of St. Albans" (p. 258, note). It would be difficult to compress more errors in a single phrase (except a recent statement of the *Times* newspaper that the only English Pope was Adrian VI., who lived in the reign of Henry VIII. !).

led the monks to repent of their election of the ex-lay-brother to be their superior.

"But the man who had passed through the great lesson of learning to obey was now to show them that he had also learnt to command. If they thought that the modest, unassuming, and compliant brother was going to rule them with a gentle hand, and tolerate any slackness in the hard duties imposed on them by their solemn vows, they were mistaken. Breakspeare showed immediately that power of command which comes at once when a man of strong will, rigid principle, and knowledge of mankind is suddenly placed in a position of responsibility. The more heavy that responsibility is, the better do such men rise to it. The easy ways into which the monks had gradually drifted were stopped, the rigid rules of St. Augustine put in force, and, by degrees, those men who had been unanimous in placing him over their abbey began to murmur among themselves."*

The consequence was a serious mutiny in the monastery, which culminated in two successive appeals to Rome, carried by Abbot Breakspeare himself and a deputation of the hostile monks to present their case against him. The Pontiff at the time was the celebrated Eugenius III., the disciple and favourite spiritual son of the great St. Bernard, who, to his own dismay, had just been thrust into his sublime office from the position of a humble monk. At the first deputation the Pope, with his wonted tact, succeeded in effecting a reconciliation between the Abbot and his unruly subjects, and the litigants returned home reconciled to each other. But very shortly—probably within a year—the disaffection broke out worse than ever. The second appeal to the Holy See, apparently in 1146, had a very different ending. The Pope answered the complaints of the monks with some severity. "I know, brethren, where the seat of Satan lieth; I know what has stirred up this tempest

* Tarleton, p. 40.

among you. Depart. Choose for yourselves one with whom you can be, or rather are minded to be, at peace ; for this one shall no longer be a burden to you." The canons of St. Rufus departed, and Pope Eugenius retained the ex-Abbot at his own Court. The startling and dramatic sequel is eloquent testimony to the keen penetration of character and promptitude of action of the Cistercian Pope ; for, almost immediately, he raised Nicholas at one bound to well-nigh the highest dignity which it was in his power to bestow, creating him straightway one of the six Cardinal-Bishops,* with the suburbican title of Bishop of Albano.

This sudden elevation of the once poor and obscure scholar and lay-brother to a rank only second to that of the Pope himself was sufficient to have turned a head less strong than that of Nicholas. It is not a little remarkable to observe how, in the providence of God, the rejection of the penniless postulant by the Abbot of St. Albans led to his becoming himself Abbot of the Canons Regular at Avignon ; and the casting off of the English Abbot by his unruly subjects led at once to his creation as Cardinal and Bishop. With this striking change of fortune ends the chapter of Nicholas's life as monk and Abbot.

III. THE CARDINAL LEGATE.

From his creation as Cardinal in 1146 to the year 1152 we know practically nothing of Breakspeare's life. Mr, Tarleton surmises—not, indeed, without some probability, though I fancy with little or no evidence—that Cardinal Breakspeare may have accompanied Pope Eugenius III. to Paris in 1147, when the Pope went to give the cross to King Louis VII. on the eve of the second Crusade.

* Nicholas Breakspeare was thus the second English Cardinal. The first had been Robert Pulleyn, Archdeacon of Rochester, created by Lucius II. in 1144. He died in 1150. Cardinal Vaughan was the thirty-fourth English Cardinal in succession (see Dudley Baxter, "England's Cardinals").

Be this as it may, in the year 1152 Nicholas was called upon to execute the first great act of ecclesiastical statesmanship for which his after-career was to be so famous. In that year Eugenius III. appointed him Apostolic Legate to the three Scandinavian kingdoms of Denmark, Sweden, and Norway. Whatever Scandinavian history we open, we shall find the name of Nicholas Breakspeare written large in the annals of those Norse kingdoms. The business for which the Legate was despatched to the Far North was connected with the ecclesiastical government of the three kingdoms, which up to 1102 had all been subject to the Metropolitan See of Hamburg. In that year Pope Paschal II., after long negotiations, had freed the Scandinavian countries from their subjection to Hamburg, and erected the Metropolitan See of Lund in Denmark. But this arrangement not unnaturally led to some jealousy between the three kingdoms, which, by the middle of the twelfth century, had culminated in a strong movement for ecclesiastical home rule, perhaps stimulated by the action of Eugenius III. in granting Ireland its four archiepiscopal sees just before. Ambassadors from the Kings of Sweden and Norway arrived in Rome, begging for the erection of such metropolitan sees in their countries. It was in reply to this request that Breakspeare was sent on his famous legation. On this journey he passed through England,* from the east coast of which he sailed for Norway, where he landed on July 19, 1152. On his arrival, the Cardinal-Legate found himself face to face with a much more extensive and serious task than that of merely settling the ecclesiastical government of the country. He found the latter in a state of great political

* Mr. Tarleton's attempt (pp. 55, 56) to trace the footsteps of his hero during his brief visit to his native country, by a few place-names containing that of Breakspeare in two or three counties, appears to me preposterous. There is surely a much more obvious and simple explanation for the existence of the name, which need not have had any direct connection with Pope Adrian.

confusion, the royal power being divided between the three sons of the murdered King Harald—Sigurd, Inge (surnamed Crookback), and Eystein—of whom only Inge seems to have been a really honourable man. The crimes of the other two had brought about a state of civil war, and the strong-minded English Cardinal, before turning his attention to ecclesiastical affairs, insisted upon settling these internecine feuds. His strong and wise efforts were crowned with success. He inflicted canonical censures upon the two criminal Princes, and finally succeeded in restoring peace to the country. His next step was to erect a metropolitan see for Norway, which he fixed at Nidaros (the modern Trondhjem), in the cathedral of which city repose the bones of King St. Olaf. He created John, Bishop of Stavanger, Metropolitan, and conferred upon him the pallium, subjecting to the jurisdiction of the new province, not only Norway, but also Iceland, Greenland, the Faroe Islands, the Orkneys, the Shetlands, the Hebrides, and the Isle of Man, detaching the last three from the province of York. But his activity did not end here. He thoroughly reformed the Norwegian Church, swept it of abuses and of many heathen practices which had been allowed to creep in. He also introduced the payment of Peter's Pence.

At the request of the Norwegian people, Cardinal Breakspeare even introduced many civil reforms—secured the public peace by causing a law to be passed forbidding the carrying of arms by private persons, and even limiting the King's bodyguard to twelve. Great was the gratitude of the Norse people. Their national historian, Snorro, relates that no foreigner ever came to Norway who was so honoured, or whose memory is so cherished, as Nicholas Breakspeare, and that after his death he was honoured by the nation as a saint. It is pleasing to add that during his brief pontificate Adrian maintained the most friendly relations with Norway, and sent thither English architects and artists to build the cathedral of Hammer, which See he had founded.

From Norway Nicholas departed, amid the lamentations of the people, for Sweden, where he was received with all honour, but where he found himself face to face with difficulties which taxed all his diplomacy. The two rival provinces of Sweden and Gothland both contended for the honour of the archiepiscopal see, and in spite of the Synod of Linköping, which he summoned, no agreement could be come to. Wisely reserving his own decision, which was to give Sweden no metropolitan see at all, the Cardinal now passed on to Denmark. Here again he had to employ no little diplomacy, for the Archbishop of Lund, Eskil, was not unnaturally aggrieved at the detachment from his jurisdiction of the province of Norway, though he received the Legate with all pomp and honour. Breakspeare propitiated the Archbishop by confirming him in the title of Primate of all Sweden, and granting him the right of consecrating and investing with the pallium the new Archbishops of Sweden, whenever the affairs of that Church should be settled. He might now have looked upon his long and difficult mission as successfully accomplished, but he was once more called upon to intervene in a serious international dispute between Sweden and Denmark, caused by the wicked conduct of Johan, son of King Sverker of Sweden. The Cardinal used all his influence to avert the threatened war between the two countries, giving the wisest advice to the Danish King. His efforts, indeed, were in vain, but the disastrous results of the ensuing war abundantly justified the wisdom of his counsels.

During its progress the Cardinal Legate left Scandinavia, and returned to Rome. Among the qualifications which had so eminently fitted him for his Scandinavian legation, over and above his natural talents and diplomatic skill, we must probably reckon also his linguistic attainments, including apparently a knowledge of the

Scandinavian languages; for among the literary works attributed to him by Pagi are said to have been, not only an account of his mission to the North ("De Legatione Sua"), but also catechisms of Christian doctrine for the Swedes and Norwegians. All these works are unfortunately lost.

IV. The Sovereign of Rome.

Cardinal Breakspeare, on his return to the Eternal City in the early part of 1154, found his great friend and patron, Pope Eugenius III., dead, and Anastasius IV., already in his ninetieth year, reigning in his place. On December 2 of the same year the aged Pontiff died, after a brief reign of seventeen months. The day after his death the Cardinals met in conclave at St. Peter's, and immediately, with unanimous voice, elected as his successor the English Cardinal, who took the name of Adrian IV. He tried to refuse the office, but clergy and laity alike, not heeding his remonstrances, cried out: "*Papam Adrianum a Deo electum!*"—a striking testimony to the unanimity of the choice.

"So at last the humble Englishman, the poor student. the modest monk, Abbot, Bishop, Cardinal, and missionary, was called to occupy the position of the greatest and most fearful responsibility upon the earth of those days. What a moment! What a life! Thirty years from poverty to Pope! And what a vista opened out before him! At this age he might reasonably hope for twenty or thirty years of power, and if he lived as long as his predecessor, forty years."*

Such was the beginning of one of the most remarkable pontificates in the history of the Church—a pontificate remarkable not only for the great and stirring events which were crowded into it, but also for its brevity, lasting as it did but four years and nine months.

"He could not tell that within five short years he would be called into the presence of the Master whom

* Tarleton, pp. 65, 66.

he had just been chosen to represent on earth; but if he had known this, and had determined to crowd into that short time all the stirring events and great deeds that he could look for, he could not have made it fuller than it actually proved to be."*

From the moment of his election to that of his death Pope Adrian was called upon to grapple with some of the most difficult and momentous questions of both home and foreign policy that have ever fallen to the lot of a Pontiff to meet. No wonder that he afterwards said to his friend John of Salisbury that "the tiara was splendid because it burnt with fire."†

"At the moment Adrian IV. took his seat behind the helm of Peter's bark the winds and waves raged furiously against her, nor ceased to do so during the whole time that he steered her course. That time, though short, was yet long enough to prove him a skilful and fearless pilot—as much so as the very foremost of his predecessors or successors, who have acquired greater fame than he, simply because a more protracted term of office enabled them to carry out to completer results than he could do designs in no wise loftier than Adrian's, and, in so doing, to unveil before the world more fully than was permitted to him characters not therefore nobler or more richly endowed than his."‡

The new Pope found his first troubles already awaiting him in the city of which he was not only Bishop, but also temporal Sovereign. These troubles, caused by the agitation of the Republican party in Rome, headed by the turbulent Arnaldo da Brescia, the disciple of Abelard, had raged fiercely under the pontificate of Eugenius III., the pupil of St Bernard. Though somewhat lulled during the brief and peaceful pontificate of Anastasius, they broke out with fresh violence on the election of Adrian. The Pope was met at his accession by a peremptory demand of the Senate, prompted by

* Tarleton, p. 66. † "Polycraticus," viii. 23.

‡ Raby, p. 17.

Arnaldo, to renounce once for all his rights of temporal government, and to recognise the authority of the Roman Republic. They had strangely miscalculated the character and temper of the new ruler. The demand was sternly rejected by the unflinching Pope. Arnaldo himself hastened to Rome, and the mob broke out into open disorder and violence, culminating in a murderous attack on Cardinal Gerard in the Via Sacra. Adrian's action at this critical moment was prompt and decisive. From Anagni, to which he had retired, he issued a stern decree, placing Rome under an interdict. Never before in history had this most dreaded weapon of spiritual chastisement been applied to the Eternal City. No wonder it was received with consternation.

" No calamity which could befall a city in those times —and they were days when calamity had full meaning, days of the storm and sack, of the plague and famine— could be more dreaded than that of interdict."*

I need not here repeat the description of the effects of an interdict. And if this dread censure produced such an impression even in England in the days of King John, what must have been its effects in the very centre of Christendom itself ? To add to its horrors, the interdict began on Palm Sunday, and lasted during Holy Week, thus seriously affecting, not only the spiritual, but also the temporal, interests of the Roman people, to whom Easter has always been a season of great profits, owing to the number of pilgrims flocking to their city. Adrian's strong action was completely successful. After some ineffectual parleying, he gained all that he demanded : the abrogation of the Republic, the banishment of Arnaldo, and the absolute submission of Senate and citizens to their lawful Sovereign the Pope. Then, and only then, did the latter return to his city, which, we are told, he entered in triumph amid the joyful acclamations of his people ; and in his cathedral of St. John Lateran he celebrated his coronation with great pomp and jubilee.

* Tarleton, p. 98.

V. The Champion of the Church.

At the very time that Adrian was engaged in this stern contest with his disaffected subjects a still more serious danger was hanging over Italy and the Papal See. This was the impending invasion of Frederic Barbarossa, "the mightiest monarch of Western Europe since Charles the Great." The motives which led the young and mighty Emperor to undertake this expedition were to reassert the Imperial claims over Italy which he professed to have inherited from Charlemagne, and to confirm them by his coronation in Rome; and also, no doubt, to check the growing spirit of freedom which was already beginning to show itself, especially among the Lombard cities of Northern Italy. To complicate the situation, Arnaldo and the Roman Republic had already sent a letter to Frederic, inviting him to come and receive the Imperial crown from the Senate; but, fortunately for the Holy See, the invitation was worded in such bombastic and insolent terms that the Emperor indignantly rejected it.

About the very time of Adrian's election Frederic, with his large army, was crossing the Alps, and, being encamped at Roncaglia, he held a great Diet to receive the homage of his Italian feudatories. A very few days after Adrian's coronation in the Lateran, Frederic received the Iron Crown in the church of Pavia. All Lombardy was now in his power, and the last city to resist—Tortona—fell after a gallant struggle. The great Emperor and his victorious army was already entering the Campagna. It was a moment of painful doubt and suspense. The new Pope might well have addressed the stern monarch in the words of the King of Israel's messenger to Jehu, as he approached at the head of his troops: "Thus saith the King: Is there peace?" (4 Kings ix. 19).

It was fortunate for the Pope that Frederic had set his heart on being crowned, like Charlemagne, by the hands of the Pontiff himself. Herein the quick glance of the diplomatic Adrian saw the advantage which he undoubtedly held in treating with the irresistible Emperor on something like equal terms.

At the same time that Frederic sent envoys to Rome to ask for his solemn coronation in St. Peter's by the Pope's hand, Adrian had despatched three Cardinals to meet Ferderic in order to ascertain his intentions, and also to induce him to aid in seizing Arnaldo of Brescia, who was engaged in his old game of stirring up disaffection against the Holy See in the Campagna. On the arrival of the two Archbishops who were Frederic's envoys, Adrian took the bold and firm stand of declining to consider the Imperial proposals until he should have received a reply to his own demands, and an assurance that the Emperor was approaching with friendly intentions. This strong attitude met with success. The Papal legates soon ascertained that the Emperor was far from supporting Arnaldo and his followers against the authority of the Holy See, and, indeed, was so much incensed against the demagogue that he was quite willing to procure his seizure, which was speedily effected.

Before passing on, we must say a word about the well-known fate of this unfortunate man. Arnaldo, on being delivered up to the Papal authorities, was imprisoned in the castle of St. Angelo, with the intention, it is said, of being ultimately tried before Frederic himself, on the latter's arrival in Rome. But the Prefect of Rome, Peter, fearful of the great danger to which the presence in a city seething with sedition of so formidable a prisoner exposed the public peace, of his own authority, and in the absence of both Pope and Emperor, caused the unhappy man to be led out on the morning of June 18, 1155, and executed by the cruel and barbarous death of burning at the stake before the Porta del Popolo. Mr. Tarleton's comment on this tragic end of the famous demagogue seems to me just and equitable :

"In judging the act of execution, we must be careful not to measure the sentiments of those days by the moral standard of our own, and Arnold's death seems to have been the only course left to those responsible to the Pope for the order of the city. On the other hand, we must apply some moral standard to acts like this, and not allow the consideration of difference in custom and thought to weigh against the sentiment of justice. Rarely, if ever, in history is there an occasion when the execution of a man without trial can be excused."*

Meanwhile Adrian still displayed great caution in his preliminary negotiations with the Emperor. He sent word to the latter at Sutri that before the favour asked was granted, Frederic would have to take an oath on the Gospels and on the Cross before the Papal envoys to protect the Pope and Cardinals against aggression, to uphold the Papal dignity, and not to usurp any of its functions. In return, the Pope promised to go and meet the Emperor, and escort him in state to Rome for his coronation. The haughty Frederic complied, and took the oath with great solemnity.

On the following day, June 9, 1155, took place the historic scene in the camp at Sutri which I am about to describe. Adrian IV., with all his retinue of Cardinals and other attendants, advanced in state from his castle at Nepi, where he had been waiting, the Pope riding, according to custom, upon a white palfrey. A splendid deputation of German Princes and Bishops received him, and conducted him to the Imperial tent. The gigantic Emperor advanced to welcome the Pontiff. And now occurred that dramatic incident, so often described in history, which to me has always appeared to be the most thrilling episode in the career of the English Pope. It was an old tradition, generally accepted in those ages of faith, that a King, meeting the Pontiff when mounted, must not only assist him to dismount, but, as a sign of supreme veneration, must hold his stirrup as he did so.

* Tarleton, pp. 106, 107.

This right of the Pope to homage was acknowledged by the old German legislation, as expressly stated in the two great codes of national law—the *Schwabenspiegel** and the *Sachsenspiegel*†—and had been observed by the Emperor Lothair towards Pope Innocent II. The proud Hohenstauffen, however, was by no means in a mood to submit to the humiliation which he felt to be involved in performing the ceremony before all his barons and troops, and, though he bowed low and offered to assist the Pontiff to dismount, he abstained from holding the stirrup. The situation had all at once become acute : it was a moment of crisis—the two strongest men in Europe, the English Pope and the German Kaiser, face to face, and a momentous question of privilege, behind which great issues were at stake, to be settled between them. Both potentates were unyielding. Adrian, unflinching before the mighty warrior King, calmly kept his seat, and refused to dismount until the due act of homage had been rendered. Frederic was angrily obdurate. Already the German soldiery were beginning to murmur aloud, and we are told that the Cardinals who formed the Papal suite were so terrified at the ominous state of things that they promptly fled, leaving the Pope alone to confront the storm. Yet Adrian retained all his cool courage, and with great dignity dismounted himself, and allowed the Emperor to conduct him to the seat prepared for him. On this he sat, and allowed Frederic to kneel and kiss his feet ; but when the Emperor arose to receive in return the kiss of peace, Adrian calmly but firmly declined to give it, declaring that until the homage had been paid to him in

* "Der Papst erhält die beiden Schwerter von Gott ; für sich behält er das geistliche Schwert, das weltliche Schwert übergibt er dem Kaiser, *und wenn er seinen weissen Zelter besteigt, muss ihm der Kaiser den Zügel halten*" (Articles 9 and 10 of Preface).

† "Dem Papst ist auch gesetzt dass er zu gewisser Zeit *auf ienem weissen Pferde reiten mag, da ihm dann der Kaiser den Steigbügel halten soll*, damit der Sattel sich nicht wende" (p. 17, ed. Gärtner, Leipzig, 1732).

full, he would withhold his blessing and decline to crown the Emperor. In vain the latter argued the question with great vehemence and every kind of argument. Adrian, feeling that he stood forth as the champion of the Holy See in a matter which, trivial as it may seem to us now, yet was in those days but a symbol of great and momentous principles of international law lying behind, remained inflexible and fearless, and, finally quitting the Imperial camp, returned unmolested to Nepi. He had proved the stronger man of the two.

After his departure, Frederic, whose great ambition, as we have seen, was to be crowned by the Pope in Rome, suffered himself to be persuaded by his entourage to yield to the Pontiff's demands. On June 11 he followed the Pope to Nepi. Adrian rode forth once more to meet him, and as he approached, the haughty Barbarossa, advancing on foot, took hold of the Pope's stirrup, and helped him to alight. The Pope then embraced the Emperor, and gave him the kiss of peace, amidst the plaudits of all the spectators. So had Adrian conquered.

"In requiring Frederic Barbarossa to pay him the typical homage of holding his stirrup, Adrian did plainly nothing but what was entirely in accordance with the spirit of the age, and, at the same time, with traditional usage as then received by Christian Princes. But Frederic did do what was contrary to both in his refusal, and that, too, while professing to be imbued with the very faith out of which the homage in question sprang. Thus, it is no wonder that Adrian should view such an inconsistency as most inauspicious for the liberties of the Church, with which those of society were then so closely bound up, and should therefore feel it imperative to pursue a line of conduct which at first glance may appear so arrogantly exacting, but which, found on closer examination to have involved the assertion of the most sacred interests against a man who was known to respect none in promotion of his ends, assumes a character calculated rather to conciliate our approval than to confirm our censure."*

The Emperor and the Pope, now reconciled, entered Rome side by side in triumph, and on June 18 Frederic was solemnly crowned in St. Peter's by Adrian, amidst a scene of great splendour and rejoicing. But these festivities were held in the midst of a city teeming with disaffection, soon to break out into open violence. Mutual exasperation existed between the Emperor and the Senate. The insolent messages of the latter had been rejected with scorn by Frederic, who had occupied the Leonine city with his troops. Immediately after the coronation a very serious riot broke out in the city, and Frederic's troops, hard pressed, had to fight all day long for their very lives. After a desperate battle, Frederic was victorious, the Romans suffering severely in both killed and prisoners, and, but for the intervention of the Pope, summary vengeance would have been executed upon the latter by the Imperial forces. But, in spite of his triumph, Frederic felt himself in not a very secure position. Not merely the ill-restrained hostility of the Roman citizens, but the difficulty of obtaining food for his large army, owing to the animosity of the peasantry and the oppressive heats of June, were sufficient reasons to make him hasten his departure northwards. At Tivoli Pope and Emperor separated with mutual expressions of goodwill, though the peace which had been made between the two powers was of rather a hollow kind. Frederic, forced by the circumstances of his position, rapidly marched northward, " not so much gratified by the acquisition of the Imperial crown as embittered by what he had gone through in the pursuit of it, and resolved not to delay longer than he could help a second invasion of Italy, which should compensate the mishaps and mortifications of the first."†

So ended the first round in the mighty struggle between Empire and Papacy—the " Hundred Years' War," as

* Raby, pp. 47, 48. † *Ibid.*, p. 54.

Alzog styles it. And it must be admitted that, on the whole, Adrian had had the best of the contest with the first and greatest of the Hohenstauffens.

Frederic's departure left the much-tried Pontiff no single moment of peace or rest. Already was he involved in yet another difficult and dangerous contest with the Norman King, William of Sicily. The feud between the Norman conquerors of Sicily and the Holy See had been of long standing, the Pontiffs claiming feudal overlordship over all Southern Italy as inheritors of the rights of the Western Empire, and this had led to frequent serious wars in preceding pontificates. Just one year before Adrian IV. was crowned Pope, William II. caused himself to be crowned King of Sicily at Palermo without obtaining previously the Papal sanction (Easter Day, 1154). On Adrian's succession, William sent him the customary congratulations ; but Adrian was not the man to brook any diminution of the traditional rights of the office which he now held, and he promptly declined to recognise William's kingly title. An invasion of Southern Italy and devastation of parts of the Papal territories was William's reply, at the very same time that Frederic Barbarossa was advancing southward in his quest of the Imperial crown. It would take too long to narrate the long and varied fortunes of this contest between the Pope and the Sicilian King, complicated as it was by the secret plotting of the Greek Emperor, who sought to turn matters to his own profit. Adrian took the strong step of excommunicating William, and though the latter at first paid little heed to the much-dreaded censure, yet the offer of the Greek Emperor to form an alliance with the Pope against him alarmed him so much that he begged for release from the sentence, and offered to do the required homage to the Pontiff for his kingdom of Sicily.

Unfortunately, Adrian's perplexity was increased by a difference among his own Cardinals, the German party among them strongly opposing any compromise with the

Sicilian monarch. They prevailed, and the war went on. The tide of success turned strongly in William's favour, whose successes at Brindisi and Bari were marked with a ferocious cruelty that struck terror into his opponents. By May, 1156, we find the Pope almost besieged in Benevento, and cut off from Rome by the victorious and ruthless Sicilian King. Adrian now negotiated once more with equal skill and firmness, and the result was a fairly satisfactory peace. The King, with great solemnity, did homage and swore fealty to Adrian as his overlord for Sicily and the various principalities in South Italy, promising to defend him against his enemies, and to pay a yearly tribute for three of the duchies. In turn, the Pope relieved William of the excommunication, and confirmed him in the feoff of his kingdom, but also conceded to him very large rights of ecclesiastical patronage and other extraordinary regal privileges with regard to the Church in Sicily, which we may be sure nothing but the stern pressure of circumstances could have induced so good a Churchman as Adrian to yield to the secular power.

So ended the long and dangerous feud with the Sicilian King. The following winter, 1156-1157, Adrian spent quietly in Viterbo, the first and last period of calm peace during his stormy pontificate. But for the troubles of the two following years there is every reason to believe that the great Pontiff would have taken in hand a work which was, after so many centuries, one of the favourite preoccupations of Leo XIII.—the reunion of the Western and the Eastern Churches. He corresponded with the Patriarch of Constantinople, the Byzantine Emperor, and Bishop Basil of Thessalonica, on the subject, and also received a deputation of several Greek Bishops to solicit his protection against certain encroachments of the Knights Hospitallers. Unfortunately, the troubles of the last years of his reign put an end to any hopes of furthering the work he had so much at heart.

VI. The Lord of the Isles.

We must here say something about Pope Adrian's relations as Pontiff with his own native country.

Immediately on Adrian's election, King Henry II. of England, who had acceded to the throne almost at the same time,* sent a deputation, consisting of the Abbot of St. Albans and three Norman Bishops, to offer his congratulations to the English Pontiff. They carried many rich gifts, including three mitres and some beautiful sandals "worked by Christina, Prioress of Markgate." The old chronicler† tells us that Adrian refused all the presents except the mitres and sandals, good-humouredly remarking that he must refuse the Abbot's gifts because the monks of St. Albans had refused to accept him when as a boy he had offered himself at their gates. The witty Abbot readily replied that the rejection must have been God's will, as He had destined the postulant for a far more exalted station. That Adrian really preserved no resentment is shown by his reply to the Abbot, bidding him ask for what favour he wanted, and adding: "You know that the Bishop of Albano could never refuse anything to St. Albans."

The envoys also presented to Adrian a letter from Henry II. It is difficult to read this rather preposterous document (preserved by Peter of Blois) without a smile. The Plantagenet King, after warm congratulations and expressions of joy upon Adrian's elevation, proceeds to lecture the Pope in somewhat paternal fashion as to his future government of the Church, and to offer him advice as to his choice of Cardinals and holders of ecclesiastical benefices. The advice given is doubtless excellent, but it reads rather oddly from one who was soon to become the persecutor of the Church in his own

* October 25, 1154; Adrian's election, December 3 of same year.

† "Chronicon Monast. S. Albani."

kingdom, and to cause the martyrdom of St. Thomas of Canterbury.

In his first creation of Cardinals, which occurred the following year (December, 1155), Adrian raised to the dignity of Cardinal-Deacon his nephew and secretary, Boso Breakspeare,* formerly a Benedictine monk of St. Albans. One of the three medieval lives of the Pope, published by Muratori, is held by Watterich and others to be from Boso's pen. This is, however, doubtful.†

But the Englishman who has left us most information about Pope Adrian was his intimate and familiar friend John of Salisbury. This celebrated English Churchman, once a pupil of Abelard, and in later life Bishop of Chartres, spent a good deal of time with Pope Adrian during the latter's brief pontificate. He has left us, in both his "Polycraticus" and his "Metalogicus," abundant and most interesting materials concerning the English Pope, which not only contain valuable information, but give us a thorough insight into his frank and straightforward character, his common-sense, and his real humility amid all the splendours of his exalted office. In the long and confidential conversations which John reports, the latter ecclesiastic spoke to the Pope with a freedom and openness in the way of frank criticism that are rather astonishing. But this criticism, and even blame, the Pontiff seems not only to have taken with humility, but even to have invited. Again, he spoke frequently in a truly touching manner of the troubles and burdens of his high office:

"The office of Pope, he assured me, was a thorny one, and beset on all sides by sharp pricks. Indeed, the burden of it would weigh down the strongest man and grind him to the earth. . . . He wished that he

* Boso was promoted cardinal-priest under the next Pope, Alexander III. He played a part of some prominence in Rome, and died about 1181.

† It is generally held to be by Cardinal Nicholas of Aragon (c. 1350). The life by Boso is probably lost.

had never left his native land of England, or at least had lived his life quietly in the cloister of St. Rufus, rather than have entered on such a narrow path ; but he dared not refuse, since it was the Lord's bidding. . . . 'It seemed once,' he said, 'as if God was constantly beating me and stretching me out as with a hammer on an anvil. Now I pray Him to aid me with this burden which He has placed on my shoulders, for I find it unbearable.' "*

After what we have heard of the troubles and worries of his stormy pontificate, we should not be surprised at this lament of Pope Adrian.

But the most famous affair in which the English Pope and the English King were brought into relation was that of the so-called Bull *Laudabiliter*, with reference to the lordship of Ireland. It would be quite impossible for me to treat at length this *cause célèbre*. I should require to write an entire article in order to treat it at all satisfactorily. Volumes have been written upon it, and even angry controversy has raged around it. Every point connected with it has been hotly denied and as hotly defended. Let me very briefly indicate merely the state of the controversy. And first of all I must dispel a very popular delusion on the subject. It is commonly enough supposed that Adrian issued a Bull giving Ireland to Henry II., and that on the strength of this document Henry straightway invaded and conquered the sister island. This is quite an incorrect statement. What history does record is as follows :

John of Salisbury writes, in the concluding chapter of his " Metalogicus " :

" At my request (Adrian) granted to the illustrious King of the English Ireland, to be held by hereditary right, as his letter testifies to this day. For all the islands by ancient right are said to belong to the Roman

* " Polycraticus," lviii., c. 23 (translated by Tarleton, pp. 151, 152).

Church by virtue of the donation of Constantine, who founded and endowed it. He also sent by me a gold ring adorned with a splendid emerald, whereby an investure should be made of the right to govern Ireland, and the said ring was ordered to be kept in the public archives of the Court."

The actual text of the letter herein referred to is professed to be given by Giraldus Cambrensis in three different works of his ("Expugnata Hibernia," ii. 5; "De Rebus a se Gestis," 10; and "De Instructione Principis"), also in several English chroniclers (Ralph de Diceto, Roger Wendover, Matthew Paris), from which sources it has been taken over into both the Annals of Baronius and the Roman "Bullarium." It seems to have been accepted unhesitatingly as genuine in Ireland and England, as elsewhere. But in course of time the controversy has arisen as to whether the supposed Bull is not, after all, a forgery, and even the very categorical statement of John of Salisbury a forged addition to his real work.

There is evidence to show that, although in 1315 the Princes and people of Ireland, in a remonstrance to Pope John XXII., mention the fact of Adrian's granting the lordship of Ireland to Henry II. (*dominium contulit*), yet so early as 1325 doubts really existed in Ireland upon the subject, as shown in a letter by the Lord Justiciary and Royal Council of Ireland to the Pope. But with that exception no trace of doubt or denial is found until the year 1615, when Father White, S.J., in his "Apologia pro Hibernia," and the learned Archdeacon Lynch in his "Cambrensis Eversus," both attacking the veracity of Gerald the Welshman, maintained the new theory of the forgery of Adrian's letter. Since then the controversy has continued. Eminent names can be cited on both sides. To be brief, it must suffice to give the following table of the chief subsequent writers for and against the authority of the Bull at home and abroad on either side of the controversy:

AGAINST THE AUTHENTICITY.

1750. MacGeoghegan (Paris).

1864. Damberger (in *Der Katholik*).

1872. Cardinal Moran (in *Irish Ecclesiastical Record*).

1882. "Analecta Juris Pontificii."

1883. Abbot Gasquet, O.S.B. (*Dublin Review*, July and October).

1885. Jungmann ("Dissertationes Selectae," tom. v.).

1890. Bellesheim ("Geschichte der Kirche Irlands").

1891. Fr. Morris, of the Oratory ("Ireland and St. Patrick").

1892. Von Pflugck-Harttung (in *Zeitschrift für Kirchengeschichte*).

1898. L. Ginnell (in *New Ireland Review*; also "Doubtful Grant of Ireland").

1903. O. J. Thatcher ("Studies concerning Adrian IV.," Chicago).

FOR THE AUTHENTICITY.

Lingard ("History of England").

Lanigan ("Ecclesiastical History of Ireland").

1849. Kelly (editor of "White and Lynch").

1884 and 1899. Rev. Sylvester Malone (in *Dublin Review*, and "Pope Adrian IV. and Ireland").

Pfulf, S. J. (in "Stimmen aus Maria Laach," xxxvii.).

1893. Miss Kate Norgate (in *English Historical Review*, vol. viii.).

Bishop M. Creighton (in "Dictionary of National Biography").

1896. Tarleton ("Nicholas Breakspear)."

In face of such a divergence of eminent names, it may seem rash indeed in an amateur to pronounce an opinion either way. I can only say that, having very carefully read all I could procure on both sides, I have become convinced that the most satisfactory conclusions have been reached by three of the writers just named—viz., Miss Norgate, Mr. Tarleton, and Father Malone. The extremely judicial summary of the controversy by the first-named writer in the pages of the *English Historical Review* has specially impressed me. To my mind these writers have succeeded in establishing satisfactorily: (1) the authenticity of the concluding passage of the "Metalogicus" of John of Salisbury; (2) the genuineness of the letter *Laudabiliter* as given by Gerald and others. I admit that some difficulties still remain, such as certain differences in several texts of the Bull, and the somewhat mysterious neglect of Henry to use it when obtained; but in spite of such obscurities, I am disposed to decide in favour of the traditional story.*

According to this, then, Henry II. applied to Adrian by means of John of Salisbury to obtain Papal approval for an expedition into Ireland in order to put an end to prevalent lawlessness in Church and State—"to root out crime and wickedness, to defend and preserve the rights of the Church,"† with an undertaking also to establish an annual tribute of Peter's Pence. It is clear that Henry must have impressed the Pope with a shocking idea of the state of things in Ireland to draw from him the approval of his projected expedition and a command to the people of Ireland to receive and obey him as their liege-lord. It is further to be noted that in granting this approval Adrian expressly bases his right so to do upon the overlordship of all Christian islands appertaining to the Holy See in virtue of the supposed "donation of Constantine,"‡ a right generally acknowledged and widely acted upon in those days.

Now, it is to be observed that this privilege of Adrian IV. *was never put into use* by Henry II. It appears to have been laid aside in the archives of

* The latest writer, Professor Thatcher, has rather novel views. He believes, indeed, that Adrian actually *did* make an offer to Henry of Ireland as a fief to be held from the Church, but that Henry "endeavoured to secure Papal recognition of his *absolute* possession of it, while the Popes regarded it as the property of St. Peter." On the other hand, he considers both the letters of Henry II. and the *Laudabiliter* as we now have them to be quite worthless and forgeries—"mere medieval students' exercises." Professor Thatcher's monograph seems the most thorough and critical study of the sources that has yet appeared.

† "Ad subdendum illum populum legibus et vitiorum plantaria inde extirpanda. . . . Pro dilatandis Ecclesiæ terminis, pro vitiorum restringendo decursu, pro corrigendis moribus et virtutibus inserendis, pro Christianæ religionis augmento."

‡ "Hiberniam et omnes insulas quibus Sol justitiæ Christus illuxit . . . ad jus b. Petri et Sacrosanctæ Romanæ Ecclesiæ non est dubium pertinere."

Winchester, together with the emerald ring sent by Adrian, just as his predecessor, Alexander II., had sent a "ring of great price" to William of Normandy when blessing his expedition into England in 1066. It was not until 1171, twelve years after Adrian's death, that Henry II. invaded Ireland, and even then with no reference to that Pope's letter, but in consequence of a series of events which began with the outrage inflicted upon O'Rourke, King of Breiffny, by MacMurrough, King of Leinster, and the subsequent interference of Robert Strongbow, Earl of Striguil. And, in order to obtain sanction for his proceedings in Ireland, Henry applied for and obtained other letters from Pope Alexander III., couched in pretty much the same strain, though without reference to that of Adrian, which became literally a dead letter.*

It is evident that the question of the authenticity or otherwise of Adrian's letter is quite distinct from that of the approval or disapproval of his action. I shall not enter into a discussion of that much-debated point. It is, however, but fair to make the following observations:

(1) With reference to the motives which led Adrian to sanction Henry's project, Miss Norgate truly observes that "our inquiry has nothing to do with the *real* condition of Ireland in the time of Adrian: all that it has to do with is Adrian's idea of that condition."† We cannot doubt that the idea was largely, if not exclusively, based upon the accounts transmitted to him by the English King.

(2) As to the actual state of Ireland at the time, however greatly Henry's agent may have exaggerated the reports about it to the Pope, the Rev. Sylvester Malone quotes evidence‡ from the native Irish annals exclusively, for the fifty years before Adrian's privilege, which give a sad picture of the state of society and

* Miss Norgate truly points out that the *Laudabiliter* is in no sense a Bull; it is a commendatory letter.

† *Op. cit.*, p. 36.

‡ *Op. cit.*, pp. 8-11.

public morality, which the "Annals of the Four Masters" concisely sum up in the statement that "all Ireland was a trembling sod."

(3) Whatever view we may take nowadays of Adrian's right to interfere in the case, it is but just to place ourselves as far as we can in the position of a Catholic of those days. To such a one the Papal action in this and other similar cases appeared not only natural but quite consonant with the public international law which prevailed. And although we now know that the so-called "donation of Constantine," upon which the Papal overlordship of all islands was based, is apocryphal, still it must be remembered that in those days it was universally accepted and acted upon with the general consent of the Christian nations.

These considerations may perhaps somewhat attenuate the censures even of those who most severely condemn the Papal action.

VII. The Last Act.

We must now hurry to a close. The concluding years of Adrian IV.'s life were darkened by a fresh and more serious contest with the haughty German Emperor. Various causes led to this fresh struggle. Frederic had departed in anything but a satisfied state of mind to Germany, and the news of the peace concluded between the Pope and the King of Sicily greatly annoyed him, for he himself claimed as Emperor feudal rights over that kingdom, as over all Italy. On the other hand, the Holy See had serious reasons to be aggrieved at the conduct of Frederic. One reason was the outrageous attack and imprisonment inflicted upon Adrian's old friend of Scandinavian days, Archbishop Eskil of Lund, by some of the Emperor's unruly knights, for which deed the Pope justly felt bound to claim satisfaction. Another was a cause which has repeatedly drawn the Holy See into conflict with Kings and Princes—the defence of the sacredness of the marriage tie, for Frederic (as, centuries after, Napoleon) had divorced his childless wife Adelaide, and taken as a fresh wife Beatrice, heiress of Burgundy. In the Diet held at Besançon in 1157 two Cardinal-Legates (one of whom, the dauntless Roland, was destined to be the next Pope) appeared from Adrian with a strong letter of complaint about the affair of Eskil. A somewhat imprudent style of address adopted by Cardinal Roland at the beginning of the interview evoked a first outbreak of wrath on the part of the Emperor and his nobles, but a single word in the Pope's letter, misunderstood or misinterpreted, fanned the flames into a serious conflagration. Adrian in this letter made use of the word *beneficium* in speaking of the favour he had granted to Frederic two years before in crowning him in Rome. It is clear that the word was used in its natural and obvious sense of a "benefit" or "favour"; but Frederic's evil genius, the Chancellor Reinhold von Tassel (whose ideal seems to have been the creation of a national German State Church, with a German Pope*), translated the word into German as if used in its technical and legal sense of a "fief." This would seem to imply that the Emperor was but the feudal vassal of the Pope. A terrible tumult was the result. The Legates narrowly escaped being cut down by the enraged Princes, and, though saved by the Emperor's personal intervention, were driven ignominiously out of the country. Adrian's subsequent negotiations were conducted with prudence and skill, and in a second legation, in 1158, he was able to explain to the Emperor the misinterpretation that had been placed upon his words, and, Frederic professing himself to be satisfied, a reconciliation was once more, though only temporarily, effected between the two Powers.

* Hefele, "Conciliengeschichte," v., p. 478. It was this Reinhold who carried away the bodies of the three Magi from Milan to Cologne, where they still repose in the Dom.

Notwithstanding this, however, in the November of the same year (1158) Frederic undertook his second invasion of Italy. The object of this expedition was to crush once for all the nascent spirit of Italian independence, and to establish the absolute and despotic supremacy of the Emperor over the whole of Italy. What this meant will be gathered from the doings of the Diet held on the plain of Roncaglia, near Piacenza (November 23), to promulgate a new code of Imperial law. At this Diet the lawyers of Bologna were induced to declare "imperatorem esse Urbis dominum." The jurist Luca di Penna is said to have affirmed, "The Emperor is on earth what God is in heaven"; and the servile Archbishop of Milan, Uberto, almost blasphemously exclaimed: "*Tua Voluntas jus est!*" No wonder that such an assembly, in which, to their shame be it said, fourteen Italian States took part, passed decrees forfeiting to the Emperor all the royalties, dues, and other customs, and exacting homage from all Bishops and nobles. Milan, the city which stood out in the cause of liberty, had been besieged, taken, and humiliated. Other cities suffered similar fates.

The year 1159 was a terrible one for Italy. "Never, perhaps, had Lombardy been so miserable as it was in the early months of 1159." It was at this juncture that Pope Adrian stepped forth as the champion of Italian liberty. In his letters he severely blamed the weakness of the Lombards, encouraged the Milanese, fearlessly bearded the ruthless tyrant, withstood him in the affair of the Archbishopric of Ravenna, and dauntlessly upheld the rights of the Church and the Holy See. He made a powerful appeal to the three Archbishop-Electors of Germany, and at the Diet of Bologna, in the Easter of 1159, practically offered to the all-powerful Emperor by his legates an ultimatum, behind which was the dread threat of deprivation of the Imperial crown and excommunication. This sturdy bearding of the lion in his den has won the just admiration of historians. There can be no doubt that to the unflinching courage and splendid example of the English Pope the Italian States owed much of that spirit of resolute independence which, years after Adrian's death, was to bear splendid fruit in the victory of Legnano.

War now seemed inevitable. The Emperor was advancing Romewards; Adrian was fortifying his fortresses. The insolence of Frederic's letters proved that all reconciliation was impossible, and Adrian was preparing to issue the dreaded Bull of excommunication against the Emperor, both for his public misdeeds and for putting away his lawful wife and taking to himself another. At this critical moment God suddenly called him by an attack of quinsy, which ended fatally on September 1, 1159. His enemies of the Imperial party spread the absurd report that he had been choked by a fly, and this ridiculous story has come down with so many other "lies of history." His body was carried to Rome, and buried in a red marble sarcophagus, next to that of Eugenius III., in old St. Peter's. In 1607 it was removed to the new basilica, where it may still be seen in the crypt, with the simple inscription, "Hadrianus Papa IIII." On the occasion of the translation the body was exhumed, and is said, together with the pontificals in which it was arrayed, to have been found entire.

So ended the remarkable career of the first and last Englishman who ever attained to the Papal throne, and one of the greatest and ablest of all the successors of St. Peter. I have endeavoured, not without difficulty, to compress within a moderate space but a jejune summary of the stirring events of his extraordinary pontificate, and even so have had to omit even reference to several other great questions in which he was involved, such as the organization of the Spanish Church, the projected expedition of Louis VII. of France into Spain, and the bringing about of good relations between France and England. It must be remembered that all the really great and important events of European history were crowded into a brief pontificate of less than five years, and we shall then have some idea of the energy, the strength of will, the statesmanship, and the political genius of this truly great man.

As regards his personal character, history records of him that he was eminent for great learning, for eloquence as a preacher, for his splendid voice, his beauty and dignity of person, and passing sweetness and kindness of disposition. Of other traits of character we have already spoken in preceding pages.

He is mentioned as having written several works, all unfortunately lost to us. One of these, it is interesting to note, was upon the Immaculate Conception of the Blessed Virgin.*

In estimating his political actions as Pope we must be careful to judge according to the notions and principles of his own times. To modern readers much of it may appear overbearing or arbitrary; but let us not forget that, as a man of the highest integrity and courage, he felt himself bound before God and man to maintain and transmit that great heritage of power and authority which he had received from his predecessors. Not only that, but in stepping forward to uphold the cause of the Church and Italy against the greatest and most formidable of all the German Kaisers, he became the saviour of Europe and of Christendom.

"His object" (writes Bishop Creighton) "was to maintain the claims of the Roman Church as they had been defined by Gregory VII. In this he showed skill, resoluteness, and decision; but he had for his antagonist the mightiest of the Emperors. He bequeathed to his successor a hazardous conflict, in which the Papacy succeeded in holding its own."†

* Translations into English of the Apostles' Creed and the Lord's Prayer (the latter metrical), attributed to Adrian, are still preserved (see Tarleton, p. 254).

† "Dictionary of National Biography," vol. i., p. 145.

Had Providence not raised up this great Englishman at the time, what would have been the result to Italy and to the Church of the West? The glorious history of the struggle for freedom of the Italian Republics would never have been written, and the Church of Europe, absorbed in a new and irresistible Cæsarism, would have been brought to the condition of the Orthodox Russian Church under the Tsars, or of Islam under the Sultans of Turkey.

It has been not unjustly pointed out that German nationality and unity, too, are indebted to the stand made by Adrian and his successors against Barbarossa's plans. For had his scheme been carried out, and had the Emperor really become "Urbis Dominus," the seat of empire would in all probability have been transferred to Rome; Italy would have become the centre of gravity of Europe, and Germany would have remained a half-civilized and outlying province of the Empire.

BOOKS TO BE CONSULTED.

ALFRED H. TARLETON. "Nicholas Breakspear (Adrian IV.): Englishman and Pope." London: Arthur L. Humphreys, 1896.

RICHARD RABY. "Pope Adrian IV.: An Historical Sketch." London: Richardson and Son, 1849.

Very Rev. SYLVESTER MALONE, M.R.I.A., F.R.S.A.I. "Adrian IV. and Ireland." Dublin: Gill and Son, 1899.

OLIVER JOSEPH THATCHER. "Studies concerning Adrian IV." Chicago: The University of Chicago Press, 1903.

IV

THE CHURCH AND THE PRINTING-PRESS*

PRINTING A CATHOLIC ART.

THERE are many people who are either not aware or will not admit that the connection between Catholic truth and the printing-press is one of ancient date and closest intimacy. It has become part and parcel of what may be styled the "Reformation myth" and the "Protestant legend" that, somehow or another, the printing-press was intimately connected with the so-called Reformation, and an English historian is supposed to have neatly summed up this view by styling the printing-press "the great hammer of the Reformers, by which they broke to pieces the power of the Papacy." The legend goes further still. According to what I will style the Luther myth—based, indeed, as will be seen later, on words of Luther himself, and still piously believed in by many an earnest Protestant and repeated in books of history—the beginning of Martin Luther's spiritual awakening was the fact that in 1505, Luther's twenty-second year, "one day he accidentally took from the shelves of the library [of the University of Erfurt, where he had studied for four years, and just taken his doctor's degree] a book he had not seen before—an old Latin Bible. Delighted with this treasure, only scraps

* Chief authorities: Janssen, "Geschichte des deutschen Volkes," Bd. I., pp. 9-20, 50-54; Von der Linde, and Falk, several articles in the *Dietsche Warande* (in Dutch), tt. I. and III.

of which he had as yet heard of, he read it—read it again and again, and committed large portions to memory." This anecdote (which I quote from Dr. Bullock's well-known manual of the modern history of Europe, in use in English schools) I beg the reader to bear in mind, as it will receive much interesting elucidation from the historical facts I am about to present to his notice.

In order to understand what follows, it will be necessary to refer briefly to what is known of the origin and the early history of the art of printing.

We may begin by asserting unhesitatingly that, whatever be the subsequent history and character of the art of printing, in its origin and early history it was an essentially Catholic art—Catholic in invention, Catholic in its use, and, above all, for long exclusively consecrated to the propagation of Catholic truth. The invention of the art of printing with movable types dates from the year 1441, or forty-two years before the birth of Martin Luther. Its inventor was almost certainly John Guttenberg of Mainz.

It will be interesting to know with what sentiments the new invention was received by the Church and her ministers at the time. The Carthusian monk Werner Rolewinck greets it in these terms in 1474: "The art of printing, invented at Mainz, is the art of arts, the science of sciences, through whose rapid spread the world has been enriched and enlightened by a splendid treasure, hitherto hidden, of knowledge and wisdom. An endless number of books which hitherto were known to only a few students in Athens or Paris, or other Universities, are now disseminated by this art through all races, peoples and nations, and in every language." The Benedictine historian of Westphalia, Bernhard Witte, monk of Liesborn, speaks of the art of printing as one "than which there hath never been in the world any art more worthy, more laudable, more useful, more holy or divine." Another contemporary, Jacob Wimpheling, wrote: "We Germans can pride ourselves on no other discovery or intellectual production so much as upon that of printing, which has raised us up to be new intellectual carriers of the teaching of Christianity, of all Divine and mundane knowledge, and so to be benefactors of all mankind." The old chronicle of Koelhoff contains the following expressions: "How many prayers and numberless inward aspirations are drawn from printed books! What great profit and happiness are derived by those who make or help to prepare printed books!"

The new art was disseminated throughout Europe with astonishing rapidity and inexpressible religious enthusiasm—not, be it observed, as a commercial speculation or for the sake of material advantages, as the telephone or the typewriter in our own days, but rather as a religious work and a means of propagating Catholic truth. From 1462 to 1500 the names of one thousand printers, mostly of German origin, have been preserved. In Mainz itself, during the very infancy of the art, five printing-presses were established, in Ulm six, in Basel sixteen, in Augsburg twenty, in Cologne twenty-one; in Nuremberg, up to 1500, five-and-twenty printers had been admitted to the rights of citizenship. Before the end of the fifteenth century over one hundred German printing-presses had been established in Italy.* By the same date Spain reckoned thirty printers, whom the Spanish poet Lope de Vega elegantly entitled "the armourers of civilization." The art reached Buda-Pesth in 1473, London in 1477, Oxford in 1478, Denmark in 1482, Stockholm in 1483 (the year of Luther's birth), Constantinople in 1490.

Those early printers who went forth from the birthplace of the new art to propagate it in various lands were looked upon by their contemporaries almost with veneration, as new missionaries and apostles of the truth. "As formerly the missionaries of Christianity," writes the before-quoted Wimpheling, "so now the disciples

* Where Dante's "Divina Commedia" was first printed as early as 1472.

of the *holy art* go forth from Germany into all lands, and these printed books become, as it were, heralds of the Gospel, preachers of the truth and of knowledge." "How much all classes of human society," wrote, in 1487, Adolf Occo, physician to the Bishop of Augsburg, "nowadays owe to the art of printing, which, through the mercy of Almighty God, has been made known in our time, any sensible man can easily judge for himself. But whilst all are under obligations to it, it is in an especial degree the bride of Christ, the Catholic Church, who hath been newly glorified by means of this art, and who now, more richly adorned, goeth forth to meet her Bridegroom, for He hath endowed her to overflowing with books of heavenly wisdom."

The View of the Church.

What, it may be asked, was the view of the Church herself, and what part did she practically take in the art of printing? The materials for an answer to this question are abundant indeed. Bishops, like Rudolf of Scherenberg and Lorenz of Würzburg, granted indulgences for the sale and dissemination of printed books. Berthold, Archbishop of Mainz, speaks of the "Divine art of printing." The following letter from Andrea de Bossi, Bishop of Alaria, in Corsica, was written in 1468, to Pope Paul II.:

"In your time, by the grace of God, has this gift been bestowed upon the Christian world, that even the poorest, for a few coins, can obtain for themselves a number of books. Is it not a great glory for your Holiness that volumes which formerly could scarcely be bought for a hundred ducats at present may be had for twenty gold pieces, or less, and are no longer full of errors, as they used to be? and that books which the reader formerly bought with difficulty for twenty ducats can now be got for four, and less? And again, whilst all the most eminent minds of antiquity, on account of the wearisome labours required, and the too great cost of hand copying, were formerly almost buried under dust and moths, they have now again, under your rule, begun to reappear, and, like a broad stream, are poured forth all over the earth. For so masterly is the art of our printers and type-engravers, that not only among human inventions of modern times, but also among those of antiquity, it would be difficult to find anything more excellent. . . . This is the reason why the laudable and pious wish of Nicholas Cusanus, Cardinal of St. Peter's ad Vincula, always was that this *holy art*, which then first saw the light in Germany, should be introduced into Rome. Already have the wishes of this man, whom you, Holy Father, loved as the apple of your eye, honoured and admired, been fulfilled in your own time, as I believe, through his intercession at the throne of our Lord Jesus Christ."

The introduction into Italy of the art of printing, here referred to by Bossi, was the work of the two German printers Konrad Sweynheym and Arnald Pannartz, who, be it noted, set up their first printing-press in the great Benedictine abbey of Subiaco, whence, later on, they proceeded to Rome, under the special patronage of the Holy See. Von der Linde, the historian of printing, has recorded that from 1466 to 1472 they published twenty-eight works, in forty-seven different editions, so that he calculates that this one press, during a space of seven years, must have issued more than 124 millions of printed pages, and truly remarks, "How many scribes would have been necessary to write out in MS. all these pages!"

"In taking a general survey of the books issued by the English presses upon the introduction of the art of printing," writes Abbot Gasquet, "the inquirer can hardly fail to be struck with the number of religious, or quasi-religious, works which formed the bulk of the early printed books. This fact alone is sufficient evidence that the invention which at this period worked a veritable revolution in the intellectual life of the world was welcomed by the ecclesiastical authorities as a valuable auxiliary in the work of instruction. In England the first presses were set up under the patronage of Churchmen, and a very large proportion of the early books were actually works of instruction or volumes furnishing material to the clergy."*

The Religious Orders as Printers.

It was not only, however, by their praise and their blessing that the clergy encouraged the art of printing; they themselves, and especially the religious Orders, took an active part in the work of the printing-press. The Brothers of the Common Life, well known as the congregation to which Thomas à Kempis belonged, set up a printing-press in their house at Rostock, and issued their first printed book as early as 1476, in which they speak of the art of printing as "the mistress of all arts for the benefit of the Church," and style themselves, "preachers, not by word, but by writing." One is reminded irresistibly by these words of the maxim of the late Cardinal Vaughan, "This is the age of the apostolate of the press;" and of the saying—attributed, I think, to an American ecclesiastic—that, if St. Paul were living now, he would be, not a preacher, but the editor of a great newspaper.

But to return: It was not only in Rostock that the Brothers of the Common Life practised the art of printing in their convents. Very early on they set up a well-appointed printing-press in their convent of Nazareth at Brussels, where we find them busily at work between 1476 and 1484. Seventeen works published at their press are known. Several of these bear the imprint "in famosa civitate Bruxellensi per fratres com. vitæ in Nazareth." The "Groto solitos sive

* "The Eve of the Reformation," pp. 315, 316.

Speculum Conscientiæ" of Arnold of Gheilhoven was the first book printed in Brussels. In their convent at Hem, near Schoonhoven, they announce in 1495 that they print books in both Latin and German.*

Monastery Presses.

The following are some more examples of these monastery printing-presses:

At Augsburg, in the Benedictine abbey of Saints Ulric and Afra, Abbot Melchior set up a printing-press (1472), in order to supply his monks with constant work in printing, correcting, binding, and publishing books. In the monastery of St. Peter at Erfurt, Abbot Gunther, with the approval and support of many other monasteries, established a press in 1479, the first work issued being a "Lectionarium," or Book of Epistles and Gospels.

The Benedictine abbey of Ottobeuren possessed an unusually extensive press, concerning which Maurus Feyerabend says in his chronicles: "At this time the immortal Abbot Leonhard, assisted by the learned Ellenbog, who was already at that time Prior of the community, set up a printing-press in his monastery, wherein, with the exception of Marc Elend, a monk from Füssen, who cleaned the formes, only monks of the monastery itself were employed."

The Cluniac monks of St. Albans in England had a press, wherein, between 1480 and 1486, eight works were printed by the unknown master called the "Schoolmaster." One of these books was the celebrated "Bokys of Hawking and Hunting" of Dame Juliana Berners, Prioress of the neighbouring convent of Sopewell, 1485.

* The same brothers set the example of printing in the Rhineland, where they opened the first of all monastery presses at Marienthal as early as 1468.

The Carthusians of Cologne printed a considerable number of books from 1490 onwards. The same Order had also a press at Strasburg.

In Italy we find a press in the Minorite monastery at Venice in 1477, and in the same year the Carthusians are printing at Parma. About the same time at Savona, near Milan, in the Augustinian convent, we find one of the brothers, known as "Bonus Joannes," engaged in printing the "Consolations" of Boëthius, whilst the Prior Venturinus corrects the proofs. Still more remarkable is the activity of the Italian Dominicans in this direction. Between 1476 and 1483, in the Dominican convent of Florence, two brothers of the Order, Domenico da Pistoja and Pietro da Pisa, as they themselves tell us, are busy producing printed books in great quantity, in so much that by the year of Luther's birth this monastery press had issued no less than seventy or eighty printed works, the highest record attained by any of these monastic printers.

In the far east of Europe the work of these convent presses was still more important. Duke George of Montenegro, whose father had founded the monastery of Cettinje in 1485, set up therein, at his own cost, in 1494-1495, a press, where the monk Macarius printed with finely-cut Venetian letters. Duke Bozidar of Servia between 1519 and 1528 had liturgical works printed at Venice, being aided in his undertaking by the monk Pacomius from Montenegro, two other monks, and a priest. Indeed, according to Schafarik, all the old Slav printed books, especially those in the Cyrillic character, were produced by the monks.

In addition to the monasteries where the monks themselves worked at the press, quite a long list could be given of other convents, both of men and women, wherein printing-presses were set up and worked by professional printers—some, masters of their art, whose names are still famous, others itinerant printers, who went about from town to town to earn their bread.

Following Falk, I will mention the following religious houses which had presses of this kind:

The great abbey of Cluny, about 1493; St. Michael's Abbey at Bamberg; the Cucufatis Monastery, Barcelona, about 1489; the convent of the discalced Franciscans at Sontheim, near Frankfort, 1511-1512; the great Carthusian monastery at Lyons, 1517; the Premonstratensian convent of Our Blessed Lady at Magdeburg, about 1504; that of the Holy Trinity at Miramar in Majorca, 1495; that of Sant' Eusebio in Rome, 1470; the Benedictine monastery of Saint Yrier de la Perche, near Limoges, and also that of Zinna, or Cenna, 1492; the Benedictine abbey of Lantenai in Brittany, in 1480; the Camaldulensian monastery at Fonte Buono in Lombardy, 1520; the monastery of Santa Maria della Grazia in Milan, 1499; and that of St. Ambrogio in the same city, 1486; at the Carthusian monastery of Namur, 1485; the Premonstratensian monastery at Schussenried in Swabia, 1478; the Hieronymites in Valladolid, and also at Montserrat; the Carthusian monastery of St. Andreas in littore in Venice, 1508; also the convent of the Sisters of Penance at the same place; and, finally, the celebrated Swedish convent of St. Bridget in Wadstena, about 1491.

Secular "Priest-Printers."

So far we have spoken only of the regular clergy as taking an active part in the work of printing; what is perhaps more remarkable is the large share taken in this practical cultivation of the art of printing by the secular clergy. Falk has compiled a list of priests, in different parts of Europe, who occupied themselves in the management of printing-presses. From this it appears that the names of thirty-one priest-printers in twenty-seven different towns have been preserved. The first of all printers in Venice—according to some, the first in all Italy—was the priest Clement of Padua, 1471, and he was a self-taught adept of the art. The names of three other priests, out of the two hundred printers who were at work in Venice before 1500, have been preserved; they are Lorenzo de Aquila, Boneto Locatello, a priest of Bergamo, and Francesco da Lucca, priest and cantor at the church of San Marco. At Milan a number of ecclesiastics encouraged, at their own expense, the introduction of printing, and one of them at least, Giampietro Casaroto, was himself a printer in 1498. In Florence three priests—Lorenzo de Morgianis, Francesco de Bonaccursi and one Bartolomeo—printed several books between 1492 and 1500, whilst the Provost of the Duomo, Vespucci, corrected the proofs. It was a German priest from Strasburg, Sixtus Kissinger by name, who first introduced printing into Naples, and who refused many honours, including a bishopric, in favour of his art. He, and also another German priest, Schenkbecker, afterwards a Canon of the Chapter of St. Thomas, both practised the art later on in Rome. At Vicenza and at Trent we find parish priests printing books. Other priest-printers are enumerated at Barcelona, Basel, Breslau, Brixen, Brün, Copenhagen, Leipsic, Lerida, in Catalonia, Metz, Mainz, Lübeck, and even in Iceland, where the first press was erected before 1534 by Bishop John Arcson.

I must not weary my readers with extending this long enumeration. Enough has surely been said to show with what enthusiasm the clergy of the Catholic Church both welcomed and practically helped in the work of the printing-press in the earliest days of its infancy. The same lesson is taught by the munificent patronage extended by the clergy to printers and their productions. Cardinal Turrecremata in 1466 and Cardinal Caraffa in 1469 invited distinguished German printers to Rome, and by 1475 the Eternal City already possessed twenty printing-presses, and by the close of the century 925 printed works had been issued from these presses. It was the clergy also who were the chief purchasers of printed books, and to their generous support the success of the art must be largely attributed.

I think I have now said enough to enable us to judge of the correctness of the statement which represents the printing-press as the "hammer for the destruction of Papacy." It would be no exaggeration to say that for full fifty years before the date of Luther's famous visit to Rome the art of printing was the favourite and most powerful sword in the hands of the Papacy. and that we may not unjustly attribute to the efficacy of this "divine art," as it was called by monks and bishops of the time, the protection of a large part of Catholic Europe from the effects of the so-called Reformation.

The Luther Legend.

Let me now remind the reader of the famous anecdote of Luther's "discovery" of a Latin Bible in the library of the Erfurt University, that familiar commonplace of the Protestant Reformation myth to which I have referred at the beginning of this address. In order to appreciate aright the worth of this story, a few more historical data must be given, not forgetting that the famous scene is placed in the year 1505. Now, the facts are these. Of all the works printed by the one thousand printers whose names are still preserved before the year 1500, no book was so often printed, especially in Germany, as the Bible. By the year 1500 no less than one hundred editions of the Vulgate, or Latin Bible, had appeared, and Janssen has shown that at this time the ordinary number of copies per edition of a printed book was about one thousand. More than this, in 1483—the year of Luther's birth—the first edition of the Bible in the German language appeared in Koburger's press, and was illustrated with one hundred wood engravings of Wolgemuth, and between that date and the outbreak of the great religious schism no less than fourteen different editions of the entire Bible in High German, and five in Low German, had already been published, to say nothing of numerous editions of separate parts of Holy Scripture, such as the Psalms or the Gospels.

How warmly the people of Germany were urged to read these editions in the vernacular may be seen from some of the quaint passages from contemporary Catholic writers quoted by Janssen. "All that Holy Church teaches," says a writer in 1513, "all that thou hearest in sermons and other instructions, what thou readest written in spiritual books, what thou singest to God's honour and glory, what thou prayest for thy soul's welfare, and what thou sufferest in trial and trouble, should encourage thee to read with piety and humility in the Holy Scriptures and Bibles, as they are nowadays set forth in the German tongue, and scattered far and wide in great numbers, wholly or in part, and as thou mayest now purchase them for but little money." The editors of the Cologne Bible of 1470-1480 declare that they have illustrated their edition with woodcuts in order to attract readers the more to the diligent use of Holy Scripture. Everything shows that the wide diffusion of the Holy Bible, in both Latin and German, at the close of the fifteenth century had given quite a remarkable impetus to the study of Holy Scripture. Adam Potken, a priest of Xanten, had, as a boy, between 1470-1480, to learn by heart the four Gospels, and later on used to read daily, with his scholars of eleven or twelve years of age, portions both of the Old and the New Testament. In 1480 a Canon of Cassel founded at Erfurt University a scholarship in favour of a student of his village, for an eight years' course of the study of Holy Scripture.

I think my readers will now have sufficient material to judge for themselves of the inherent probability of the Luther legend. By the year 1500, five years before the Erfurt episode is alleged to have taken place, the printing-presses of Europe (all Catholic, be it noted, and many of them monastic) had issued one hundred different editions of the Vulgate or Latin Bible, equivalent to at least one hundred thousand copies. In addition to this, at least five or six translations of the complete Bible into German had also been printed, and the reading and study of Holy Scripture was widely diffused and warmly encouraged throughout Germany. At such a time and in such surroundings Martin Luther, a talented student of the University of Erfurt, having already taken his bachelor's and doctor's degree, and being in his twenty-second year, is supposed to make an accidental discovery of a Latin Bible in the University library, a book he had never seen before, and the unexpected discovery and reading of which, we are asked to believe, effects a crisis in his intellectual and spiritual life!

The extraordinary thing is, that this incredible tale is directly based on Luther's own words, who says: "When I was twenty years old I had never seen a Bible; I thought there were no other Gospels or Epistles except those in the 'Postillæ'" (*i.e.*, "Commentaries"; see his collected works, edited by Plochmann and Irischer, Erlangen, 1826-1868, vol. lx., p. 255). What are we to think of the veracity of this statement? The judgment of Janssen seems but mildly expressed when he introduces the quotation with the phrase "if one may believe his words," and adds: "These words are all the more wonderful, as, when he was twenty years old, he had already been two years at Erfurt University, and cannot have failed to have many opportunities to get to know the Bible. For at Erfurt Biblical studies had flourished since the middle of the fifteenth century; among the MS. theological works existing in one of the town libraries about one-half consist of exegetical works."

I would venture to submit that the only charitable explanation for so fantastic a tale would be to imagine the young doctor of Erfurt as a kind of intellectual Rip Van Winkle, who had been sound asleep all those years of his student life, whilst the noise of over a thousand printing-presses in monastery, cathedral, and printing works was filling the intellectual atmosphere of Germany, and stirring up a new and warmer intellectual life throughout the ranks of clergy and laity alike, and most of all by the diffusion and diligent study of the Holy Scriptures.

Subsequent abuses of the printing-press, and evils which it may afterwards have given rise to, whether in the intellectual or moral order—and no one can shut his eyes to the serious extent of such evils—can therefore never deprive the art of printing of the title it inherited at its birth of a truly Catholic art, and of one of the noblest instruments of the Catholic Church. The existence of the Catholic Truth Society in our midst is a living proof that the printing-press has not yet lost, and never will lose, its efficacy for doing good by the spread of Catholic truth.

V

THE DUTCH POPE

1459 — 1523 = 64

I. The Scholar and Professor.

One dark winter's evening, somewhere about the year 1480—so runs the charming legend*—the Princess Margaret of York, sister of Edward IV. of England, and widow of the ill-fated Charles the Bold, Duke of Burgundy,† at that time residing at the Flemish University town of Louvain, was returning to her residence in the ancient castle on Mont-César‡ (where nowadays rises the new Benedictine abbey of Regina Cœli) when she called into one of the town churches to offer a prayer.

> " There was no light,
> Save where the lamps that glittered, few and faint,
> Lighted a little space before some saint."

She was struck by the sight of a young and impecunious scholar poring over his books by the aid of one of those lamps, too industrious to waste the precious hours

* The story is not found in either Moringus, Adrian's first biographer, Valerius Andreas, Vernulaeus, or Molanus.

† See genealogical table, p. 115.

‡ There is, of course, no foundation for the popular legend that the original structure was one of Cæsar's camps. It had, however, a very interesting history as the feudal castle of the Counts and Dukes of Brabant. In 1338, Edward III. of England and his queen wintered here on their way back from Germany.

which might still be devoted to study, too poor to "waste the midnight oil" in his own humble lodgings. Touched by the youth's zeal and poverty, the widowed English Princess—continues the story—immediately took upon herself the care of his future, and provided him with the means to pursue his further studies at the University founded some half-century before by John the Good, Duke of Brabant.

The pretty story in this form unfortunately seems not to bear the test of historical accuracy; nevertheless, there is this much of truth underlying it, that Margaret of York actually did afford substantial support and patronage, though in somewhat different form and at a later date, to this modest scholar, who was one Adrian of Utrecht, a young Dutchman, whose name is one of the brightest ornaments of the Flemish University.

Adrian was born in Utrecht in 1459. His father was one Florent, or Florensz,* whence he came to be styled in after-life Master Adrian Florisze, though this latter name was no surname, but simply meant "son of Florent," exactly as the latter is sometimes styled "Florent Boeijens," or "Bouwens"—*i.e.*, son of Baldwin; for at this time the common people of the Netherlands had no family surnames, a distinction reserved to the nobility. This fact is of interest, for it indicates that Adrian was of humble plebeian origin, just like the English Nicholas Breakspeare, who eventually became Pope Adrian IV. It does not, however, seem correct to say that he was actually very poor, like the English lad of Langley, for in the register of Louvain University—still preserved—the epithet "pauper," which it was at the time customary to place beside the names of indigent scholars when matriculated, does not appear, and in 1469 and 1474 we find his widowed mother, Gertrude, selling two houses, which indicates

* And not Floris, as Creighton writes it ("History of the Papacy," vi., p. 222). Floris is the genitive form of Florent, and used as a patronymic, as explained in the text.

the possession of some property on her part. However, it is certain that Adrian's parents were not much blessed with the goods of this world. The father, who seems to have been a small artisan, probably a weaver of tapestry or of silk,* died by the time the boy was ten, and once more, like Nicholas Breakspeare, the lad owed his early training in both letters and piety to an excellent mother. Gertrude, we are told, taught him to love visiting the churches, to serve Mass, and to listen attentively to the sermons, which she made him repeat to her on his return home. As he had manifested from his tenderest years unusual aptitude for learning, she did all she possibly could to encourage and develop his talents, and sent him to school to learn the *trivium*, as it was then called, comprising probably Latin, with arithmetic and logic. He learnt his first elements of Latin at Delft, in the school of the Brothers of the Common Life, a fact of considerable importance for his future development. These Brothers of the Common Life, whose name will ever be held in blessing for having given to the world Thomas à Kempis, had been founded in 1396 by Gerard Groote as a reaction against the excesses into which scholasticism had fallen. "Let the foundation of thy studies," said the pious founder, "and the mirror of thy life be first of all the Gospels, for they contain the life of Christ, then the lives of the Saints and the sentences of the Fathers, the Epistles of St. Paul and the Acts of the Apostles. . . . Lose not thy time in geometry, rhetoric, dialectic, grammar, poetry, and astrology. All that doth not render us better or turn us away from evil is harmful."

Like most reactions, Gerard's teachings went to extremes, and after his death his Order considerably modified them, and cultivated science and literature with success. But it inherited his practical tendencies

* Lord Bacon makes him a brewer ("Historia Henrici VII.," p. 1037). I do not know where Creighton (*op. cit.*, p. 222) got the idea that he was a "ship's carpenter."

in education, and his aversion to the exaggerated subtleties of the later scholasticism. In such a school as that of Delft we see the source of that love of Scripture and the Fathers, that good common-sense in philosophy, and that dislike of pedantry which distinguished Adrian through all his life. After the school of Delft, Adrian completed his preliminary studies either at Zwolle, where Thomas à Kempis had lived his religious life of seventy-one years, or, according to others, at Deventer. Everywhere distinguished by his brilliant successes, which placed him far ahead of all his competitors, he was ready at the age of seventeen to enter the flourishing University of Louvain, just fifty years founded, and at the time one of the most celebrated in Europe. Adrian was enrolled on June 1, 1476.

The Flemish University had lately received large additions to its ranks in the numerous students who had fled from the University of Prague, which had been destroyed in the Hussite wars, and in the four hundred Burgundian subjects expelled from that of Paris by Louis XI. Erasmus, who a few years later was Adrian's own pupil at the University, declares that it was the most numerously frequented of all except Paris, the students surpassing three thousand in number, and increasing day by day. "The climate," he boasts, "is preferable to that of Italy, being not only delightful but also healthy. Nowhere," he continues, "are studies pursued with more success and quietude, nowhere is the intellectual output more abundant, nowhere a larger or better equipped staff of professors." The discipline, if we may believe the descriptions of the time, was not only severe but very well observed. After curfew the students were forbidden to go out in public places without carrying a lantern at the level of their face, and, as at the Oxford and Cambridge of to-day, both masters and students had to wear their gowns whether at church or at lectures. Extravagant and worldly costumes were forbidden, and when the students saw any of their number contravening this rule they ran after them, hooting and crying, "Barbara! Barbara!"

The University comprised five faculties—Theology, Canon Law, Civil Law, Medicine, and Arts, the latter being a preparation for the other faculties. The wave of the Classical Renascence had not yet made itself felt in Louvain, and the study of philosophy was the chief occupation of the faculty of Arts, the Humanities being but little esteemed. Neither the rhetoric which was taught at this time, nor the Latin which was in use, seems to have been of a very high order, though things were very soon after destined to be much changed for the better. Four colleges or hostels, abundantly endowed with charitable foundations for poorer pupils, were attached to the faculty of Arts, and bore the curious names of the Pig, the Castle, the Falcon, and the Lily. Life in these colleges was sufficiently strenuous and severe. The students rose before daybreak, assembled in the great hall for prayers, then attended a lecture, after which, at six o'clock, they heard Mass. The rest of the day was passed in lectures, repetitions, and public or private disputations. The course lasted two years, apparently without any vacation. Notes were not taken, and the whole work appears to have been a gigantic effort of memory.

It was into the first-named of the four hostels (the Pig College) that young Adrian made his entrance. His exceptional gifts of intellect, his unusually powerful memory, and his extraordinary zeal for study, soon rendered him master of all that the faculty of Arts could teach him at the time—philosophy, physics, rhetoric. His Latin style, though not adorned with the graces which characterize the authors of the Renascence, was sufficiently elegant to escape the biting criticisms of Erasmus. For mathematics he showed a special aptitude, and soon was called upon to teach them. No wonder his fame rapidly spread in the University. When the Venetian Ambassador, Hermolaus Barbarus

—accounted one of the leading Italian humanists of the day*—visited Louvain, and asked to be introduced to an eminent member of the faculty of Arts, in order to discuss philosophy with him, Adrian was at once chosen, and we are told that the Venetian scholar was charmed with the penetrating intelligence and varied erudition of the young Dutch student.

One of the greatest events in the old University of Louvain was the annual competitions at the close of the Arts course for the much-coveted title of Primus, or first in the faculty of Arts, a distinction which was apparently as highly valued as the Senior Wranglership in modern Cambridge, and celebrated by festivities, both at the University and in the native place of the successful candidate, in a style of which we have little notion at the present day. We are not surprised to learn that the Primus in 1478 was Adrian, then nineteen years of age, on which occasion he made a public triumphal entry into his native town of Utrecht. Immediately after he passed the solemn act entitled *inceptio*, and thereby became a fully-fledged Master of Arts.

His liberal education now completed, Adrian at once began his course of Theology, which in those days lasted no less than ten years. For this purpose he entered the Collège du Saint-Esprit, founded in 1442 by Louise de Rycke for theological students, and which, then as now, was a hostel, giving board and lodging, though not teaching. Of Adrian's long course of studies in this faculty we have not many details. We know, however, that he threw himself with all the ardour of his nature and the keenness of his intellect into the study of the Fathers and theologians, and also of Holy Scripture; and, not content with the varied studies of his own faculty, he applied himself to those of both Civil and Canon Law. No wonder that his biographer, Moringus, expresses his astonishment that Adrian was able to pursue with such success so many different

* See Abbot Gasquet, "The Eve of the Reformation," p. 29.

branches of study at the same time. The explanation, he tells us, is to be found in his methodical use of time: every hour was employed by rule, and every occupation had its fixed time. No wonder that he soon became known as the most brilliant ornament of the University, and eventually one of the greatest Catholic theologians of the Reformation epoch. "Magnus sine controversia theologus," writes Erasmus, his pupil.

At the end of ten years of this strenuous student's life (in 1488) Adrian was appointed to teach philosophy in his old college, the Pig, and also elected a member of the General Council of the University; and two years later (1490) he was promoted to a professorship of Theology, carrying with it a prebend and a stall as Canon of St. Pierre. This promotion is the more remarkable as he had not yet obtained his degree as Licentiate in Theology, owing probably to his want of means to meet the expenses of the examination. Patronage, however, now began to flow in upon him in a steady stream. In the same year (1490) he received the appointment of Curé of the Béguinage,* and his resources now permitted him to proceed to the Licentiate's degree in 1491, on which occasion, we are told, the magistracy of Louvain offered him two measures of Rhine wine as a mark of their esteem.

On June 21, 1491, Adrian at last crowned his career by obtaining the coveted degree of D.D. The public examinations, or "defensions," as they are styled, for the obtension of this crowning academic honour, and the elaborate function of its actual conferment, are sufficiently imposing in the actual University in our own times, lasting as they do three full days, and

* The Curé of the Béguinage in which Adrian dwelt—No. 153, Rue des Moutons—is now the residence of my venerated master, Mgr. T. J. Lamy, Emeritus Professor of Holy Scripture and Semitic Languages, and well known by his numerous writings. The house itself has been rebuilt since Adrian's time, but the cellars and the garden are much the same as when he dwelt there.

involving public celebrations in the town, as well as in the academical premises. But in the early University of the fifteenth century they were far more elaborate, lasting no less than five days, and terminating with a banquet given by the new doctors. The expenses, therefore, were very considerable, and beyond the reach of many a poor scholar. Here it is that we come into actual historical contact with the English Princess, Margaret Plantagenet, concerning whom we related a pretty, though probably apocryphal, anecdote at the beginning. What is certain is that, whether she knew Adrian and had benefited him before or not, she now stepped forward and generously defrayed all the expenses of his doctorate. On this occasion also the Louvain magistracy, according to a custom frequently honoured at the time, contributed no less than forty-eight measures of Rhine wine, costing thirteen gold florins, in honour of the new doctor.

More substantial favours rapidly followed. Margaret of York conferred upon Adrian the benefice of Goerzee, in the island of Zealand, which he was allowed to retain *in absentia*, whilst administering it by means of a pious and capable curate whom he suitably maintained. Several times a year Adrian visited his distant parish to preach and shrive his people and reform abuses. Other preferments quickly followed. It must be remembered that those were the days of pluralities, before the reform of the Council of Trent. We need not, therefore, be surprised to learn that Adrian had conferred upon him successively the benefices of Canon of St. Peter at Anderlecht (Brussels), of Provost of St. Quentin (Maubeuge), of Dean of Notre-Dame at Antwerp, and of Canon and Treasurer of St. Mary's in his native town of Utrecht. No doubt such cumulations of ecclesiastical benefices *in absentia* were essentially an abuse, though quite in the ordinary course of events. But in Adrian's case the abuse was greatly diminished by the personal sanctity of his life and the scrupulous justice of his administration. His own household was as simple, his table as frugal, as ever. The large revenues of his various benefices were spent, not on himself, but on the poor of his flock, or on indigent students, and in munificent foundations. Moreover, his intellectual gifts, his theological and canonical abilities were placed unstintedly at the disposal of all. People flocked to consult him from all parts—from Holland and Flanders, from Hainault and from Zealand.

In the University he was now by far the man of greatest mark. For full twenty years, from 1492 to 1512, he held the post of ordinary Professor of the Theological Faculty. His lectures became renowned for the solidity of their matter, and the clearness of their style. His elocutionary gifts were remarkable. He did not, indeed, publish much, though he wrote a great deal. His principal theological work, entitled "Quæstiones in Quartum Sententiarum Librum,"* which was the résumé of his lectures up to 1509, was first published surreptitiously, and without the author's knowledge, at Paris in 1516 by Godocus Badius, under the editorship of a professor of the Sorbonne, Jacques d'Assoneville. The following year it was republished at Louvain itself by Martin Dorpius, a pupil of Adrian, and the work soon became popular, for other editions followed at Paris, Louvain, Venice, Rome, and Lyons all without any participation on Adrian's part. Its merits were its simplicity and clearness, a return to the method of St. Thomas Aquinas from the exaggerated subtleties and quibblings of the later decadent scholastics. Not less was the success of another work, "Quæstiones Quodlibeticæ," which ran through several editions in Louvain, Venice, Lyons, and Paris.

The theological teachings of Adrian, collected from all available sources, were skilfully edited and arranged by my old master, Professor E. H. J. Reusens of Louvain,

* In spite of its name, not "a commentary on Peter Lombard," as Creighton calls it (*op. cit.*, p. 222); see Lepitre, p. 29.

lately deceased,* in his doctoral dissertation published in 1862,† a mine of curious and useful information.

The highest University honours naturally fell to the now famous theologian. In 1497 he was elected Dean of the Chapter of St. Peter's, which carried with it the functions of Chancellor of the University. On two different occasions, in 1493 and in 1500, he was chosen for the highest academic post, that of Rector Magnificus of the University, which office in those days was tenable for only six months at a time, but which carried with it exceptional privileges and jurisdiction, both civil and ecclesiastical.

Before quitting this first chapter of Adrian's life it will be of interest to quote the descriptions which his admiring contemporaries have left us of his personal appearance and character.

He was tall, we are told, and well proportioned, his eyes full of fire and intelligence, his eyebrows bushy, his countenance ruddy and full of grace, the forehead somewhat sloping, the nose aquiline. His manner was dignified, grave, and modest, his lips ever graced with a smile, his gestures calm, his eyes ordinarily cast down. His eloquence was extraordinary, without either hesitation or precipitancy, his diction slow and majestic, his voice both soft and penetrating.

To such a gracious exterior corresponded still more precious gifts of soul and mind. His life was exemplary, his fare frugal, though his table was always hospitable, without luxury or excess. He abhorred the long drinking bouts so dear to German students then as nowadays. His meals were brief. He rose at midnight to recite his breviary, and then returned for a brief repose. By daybreak he said his daily Mass with the

* Died December 24, 1903. For biographical notice, see "Revue d'Histoire Ecclésiastique," vol. i., pp. 150-152 (Louvain, January, 1904).

† "Syntagma Doctrinæ Theologicæ Adriani VI." (Lovanii, 1862).

deepest piety. He was affable and kind to all who came to seek his advice or aid. By practising strict economy in his household, he was able to dispose of considerable means, especially in favour of poor students, whose needs he knew by personal experience. He bought them books, paid for their board, encouraged their industry—not only by words, but by substantial rewards.

But Adrian's most munificent benefaction to his Alma Mater was the erection of the splendid college which still bears his name.* His own resources and the help of his friends were severely taxed to erect such fine buildings, which called forth the surprise of his contemporaries. In one way this generous creation had an influence on his future career. The celebrated Bernardino Carvajal, generally known as the Cardinal di Santa Croce (from his titular Church), sent by Pope Julius II. as his legate to Germany, visited Louvain, and inspected the newly-finished college. He expressed great surprise that a simple Dean should have succeeded in erecting so splendid an edifice. On his return to Rome, the Cardinal spoke to Pope Julius in such high terms of the Louvain professor that the Pontiff endeavoured, though without success, to draw him to his Court. Adrian steadfastly declined, but events of a different kind were rapidly approaching to put an end for good and all to his academic career, and to draw him into the vortex of public life, and eventually to the highest attainable careers in both State and Church.

We have already seen Adrian's indebtedness to one royal Margaret, the widow of Charles the Bold and sister of Edward IV., our English King. We are now to see a still more important act of patronage on the part of another royal Margaret.

Margaret of York, the early patroness of Adrian, was godmother to the young Prince Charles, her step-great-

* Collège du Pape Adrien VI., in the Place de l'Université. Restored in 1775. It was originally built for theologians; it is now appropriated to Arts and Law students.

grandson, now, owing to the death of his father Ferdinand, heir to his grandfather, the Emperor Maximilian.* Up to her death, the royal lady had charge of the infant Prince, and afterwards he was in the care of a succession of tutors, none of whom was very satisfactory or successful. For the wilful young Prince—destined one day to be the famous Emperor Charles V.—had little or no aptitude for learning. He hated Latin, never learnt to speak German, and had but a poor knowledge of Spanish and Italian.† He had equal difficulties with mathematics, in which science he was many years later "coached" by his favourite companion, the Marquis of Lombay, afterwards glorious in the annals of the Church as St Francis Borgia. On the other hand, Charles excelled in all military and physical exercises. In the year 1512 his aunt, Margaret of Austria, daughter of Maximilian (and therefore step-granddaughter of Margaret of York)—who in her second widowhood presided over a little Court at Mechlin, rendered brilliant by the scholars and artists who frequented it—selected the famous Louvain professor Adrian to undertake the weighty task of educating and training the young Prince,

* The following table will serve to render somewhat more intelligible the rather complex genealogies mentioned in this article:

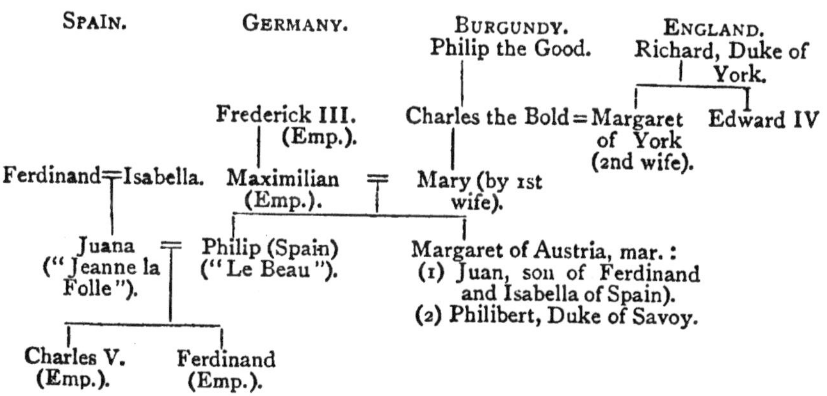

† It may have been a realization of his own defects that caused him to utter in after-life the oft-quoted dictum: "Plus de langues qu'un homme sçait parler, plus de fois est-il homme."

then in his twelfth year, as well as his sisters, the Infantas Leonora, Maria, and Isabela. This new and honourable charge was the turning-point in Adrian's career. He had now to quit for ever his Alma Mater, where he had resided for no less than thirty-six years, and lay aside his beloved studies, to take up his residence at Mechlin.* Whatever regrets he may have felt at this sudden break in his career at the age of fifty-three, he threw himself whole-heartedly into his great task. For a great task it was. In the youthful Charles he was to train him who was destined one day to unite the triple sovereignties of Germany, Spain, and the Low Countries, and to become the mightiest monarch in Christendom. If Adrian did not have much success in the intellectual training of his somewhat refractory pupil, at least he seems to have produced a profound impression upon his mind. Austere and severe in himself, with the highest ideals of duty and responsibility, he strove to form the young Prince's heart upon the noblest maxims of Christianity. He found his pupil, says Vicenzo Quirino, hot and impetuous in character, like his celebrated ancestor, Charles the Bold. Adrian did not flatter his faults. He impressed upon him the emptiness of riches, honours, and success;† he warned him against the tongues of flatterers; taught him that God had chosen him solely for the welfare of his people, and would one day demand of him a rigorous account of his stewardship. It is true that there was much in the subsequent career of Charles that belied these noble maxims, as we shall

* This would seem at first to dispel the popular Louvain tradition that Adrian and his royal pupil lived during this time in the Castle of Mont-César alluded to above. Yet, according to Reusen's account (p. xiv), Adrian had already been teaching Charles, as a little boy from his seventh to his twelfth year, during the greater part of the year which the young Prince was wont to spend in the castle of Mont-César, whilst Adrian was still Professor of Theology. In 1512 he removed altogether to Court.

† Did Charles's mind recur to these teachings of his old master when, at the close of his reign, he resigned his crown and passed his last years in religious retirement?

see in the course of this recital; but he frequently referred with gratitude to the teachings of "Master Adrian," to whom he declared he was indebted "for what little of letters and good morals God had given him." He showed his gratitude, indeed, very soon; for, on attaining his legal majority, his fifteenth year, in January, 1515, he at once nominated Adrian to a seat in his Council as Sovereign of the Low Countries. One of his fellow-councillors, William of Croÿ, Marquis of Chièvres, seems to have resented this nomination, perhaps because of Adrian's plebeian origin, perhaps fearing his influence over the mind of his pupil. He sought and found opportunities of removing the favoured tutor from the Court on various honourable missions, twice to Holland, and a third time, in the September of the year, on a highly weighty embassy to Ferdinand the Catholic, King of Spain, Charles's maternal grandfather. In thus, through motives of jealousy, sending Adrian far away from the petty Court of the Low Countries, the ambitious courtier all unconsciously provided a stepping-stone to the most exalted dignity which the Dutch tutor was destined, in the brief space of seven years, to attain. Adrian, little dreaming that he would never again see his native land, far less of the high destiny that Providence had in store for him, quitted Flanders, and, passing through France, visited the famous Sorbonne of Paris, where his fame as a theologian had long preceded him, and even engaged in a public philosophical discussion in that ancient University.

II. The Ambassador and Statesman.

The object of Adrian's embassy to Spain was kept a secret; it was announced that he was going "par devers le roy d'Arragon, pour aucuns grans affaires secretz dont n'est besoin icy faire declaration." In reality, he was to treat of the highest matters of State, which were to effect the whole future of European politics. Adrian's task was no other than that of winning over the old Spanish King to consent to his grandson Charles succeeding to the Spanish Crown, instead of his younger brother Ferdinand, whom the King, irritated by the action of his son-in-law, would have preferred as his successor. It would be too long to narrate the difficult negotiations which Adrian had to conduct with the aged and infirm King, whose last days were rapidly approaching. His difficulties were the greater in that he had first to gain the support of his all-powerful Minister, one of the greatest politicians of his day, and the greatest Minister that Spain has ever seen, the famous Franciscan Cardinal Ximenes. It speaks volumes for Adrian's tact and prudence, as well as for the high reputation for sanctity and learning which had preceded him, that he won over both the great Cardinal and the aged and suspicious King, who was delighted with the Ambassador's prudence and virtue, mingled with firmness. He succeeded in negotiating a treaty, by means of certain prudent concessions, and before the King died had secured for his pupil and Sovereign the succession so much desired. The death of the King rendered Adrian's position still more delicate. Ximenes was appointed by Ferdinand's will as Regent of Castile, for which post Charles now designated Adrian himself. Nevertheless, by a friendly agreement, Ximenes and Adrian undertook the government jointly, though Adrian was not to bear the title of Regent, but only of Charles's Ambassador. It cannot be denied that Adrian's position at this time was one of great difficulty. Whatever his talents, there is no doubt that as a politician and statesman the ex-professor of Louvain could not in any way compete, either in political genius or experience of affairs, with the great Cardinal. Add to this that the latter was a native Spaniard of whom his countrymen were justly proud, whilst Adrian was a foreigner, only just arrived in the country from the "barbarous North," and the haughty Castilian nobles were little likely to brook the interference in their affairs of an obscure and humbly-born foreigner. The views of the two Regents on many subjects were often diverse, the interests they represented often opposed. For, whilst Ximenes may be said to have championed those of Spain, Adrian's task was to protect the interests of the youthful Charles, himself a foreigner, and as yet totally unknown to the Spanish people. Once more Adrian's good sense and tactfulness, his evident sanctity of life and honesty of purpose, steered him through shoals on which many a more promising statesman would have been wrecked. Sometimes Adrian won over the Cardinal to his views; at others, by sage concessions, he avoided conflicts. For one thing, the two men had much in common, and were able to live together as sincere and even intimate friends. Both were ecclesiastics of great personal piety, both devoted lovers of theological science. Common tastes and mutual admiration for one another's virtue drew them together. The great Cardinal often invited his Flemish colleague to his table to discuss with mutual friends their common studies. Ximenes consulted the experienced Louvain professor in drawing up the constitutions of his own University of Alcalá, which he had recently founded.

Adrian found a new and powerful friend in the dowager-queen Germaine, the second wife of the last King. She wrote to Charles urging him to obtain from Rome for Adrian the important bishopric of Tortosa. Ximenes generously seconded her efforts, and Leo X. conferred upon Adrian the above-named see, one of the best-endowed in the whole kingdom. Adrian, now placed in comparative affluence by his Spanish revenues, at once resigned nearly all the benefices which he had hitherto held in the Low Countries. Once more it was, owing to Ximenes' influence that the Pope, at Charles's request, in 1516 nominated the new Bishop of Tortosa to the important office of Grand Inquisitor of Arragon and Navarre. In this new and delicate office Adrian displayed those qualities of gentleness and prudence which were all the more needed at the time, as his predecessor Deza had been forced to resign through the public odium excited by his rigour and excessive severity. Indeed, one of the greatest merits of Adrian during his stay in Spain was the moderating influence that he exercised over that dreaded tribunal, which had become in the hands of the Spanish Kings an instrument of political, rather than of religious, government.*

Further preferment quickly followed. On June 25 of the following year (1517) Leo X. created on one day the unprecedented number of thirty-one Cardinals,† among them Lorenzo Campeggio, so well known later on in the affair of the divorce of Henry VIII., and also, on the special petition of Charles, Adrian of Utrecht.

The letter of Leo to Charles is a high testimony to Adrian's reputation. "We have very willingly admitted into the College of Cardinals Adrian, Bishop of Tortosa, on account of his singular knowledge of sacred sciences, his stainless character, and his eminent virtues; also out of condescension for you, and to cause you great joy, since we have raised to the highest dignity of the Church a virtuous, learned, and prudent man, your former master and tutor." Furthermore, the Pope urges upon Charles as a duty that he should supply the new Cardinal with means suitable to support his new dignity, and not leave him "with such limited means, or, to speak more accurately, in that poverty which has so long been the companion of his life"—a striking testimony to Adrian's reputation for frugality and disinterestedness, which had already made him known in Rome, though he had never visited that city.

Cardinal Ximenes did not long survive the nomination of his colleague to the Sacred College. Worn out with

* It is surprising to find Creighton stating that as Inquisitor Adrian exercised his office with rigour, and even "sharpened" its methods (p. 224). Exactly the contrary was the case, as shown in great detail by Lepitre, pp. 155-163. (See also Höfler, p. 112, n. 2.)

† And not thirty-nine, as Creighton incorrectly says (p. 223).

disease, pursued by popular suspicions and calumnies, slighted and disliked by Charles, the great Cardinal, at the very moment of the new King's arrival in Spain, breathed his last, at the age of eighty-two, in the monastery of Aguilera, "leaving behind him," says Peter Martyr, "a glory unequalled in history." "The only Minister," says Robertson, "whom his contemporaries have regarded as a saint, and to whom the people governed by him attributed the power of working miracles." His death was a great loss for Spain. Had he lived longer, to mould and direct the policy of the new King, that country would have been spared many miseries. It was high time that the new King should visit his Spanish subjects, but unfortunately his visit, entirely under the influence as he was of his unscrupulous Minister, de Chièvres, the old rival and enemy of Adrian, only led to dissensions and civil war, in which Cardinal Adrian had later on to play a difficult and most ungrateful part.

It would take too long to narrate the miserable bickerings and disputes, chiefly concerning money matters, which marred Charles's sojourn in his new kingdom, owing largely to the cupidity of his Minister, which led Charles, as has been said, to treat Spain almost as a conquered country. The Cortes of Castile, Arragon, and Catalonia; summoned to recognise the new King and vote him the customary *servicios*, or monetary contributions, were the cause of still further dissatisfaction. At this moment, news suddenly arrived from Germany that the Electors had designated Charles for the Imperial Crown in succession to his grandfather, and Charles was only too glad to give effect to their pressing invitation to leave at once for Aix-la-Chapelle for his installation. He hastily delegated Cardinal Adrian to preside in his name over the Cortes of Valencia, and quitted without further delay a country for which he cared little, whose language he would not speak, and for which he did not conceal his dislike. He left his old master Adrian a legacy of serious troubles and dangers. The Cortes of Valencia showed themselves entirely refractory, and within a short time of Charles's departure Adrian, now named Viceroy of Castile, found himself face to face with a general rising of the kingdom, which rapidly developed into the terrible civil war of the Comuneros, in which much blood was shed, and fortune vascillated from side to side, sometimes in favour of, sometimes adversely to, the royal authority and arms. During all this stormy period the Cardinal of Tortosa employed all his habitual tact and prudence, his natural mildness and placability; and when actually forced by circumstances to take up arms, manifested no less firmness and decision.* It is instructive and edifying to remark how, in the midst of all these troubles, Adrian retained the personal veneration of the Spanish people, in spite of his foreign origin, and in spite of the powers, unconstitutional as they were held to be, which Charles had conferred upon him. Spanish writers always refer to him as a holy man—a saint. The civil war of the Comuneros lasted during the years 1520-1521, and were only ended by the crushing defeat of the rebels at the Battle of Villaler in the latter year. The Cardinal and the two colleagues whom Charles had given him in the government received the submission of all the cities except Toledo, which still held out for a considerable time under Doña Maria Pacheco, and the Comuneros accepted all the conditions imposed upon them by Charles V., conditions which modern historians consider to have compromised the traditional liberties of Castile, and introduced a royal absolutism which has had regrettable results in the subsequent history of Spain. For such results Adrian cannot be blamed. Faithful to the behests and interests of his royal master, his influence all through was exercised in the direction

* I do not think Creighton has any justification for his opinion that Adrian "played a somewhat ignominious part during the rising ot the Comuneros" (p. 223).

of moderation and clemency. We may rather pity him as the victim of the headstrong and tyrannical policy of Charles and his ill-omened adviser. But internal troubles were not all that Adrian had to contend with. He found himself at almost the same time face to face with the active hostility of France, under the unscrupulous and ambitious King Francis I. Pursuing his claim to the kingdom of Navarre, Francis in the spring of 1521 sent his army, under André de Foix, to invade that kingdom. The campaign was rapid and, for a time, decisive, for in a fortnight Navarre was conquered. One of its most striking episodes was the siege and gallant defence of Pampeluna, in which a Guipuzcoan gentleman, Don Inigo de Loyola, received those serious wounds which were to change the current of his life, and make him for ever known as St. Ignatius, the founder of the Society of Jesus. But the attempt of the French to push on into Castile was, largely owing to Adrian's courage and firmness, a failure. The Battle of Exquiros ended in the rout of the French; Pampeluna was retaken, and the French army captured or scattered. A second French invasion, however, followed in the winter, though it was of short duration, and the French once more withdrew. Cardinal Adrian passed the rest of the winter busily occupied in the administration of Castile.

III. The Pope Elect.

In the January of 1522 Adrian was residing in Vitoria. The winter was one of unusual severity, the excessively heavy snowfall having rendered the mountains almost impassable, whilst severe wintry storms swept the sea. On the 25th Adrian had been to visit his colleague in the government, the Admiral of Castile, who was confined to his bed by sickness. As he returned to his home, a courier, half dead with cold, rushed into his presence, holding out a letter and crying out: "Holy Father!

Holy Father!" at the same time throwing himself on his knees and trying to kiss Adrian's feet. The Cardinal endeavoured to repel him, asking in amazement, "Where is the Holy Father?" The stranger answered in Italian, "Voi, Padre Santo, e non altro!" Adrian, who was not even aware of the death of Leo X., which had occurred as far back as December 1, opened the despatch, which proved to be from the Spanish Bishop of Girona, then in Rome, and learnt the astounding news, not only of the Pope's death and the subsequent conclave, but also of his own unanimous election to the Papal See on January 9. Adrian, with his customary calmness and without changing colour, turned to his friends and said: "If the news be true, I am very much to be pitied."*

It gives us some idea of the difficulties of communication in those days to learn that, in the case of such important news as that of the death of a Pope, the holding of a conclave, and the election of a successor, out of five messengers sent off to Adrian immediately after his election, three, who chose the road by land, were stopped and held captive in France; a fourth was driven back by contrary winds to Cività Vecchia, kept there ten days, and, having sailed again, was driven back by pirates to Italy, finally arrived at Nice, but was prevented from proceeding further by the French; whilst of the fifth nothing more was ever heard.

Even towards the end of February Adrian was not yet sure whether the news of his election was true, and the Cardinals in Rome were ignorant whether Adrian was alive or dead! It was merely by a lucky chance that the new Pope had received the news on January 25. A messenger of the Bishop of Girona had succeeded in bringing it as far as Logroño, where he communicated it in secret, upon which Ortiz, provisor of the Bishop of Calahora, himself set out for Vitoria, and, with the greatest danger to his life, managed to make his way over the snow-covered mountains, and so reached

* Letter of Pace to Wolsey, February 22, 1522.

the presence of Adrian as we have described. The news rapidly spread through Vitoria and the neighbourhood. The inhabitants of all classes crowded to the viceregal palace to congratulate the new Pope and kiss his feet, which Adrian endeavoured to prevent, declaring that the news was by no means certain. At night the streets were illuminated, and a cavalcade traversed the city to celebrate the joyful event. Yet Adrian's suspicions seemed almost justified. Sixteen days passed, and no official confirmation of the news arrived. People began to ask whether the letter of the Bishop of Girona was not a hoax. It was even suggested that it had been forged at the Court of Francis I. in order to turn Adrian into ridicule; but at last, on February 9, the *cameriere* of Cardinal Carvajal, who had succeeded in making his way through the snow-covered, mountainous roads, arrived with the official letter from the Sacred College. Adrian read the document with his accustomed calm, and, making no comment upon the contents, simply bade the messenger to go and take the rest which he so much needed. For some days those around him were in doubt whether or not he would accept the nomination. Once more the population crowded in to ask his blessing or to seek his favour. Adrian, to escape them, took refuge in the monastery of St. Francis, and continued to devote himself to the ordinary affairs of State, refusing to see anybody. Not till the 16th did he, after saying his Mass, summon his physician and two other attendants, and declare to them his decision. Although, he said, he was well aware of the dangers of so exalted a position, yet he felt that if he refused the election he might cause still greater confusion in the Universal Church. Called by the inscrutable designs of Providence to this new dignity, he had decided to accept it, relying on the Divine assistance, and hoping to become a not unworthy servant of Divine grace. He then gave instructions for the legal act of acceptance to be drawn up, though all in the greatest secrecy. Meanwhile, however, as early as February 2, Adrian had written both to King Henry VIII. and to Cardinal Wolsey. Referring to the rumours of his election, he declared that he had neither sought nor desired the Papacy. His strength was insufficient, and he would have declined it did he not fear to offend God and the Church. In his letter to the English King he struck what was to be the keynote of his whole policy—Peace. He begged the King to labour for the restoration of peace in Christendom, and for this purpose to come to an understanding with the Emperor Charles V. The same idea appears in his letter to Wolsey, whom he designated one of the pillars of the Church. His first letter to Charles V. is dated February 11. In it he clearly expresses his intention of accepting the election. The tenor of his letter, on the whole, is much the same as those just quoted.

What Adrian's private sentiments were at this moment will be clearly gathered from his familiar letter to his intimate friend, Dr. Florencius Oem, Syndic of Utrecht:

"There will certainly be no one who will not be surprised and annoyed that a poor man, almost unknown to everybody, and at so great a distance, should have been unanimously chosen by the Cardinals as the Vicar of Christ. But for God it is an easy thing suddenly to exalt the poor man. I am not rejoiced at this honour, and am afraid to take upon myself so great a burden. I would much rather, instead of the dignities of Pope, Cardinal, and Bishop, serve God in my provostship at Utrecht. But I dare not resist the call of God, and hope that He will perfect what is wanting in me, and grant me sufficient strength to bear the burden. I beg you pray for me, and obtain for me by your pious prayers that God may teach me how to carry out His commandments, and make me worthy to serve the welfare of His Church."

Similar sentiments of humility appear in other letters

to his personal friends, of whom, in his exalted position, he never showed himself at all ashamed. "Votre bon ami et esleu pape" is his homely signature. Writing to another, he says: "The Prince who sets anything above his princely good name and the welfare of his subjects is no Prince, but a tyrant. I myself have learnt to satisfy myself with common food and little drink, to clothe my body with cheap garments; all else, however much it may be, must be employed for the common weal of Christendom." Such was the man, humble, earnest, frugal, unworldly, whom a College of Cardinals, one of the most worldly, ambitious, luxurious, and mercenary that Christendom had yet seen, at a time of general worldliness, pride, dissoluteness, and intrigue, had unanimously chosen to be the successor of the sumptuous, ambitious, and worldly-minded Leo X.

Surely here was the finger of the Most High.

This is the place to say something of that extraordinary conclave—one of the most disgraceful in history, as it is not unjustly styled in the Cambridge Modern History*—in which this marvellous election occurred.

Christendom in this first quarter of the sixteenth century was sick unto death. Ruin and devastation from without threatened it in the ever-growing power of the irresistible Turk, whose legions, under the redoubtable conqueror Suliman II., were thundering at its gates. Within, Luther and his adherents were kindling those religious and civil wars that were soon to rend Christianity in twain. The Christian Princes were at bitter enmity among themselves—Charles V. of Germany and Henry VIII. of England, on the one hand, arrayed against Francis I. on the other; the States and cities of Italy torn by contending factions, Imperialist or French; whilst petty Princes were fighting for their own hand, until the whole peninsula was in a state of inextricable confusion and hopeless strife. A succession of worldly-

* "The Reformation," vol. ii.

minded Popes had left behind them a worldly-minded College of Cardinals, which exemplified all the vices of the times, and in which were reflected only too faithfully the varied feuds and jealousies that distracted the whole of Europe. Most of the Cardinals, Italian Princes of high rank, were men full of personal ambition, seeking their own exaltation, greedy of power and wealth, carrying the internecine feuds of the Medici, the Orsini, the Colonna, into the sacred precincts of the Church; or else creatures and secret agents of the German Emperor or the French King, all alike blind and deaf to higher interests and to the welfare of the Bride of Christ.* The deplorable result was that the conclave which followed the death of Leo X. was an unprecedented scene of intrigue, quarrelling and faction, which even threatened schism in the Church. The various Princes and States of Europe endeavoured by their agents to promote the candidature now of one, now of the other, of the Cardinals. Henry VIII. of England and, secretly, the Emperor Charles V., supported Cardinal Wolsey. Clerk, the English Ambassador in Rome, writing to Wolsey at the time, declared: "I assure your Grace here is a marvellous division, and we were never likelier to have a schism"; and again: "The Papacy is in great decay; the Cardinals brawl and scold; their malicious, unfaithful, and uncharitable demeanour against each other increases every day."

The conclave opened on December 27, numbering thirty-nine Cardinals, and lasted till January 9. So "marvellous," indeed, to use Clerk's words, were these divisions among them, that after ten scrutinies it seemed absolutely impossible for any one name to secure the

* Creighton remarks, with some truth, that the large addition by Leo X. to the Sacred College of men from every State in Europe made it more amenable to political considerations (p. 214). The evil beginnings of this corruption of the Sacred College, especially under the reign of that weak nepotist Sixtus IV., are most strikingly portrayed in the second volume of Pastor's "History of the Popes."

necessary number of votes. At one moment the conclave was almost in despair, and it seemed as if all must end in an absolute fiasco. Then a wonderful thing happened. Cardinal Medici, himself one of the principal candidates, and all through one of the least scrupulous intriguers, suddenly arose and proposed the election of one of the Sacred College, " who was absent from Rome, but who was a just man "—Cardinal Adrian, Bishop of Tortosa. He was a man almost absolutely unknown to Rome, and whom but one of the Cardinals had ever seen. But, wonder of wonders, as if by a sudden inspiration, at the eleventh scrutiny Adrian was unanimously elected. So unexpected, in fact, was this choice that the Cardinals themselves seemed hardly to realize what they had done, and none were more astonished than themselves at their own handiwork. Yet, indeed, it was not their work. If ever in the history of the Church there was an evident and almost visible interposition of the Holy Ghost, setting at nought the follies and intrigues of men, it was in the election of Adrian VI.

The news was received by the people of Rome with amazed incredulity, succeeded by indignation and rage. As the first of the Cardinals left the conclave, he was received in the front of the Vatican Palace by a mob of 6,000 persons, howling, yelling, and hissing. Disgraceful scenes occurred all over the city; men and women hooted the Cardinals wherever they appeared. The next day Pasquino was posted over with the bitterest squibs, sonnets, and lampoons. The Cardinals were declared " betrayers of the Blood of Christ," and covered with every species of outrage. The Romans were furious that no Italian had been elected, but a low-born, obscure foreigner, whom they already dubbed a " barbarian." Yet the Cardinals were themselves as much distressed and alarmed at the result as the Roman mob. " They had done," says one writer, " not what they wished to do, but what they were obliged to do,

9

and therein was their rightful chastisement."* "The election of the Pope," wrote the Swiss Cardinal Schiner to Cardinal Wolsey, "was the work of the Holy Spirit, whose dictates we are all bound to obey." But the work once done could not be undone. Wherefore the Sacred College determined, as the newly-elected Pope was still absent, to make things as comfortable as possible for themselves by dividing amongst themselves all the various lucrative posts and the governorship of the cities and territories in the Papal States, besides drawing up quite a long list of conditions and requisitions ("capitulations") to be imposed, if possible, upon the new Pope, so as to fetter his independent action, and, as has been said, to turn his Papal monarchy into an oligarchy.† How far they succeeded the sequel will show.

The news was received throughout the rest of Europe with varied feelings. The French—especially King Francis I.—were furious. They looked upon Adrian as an "Imperialist," and his election as their own defeat and the triumph of the Germans. Even a French schism seemed not unlikely. Henry VIII. and Wolsey were, of course, greatly disappointed at the latter's failure. The Low Countries were wild with enthusiasm at the election of their countryman. The news reached Brussels on January 18, whilst Charles V. was hearing Mass in the Church of Ste. Gudule. The Emperor opened the despatch, read it, and, turning to the bystanders, said: "Master Adrian is made Pope." All the bells in the city were rung; joyful processions and bonfires and a solemn High Mass in Ste. Gudule expressed the popular satisfaction. Spain was no less flattered and delighted. The good were everywhere rejoiced. All Christendom felt that the election had contravened all political combinations, and put to

* Höfler, p. 96.

† "The Cardinals felt themselves a powerful aristocracy," remarks Creighton, p. 214.

shame all worldly calculations. "Thy absolutely blameless life hath alone raised thee to the highest position in human affairs," wrote Vives, full of enthusiasm. "Thou hast shown that there is still a place for virtue, and men's minds have not yet lost all consideration for it. The lives of preceding Popes have brought it about that the highest dignity on earth receives fresh lustre from thy own person." "This is the day of the Lord!" cried out William Van Enkenvoert. "We have a Pope who has been elected without any canvassing and in his absence. No better, no more blameless, no holier Pope can be found, or even desired." "We have a Pope," says another contemporary, "who is a father of all goodness, a fountain of all doctrine, the glory of learning, the patron of the learned." Even his enemies and critics had to bear testimony to his virtues and spotless life.

It was only likely—and many historians have taken the fact for granted—that Adrian should have been supposed to owe his election to the influence of his old pupil and actual Sovereign, Charles V. And when the election was made known, that Monarch and his Ministers endeavoured to make capital out of so probable a belief, and to inculcate it as a fact upon the mind of the Pope himself. But Adrian was too keen and too well informed to give credit to the claim, and there is documentary evidence in abundance to show that in this matter Charles played no very honourable part, but rather that of an astute dissembler. For before the election he was secretly pledged up to the hilt to support an entirely different candidate—Cardinal Wolsey; and there is everything to show that the name of his Viceroy in Spain never even occurred to him as a likely candidate for the tiara, but that the election took him completely by surprise. As soon as Charles learnt of the death of Leo X., he took steps to carry out his promises towards Wolsey. On December 28 he wrote to the latter:

"Monsieur le Cardinal,—Mon bon amy, vous savés les devises que autrefois vous ai tenues de ce que voudrais faire pour vous. Avisés ce que pourray, et me les faites savoir, car je m'y emploiray de très-bon cœur." Richard Pace, sent by Henry VIII. to Rome to support the candidature of the Cardinal of York, called upon Charles at Ghent, who gave him a letter for his ambassador, Don Juan Manuel, in Rome, in which he said: "We have written to the Sacred College, and to several Cardinals in particular, to exhort them to give to the Christian commonwealth the Pontiff who shall appear the best suited. . . . In our judgment, the Cardinal of York is the man most worthy of this high pastoral office. . . . Do, therefore, with diligence and dexterity . . . all that may be necessary to arrive at this desirable end." And at the same time, writing again to Wolsey himself: "Vous pouvez estre schur qu'il ne sera riens épargné pour parvenir à l'effect désiré, *et ne m'a point semblé convenable d'escripre en faveur d'autre que vous*, car toute mon affection est à vous." And to Henry VIII. on December 27: "Par quoy incontinent que ay sceu votre intention et la sienne (Wolsey's), ay depeche sur ce mes lectres patentes en la meilleure forme que l'hon a sceu devise pour promouvoir le dit seigneur Cardinal aussis que en cest affere tant que en moy sera, n'espargneray chose quelcunque pour la conduire en bon effect."

When the intrigues of Charles V. and his Minister, Don Juan Manuel, had failed, every effort was made by them to induce Adrian to believe that his election had been their work only. Don Juan wrote to the new Pope on January 11 to the effect that in his election "the will of the Emperor had coincided with the will of God" (!). He goes on to give the Pope a very large dose of advice as to his future conduct of affairs. In one curious detail Adrian followed the Spanish ambassador's advice; it was in retaining his own baptismal name as Pope, contrary to the custom which had been invariable for many centuries. Hence it was that Adrian of Utrecht became Pope Adrian VI., the last instance on record of such a departure from the traditional practice, which is said to date from A.D. 956, when Ottaviano Conti on his election took the title of John XII.

Charles V. himself wrote to the Cardinals to thank them for an election by which they had "shown their piety towards God, and their benevolence towards himself." He sent his ambassador, de la Chaulx, to venerate the new Pope in his name, and instructed him to declare that he "could not desire a choice more worthy, more suitable to the service of our Lord, and the prosperity of His Universal Church, than that which had been made by the grace of the Holy Ghost." And later on, in a letter of March 7, he tries hard to persuade Adrian of the falsity of the reports (which were perfectly true, we have seen) that his ambassador Manuel had supported any other candidature : "Je ne sçauroye croire qu'ainsi fust, ne que Votre Saincteté deust adjouster foy à une chose si contraire à vérité . . . mais soyez asseuré que jay esté cause de votre dite ellection, et en ay eu austant plesir et joye que si elle m'eust esté donnée avec mon empyre." Adrian, in his very courteous and friendly reply, accepts all the Emperor's assurances of joy and friendship : "et me suis toujours tenu pour asseuré que si, par vostre pure affection et entière amour, vous seul eussiez deubt eslire ung pape, vous fussiez incliné vers moy et m'eussies donné vostre vot." But a few lines lower down, in the quiet manner peculiar to himself, Adrian clearly gives the Emperor to understand that he knew exactly what had happened, and how little Charles or his ambassador could take credit for the result. "Je suis toutesfois joyeux *non estre parvenu à l'élection par vos prières*, pour la pureté et sincérité que les droits divins et humains requièrent en semblables affaires. Je vous en sçay néantmoins aussi bon gré ou meilleur, que si par vostre moyen et prières vous me l'eussiez impétré." Adrian had seen clean through the duplicity of Charles and his Minister, and did not conceal the fact from them.

In all this matter Charles's conduct shows but little to his credit.

But Adrian checkmated his wily pupil in other matters. Charles jumped to the conclusion that the new Pope would be his man, and that he would easily be able to make use of him and the vast influence of the Holy See as an all-powerful weapon against Francis I. and France. Like his famous predecessor Frederic II., he had much to say about the "Unity of the Papacy and the Empire." He spoke of the Pontiff as of a person "whom he thought he could command as one brought up in his household." Writing to Adrian on March 7, he let it appear pretty plainly that he counted on the Pope to help him in confounding the designs of the French King: "J'ay espérance que à ce cop ma requeste ne me sera refusée ny dylaiée, et que ferez plus à ma requeste que à celle de nul prince chrétien, de craint que aucun savançast de vouloir mener quelque pratique entre vous et le roy de France, et que par leurs doulces parolles vous cuidassent endormir." In his instructions to his Minister de la Chaulx, Charles had the audacious impiety to suggest that a triple league between the Pope, the Emperor, and the King of England might be likened to a Trinity, in which Adrian should be the Father, Charles the Son, and Henry VIII. the Holy Ghost (!).

The new Pope was too wise and too righteous to fall into the Imperial snare. He did not hesitate to refuse one or two favours asked from him by Charles. He declined to take sides with the latter against Francis I.; on the contrary, he strove to enter into friendly relations with the French King, and wrote at once to him, to his mother, and to his sister, and in spite of much suspicion and unwillingness on the French side, succeeded in moderating at least to some extent the hostile views of the King. Adrian's cry in all this correspondence with Charles, with Francis, with Henry, with Venice, and the other Italian States was "Peace, Peace!" He longed to come forward in the capacity of a Prince of Peace. His great hope and desire was to induce the three great rival Sovereigns of Germany, France, and England to agree, if not to a permanent peace and alliance, at least to an armistice of two or three years, and to common action against the ever-growing dangers of the Turkish invasion of Europe. And all through his brief pontificate this was one of the chief pre-occupations of his policy.

IV. The Sovereign of Rome.

Although Adrian received the official news of his election on February 9, it was not until July 10 that he was able to take ship from the Spanish coasts. There were many reasons for this extraordinary delay. One was the difficulty of obtaining ships to escort the Pontiff and his suite across the Mediterranean. Strange as it seems to us, all kinds of reasons, chiefly political, interfered with the plans that were successively proposed for setting the Pope across the waters that divided Spain and Italy. At one time there was a possibility of his going overland through France, but the Pope and his counsellors dared not trust themselves to the mercy of the French King, however fair his words. To cross the sea, it must be remembered, was no easy matter. Not only during the wintry season was the voyage often rendered impossible by terrible storms, but at all seasons a strong naval escort was required, for the waters were infested by the constant raids of corsairs and pirates, who often threatened the very coasts of Italy; and even the presence of the French vessels was itself a danger. Negotiations were carried on at one time with Venice, at another time with the Emperor, or with other Powers to supply the needed fleet. At one time it was even seriously proposed by the Imperial party that Adrian should sail to England, and thence, viâ Flanders and Germany, make his way overland to Italy. With his usual prudence Adrian refused all these combinations. Yet time dragged slowly on. The Romans began to fear that the Pope would never leave Spain, and that a second "Avignon captivity" would ensue. Meanwhile the Pontiff pursued the calm and even tenor of his way. The three Cardinal-legates who had been deputed to go to Spain, formally salute the Pontiff and escort him to the Eternal City, still tarried in Rome, and, as a matter of fact, only one of them, Cardinal Cesarini, ever crossed to Spain. In March Adrian, passing through various Spanish cities, made his way, amid demonstrations of universal veneration, to the city of Saragossa, where he abode from March 29 to June 11, and whence, for a good part of three months, he governed the Church. During this long stay at Saragossa he received the homage, one by one, of all the Christian States by means of their ambassadors. He himself was not rich enough to provide a sufficient number of galleys to undertake the voyage, which he longed to accomplish, to his own capital. Finally he reached the sea-coast at Ampolla, whence, on July 10, he set sail for Tarragona, where he had again to wait until August 5. On the evening of the latter day, after vespers, with a large squadron of fifty sail, and accompanied by his suite and a number of the representatives of the various Powers, he set sail on his long and slow voyage. He touched at Barcelona, then, passing through French waters in the Gulf of Narbonne, he passed Antibes and Marseilles, touched at Nice and Villefranche (August 13), where he received the salutations of the French King through his secretary, then on to Porto Marino and Savona, and on August 17 the thunder of cannon announced his arrival at Genoa; finally, on August 26, he first reached his own territory at Cività Vecchia, one hundred and sixty-nine days after he had left his residence at Vitoria. On the very same day on which the Pope first set foot on his own territory (August 27) the Lutheran faction in Germany began the civil war which was destined to last for so many years and to cause so much misery. A number of Cardinals, representatives of the Roman nobles, and many Bishops hastened to meet the Pontiff. The Cardinals tried to dissuade him from proceeding to Rome, where at this moment the plague was raging; but Adrian, with his usual calm determination, and in spite of a furious storm which broke out, again betook himself to his galley, leaving a great part of his suite and luggage behind, and reached the mouth of the Tiber at Ostia. He found the shore crowded with Cardinals, Bishops, nobles, scholars, and knights to welcome him. So great was his eagerness to reach the Eternal City that towards evening of the same day the Pope and Cardinals mounted their horses, and, hastening towards Rome, arrived the same day (August 28) outside the city, and took up their abode at the sanctuary of San Paolo fuori le Mura. So rapid had been his movements that everything was in confusion. Cardinals and people alike had quickly to grow accustomed to the new Pope's calm decision and determination of character, as well as to his simplicity of life and speech; they had indeed found their lord and master. The following day he was up by six o'clock and said Mass as usual, and during the forenoon he received the solemn homage of the Sacred College in the magnificent basilica of St. Paul. Here he listened to a tedious address from Cardinal Caravajal, who endeavoured to lay down for him a programme of action and policy. Adrian's reply, as usual, was short, simple, and practical. He referred briefly to certain abuses which he desired to see reformed, summarily refused a number of favours and privileges asked for by various persons, and, in spite of the burning sun, towards evening mounted his mule and began his entry in solemn procession to the holy city. Passing the little chapel where SS. Peter and Paul are said to have taken leave of each other on the day of their martyrdom, by the Porta di San Paolo and the Aventine, the magnificent cavalcade—the Pope carrying the Blessed Sacrament and surrounded by the Swiss Guard—wended its way through the plague-stricken city, by the Ghetto and the Campo dei Fiori, on to the Vatican. The houses were decorated with tapestry, a triumphal arch spanned the street; the clergy of the city met him, singing the *Te Deum*. At St. Peter's Adrian dismounted, threw himself on both knees on the threshold, and then proceeding to the altar of the Confession, once more received the obedience of the Cardinals. The whole city was in an uproar of jubilation; cries of joy drowned the thunder of the cannon; women wept, and the populace, decimated by plague and famine, cried out "Adriano! Adriano!" as though their deliverer had come. On Sunday, August 31, the solemn crowning took place at St. Peter's. It was remarked that the Pope, now sixty-four years of age, read the prayers without glasses, and an eye-witness declares that whosoever saw the angelic countenance of the Pope and heard his melodious voice must have felt that something Divine rather than human was here. Then followed the customary banquet, after which the Pope spoke of his plans for completing the Church of St. Peter, and of reforming the Rota, the supreme tribunal of Rome. A curious little instance of the influence of Adrian's example is that all the Cardinals except two at once shaved off their beards, which they had been accustomed to wear under the preceding Pontiff. "Never," wrote Campeggio to Wolsey, "had there been greater joy than at Adrian's entrance. All concluded from his expression, his words, his manner, that he would be an excellent Pope. All were astonished that at his age he bore so well the fatigues and excitements of the past few days." Thus did Adrian VI. enter upon his short but well-filled administration of the Holy See.

V. The Reformer.

One word sums up the leading idea of that administration—reform. Never perhaps had there been a time when the Church and her clergy, especially the higher clergy, were more in need of reform. Luther and his partisans had raised, under the name of reform, which was in the mouths and the hearts of all earnest thinkers, the standard of religious and civil revolt, and were setting the North of Europe ablaze. But the true reform of the Church was to come, as ever, from within, and Adrian VI., himself of Teutonic blood, like Luther, was the first, during the short year of pontificate that remained to him, to begin that great religious reformation which culminated in the Council of Trent, and of which we are all enjoying to-day the spiritual benefits. Truly had the election of Adrian been the work of Divine Providence.

We cannot pretend to narrate in full the complete history of his short but ever memorable reign. We must, however, briefly touch upon four chief questions which occupied the remaining months of his strenuous and indefatigable pontificate—the reform of the Church, the protection of Europe against the Turkish peril, the defence of the Church against Lutheranism, and the international feud between Charles V. and Francis I.

We have said that the word reform was in all hearts and mouths. At this very time secret spiritual forces were at work in the Church herself that were to be the Divine means of working out this reformation. St. Jerome Emilian was laying the foundation of the Order of the Somaschi ; three Italian noblemen, that of the Barnabites ; Ignatius of Loyola had just completed his long retreat at Manresa, where he conceived the plan of his famous Company of Jesus ; St. Gaetano was exercising his zeal in Rome, and about to establish his Congregation of the Theatines. The pious Cardinal

Egidio of Viterbo submitted to Adrian, perhaps at the latter's own request, an elaborate project of reform, nearly all of which the Pope adopted. These reforms had reference to abuses in benefices, indults, concessions and indulgences; concordats with Princes, the administration of justice, the government of the Papal States, the extravagant expenditure which had burdened the Papal treasury. One of Adrian's first acts, and it was a drastic one, was to annul all the "provisions" that had been made by the Sacred College in his absence. So radical a measure provoked many murmurs; but Adrian was not the man to be disquieted by them. He published new laws of the Papal Chancellery, which he had elaborated some time before, and by which he regulated the collation of benefices.* More especially did Adrian suppress with all severity that great curse of the Church under so many of his predecessors—nepotism. Adrian himself set the example in his own case, and sternly refused to confer honours and benefices on those of his own kin. The revocation of indults left vacant, it is said, nearly 5,000 benefices, and Adrian employed himself actively in providing these with worthy and deserving incumbents.

Rome and the Curia itself were among the first objects of Adrian's reforming zeal. He found the Holy See heavily laden with debt owing to the extravagance and luxury of Leo X., who did not even leave enough to pay for his own funeral. Rigid economy now became the order of the day. The ranks of court officials and servants were considerably reduced. The hundred grooms who had served Leo X. begged to be taken again into service. Adrian replied that four were quite enough for himself, and was with great difficulty persuaded to take on twelve. Naturally enough these retrenchments caused much discontent in the city, and

* These rules, published at Antwerp 1522, are now exceedingly rare.

tended to procure for Adrian the reputation of avarice. Yet when he died only 3,000 ducats were found in his coffers.

The Pope himself set the example of personal frugality, and continued just the same kind of life as he had led at Louvain. An eye-witness, Luigi Gradenigo, Venetian Ambassador, wrote of him:

"Pope Adrian VI., who has refused to change his name, leads an exemplary and devout life. Every day he says the canonical hours; he rises during the night to say Matins, and then returns to bed to take a little sleep; before dawn he rises again to say Mass, and then gives audiences. He dines and sups very frugally, and spends, it is said, but one ducat for his meals. He is of good and holy life, and sixty-one years old.* He is slow in deciding, and acts with much circumspection. He is learned in Holy Scripture, speaks little, and loves solitude."

Other Venetian ambassadors confirm this description point by point, adding that, when asked any request or decision, great or small, his invariable answer is *Videbimus*, "We will see."

"He gives a good deal of time every day to study, for, not content with reading, he still wishes to write and compose, and thus distracts himself from the cares of the pontificate. His day is largely occupied with exercises of piety, study, and needed repose, so that it is not possible to give many audiences. . . . They say that his daily expenditure for meals is a ducat, which he takes every evening from his pocket, and gives secretly to his majordomo, saying: 'Here is for to-morrow's expenses.' His meals consist of veal, beef, or chicken. Sometimes he has a thick soup; on abstinence days he lives on fish; but of everything he eats with moderation. A woman from his own country cooks and washes for him, and makes his bed."

These homely details of a simple life must have

* This is incorrect; he was past sixty-four.

appeared a strange contrast indeed to the extravagant luxuries of the princely Court of a Leo X.; they excited ridicule and dislike, for they were a silent reproach to many of the clergy of the Eternal City. His love of learning was another useful lesson to his contemporaries. "He could not bear an ignorant priest," writes Girolamo Negro. His only amusement was gardening.

Yet simple and frugal in his own life, he could be magnificent when his duties as a Sovereign required it. The poor idolized him and crowded round him, as, alone on foot, he traversed the streets of Rome. He was the first Pope to repair the Roman aqueducts.

Still his unpopularity among the higher classes, and especially in the world of secular learning and art, steadily grew. Pasquino was often covered with bitter epigrams directed against the saintly Pontiff. In one of these it was said that Rome had always been ruined by a "Sextus" (Sextus Tarquinius, Sextus Nero, Adrianus VI.).* At one time Adrian was disposed to break up both statues, Pasquino and Marforio, and throw them in the Tiber, but was dissuaded by a witty ambassador. Adrian was certainly the *bête-noire* of the humanists and the poets of his day. They loved to represent him as a "barbarian" and the enemy of learning. This charge was unjust. Adrian was no enemy of good letters. He had been years before one of the supporters of Busleiden in establishing his celebrated Trilingual College of Humanities at Louvain.† He maintained his friendship with Erasmus, and as Pope urgently pressed him to come and settle in Rome. Erasmus declined in a curiously artificial and exaggerated letter, in which he declared he could not stand the snow of the Alps, the odour of Italian cookery, and the sourness of the wines! There is no doubt, however, that Adrian keenly realized the abuses and dangers of

* "Sextus Tarquinius, Sextus Nero, Sextus et iste:
Semper et a Sextis diruta Roma fuit."

† See later, Article VII.

the Renascence movement. The exaggerations of humanism had led to a paganizing even of Christianity itself. Many of the leading humanists distinguished themselves by indecent and even obscene writings; and the undue importance attached to the pagan literatures and philosophies had caused a widespread neglect of theology. Adrian's ambition, like that of Leo XIII., seems to have been to bring about a Renascence of Christian philosophy and theology as a means of meeting the intellectual dangers which threatened the Faith then as now.

It is true that, with his practical and serious turn of mind, Adrian seems to have lacked the love of art for art's sake, and also the appreciation of poetry. Hence artists and poets, who had enjoyed an elysium at the Court of Leo X.,* found no patronage under his austere successor. No wonder that the poets were the Pontiff's bitterest enemies, and attacked him with vehement scurrility. The bitterest of all was Berni, whose outrageous invective is yet a testimony to Adrian's virtue, for he incidentally styles him "a saintly Pope, who says Mass every morning."

We may well say, with Erasmus, that ten years of such a pontificate would have changed the face of Rome and Italy.

VI. The Watchman of Christendom.†

Long before his departure for Italy Adrian's mind was preoccupied with the Turkish danger which

* Yet Professor Kraus, in his chapter on "Medicean Rome" in the Cambridge Modern History (vol. ii., "The Reformation"), questions seriously whether Leo X., the patron of Raffaele, was a true encourager of the arts.

† It will doubtless strike many readers how much similarity there existed between the aims and aspirations, as well as the disappointments and troubles, of Adrian VI. and those of his predecessor Pius II. in the preceding century, as so vividly depicted by Pastor in his classical "History of the Popes"; and this in spite of the great dissimilarity of personal character and history.

threatened all Europe. Christendom was distracted with internal jealousies and dissensions, and seemed heedless of the growing power of the terrible Suliman II. The Pope alone was on the watch-tower, solicitous for the common weal of Europe. This was one of the chief motives of his constant appeal for "peace" in all his correspondence or negotiations with Christian States and Princes. He longed to unite them in a common league of defence, as in the old Crusading days, and to turn back by their united arms the Moslem tide of conquest. But his efforts were all in vain. Fair words and promises were all he could obtain. Charles V. and Francis I. were implacable in their mutual hostility; Henry VIII. was bound to Charles; Venice's commercial interests in being free to carry on her trade with the East made her unwilling to break with the Turk: she was even accused of secretly abetting the Moslem. Meantime Suliman was gathering together vast naval and military forces, and nobody knew what would be his first point of attack. At last, in the summer of 1522, all Europe learnt that the Sultan with his forces was investing the island of Rhodes, then held by the gallant Order of the Knights Hospitallers of St. John. In vain did the heroic defenders call on the Pope and the Princes of Europe to come to their succour; in vain did Adrian redouble his efforts to bring about at least a temporary truce in Europe, so as to enable the Christian States to send aid to the little band of Christian knights hard pressed by all the legions of the Great Sultan. Charles refused point blank; Genoa made a feeble effort to send a couple of vessels; there was no hope from any earthly power. All that year the terrible siege dragged on. The heroic defence of Rhodes, under the Grand-Master Villiers de l'Île-Adam, is one of the golden pages of history. More than once Suliman was actually on the point of abandoning the attack. The intrepid heroism of the Knights of St. John excited the genuine admiration of the Moslem; and when at last, after enduring unheard of hardships and displaying superhuman valour, the Grand-Master found himself obliged to capitulate on Christmas Day, the Sultan accorded the most honourable terms. The Knights were allowed to leave unmolested with their arms and baggage, and any Christians who liked to follow them, to Candia; to the inhabitants of Rhodes the free exercise of their religion was guaranteed. On the first day of 1523 the Christian fleet set sail for Candia. The heroic Villiers de l'Île-Adam and his Knights wished to visit Adrian VI., and place themselves at his disposal. But when they reached Italy the Pope was lying on his sick-bed and unable to receive them. He assigned them Cività Vecchia as a residence, and it was the Knights of St. John to whom was confided the care of the conclave in which Clement VII. was elected. Later on Charles V. granted them the island of Malta, where they remained till dispossessed by Napoleon I.

The impression made upon Adrian by the fall of Rhodes was a deeply painful one. It was remarked that he was never cheerful again. Whenever he spoke of it tears filled his eyes.

Adrian's preoccupation for the defence of Christendom from the external perils of the Moslem invasion did not in any way interfere with the anxieties concerning the internal perils which threatened it from the Lutheran revolt in the North of Europe. His election coincided with the rapid growth of Lutheranism, and Adrian, who was as convinced as Luther of the urgent necessity of a reform in the clergy, whether in Germany or in Italy, was clear-sighted enough to perceive that Luther's so-called Reformation was as much a political as a religious movement, and that it threatened both the political and social, as much as the religious, disintegration of Christianity. To a large extent it was a continuation of the old feud of the Guelphs and the Ghibellines, and when Luther, in his coarse diatribes, called upon the German people to reject the Pope because he was Antichrist, he was exploiting the national tendency of the Teutonic race to enfranchise itself from an authority which to them was "ultramontane" or foreign. Luther had the talent to excite the German nobles against Rome and the Emperor, and at the same time to excite the people against their Princes. A recent critic of the Cambridge Modern History, commenting on Professor Pollard's account of the Reformation in Germany, writes: "Luther does not cut a heroic figure in his relations with the democratic movement of the peasants against the Princes, and (quoting Pollard's own words) 'from the position of national hero now sank to be the prophet of a sect, and a sect which depended for existence upon the support of political powers.'" With the exception of Duke George of Saxony, the German Princes seemed blind to the dangers which threatened them. Some, like the Archbishop-Elector of Mainz, were timid, and feared a condemnation of Luther at the Diet of Worms; others, like the Elector Frederick of Saxony, openly favoured the innovator. The secular Princes also were not sorry to emancipate themselves from the authority of the Emperor and to seize upon ecclesiastical property, as Luther encouraged them to do. At this time robbery and spoliation of convents and benefices was called by that name of "secularization" that has been found so convenient a term even in our own times. Adrian was in season and out of season in his efforts to open the eyes of the German Princes, by his able letters and despatches, to the growing danger. These documents are remarkable both for the firmness of their tone and the solidity of their arguments. He describes in graphic terms the evils already wrought by Luther's preaching—the churches abandoned; the people in revolt against their clergy; a portion of the clergy seduced and unfaithful to their vocation; the Sacraments despised, Christians dying without confession; and the clarion of civil discord re-echoing throughout Germany, summoning the populace to pillage, murder, and fire; nuns drawn out of their convents; the priests of Christ induced to violate their vows and contract marriage; and all obedience, both secular and religious, trodden under foot. But all his efforts remained sterile. Charles V. himself would take no active part in suppressing the evil except on conditions of monetary advantage to himself. He desired the Pope to authorize him to retain for his own use the annates, and to impose for his own benefit tithes on the cathedrals, the collegiate churches, the monasteries, and even the houses of the mendicant Orders, under the pretext of using them for the war against the Turks. Adrian was too prudent to grant these requests, and the Diet which assembled at Nüremberg, perhaps partly owing to the incapacity and imprudence of the Papal Legate, Francesco Cheregato, entirely failed to produce those results which Adrian desired. Soon after the "Centum Gravimina" appeared in Germany, according to some the work of the Diet itself,* according to others, more probably that of Luther, or some of his adherents. This document ridicules Purgatory and the cult of the Saints, calumniates the mendicant Orders, demands the suppression of ecclesiastical feasts, condemns the consecration of churches, cemeteries, and bells, and many other sacred rites, as so many superstitions. Luther was triumphant; he felt that his cause was gained. He poured forth with more than usual scurrility attacks upon the Pope and his letters, which he called "truly Papistical, monkish, and Louvanian." Adrian could not but feel that, in spite of his conciliatory words, he had failed on all points. He resolved as a last and supreme resource to summon an Œcumenical Council, which the Lutherans had long demanded, and for which Catholics like the celebrated Louis Vives were

* So Creighton: "The Lay Estates brought forward the Hundred Grievances" (p. 262), and thinks "this was no token of sympathy with Luther's opinions."

pleading. But death prevented his carrying his great project into execution. It was reserved for a later pontificate to realize Adrian's design in the great Council of Trent. In 1523 Adrian canonized two illustrious saints—the great Dominican, St. Antoninus, Archbishop of Florence, and St. Benno, whose memory is venerated all through Saxony.* Luther replied by one of his most infamous libels, entitled, "Against the New Idol and the Old Devil who is to be glorified in Misnia."

One more project which Adrian VI. had deeply at heart was also destined to failure, partly owing to the duplicity of his own pupil Charles, still more to the implacable hostility of Francis I. We have already seen the untiring efforts made by Adrian from the very moment of his nomination to bring about a reconciliation between Francis I. on the one hand and Charles V. and Henry VIII. on the other, or at least to induce them to consent to a truce of temporary duration. We have also seen the insidious efforts of Charles to involve Adrian in a common alliance with himself and Henry against the French King, and we have noted the steady refusal of the clear-sighted and just Pontiff, who felt himself in reality the common Father of Christendom, to allow himself to be cajoled into becoming the cat's-paw of the wily Emperor. Adrian spared no efforts to secure the goodwill of Francis I, but, at the close of his brief pontificate, what the diplomacy of Charles had failed to obtain was brought about by the injustice and violence of the French King himself. Already Charles and Henry, the latter probably influenced by Cardinal Wolsey, whom Adrian seems to have won over, appeared disposed to listen to the Pope's propositions of peace. But Francis's unjustifiable arrest of the Papal Nuncio in France, which was a violation of international law, his recall of his own ambas-

* Creighton, oddly enough, calls this the canonization "of two German Bishops" (!) (p. 273).

sador from Rome, and his evident determination once more to invade Italy and renew all the miseries of war in that ill-fated country, finally drove Adrian to abandon his neutrality and conclude a defensive league with the Emperor, the King of England, the Archduke Ferdinand of Austria, the Duke of Milan, and the republics of Florence, Genoa, Siena, and Lucca. That of Venice acceded to the league under certain reserves. Even as it was, an opportunity was left for the headstrong French King himself to enter the league upon certain conditions. Francis, however, declined to accede to this treaty of peace, and began his preparations for the invasion of Italy. Adrian was already taking active steps to provide for the defence of Italy when death put an end to his career.

VII. "Magis ostensus quam Datus."

On the very day (April 3, 1523) on which the international league was solemnly published in the Church of St. Mary Major, Adrian, who had been for a long time unwell, was taken seriously ill. Rome at the time was in a most unhealthy condition. The plague, which had raged in 1522, broke out again with renewed virulence in the summer of 1523. In spite of this, Adrian continued to reside in the city, in order to restore the courage of the Roman people. Ill as he was, he occupied the last few months of his life with his wonted restless activity. Touched by the entreaties of King Louis of Hungary, whose States were already being invaded by the conquering Turk, the Pope, by a great effort and at the sacrifice of many jewels, silver-plate, and precious objects, succeeded in raising a sum of 50,000 ducats, which he despatched to Hungary to furnish resources against the Turks. For the same purpose, he sent large provisions of corn and gunpowder to the frontiers of Croatia and Dalmatia, which were in the greatest peril. But the Papal solicitude extended to far-distant parts of the world. He conferred upon the Franciscan missionaries special powers and privileges for the work of evangelization in Central and Southern America. He took much interest also in the welfare of the Order of the Dominicans, establishing, among others, a home of the Friars Preachers at Elgin in Scotland. He interested himself in the Eastern Church, and had the consolation of receiving the letters of Theophilus, the schismatic Patriarch of Alexandria, begging to be readmitted into communion with the Roman Church. On Palm Sunday he received in audience Ignatius of Loyola, who came to beg his blessing on the pilgrimage he was about to undertake to the Holy Land.

Meanwhile his sickness grew rapidly worse, and as the summer wore to its close he felt that his last hour was swiftly approaching. On September 8 he summoned the Cardinals round his bed, and announced to them his desire of raising to the cardinalate his faithful friend and countryman, William Enkenvoert, the only Cardinal whom he created during his reign. It is a striking instance of his simplicity and uprightness of character that he also begged the Cardinals' consent to his bequeathing to his relations in the Low Countries such movable property as he had brought with him from Spain.* "This is enough," said he, "to relieve their poverty and future necessities. I have not wished to enrich them with benefices or with the goods of the Church, and I desire that my successors should imitate me"—words which recall those of another Adrian, the English Pope. He then charged Cardinal Enkenvoert to dispose of all his property in Louvain and Utrecht for pious works, among these chiefly the endowment of the college he had founded at the Flemish University. Lastly, he begged that his funeral might be one of the

* The "hideous scene," as Creighton calls it, made by the Cardinals around Adrian's deathbed, narrated by the Duke of Sessa, is discredited by Höfler (p. 536, n. 5). Nor is there any truth in the rumour of Adrian's having been poisoned.

greatest simplicity. On the morning of September 14 he begged for Extreme Unction, and soon after calmly expired in the arms of the Archbishop of Durazzo. "As he had lived," writes Lochorst, "so he died—peacefully, calmly, devoutly, and holily." The words of the Venetian historian Marino Sanuto might be taken as his epitaph: "He was a good Pope, our friend, and a lover of peace." No sooner was his death known in the city than the Roman people came in crowds to venerate the Father they had so much esteemed. The poor, especially, all devout Christians, and the religious Orders, deplored his death as a public calamity. But those who had felt the lash of his reforms—usurers and corrupters of youth, men who had lost their offices in the Papal Court, and with whom the "barbarian" Pope had ever been unpopular—rejoiced in his death as in a deliverance. After its temporary repose in the basilica of St. Peter, the body of Adrian was eventually laid to rest in the magnificent mausoleum in the Church of Santa Maria dell' Anima, erected by his friend and executor, Cardinal Enkenvoert, who also is buried in the same church.*

Adrian VI.'s pontificate had lasted not quite twenty months, of which little more than one year in Rome

* On the medals of Adrian VI. see Bonnani, "Numismata Pontificum Romanorum" (Romæ, 1699, t. i., pp. 181-184). He figures and describes five medals, two being coronation medals, the reverse representing Adrian being crowned by one and two Cardinals respectively, with the motto *Quem creant adorant*. A third represents the Holy Ghost descending upon the tiara and keys, beneath which are a number of volumes of books—motto *Spiritus Sapientiæ*—probably in compliment to Adrian's theological learning. A fourth (of which a specimen is in the Hanmer Collection in the Library of St. Bede's College) represents the two Princes of the Apostles side by side, with the words *Sanctus Petrus, Sanctus Paulus*. Lastly, the fifth depicts a tower in process of building, with scaffolding round, and the motto *Ut ipse finiam*. Does this refer to Adrian's desire to finish the building of St. Peter's, or to his project of ecclesiastical reform? Bonnani tells a curious story of the attempt ("somnium") of a Capuchin writer, Matt. Bellintonus (1586) to make out Adrian to be an Italian, born at Renzano, in the diocese of Brescia, his father being one Giovanni Bono (!).

itself.* Short as it was, it was a well-filled reign, of which it may justly be said not one hour was wasted.† It stands forth as a bright page in the disordered and often disedifying history of the sixteenth century, and it was the first step towards that great internal reformation of the Church, which was to see its culmination half a century later under St. Pius V., for whom it was also reserved to realize Adrian's scheme of turning back the Moslem power and saving Europe from the Turkish peril.

I do not think that Creighton's estimate of Adrian VI. is generous, or even fair. We may all indeed agree with him when he styles Adrian "a pathetic figure" (p. 271), and in his true statement that the Dutch Pope had the wisdom to see "that contemporary opinion was wrong, in putting political questions in the front place instead of reform" (p. 269). But he accentuates Adrian's slowness and want of prompt decision. "He had not the boldness of constructive genius. He went so far in his boldness that it would have cost him little to be bolder. As it was, he irritated and alarmed every interest, while he gained no allies and awakened no enthusiasm. . . . No one paid much heed to him" (p. 270). "His attitude was rather negative than positive" (p. 234). There is a degree of truth in this judgment. Certainly as a politician and statesman, as before remarked, Adrian stands at a disadvantage compared with a contemporary like Ximenes. But Creighton scarcely takes into sufficient account the extreme difficulty of his position, his isolation as a foreigner, the shortness of his reign, his ill-health, and many other distressing

* Except Adrian I. (24 years), all the Popes of that name had short pontificates: Adrian II., 4 years 10 months; Adrian III., 1 year 4 months; Adrian IV., 4 years 8 months; Adrian V., only 1 month 9 days.

† One of the greatest misfortunes which have pursued the memory of Adrian VI. is the loss of his Regesta. They were all carried off after his death by his Flemish secretary, Dietrich Hetzius, to Liège (not Louvain, as Creighton says), and he refused to restore them to Clement VII. Where are they now?

circumstances of his life, which might have crippled the best efforts of a much stronger man.

There is much in the career of Adrian VI. that recalls that of his English namesake, Adrian IV. Both these Teutonic Popes were humbly born; both distinguished themselves as brilliant scholars in spite of lack of means; both received unexpectedly rapid promotion to the highest ecclesiastical honours; both were unanimously elected to the Papal See in the most unlooked-for manner; both were men of strenuous, simple, frugal, austere life; and both displayed in their high office the combination of firmness and decision of purpose with personal humility.

But there is another obvious parallel. Like Adrian VI., our present Holy Father, Pope Pius X., is essentially a man of the people. Of lowly origin, by sheer force of intellectual talent, of personal virtue, of high character, he has been raised by Providence from the humblest rank to the supreme dignity on earth; and although, thank God, in far better times and in purer surroundings, the outcome of the conclave of 1903 was almost as great a surprise to the Christian world as that of the conclave of 1522. Of both it may be said: "Digitus Dei est hic." The simple frugal life and homely tastes, the dislike of unnecessary court ceremonial, of the peasant's son of Riesi, recall those of the weaver's son of Utrecht. And if Adrian VI. during his brief pontificate showed himself a true reformer, what have we not been led to expect in the way of reforms in the short space that has already elapsed since the election of Pius X.?

Adrian VI. was surely a Pius X., born four centuries before his time.

BOOKS TO BE CONSULTED.

Constantin Ritter von Höfler. "Papst Adrian VI." Wien: Braümuller, 1880.

L'Abbé A. Lepitre. "Adrien VI." Paris: Berche et Tralin, 1880.

E. H. J. Reusens. "Syntagma Doctrinæ Theologicæ Adriani Sexti, Pont. Max." Lovanii: Vanlinthout, 1862.

VI

THE ENGLISH UNIVERSITIES AND THE REFORMATION

THE decision of the Holy See of April 2, 1895,* removing the ecclesiastical embargo hitherto laid upon the access of our Catholic students to the national Universities, marked the beginning of a new epoch in the history of Catholic education, or, to put it perhaps more correctly, indicated the closing of an era which had lasted for some three centuries. It will be fittingly recorded as signalizing the same year of grace which had seen the publication of the Apostolic Letter "Ad Anglos." We are much too near both events to properly appreciate their significance and probable results. We cannot be mistaken in thinking that both will be one day estimated as of unusual magnitude.

At any rate, the mind is irresistibly carried back, across the desolate span of three hundred years of conscription and persecution, to the times when the two national Universities were not only accessible to Catholic students, but were themselves Catholic institutions in as true a sense as Louvain and Washington and Fribourg are at the present day. To some minds this will not be easy to realize. Every Catholic boy and girl knows how we have been robbed of our grand old cathedrals, and a visit to Canterbury, York, or Lincoln recalls memories of a glorious past, associated with a keen sense of loss, even to the least imaginative mind. But somehow or

* *Tablet*, April 27, 1895, p. 647.

other we seem almost to have forgotten that Oxford and Cambridge are as truly lost heirlooms of our Church, so identified have they become with the ideas of Protestantism, or even of free-thought and scepticism. Yet the material and artistic loss of our beautiful cathedrals, great as it was, has been far less than the intellectual loss of the ancient seats of learning, the homes of culture, and the national schools of theology. It seems appropriate at this juncture to rehearse the sad history of the process by which these national Universities were lost to the Catholic Church, not without a long and gallant struggle. To do this in a brief and commodious manner, we purpose to select as our guide the short and excellent monograph of Father Zimmermann, S.J., published already some sixteen years ago, but which, like too many admirable publications of its kind bearing upon English Church history, has not yet found a translator in England or America.* Father Zimmermann will prove a conscientious and reliable guide. He has diligently utilized the best sources of information up to the time of his writing—Abbot Gasquet's star had scarcely appeared above the horizon—and, as every page shows, has carefully and critically digested both the older authorities, like Wood, Cooper, Dugdale, or Spelman, and the modern ones, like Mullinger, Brewer, Bridgett, or Seebohm.

* There is ample opening for the publication of a whole library of valuable monographs, for instance, on English Churchmen, translated from foreign languages. I will instance only a few: Abbé Martin, "St. Etienne Harding et les premiers Recenseurs de la Vulgate" (Amiens, 1887); "La Vulgate latine d'après Roger Bacon" (Paris, 1888); and "Etienne Langton et le Texte parisien de la Vulgate" (in the Muséon, 1889-1890); Dr. J. Felten, "Robert Grosseteste, Bischof von Lincoln" (Freiburg-i.-B., 1887); Dr. K. Werner, "Beda der Ehrwürdige und seine Zeit" (Wien, 1875); "Alcuin und sein Jahrhundert" (Paderborn, 1876); Alberdingk Thijm, "H. Willibrordus Apostel der Nederlanden" (Amsterdam, 1861). Here are able and scholarly studies, all comparatively short, of seven great English Churchmen, all well deserving of translation and publication. It seems a pity that they should not be better known and utilized in this country.

This will serve as an excuse for presenting in this paper little more than the summary of a book, itself not exceeding 140 pages in extent.

I.

Mr. Gladstone's ingenious and curious contention in his brilliant Romanes Lecture that the Universities of the early Middle Ages were the outcome of "a great systematic effort (of the) lay mind to achieve self-assertion and emancipation"* as against the predominance of ecclesiasticism, hardly commended itself at the time to his hearers,† and probably will not do so to his readers at the present moment. It is, indeed, highly probable that the early universities, like Topsy, mostly "growed." Zimmermann altogether discountenances the old-fashioned idea that they were a continuation of either the old cathedral or monastic schools, from which they differed not only in the subjects and methods of study, but still more in their entire organization. Mr. Gladstone opines that the Papal authority may have been used "as a defensive measure to keep in check the separate action of the lay element." But, although it may be true enough that the very earliest Universities, such as Salerno or Bologna, as well as Oxford and Cambridge—ten altogether, according to Mr. Gladstone—were called into existence before either Papal or regal authority began to intervene, yet there does not seem to be much evidence for the supposed organized system of "emancipation." The more probable solution appears to be that these schools, sprung from what Mr. Gladstone more happily styles "professional exigencies," were at first under local episcopal

* P. 10.

† "Unless the accepted view in these matters has been modified by very recent researches, the accepted view is not quite that of Mr. Gladstone," is the sensible criticism of a very scholarly article in the *Manchester Guardian* of October 25, 1892, evidently from an able though anonymous pen.

control. Green, indeed, by whom Mr. Gladstone seems to some extent to have been influenced, points out that at first the Chancellor of Oxford was simply the local officer of the Bishop of Lincoln,* but that later on "Popes, seeing in them the possibility of an intellectual tool and weapon that the Church needed, gave them privileges and immunities."† Be this as it may, the early English Universities, although true "republics of letters," were thoroughly Catholic institutions, and for all practical purposes may be styled ecclesiastical ones. The famous "secession" of the students in 1209 is the first certain date in the history of Oxford, whose foundation almost certainly preceded that of Cambridge. From the first the history of both Universities was intimately bound up with all that was best and holiest in the English Church. The Oxford career of St. Edmund Rich, so beautifully told by Green,‡ falls between 1219 and 1226, and it was the Saint of Abingdon who first taught Aristotle at Oxford. But it is more especially with the coming of the friars of the Orders of

* "History of the English People," book iii., chapter i. (Library edition, vol. i., p. 205).

† The most recent, as well as the most complete statement of the origins of the European Universities before 1400 is that of the great historian of these Universities, the late F. Denifle, O.P. His conclusions may thus be summed up: Four categories may be made according to the manner of foundation: (1) The eleven which arose without any formal diploma of foundation, some of these being the outcome of pre-existing ecclesiastical schools: among these are some of the most illustrious of all, including Paris, Bologna, and Oxford; (2) sixteen created exclusively by Papal diploma, among which Denifle places Cambridge; (3) ten created exclusively by imperial and royal charters; (4) nine, created simultaneously by both Papal and royal decrees ("Die Universitäten des Mittelalters bis 1400," von H. Denifle, vol. i., pp. xiv, 814). These significant statistics confirm the truth of Paulsen's dictum: "In the erection of the Universities there was formerly absolute liberty, not outside the Church, but inside the Church, and the Church blessed without reserve and with equal affection both the good she did herself and the good which was done in her" (see P. Berthier, O.P., "Projets anciens des hautes Études catholiques en Suisse").

‡ *Op. cit.*

both St. Dominic and St. Francis that the early glories of Oxford are so intimately bound up. It was immediately after his second general Chapter in 1221 that Brother Dominic despatched his first party of friars to England, and it was at Oxford, on the Feast of the Assumption, that they first settled and opened schools. Very soon learned men flocked to their Order, including Robert Bacon, uncle or brother to the still more famous Roger, and his dearest friend, Richard Fishacre, "the most learned among the learned," as Ireland calls him, and who ever carried the works of Aristotle in his bosom; also Robert Kilwardby, eminent as philosopher and theologian, a future Archbishop of Canterbury and Cardinal; and John of St. Giles, called by Matthew Paris "a man skilful in the art of medicine, a great professor of divinity, and excellently learned." In 1229 took place another curious "secession" of students, this time to Oxford, from the mother University of Paris, as a protest against the violation of certain privileges. Among these were the Dominicans of St. James's Convent, and with them their General, Blessed Jordan, who wrote to the nuns at Bologna, "Our Lord gives me hopes of making a good capture in the University of Oxford, where I now am." The Dominicans, indeed, contributed some of its brightest ornaments to the University.* But, as Mr. Gladstone points out, the greatest names belonging to Oxford in the thirteenth and fourteenth centuries "are not of the Order of St. Dominic, to whom Dante awards the intellectual brightness of the cherub (*Paradiso*, xi. 39-41), but in the ranks of the seraphic Francis, who could not abide the world, even in its academic form."†

The Franciscan Order (he says elsewhere) gave to Oxford the larger number of those remarkable, and even

* See the late Mother Augusta Theodosia Drane's admirable "History of St. Dominic," chap. xxxii., pp. 442-446, on the Friars Preachers at Oxford.

† *Op. cit.*, p. 18. The Franciscans came to Oxford in 1225.

epoch-making, men who secured for this University such a career of glory in medieval times.* These men were of English birth, but the fame of their school was such that Franciscans flocked to it, not only from Scotland and Ireland, but from France, Italy, Spain, Portugal, and Germany.

The most famous of these luminaries whom Mr. Gladstone cites in his generous eulogium on the Oxford Friars Minor were Alexander of Hales, Adam Marsh, Archbishop Peckham, Duns Scotus, William of Ockham, and, greatest of all, "perhaps the most striking British intellect of the Middle Ages," the earlier and the greater of the two Bacons, Roger.† Mr. Gladstone goes on to point out how the fame of the early Oxford Franciscans were consecrated by "that superlative distinction" of a special epithet attached to their names, "coin of European rather than of British currency," such as "Doctor irrefragabilis" (Alexander of Hales), "Doctor subtilis" (Scotus), "Doctor mirabilis" (Bacon), and others.‡ Thus it was that the very foundations of Oxford's greatness, which won for her, already as early as 1252, the epithet *aemula Parisiensis*, are owing to the two mendicant Orders,§ not merely for their own scientific achievements, but also because they stimulated by their example the secular and regular clergy. Very soon the Bishops and the Benedictines had founded colleges at Oxford. Merton, the first Oxford college, dates from 1264; the first Cambridge foundation was Peterhouse, 1274.

* *Op. cit.*, p. 12.

† Sir John Herschel, Mr. Lewis (quoted by Mr. Gladstone), and, we may add, Professor Jevons ("Logic," p. 229), estimate Roger above his famous namesake, Francis Bacon. The same estimate of the great Franciscan is warmly maintained by Mr. J. Vellin Marmery in his book entitled "Progress of Science: its Origin, Course, Promoters, and Results" (London: Chapman and Hall, 1895), in which he spiritedly defends the Middle Ages from the old-fashioned charge of intellectual stagnation.

‡ *Op. cit.*, p. 19.

§ *Op. cit.*, p. 17.

I have dwelt perhaps too long upon these early facts, but my object is to emphasize the essentially Catholic character of our national Universities from their inception. The same is true from the point of view of their character and discipline, so unlike what they have come to be in these last three centuries. To begin with, the ancient University offered access to the poor, even to the very poor. The penniless student athirst for knowledge was not an object of contempt, but was on a perfect level with the richest and the noblest. His life was hard enough, though he generally had sufficiency of food, and there were many charitable foundations to assist, not to pauperize, him. The discipline was severe.* The course was much longer: seven years' study was required to reach the Master's degree; theology took ten years.† The student was not merely receptive; on attaining his degree, he was obliged himself to teach "cursorie." Public disputations were frequent, as still in Catholic Universities and seminaries abroad. This system may have had its weak points, but it was well suited to the times. It may be questioned whether we are not slowly coming back to some part, at least, of the old ways of the thirteenth, fourteenth, and fifteenth centuries.

The opening of the fifteenth century was characterized, as our own days, by a remarkable devotion to learning on the part of the lower classes. A statute of 1406 laid down the grand principle, which the nineteenth century believed itself to have established, that it is free to any man, of whatever social rank he may be, to have his son or daughter educated in any school of the kingdom. Numerous colleges were founded during the century: Lincoln, 1427; All Souls and Magdalen, 1457; King's, 1440; Queen's, 1458; Catherine Hall, 1475; Jesus, 1497. Henry VI. and his Queen were special patrons of

* As late as 1540 undergraduates could receive the birch-rod (Zimmermann, p. 65).

† So in old Louvain (see "The Dutch Pope," p. 109).

the universities. Let it be remembered that colleges at this time were really charitable foundations to aid poorer students, and in each case established out of pious motives, for God's glory and to obtain prayers and masses for the souls of the founders. During this century also began the close connection between the universities and the great public schools, such as Winchester and Eton, so that "young men at the English universities were better prepared than elsewhere."*

The close of the century saw the rise of "Humanism," or the "New Learning,"† the cradle of which was in Italy. Oxford men, like Robert Fleming, William Grey, John Gunthorp, John Free, Tiptoft, Earl of Worcester, and William Snelling, O.S.B., went to Italy to become learners.‡ In 1488 three Italian humanists, one of whom was Cornelio Vitelli, were at Oxford, boarding at Magdalen College. Vitelli taught Greek to Grocyn, perhaps also to Linacre. Both these great English humanists were good and zealous Catholics. Grocyn was an ascetic, devout man, much attached to the scholastic philosophy. Linacre, distinguished for his studies in medicine, and worthy of record as the founder and first President of the Royal College of Physicians, was no less celebrated for his piety, and late in life (1509) became a priest. The illustrious pupils of Grocyn and Linacre were Erasmus and Sir Thomas More. Other eminent names among the Oxford humanists of the day were William Latimer and William Lyly, and, above all, John Colet. A Londoner (b. 1466), Colet visited Italy for purposes of study, but his strongly ascetic mind saw and realized more easily than many others the intellectual and moral dangers of Humanism, of which, however, he himself became one of the brightest orna-

* Zimmermann, p. 8. To the same writer we are also indebted for an admirable monograph on "Our Public Schools" ("England's Oeffentlichen Schulen," Freiburg, 1892).

† For another meaning of this term, see Gasquet's "Eve of the Reformation."

‡ *Ibid.*

ments. In 1496 he returned to Oxford, and soon gained great fame and influence by his eloquence and learning, not only in Greek, but also in the interpretation of Holy Scripture. Two years later we find the famous Erasmus of Rotterdam at Oxford, studying Greek under Grocyn and Linacre. Together with his friend More, with their two teachers, with Charnock and Colet, he formed the never-to-be-forgotten coterie of classical scholars which graced Oxford at the close of the fifteenth century. Up to this, as Mr. Gladstone is justified in claiming, Oxford had far and away surpassed her sister of Cambridge, giving to England nearly all her great theologians, bishops, and statesmen. Cambridge seems to have been marked by a kind of apathy. Even in Greek learning, scarce one or two names of note can be recorded.

During the following century, however, things altered, and eventually—at least, as regards humanities—the positions were almost reversed. Cambridge owes her awakening almost entirely to Blessed John Fisher. It would be useless here to repeat the well-known story of his life. Suffice it to say that, born in 1469, he entered Cambridge in 1483. As confessor of the Lady Margaret, Countess of Richmond, the pious mother of Henry VII., he was soon able to exercise great influence in favour of his Alma Mater. To him is owing a novel institution, the establishment of salaried professorships, independent of the colleges. The Lady Margaret Chair of Divinity was founded at this time. The university awoke to new life and activity. In 1503 Pope Alexander VI. empowered the Chancellor to send out yearly twelve priests, either Doctors of Divinity or Masters of Arts, to preach all over England, Ireland, and Scotland. The next year Fisher himself became Chancellor. In 1506 Erasmus, probably induced by the new Chancellor, came to Cambridge. The great humanist does not appear to have had the gifts of a successful teacher. His great faults of character, too, his vanity, frivolity, love of ridicule and invective, all of which render his testimony about his contemporaries eminently suspect, might, but for the goodwill of Fisher, have led to unpleasant strife at Cambridge.* Fisher esteemed his real talents, and, wishing to utilize them for the Church, avoided doing anything to drive him into the hostile camp. Several eminent men at the university—Bullock, Gonell, Bryan, Aldrich, Waston—were among his pupils, and others were encouraged by him to take up the study of Greek. Fisher himself, in 1518, then in his fiftieth year, learnt Greek. Thus, as the classical studies began to decline at Oxford, they grew in favour at Cambridge.

Whilst Fisher was thus making himself the real father of the greatness of Cambridge, three well-known Churchmen were doing much for Oxford. The first of these was Fox, Bishop of Winchester, than whom few prelates have merited better of the universities. The college of Corpus Christi, founded by him, shows in its statutes the strong influences of the Renascence.† Great stress was laid upon the reading of the classical authors. Scarcely less important was the influence of Archbishop Warham and of Cardinal Wolsey, of whom it will be necessary to speak later, when on the subject of the great religious separation. In several important points Wolsey displayed really marvellous breadth of view. He munificently endowed professorships, and one of the men he brought to Oxford to fill a chair was the celebrated Louis Vives. Still more remarkable was Wolsey's grandiose scheme of establishing schools in all the chief towns of the country, as preparatory schools for the universities. His foundation of Cardinal College, which he was never able to complete, and which scarcely survived his fall, is too well known to repeat here. He has been severely blamed by Protestant and Catholic writers alike, from Spelman to Mullinger, for his action in utilizing the revenues of the suppressed minor monas-

* For an excellent estimate of Erasmus, see Gasquet's "Eve of the Reformation."

† See p. 192.

teries to endow his college. Zimmermann, however, is inclined to defend him, and invokes Pope Clement VII., whose permission was granted for the purpose, as had been done in other cases of a similar kind. Wolsey's misfortune, he thinks, was to have had such a tool as Thomas Crumwell to employ for the purpose.*

But Oxford had fallen upon evil times. To begin with, visitations of sore disease wellnigh threatened her existence. From 1509 to 1528 constant outbreaks of epidemics, generally the dreaded "sweating sickness," drove away the students in crowds. More tells us in 1523 that the abbots had almost ceased to send their monks to the university; neither the nobleman would send his sons, nor the parish priest his subjects or kinsfolk. Many hostels were altogether closed. This sad state of things was doubtless owing to the unhealthy position of the city and its shocking sanitary arrangements, or rather utter want of sanitation. Vives complains bitterly of the unhealthiness of the place.

Intellectual dissensions also broke out with considerable bitterness. It is a reproach to be made against the early humanists that, in the pride of their New Learning, they too often showed themselves narrow-minded, insolent, and overbearing, and affected contemptuous scorn of the scholastic philosophy, chiefly on account of their own ignorance of anything outside the narrow circle of their own philological and literary studies.† At first they seem to have been received by the theologians and philosophers with good humour and deference, but later on the opposition of the theologians to the New Learning was stimulated to regrettable exaggeration. So arose the feud between the "Greeks" and the "Trojans," as the anti-humanists came to call themselves. More had to invoke the

* Zimmermann, p. 24. But see Gasquet, "Henry VIII. and the English Monasteries," vol. i., pp. 78 *et seq.*

† See Pastor, "Geschichte der Päpste" (4th edition, 1901), vol. i., pp. 15-41.

intervention of the King, and Greek was at last duly recognised as a regular branch of study.

Such was the state of things at the national universities at the dawn of the dark day of the religious troubles under Henry VIII.

II.

Mr. Gladstone does but formulate the universal verdict of history when he tells us that in the new epoch which now opened Cambridge was to become the cradle of English Protestantism,* to which we may add that Oxford was long to remain the citadel of English Catholicism.† This fact is not without its explanation. Wycliffism, it must be remembered, was still existent in the country as a religious faith, and its home was chiefly in the eastern counties, which, moreover, owing to their geographical situation, were in easy and constant communication with the Netherlands and Germany. It cannot surprise us, then, that in these districts the writings of Luther and other Continental "reformers" came to be circulated by the agency of booksellers, bankrupt traders, and various kinds of smugglers. They made their way soon enough to the University of Cambridge. As early as 1517 Luther seems to have found there an imitator in his denunciation of indulgences. This was a Norman, Peter de Valence, who was eventually publicly excommunicated by the Chancellor, Bishop Fisher, and who, though not an Englishman, may be claimed as the first English Protestant. The first head of the Protestant party was, however, the talented, but eccentric, and (like Luther) originally scrupulous, "Little Bilney," who by a secret propaganda won over by degrees to the Lutheran doctrine a knot of men — Arthur, fellow of St. John's, Smith, a doctor of canon law, Forman of Queen's, and one or

* "Romanes Lecture," pp. 23-25. † Zimmermann, p. 31.

two others. But his most celebrated conquest was that of Robert Barnes, prior of the Augustinians. Both Bilney and Barnes, it is worth noting, were Norfolk men. Barnes had been a student of Louvain, and was an enthusiastic humanist. His worldly and lax character would seem to have little fitted him for a "reformer," but he really became the leader of the party. It is remarked that, at least for the present, these English Lutherans did not go so far as Luther himself in all points, refraining, for instance, from attacks on the Catholic doctrine of the Holy Eucharist. Bilney's next successful move, the winning over of Hugh Latimer, was of a character very shocking to a Catholic mind. He went to confession to Latimer, and under the pretext of seeking advice in his mental and spiritual doubts, difficulties and trials, succeeded in winning the confidence and esteem of Latimer, who seems to have been up to this of a guileless and unsuspicious nature, and hitherto had enjoyed the reputation of piety and str ct orthodoxy. Very soon he was entirely under Bilney's influence and guidance. Latimer's character does not certainly seem to have gained by the new direction under which he fell. Duplicity and a decided want of steadfastness are stamped on his subsequent career. Summoned before Bishop West of Ely to answer for preaching Lutheran doctrine, he declared that he knew nothing about Luther's teachings as it was forbidden to read his books. In 1531 we find him, after some show of manful resistance, on his knees at Lambeth admitting having preached error, declaring that his hasty speech had led him into errors and want of discretion, and begging pardon for the scandal caused. Two years later he was again accused of the same errors, and declared he had been misunderstood. Arthur and Bilney too, after some hesitation, are found recanting their errors, and altogether these early English Protestants show a decided want of constancy and much moral weakness as compared with their predecessors, the Lollards.

It is difficult to explain Wolsey's want of firmness and foresight at this juncture. When Barnes and Latimer were cited before him, he not only, led astray by Latimer's skilful pleading, reversed Bishop West's prohibition to him to preach, but with his legatine power gave him general faculty to preach everywhere.

From Cambridge the infection of the Lutheran heresy was carried to Oxford in 1526 by a small band of students, whose leader seems to have been one John Clarke. The importation of the dangerous doctrines into his own university alarmed Wolsey, and roused him at last into some activity.

The curious history of the attempts to arrest Thomas Garrett of Magdalen, the most zealous propagator of the writings of the Continental reformers, as related by his friend Dalaber, is a tragi-comic story of adventures. Dalaber himself does not come very honourably out of it, for we find him, when brought up before Dr. Loudon, the head of New College, whom he styles "the worst Papist Pharisee of all," himself playing a highly discreditable part. After long opposition he finally promised, and even swore on the Mass-book, to answer according to the truth, "but in his heart resolved the opposite." He ended by betraying his twenty-two companions, and was then set at liberty. On the other hand, it impresses us unpleasantly to find the University Commissioner, Dr. Cottisford, having recourse to an astrologer to find out the whereabouts of the fugitive Garrett !* The latter being eventually incarcerated wrote a suppliant letter, begging not so much for delivery from the fetters he had merited as from the terrible fetters of excommunication.† Several of the other innovators were apprehended, but the authorities displayed considerable mildness in their treatment of them. Dr. Higdon (Dean of Cardinal College), who himself caused their apprehension, writes to Wolsey

* Zimmermann, p. 41.
† "Letters and Papers" (Brewer), iv., 1804.

begging for absolution for them, and permission to make their Easter duties. Longland, Bishop of Lincoln, apparently expecting their amendment, also pleaded for them. More than a dozen of these suspects took part in the penitential procession from St. Mary's to St. Frideswide's, and as they passed the Carfax cast there a book into the fire. Foxe's harrowing tales in his "Book of Martyrs" about noisome underground dungeons and salt food are manifestly apocryphal.* Three of them died in August of the sweating sickness, and seem to have shown some repentance. Altogether, as before remarked, these early Protestants did not display much of the stuff of which martyrs are made.

More than this, men of the eloquence of Luther or the wide learning of Melanchthon were wanting in their ranks. Some of them were coarse and vulgar in their expression, and not likely to exercise much influence among the more cultured. Indeed, the whole movement would probably have died out without leaving any appreciable traces, as it did in Italy and Spain, but for the lamentable affair of the Royal Divorce—that true *fons et origo malorum* of the English Church. The effects of the divorce case may be thus summed up in a sentence—the numerically and intellectually weaker party got the upper hand, and the universities were reduced to a state of servitude.

It was in 1530, two years after the events just narrated, that Henry VIII., being determined upon his divorce from Queen Catherine, appealed to the two universities for a favourable decision. From what has gone before, we can hardly wonder that he appealed first to Cambridge. Cranmer, Fox, and Gardiner, his chief tools in the matter, were Cambridge men. It is remarkable that the older men were inclined to yield to the very urgent arguments of the King; the younger held out more manfully. Now every kind of pressure was brought to bear. The King's party, not daring to

* Zimmermann, p. 42.

challenge a vote of the university at large, brought about the appointment of a Special Commission. But even in this Commission, partial as it was, things did not go smoothly, and the final decision that was extorted ran thus: "Ducere uxorem fratris mortui sine liberis *cognitam a priori viro per carnalem copulam*, est prohibitum iure divino ac naturali." Practically the verdict was dead against the King, for it was exactly the consummation of the marriage with Prince Arthur that was steadfastly denied by the Queen. We know, therefore, what value to attach to Froude's eulogy of the spirit of independence and liberality of Cambridge in favouring the divorce* as compared with the narrow-mindedness of Oxford. As a matter of fact, both the national seats of learning rejected it.†

Oxford, however, was certainly much more strongly Catholic, and so remained for several generations. And whilst the Protestant party was very unpopular there, the party of the Queen was especially popular. Mr. Gladstone is correct in maintaining that there was a difference in the prevalent theological cast of the two universities. "Oxford was on the losing side. . . . It might be said, without any great perversion of historical truth, that in the sixteenth century the deepest and most vital religious influences within the two universities respectively were addressed at Oxford to the making of recusants, at Cambridge to the production of Zwinglians and Calvinists."‡

No wonder that extraordinary efforts were made by Henry to coerce the Oxford intellect and will. The younger generations here again, especially the Arts men, held out gallantly, and drew down the royal wrath, expressed in no measured language in Henry's letters. He concludes by reminding them, in words which recall our Latin exercise books, "Non est bonum irritare

* "History of England," i., 257-262.
† Zimmermann, p. 44.
‡ "Romanes Lecture," p. 25.

crabrones."* Unfortunately, it must be admitted that the part played by Archbishop Warham in this matter was a discreditable one. He did not hesitate to assert that the Universities of Cambridge and Paris had already pronounced in favour of the divorce, which was a falsehood. Cambridge's decision we have seen above; that of Paris had not been given at this time. After this we can scarcely be surprised at Henry's false citation in his letter of March 17, of the Cambridge decision, by *simply omitting the crucial clause italicised* in our quotation above.

In spite of all, of King and Primate, and even of the threatened weakness of the theological faculty under tremendous pressure, it is refreshing to find the M.A.'s holding out gallantly. After eight weeks' strenuous contest and every kind of intrigue, nothing further could be squeezed out of the university than a decision practically equivalent to that of Cambridge—for which, of course, Oxford falls in for the censures of Mr. Froude.†

Henry's wrath descended heavily on the university, whose great Chancellor, Cardinal Wolsey, had already fallen into disgrace in the preceding October. It was his famous college, Cardinal College, that was to feel the full fury of the storm. And after various efforts to ward off the blow, spoliation and suppression rapidly followed one another—perhaps among the bitterest of the dregs that the fallen Chancellor had to drink.

Five years later the great Chancellor and benefactor of the sister university, Blessed John Fisher, died the martyr's death upon the scaffold (June 22, 1535). Unlike Wolsey and Warham, the saintly Bishop had early on foreseen the dangers for the English Church which the spread of the Lutheran heresy only too surely threatened, but his warnings had been unheeded by these mighty prelates. His own services to Cambridge slackened not until the end. His new statutes,

* Letter of March 6, Zimmermann, p. 46.
† "History of England," i., p. 279.

to some extent borrowed from Oxford, were directed partly to elevating the level of the studies, partly to remedying the evergrowing indiscipline and recklessness of the rising generation. He is therefore very far from meriting the charge of narrow-mindedness which even Mullinger makes against him,* and not only St. John's College, as that historian truly claims, but the whole university may justly look back with gratitude and pride to Bishop Fisher as the greatest of her benefactors.

The remaining years of Henry, from 1535 to 1547, are rightly summed up by Father Zimmermann in reference to our subject as the epoch of the plundering and enslaving of the universities. The meanness and greed which disgraced the policy of the latter years of the reign do not always, or even generally, mark the policy of the "Turkish Sultans" to whom Zimmermann compares him. Henry has been praised as a patron of the universities, and a declaration of his is often quoted to the effect that no foundations are more to the general good than those in favour of colleges, and sharply discriminating between the universities and the monasteries. There is good reason to suspect the sincerity of these expressions, and to believe that a systematic spoliation of the universities was originally intended to follow in due course that of the monasteries. In spite of his foundation of Trinity, Cambridge, from purely political motives, Henry cannot be said to have esteemed either learning or learned men for their own sake.† But what is a much more serious charge is that his policy was directed to a systematic enthraldom of the intellect. Never were independent thought and freedom of research so much kept in fetters as at this epoch. The King's changeableness of disposition and views rendered this mental servitude the more galling. The universities were called upon to change the opinions they had to defend according to the royal humour.

* "History of England," i., p. 624.
† Zimmermann, pp. 53, 54, 67.

Thomas Crumwell was made Visitor of both the universities, and an elaborate document containing detailed instructions was drawn up, which Zimmermann analyses. The first article expressly stipulates that the members of the university are to promise obedience not only to the rules of succession established by the King, but also to all statutes directed to the uprooting of the Papal claims and the confirmation of the King's supreme authority. No lectures were to be permitted upon the Master of Sentences and his commentators; only the Old and New Testament in their literal sense were to be expounded. This was, of course, directed to the abolition of the scholastic philosophy and theology. Both lectures and degrees in canon law were to be abolished, "as all England (!) had acknowledged the ecclesiastical supremacy of the King." Melanchthon's name is inserted among the authors to be expounded in philosophy. All heads of houses and professors must swear obedience to these new statutes. Two pliant tools, Dr. Layton and Dr. Legh, were deputed in place of their master, Crumwell, as Visitors to Oxford and Cambridge respectively. Then followed a veritable panic, a reign of terror. With what high-handed violence the new ordinances were carried out we can learn from Layton's letters to his master. Duns Scotus was the object of special ill-treatment. His books were torn up and scattered about with every circumstance of ignominy. This was practically the banishment of sound logic from the English universities, remarks Zimmermann caustically, and so things have remained till quite recent times. Legh proceeded with somewhat more moderation in Cambridge.

No wonder that these measures, and the general uncertainty which prevailed, rapidly tended to diminish the number of students. But the severest blow which the universities received was in the suppression of the great monasteries between 1536 and 1539. Dr. Loudon was commissioned to suppress the nine colleges of the regular orders—Benedictines, Cistercians, Augustinians, Franciscans, and Dominicans in Oxford. Nobles, townsfolk, and heads of secular colleges threw themselves greedily upon the plunder; the subjects were bettering the unworthy example of their sovereign. The few regular colleges at Cambridge had no better fate. But the effects of the suppression of the monasteries were more far-reaching. Among these was the destruction of so many of the middle schools which had served as feeders for the universities by affording training for talented boys of the poorer classes. Now began that gradual change which eventually led to the practical shutting out of the poorer classes—who before this epoch had been in the *majority* at the universities—and the exclusive reservation of these national institutions to the rich and the noble. A little later than this, as Mr. Gladstone reminds us, "Ascham says that among the prevailing evils there was none more grave than the large admission of the sons of rich men indifferent to solid and far-reaching study."* But this was the process which now began and went steadily on for three centuries.

On Crumwell's fall in 1540 Bishop Gardiner succeeded as Chancellor. It is not our business here to discuss the somewhat ambiguous character of Stephen Gardiner. As bishop he appears to have shown a less pliant disposition than Henry had expected from his former behaviour. He was at any rate a scholar of some merit. During his chancellorship occurred his famous quarrel with the gifted Hellenist, John Cheke, concerning the pronunciation of Greek, which led to a strife as bitter as (to us) it is amusing. Here we meet with the first beginnings of the "pedantry," which for some time was to cling to English learning. The chancellorship of Gardiner, however, to some extent appears as a time of comparative prosperity to the university. The new regulations published in 1544 were wise and useful.

* "Romanes Lecture," p. 23.

The foundation of Magdalen College, although the complete carrying out of the original plan was not possible till Mary's reign (1584) falls in this time, and, at length, also Henry's own long promised foundation Trinity, Cambridge. In spite of all the misery and uncertainty of the times there was still a certain number of scholars of note at the universities, but of these the majority were true to the Old Faith.

At the death of Henry VIII. the country was in a state of the greatest anarchy that it had seen since the Conquest. Never had there been such a severing of classes and such divisions of men's minds. The people were in a temper of despair, and, but for the paid army at the King's command, a revolution would probably have broken out. The short reign of the boy-king Edward VI. was to mark the victory of Protestantism—a victory which, in spite of the temporary Catholic reaction under Mary, was to be continued and consolidated under Elizabeth. The Protector Somerset was a convinced Calvinist; Warwick, later Duke of Northumberland, though at heart a Catholic, relied for the success of his schemes on the Protestant party, as the Catholics naturally favoured Mary.

From the intellectual point of view, the Protestants at this time were decidedly weak, especially in theologians. Cranmer and his friends could not help feeling that they had no men at the universities who could be considered a match for scholars like Dr. Richard Smith, Mallet, or Chedsey at Oxford, Young and Bullock at Cambridge. As Mr. Gladstone points out, "A proof of this relative weakness is supplied by the single fact that to reform our service-books, and to instruct our candidates for holy orders, we were driven to invoke the aid of foreigners."* Already in Henry's lifetime unsuccessful overtures had been made to Melanchthon, and now Bucer and Fagius were imported to Cambridge, and Peter Martyr (whose name was Vermigli) to Oxford.

* "Romanes Lecture," p. 25.

In 1548 and 1549 a new Commission of Visitation was issued for both universities. The statutes, under the sanction of all kinds of penalites, fines, imprisonment, etc., were to effect a thorough revolution in the Protestant sense. The old doctrine was to be extirpated, foundations for masses to be commuted, the forms of Divine service to be altered. Some changes were introduced into the prescribed courses of study, and efforts made, not, indeed, with success, to encourage the study of civil law. Further confusion was a necessary result.

Peter Martyr began his lectures at Oxford in 1549. He was the first in England to deny the Real Presence. His crude Zwinglian teaching regarding the Holy Eucharist disgusted the Catholics. Quarrels, and even physical strife, were the result. Shocking scenes of profanity and desecration occurred in some of the college chapels, especially Magdalen. At Cambridge Dr. Cox was the bitterest enemy of the Catholics. He displayed a literal fury in the wholesale destruction of books and MSS. A new feature in the strife was the introduction of public disputations between the parties. Dr. Richard Smith challenged Peter Martyr to such a trial of skill, but his crafty adversary eluded every attempt to make him face so able a disputant with quite an amusing variety of subterfuges. The end was that Smith, like so many other of Oxford's ablest men, was forced to seek refuge in flight to the Continent. Other Catholics, however—Tresham and Chedsey—took up the cudgels in his place, and Peter Martyr, forced at last to a disputation, cut such a sorry figure that Dr. Cox, after four days, adjourned the meeting *sine die*. Bucer, also at Cambridge, had to face the challenge of Young, Sedgwick, and Andrew, and came off with little credit in a public disputation on theology. Other such intellectual contests followed.

Somerset and Northumberland were meanwhile gradually getting rid of the Catholic professors and officials, whilst Catholic parents (who were still in the majority) were withdrawing their sons from the national universities to have them educated privately at home or at foreign seats of learning. The lecture-rooms were steadily emptying, and the diminishing ranks of students were recruited only from the sons of the richer classes, whose chief aim was pleasure, not study. We have Latimer's and Lever's lamentations to bear out these statements.* Huber† is therefore fully justified in maintaining that the "Reformation" had injured the universities, both externally and internally. But we cannot agree with him in comparing the reign of Henry VIII. with that of Edward VI., to the advantage of the former. Although the evils grew under the latter reign, it was precisely Henry's policy which was responsible for them in their origin. Yet even Edward does not seem to have merited all the praise which has been bestowed on him as a patron of learning. The funds for the schools of which he is reckoned the founder were for the most part derived either from Church property or the contributions of the local burgesses.

In the statutes of Trinity College, Cambridge, published by the visitors at this time, we find first fully developed the systematic plan of making the colleges independent of the university, an innovation which had serious consequences later on, as we shall see. The President is also to take an oath to maintain the Protestant doctrine, and the fellows are to be obliged to abjure the Old Faith, whilst the scholars are to take an oath recognising the Bible as the sole rule of Faith. We are already in the full swing of those penal regulations which long kept the doors of the universities locked against Catholics from the inside.

From 1553 to 1558 the reign of Mary was marked by the short-lived Catholic reaction. The circumstances of her early life, the fanaticism of her religious opponents, the personal affronts she had to endure under Edward's

* Letters quoted by Zimmermann," pp. 80, 81

† "English Universities," vol. i., p. 284.

reign, and the violence of the innovators even after her accession, must go a long way to account for the bitterness and intolerance she herself displayed when in power. At least, the universities flourished under her reign. She stands out favourably from the other Tudors in her patronage of learning, and in her personal munificence to the universities. Two zealous Catholics, Sir Thomas Pope and Sir Thomas White, founded at this time the two Oxford colleges of Trinity and St. John's respectively; whilst the Queen's physician, the celebrated Dr. Caius, also an earnest Catholic, by remodelling Gonville Hall, Cambridge, merited the title of the founder of Gonville and Caius, now generally known by his own name alone. The statutes display broad-minded zeal for the promotion of the study of medicine, for which foundations are provided to be enjoyed at Padua, Bologna, Montpellier, or Paris. The careful disciplinary regulations show us how far the moral tone had descended already at the universities. The keeping of horses and dogs, as well as bull-baiting and bear-baiting, have to be prohibited to the students. In spite of Mullinger's contrary opinion, based upon such partial witnesses as Ascham, Jewell, and Peter Martyr, Oxford under Mary compares very favourably with Cambridge. The number of students increased—a good sign of prosperity. The B.A.'s who graduated during the reign at Oxford were 216, as against 176 at Cambridge.

At the latter university Gardiner was reinstated as Chancellor, and we cannot but regret that his reversal of all that had taken place under Edward was carried out with much of the same spirit in which it had been introduced. Some of the Protestant party, like Perne, Cheke, and Cecil, yielded and became Catholics. Others were driven out. Those were not days of toleration on either side !* At the same time, we may remark that 125 M.A.'s

* "It was not only Mary who thought that heretics should be burnt. John Rogers, who was the first to suffer, had, in the days of Edward, pleaded for the death of Joan Bocher" (S. R. Gardiner, "Student's History of England," vol. ii., p. 424).

and 195 B.A.'s graduated during five years of Mary, as against 90 and 167 respectively during five years of her predecessor. Gardiner died in 1555, and Cardinal Pole succeeded him as Chancellor. Visitors were now sent to both universities for the "extirpation of heresy," but their new statutes were never carried out, for the Queen's death followed immediately. Whatever views may be held of her policy, it must at least be said that she did more for the universities than either her predecessor or her successor.

Over the reign of Elizabeth we must pass more rapidly. It was the period, not only of the final triumph of Protestantism, but of the remodelling of Protestantism into the form of Anglicanism, and the consequent beginning of the long struggle between that form and Puritanism. Elizabeth herself cannot be said to have had strong religious convictions, and, like Cecil, who could easily change his religion, was influenced rather by political, or we may say national, motives.* Her endeavour all along was to found a kind of middle party, a species of Protestantism amalgamated with Catholic discipline. This was "Anglicanism." As usual, a visitation of the universities was carried out, with the inevitable new regulations and the usual serious interference with the rights and liberties of the ancient "republics of letters," which would never have been tolerated in the Middle Ages. The Catholics showed great steadfastness, and nearly all the heads of colleges and many of the fellows at Oxford either resigned or suffered expulsion. The new men put into their places were mostly very inferior. The test oath, and the system of espionage and persecution which followed it, found some, indeed, not quite so stanch, and these few formed the kernel of the new "Anglican party." But the new doctrines had seriously

* "She cared nothing for theology, though her inclinations drew her to a more elaborate ritual than that which the Protestants had to offer. She was, however, intensely national. . . . For this end she must establish national unity in the Church" (S. R. Gardiner, *op. cit.*, p. 428).

lowered the general estimation of the ecclesiastical character, and both the clergy and the universities sank under Elizabeth into a pitiful condition. " Sunt mutæ musæ nostraque fama fames " was the all too true complaint of the state of things at Oxford. As to the ignorance of the clergy, we have the emphatic testimony of Pilkington, Bishop of Durham, and of Cecil.* The former in 1561 reported that the heads of colleges were so bad that he could not say whether their absence or their presence were more harmful, for that none of them did any good ; whilst " his heart bled " when he thought of St. John's College. Next year Cecil wished to resign the Chancellorship, out of disgust at the state of things ; for the heads had no care to second him in either controlling disorderly youth, enforcing discipline, or encouraging science and godliness. Probably with the design of improving the state of things at the universities, Elizabeth paid her famous State visits to Cambridge in 1564 and to Oxford in 1566. As a matter of fact, these sumptuous pageants did vastly more harm than good. They tended to encourage the taste for luxury and frivolous amusement, and especially to develop a love for dramatic entertainments, which, whilst directly beneficial to the rise of the English drama, was certainly ill-calculated to improve study or academic discipline.

In 1572 the celebrated Dr. Caius, who for a time had been inclined, with some others, to favour the new *via media* of Anglicanism, and had so kept his place, became a victim of persecution. His college was broken into (by the Vice-Chancellor and Dr. Whitgift, the future Archbishop), and all his vestments, sacred vessels, statues, and other objects cast into the flames. He did not long survive the blow, dying in London, after a life spent in doing more for the promotion of study at his university than any of his contemporaries.

In spite of all, there was still considerable vitality in

* Zimmermann, pp. 96, 97.

the Catholic party—at least, at Oxford. Merton and Corpus had already shown considerable pluck in defending their privileges against Leicester in 1564. There was even a certain Catholic reaction set in.

It would be interesting (says Zimmermann) to show in detail how many professors and students at both universities, little by little returned to the bosom of the Catholic Church; how, in very many instances, the reading of Catholic writings converted zealous Protestants and timid Catholics; with what zeal Catholic booksellers or private persons strove to disseminate Catholic tracts of devotion or controversy among the students; how often Protestant bishops or heads of houses caused domiciliary visitations to be made, destroyed Catholic books, or severely punished Catholic booksellers or colporteurs.*

One of the best known of these latter cases was that of Rowland Jenks. In 1592 the heads of houses at Cambridge established a commission to prosecute Catholics for "seducing the young," complaining that no books were so widely circulated as Catholic ones, and that in many of the rooms of Anglican professors the majority of the books found were those of scholastic theologians, writings of Franciscans, Dominicans, and Jesuits. Indeed, Anglicanism was no more able to produce a scientific school of theology then than it has been since. And there can be little doubt that, if the contest had been fought out with intellectual weapons only, the Catholic party would have come off easily victorious. Mr. Gladstone admits that "the very ablest men among those [Oxford] reared, such as Allen, Campion, Stapleton, and the rest, were ejected and suppressed."†

It is hardly cognate to our purpose to follow Fr. Zimmermann in his history of the struggle between Anglicanism and Puritanism. "Nonconformity," indeed, took its rise at Cambridge, as Mr. Gladstone points out.‡ Browne and Cartwright, the leaders of the

* Pp. 100, 101. † "Romanes Lectures," p. 25. ‡ *Ibid.*

movement, were Cambridge men of note. The latter's election as Professor in 1569 and subsequent exclusion by the Vice-Chancellor Mey led to a serious storm; the situation became so critical that a fresh revision of the statutes was decided upon. It was John Whitgift who was charged with this revision. This remarkable man seems originally to have been a Calvinist, but his skilful trimming made him a valued ally of the Queen. It is well known to what importance he eventually rose as Archbishop of Canterbury. Indeed, Fr. Zimmermann does not hesitate to declare that to him and Elizabeth is owing the foundation of the Anglican High Church system, and that Laud (to whom, by the way, Mr. Gladstone assigns so high a position as a Churchman*) merely followed in their footsteps. Whitgift's new statutes transferred the centre of gravity of university authority. The heads of colleges formed a new body of very great power, into whose hands almost all practical control was transferred. This also had much effect upon subsequent developments. Little by little the universities were becoming mere seminaries for Anglican divines. Yet, although Cartwright had to fly to Geneva, the Anglican bishops were in an awkward position, and did not dare to proceed to extremities against the Puritans, as against the Catholics. There is a curious memorial of complaint from them about the state of things at the universities, chiefly interesting to us, as it incidentally refers to civil law and natural science as "useless branches of study"! The fact is, the universities were once more in a state of intellectual decline, of which we have contemporary testimony in Traver's "Ecclesiasticæ Disciplinæ Explicatio" (1574). Most of the best men fled abroad. So in 1583 some eighty professors and students followed Dr. Allen to Rheims, and most of these were from Oxford. Leicester's influence at Oxford as Chancellor was for evil. Though the number of students increased under his rule, good discipline and study rapidly declined, and Oxford

* "Romanes Lecture," pp. 37-39.

was soon outstripped by Cambridge. The centre of intellectual life had meanwhile been transferred to London.

To sum up the results of the Reformation in the universities. The independence and rights of the national seats of learning had come to an end with freedom of research and opinion. The authority of the Senate had been superseded by that of the heads of houses, as we have seen, and these colleges were merely seminaries for training Anglican clergymen. The students were made up of two classes—the sons of the nobility, idlers, and pleasure-seekers, on the one hand; and Protestant divines, on the other, to whom theology was merely a "bread-study" leading to prospective benefices. The best class—the poorer middle class—had disappeared. The real talent of the universities was to be sought abroad in the flourishing colleges founded by Allen, or after his example, especially at Douay, which at the time far surpassed Oxford. The study of law and medicine had almost disappeared, and the professors could get no hearers. In seven years Oxford could produce but one doctor and eight bachelors in law. The natural sciences and mathematics were treated with the utmost contempt, as dishonourable for university students!* Greek was almost forgotten. During the last forty years of the century Mullinger admits that only two men at Cambridge certainly knew Greek, and perhaps three others had a smattering of it. Things were worse at Oxford. Latin, too, was far less known at the close than at the beginning of the century. Hebrew, owing to the importance now attached to the text of Scripture, had received some more attention; but the most distinguished Orientalist at Oxford, Robert Wakefield,† had been a Catholic; and his brother

* See the quotations and examples, Zimmermann, p. 122.

† He became the first Professor of Hebrew at Louvain. He had, however, supported the Royal divorce and shared in the plundering of the monasteries (Nève). See pp. 194, 195.

Thomas, who also remained true to the faith, was the first public professor of Hebrew at Cambridge, where, however, Protestant bigotry forbade his lecturing. Foreigners or Jews were the chief teachers of Hebrew after them. Rhetoric had taken the place of solid learning. History has only the name of Camden (Oxford) to show; Leland, the antiquarian, had been suffered to die in neglect and poverty. In a word, learning had not gained in a single branch by the Reformation. And no attempt at improvement was made till the reigns of the Stuarts.

College life and discipline had fared no better. An entire change had come over society. The rural population, flocking to the towns, had become spoilt and corrupted.* The character of the bishops, clergy, and heads of colleges had descended both intellectually and morally. The abuses of the collegiate system of university "graces" and of the tutoral system had most serious results upon the universities. The students came up much too young—lads of twelve or thirteen, Peacham tells us—and were badly prepared. The heads of colleges abused their autocratic powers. The material prosperity of the colleges (greatly augmented by Sir Thomas Smith's wise regulations) was accompanied by general intellectual stagnation. Poorer students, sizars, were systematically degraded into the position of drudges. How different from the state of things in the Middle Ages!

"What the Reformation meant for the entire nation was also what it meant for the universities—the robbery of the poor, the enrichment of the great, the almost absolute exclusion of talent and industry from place and honour. A brilliant university career had formerly opened a path to high office in Church and State; this was now reserved for a privileged class. Formerly the university professor was able, by one or more livings, which laid upon him no obligation of residence, to secure

* Hall, "Society in the Elizabethan Age" (1887), pp. 104, 105.

an existence free from anxiety; now the stipend of a professor was far too little. Formerly, by the study of philosophy, by public disputations and other scholastic exercises, not only the memory, but also the thinking powers, had been developed; now study was directed almost exclusively to cramming the memory. Formerly there was freedom of research, so far as it did not run counter to the dogmas of the Catholic Church; now the narrowest compulsory teaching prevailed. Formerly ideal ends were united with science; now science was esteemed only so far as it served practical ends. From the continental universities nothing had been borrowed but unrestrained polemics and party passion. The warning of Bacon* and others fell on deaf ears. Not till the beginning of the present century were some of the crying abuses which had crept in during the sixteenth century done away with, and the universities brought nearer to their true end and object."†

It is not without significance that the vast reforms in the national universities which signalized the latter half of the nineteenth century have all been in the direction of the state of things in pre-Reformation times. There has been a casting down of barriers—first religious, by the abolition of test-oaths; then social, by the gradual readmission of the middle and poorer classes. The tendency nowadays to build a procession of bridges from the primary school, across the middle school and grammar school, up to the university itself, is merely a reversion to what existed on a much larger scale in Catholic times. Even for the poor boy, gifted by talent and industry, there is now ever-increasing opportunity for rising to an academic career, but as yet to a far less extent than there was in the Middle Ages. The intellectual revival in every department has been extraordinary indeed; here, again, we are going back to the Oxford and Cambridge of old England. During the last thirty

* Works, ad. Spedding, vol. iii., pp. 326-328, 597.

† Zimmermann, p. 138.

years, we are assured by unquestionable authority, the growth of earnestness and the spirit of work, the decline of luxury and frivolity, the greater simplicity of student life, have made the Oxford and Cambridge of to-day something very unlike that of even the seventies. Here, again, we have a reversion to the thirteenth and two subsequent centuries. This being so, it appears providentially timed that a beginning should be made of once more opening the road towards those old Catholic foundations, the national universities, for the spiritual and intellectual heirs of their founders, who have been exiled from them for three hundred years. But the restoration will scarce be complete till we can see the successes of St. Edmund Rich, of Stapleton, and of Allen —and, may we hope, those of Kilwardby, Roger Bacon, and Duns Scotus—pursuing the same paths of study, Divine as well as human, by the banks of the Isis and the Cam.

BOOKS TO BE CONSULTED.

ATHANASIUS ZIMMERMANN, S.J. "Die Universitäten Englands im 16 Jahrhundert." Freiburg im Breisgau: Herder, 1889.
RIGHT HON. W. E. GLADSTONE, M.P. "The Romanes Lecture, 1892: an Academic Sketch." Oxford: Clarendon Press, 1892.

VII

TWO ENGLISH SCHOLARS AND THE BEGINNINGS OF ORIENTAL STUDIES IN LOUVAIN

It ought not to be necessary to plead before an audience of Catholic theologians the great importance of Oriental studies in the cause of theology and apologetic. The value of Semitic languages for Scriptural exegesis has been an admitted fact in all ages from St. Jerome downwards. But exegesis is only one of the many points—vital points all of them—where Oriental science touches the domain of theology. In the century of Strauss, Renan, and Kuenen, and—*sed longo intervallo*—of popular writers like Mrs. Humphrey Ward and the late Professor Huxley, the very fundamental bases of "the Impregnable Rock of Holy Scripture," to borrow Mr. Gladstone's phrase, suffer attacks from the side of a newer kind of Orientalism, and require us to call in for our defence not merely the "higher criticism" of the more familiar Semitic tongues, but also the results of those eminently nineteenth century developments, Assyriology and Egyptology. Nor is this by any means all. The century of Max Müller, Tiele, de Gubernatis, and Sir Edwin Arnold has developed yet new and perhaps more insidious methods of attack not on Christianity only, but on all the history of revelation, from the side of the new sciences of "Comparative Mythology" and the "History of Religions." In the teaching of those sciences both the religion of the Old Testament and the Christianity of the New are supposed to find their place as merely some out of the many phases of a mental and spiritual evolution, which begins in a primitive animism and fetish worship, to end in the Sermon on the Mount and the Epistles of St. Paul, and in which Yahvê and Christ hold a place with exactly the same rights as Obatala, Thoth, Varuna, or Heraklês. It would, perhaps, be difficult to indicate any other field of research on which it is more urgent for Catholic scholars to employ their talents and energy than that of the "Comparative History of Religions," with its concomitant branches, such as Mythology and Folklore. But all this means a wide and thorough study of various departments of Orientalism. And what we want is an army of specialists in each of these branches.

These general remarks may serve to introduce and explain the appearance of the following historical sketch of the earliest Oriental teachers and schools of Louvain. Among Catholic centres of learning the Belgian University has always held an honourable place for its cultivation of such branches of Orientalism as have been of importance at different epochs. In the fifteenth and sixteenth centuries the Alma Mater was publishing Hebrew Grammars and Commentaries on Ecclesiastes; in the nineteenth she is translating the "Avesta," commenting the "Vedas," and solving for the first time in literary history the riddles of the "Yih-King." I venture to think that the work she has done and is doing will be found no mean contribution to the advance of Christian learning.

It may be well here to point out that the history of Louvain falls into two quite distinct periods, the old and the new. The old University, entirely medieval in form and constitution, founded by Pope Martin V. and Duke John the Good of Burgundy in 1426, was brought to a violent end by the French Revolutionary invasion and the decree of suppression of October 27, 1797. In the interval of thirty-seven years which elapsed an attempt was made, it is true, by the Dutch rulers of Belgium to revive a University, governmental in character, in the old city, but the attempt was a failure (1817-34). It was in 1834 that the Catholic Church, by the hands of the Belgian hierarchy, modestly began a revival of the old Alma Mater—for a few months in Mechlin, and then in Louvain itself, and with such happy success that the eighty-six students of the first year have grown to over 2,000 at the present moment, with all the modern equipment, especially in the domains of Natural and Applied Science, of a great European seat of learning.

For old Louvain I have had little more to do than condense the elaborate history of its Oriental teachers contained in the exhaustive monograph of the venerable Orientalist of the present Alma Mater, the late Professor Félix Nève, entitled "Mémoire Historique et Littéraire sur le Collège des Trois Langues à l'Université de Louvain," which was crowned by the Royal Academy of Belgium in 1856 (Bruxelles, Hayez, 1856, 4to., pp. xviii and 425*). For the earlier part, of course, I have also used Valerius Andreas' "Fasti Academici Studii Generalis Lovaniensis" (Lovanii, 1650).

I. Orientalism among Catholic Scholars before the "Reformation."

At the beginning of the sixteenth century Hebrew and Rabbinical studies began to penetrate from the Jewish to the Christian schools. Up to this date, during the course of the Middle Ages, there were but a few isolated scholars who ventured into the study of Hebrew, and of these most were actually converted Jews. There were serious difficulties which met the first students of Hebrew. One was that it was necessary to take lessons from Jewish rabbis, who exacted a great price for their teaching. Moreover, such a proceeding too often exposed the student to serious suspicions con-

* Tome XXVIII., "Mémoires Couronnés," etc.

cerning orthodoxy on the part of his fellow Christians. Lastly, there was the great dearth of books and texts.

Notwithstanding such drawbacks there is plenty of evidence to show that Catholics cultivated Hebrew and even its kindred tongues before the so-called Reformation. A well-known instance is that of Pico della Mirandola (1463-94), whose acquaintance extended to Arabic and Chaldaic, besides Hebrew. Reuchlin (1455-1522) published his "Rudimenta Linguae Hebraicae" in 1506; and when his frequent intercourse with Jewish rabbis and his resistance to the decree for burning all the rabbinical books of a converted Jew got him into serious suspicion of heterodoxy and prosecution on part of the Inquisition, he owed his protection to Leo X. Spite of his persecution, he resisted the overtures of Luther. Elias Levita, "the last and most celebrated of the native (Jewish) grammarians" (1470-1549), had Cardinal Egidio for his pupil and patron at Rome. The great Polyglot of Jimenes (Ximenes) was published between 1514-17, and contains the Hebrew and Chaldee texts of the various parts of the Old Testament. The still superior Antwerp Polyglot, published by Plantin under the auspices of Philip II. (1569-72) contains, in addition, the Syriac version of the New Testament.

Long before the above writers, Nicolaus de Lyra, a converted Jew (died 1340), had published his "Postilla Perpetua in Biblia Universa," which were found so useful by Luther.*

II. The Beginnings of Orientalism at Louvain.

The earliest beginnings of Orientalism at Louvain carry us back to nearly a century before the Antwerp

* For much of the above, see Gesenius, "Geschichte der Hebräischen Schrift und Sprache" (Leipzig, 1851). For Roger Bacon's knowledge of Hebrew and his Hebrew grammar, see Nolan's and Hirsch's "The Greek Grammar of Roger Bacon, and a Fragment of his Hebrew Grammar." Cambridge: University Press, 1902.

Polyglot above alluded to. And curious to say it is not in the professional chair or the lecture-room that we come across these beginnings, but in the printers' office. Louvain has all along been well equipped with an Oriental press, never so well as at the present day, with its double set of founts, owing respectively to Beelen and de Harlez, of which we speak elsewhere. The remote ancestor of this press must have existed there almost at the time when Luther was born (1483), for in the year 1488 there was issued a quarto volume entitled "Epistola Apologetica Magistri Pauli de Middleburgo ad Doctores Lovanienses," which is stated to be printed *in Alma Universitate Lovaniensi, per Joannem de Westphalia.* Now the curious fact is that "the Hebrew quotations of this book are printed in characters of a massive form and German cut, whilst the Greek passages are written by hand" (Nève). Evidently, then, there was in the Alma Mater a fount of Hebrew type even before one of Greek characters. It is easy to suppose who brought it. This John of Westphalia (he died, by the way, next year, 1489), was John Wesel or Wessel, of Gröningen in Westphalia, brought up at Zwolle under the influence of Thomas à Kempis and the Brothers of the Common Life.* "In the course of his wanderings he made a long sojourn at Louvain, and must have taught Hebrew there, as he did in other cities he visited—Cologne, Heidelberg, Paris, Rome, and Basel."† J. Wessel, then, would appear from this to merit the honour of having been both the first teacher of Hebrew and the first printer of Hebrew at Louvain.‡

* He remained a staunch Catholic, and is not to be confounded with John Wesel of Oberwesel, who fell away from the Church, and died 1481, a prisoner of the Inquisition.

† See Hetzel's "Geschichte der Hebräischen Sprache und Litteratur," p. 135 (Halle, 1776).

‡ Or were the printer and the Hebrew scholar different persons? This would seem to follow from a paper of Ed. van Even in the "Dietsche Warande," vol. iii. (N.S.), p. 167, for the year 1890,

It is probable that in 1506 the press of Theodoricus Martinus Alostensis (Thierry Martens of Alost) issued a "Dictionarium Hebraicum sive Enchiridion Radicum seu Dictionum Hebraicarum ex Joanne Reuchlino," a quarto without name of author or year. This Martens had printed at Louvain up to 1501 in partnership with Hermann of Nassau.

Ten years later the first step was taken towards the foundation of the first real Oriental school of Louvain.

The Trilingual College.—Matthæus Hadrianus.—In 1516 Erasmus came to Flanders, and the same year was inscribed in the matriculum of the university, bringing with him his doctor of theology's degree from Padua. "Vivo," he writes next year to Pirckheimer, "versorque Lovanii; coöptatus in consortium Theologorum, licet in hac Academia non sim insignitus titulo doctoris." Indeed, as Valerius Andreas tells us,* he was engaged in perpetual squabbles with these same theologians. However, he did one good thing for them; he brought about the establishment of their first chair of Hebrew. The very year of his arrival, 1516, he wrote to invite over from Germany Matthæus Adrianus (Erasm. "Epist.," lit. iii., ep. 39, "Opera," t. iii. 353). This man was a converted Jew of Spanish origin (born between 1470 and 1480). At Heidelberg he had proceeded to the degree of doctor in medicine, and was there teaching Hebrew. Erasmus in the above quoted letter recommended him to Ægidius Buslidius (Giles Busleiden), for the new "Trilingual College" just founded by the will of his distinguished brother Jerome.

Here we must turn back a moment to say a word of this celebrated college of the three languages ("des Trois Langues"). Jerome Busleiden was a wealthy

when he records a printer, John of Westphalia, who, born at Aken, near Paderborn, settled at Louvain in 1474, and worked there till 1496. (Postscript to Frank's paper, "De Boekdrukkunst en de Geestelijkheid tot 1520.")

* "Fasti Academici Studii Generalis Lovaniensis," p. 85 (Lovanii, 1650).

and enlightened ecclesiastic who had held high offices in Church and State.* His love of learning induced him to leave all his property to found a college at Louvain for the special study of the three languages—Latin, Greek, and Hebrew. There were to be burses for the support of the three professors and ten students. They were to devote themselves to the study of grammar and philosophy "up to the degree of master," and were to learn also the rudiments of Greek and Hebrew. The idea was entirely new. It excited dreadful scandal and opposition among the old-fashioned fogies of the university. It was decried as "heretical" and whatnot. Erasmus fought hard for it; but there was every chance of this "unicum nostrae regionis, imo totius Cæsareæ ditionis ornamentum," as Valerius Andreas styles it,† coming to an untimely end, but for the interposition of Cardinal Adrian, an old Louvain student and professor, soon after (1522) to ascend the Throne of Peter as Pope Adrian VI. He summed up the whole matter in a very simple, if somewhat obvious, "oracle," as Valerius Andreas calls it: "Bonas litteras non damno, hæreses et schismata damno." The college was therefore opened—near the fish-market—and the academical historian boasts with reason that "this praise is due to our Busleiden: he was the first in Christendom to establish a Trilingual College, though his example was followed by others afterwards, as Francis I., King of France, in Paris, Richard Fox, Bishop of Winchester, at Oxford;‡ Francis, Cardinal Ximenes, Archbishop of Toledo, at Alcalá," etc.

* Jerome Busleiden was the esteemed friend of the great English Chancellor and Martyr, Blessed Thomas More, who wrote three elegant little Latin poems in his honour, published in his "Epigrammata," to be found in several editions of his works. They are given in full by Nève, Appendix C. (pp. 384, 385).

† "Fasti Academici," p. 277.

‡ *I.e.*, Corpus Christi, 1516-17. Fox compared his college to a beehive, and called his three professors "three gardeners." See A. Zimmermann, S.J., "Die Universitäten Englands im 16 Jahrhundert," pp. 16-18 (Freiburg: Herder, 1889).

We have said above that Erasmus got the Chair of Hebrew for Matthæus Adrianus, who accordingly gave his first lesson in the new college on September 1, 1518.

It is noteworthy that the first regular teaching of an Oriental language at Louvain began under the auspices of the Faculty of Arts, and not of that of Theology. This is a fact of some significance. It indicates, on the one hand, that the study of Hebrew and its kindred tongues was not looked upon at Louvain merely as an appendage to the exegesis of Holy Writ, which has been so long a popular impression among Catholics, but that it had another and independent basis to stand upon—viz., that of a philological branch of learning; and, on the other hand, it indicates the strength and the breadth of the spirit of the "new learning," the humanitarian learning, which Erasmus did so much to foster at Louvain as at Oxford and Cambridge. The position thus assigned to Oriental studies has been maintained, and whilst at all times they have been largely drawn upon at Louvain to strengthen and elucidate exegetical and theological studies, they have always enjoyed, over and above, a position of their own as philological disciplines.

Matthæus Adrianus does not seem to have got on very well in his new home. He complained that he lived there "for two years without resources." As a matter of fact he taught for only a year and three months. In July, 1519, he resigned his chair, and in the December of the same year he went off to Wittemberg. "Conductus est Hadrianus, professor Lovaniensis," writes Melanchthon to Langius next year, 1520, "qui apud nos Hebraica doceat."

We do not know much more of this primeval ancestor (in the academic sense) of Mgr. Lamy. Did he become a Lutheran, as Paquot says? Where did he die?

His Oriental works were not numerous. We know only of (1) "Introductio Brevis in Linguam Hebraicam," 8vo., no date; also (2) "Oratiunculæ tres: Dominica,

Salutatio Angelica et Salve Regina hebraice redditæ," 4to., both published by Gryphius at Lyons.

As to his abilities, we have a glowing eulogy pronounced upon him by Erasmus, in the already quoted epistle to Busleiden. He speaks of him as "so learned in the whole Hebrew literature that, in my opinion, there has not been any other in this age to compare with him. He is not only a perfect master of the language, but is so familiar with the most abstruse parts (*adyta*) of the authors, that he has all their books at his fingers ends" ("*ac libros omnes sic habet in promptu ut digitos unguesque suos*").

Two Englishmen at Louvain.—It is an interesting fact that the two occupants of the newly-founded chair of Hebrew who immediately succeeded Adrianus were both Englishmen, and connected with the national English universities. Upon the withdrawal of Adrianus the vacant professorship was conferred upon Robert Wakefield. This person was a north of England man, possibly a native of Yorkshire.* He had been educated in his youth at Cambridge, where he had studied arts, philosophy, and theology. Afterwards he, like so many other scholars in the Middle Ages, went abroad to various seats of learning; but in his case it was a particular taste for Oriental languages that was the moving power. It is said that he had mastered Hebrew, Chaldee, and Syriac.

Very short, however, was his stay at Louvain, for he occupied the Hebrew Chair only four months—August to December, 1519. The next place we find him at is Tübingen, where in 1522 he succeeded the very celebrated Orientalist, Reuchlin; but he did not stay there long, either, in spite of the efforts of Duke Ferdinand of Wirtemberg to keep him. He seems to have been of a roving disposition.

A word may be said of his subsequent career, which is not very creditable. In 1524 he was back in Cambridge,

* See *ante*, p. 182.

and his Oriental and Biblical learning soon brought him into the notice and favour of Henry VIII., to whom he became chaplain (*a sacris*). Later on he taught at Oxford. It is regrettable to record that he strenuously supported the King in the divorce case, writing a work in favour of it (" Kotser Codicis," London, 1528) ; and took an active part in the suppression of the monasteries. Indeed, he was supposed to have plundered the library of Ramsgate, and carried off, among other tomes, for his own use, the Hebrew dictionary of Laurentius Holbeccius. Fr. Zimmermann speaks of him as though he had remained staunch to the Old Church, like his brother Thomas, the first public professor of Hebrew at Cambridge.* But at least his books were suspected of dogmatic errors, and his conduct we have already seen.

He died in London in 1537 or 1538. Of his writings we may record the following :

1. " Oratio de Laudibus et Utilitate trium Linguarum Arabicæ, Chaldaicæ et Hebraicæ, atque Idiomatibus Hebraicis quæ in utroque Testamento inveniuntur." 4to. Cantab. 1524. (This was his inaugral lecture at Cambridge, and Nève says of it, " An interest of novelty must no doubt have attached in his days to his comparison of the three languages.")

2. " Paraphrasis in librum Koheleth (vulgo Ecclesiasten) succincta clara atque fidelis." 4to. (We shall see further what a favourite study at Louvain was that of Ecclesiastes.)

3. " Syntagma de Hebræorum codicum incorruptione." 4to. Oxonii. 1552 (posthumous).

We need not mention his theological and canonical writings.

On leaving Louvain, Wakefield recommended a fellow-countryman, Robert Shirwood, to succeed him. This person was a native of Coventry, and had studied at Oxford. His career at Louvain is summed up by Valerius Andreas in a single sentence : " Post mensem

* " Universitäten Englands im 16 Jahrhundert," p. 124.

unum professionem inglorius deseruit." We know nothing of his subsequent life, except that he probably lived on for several years in Belgium, though he does not seem (in spite of Pitts) to have taught again at Louvain. As an author he was "a man of one book," viz., "Ecclesiastes Latine ad veritatem Hebraicam recognitus, cum nonnullis annotationibus Chaldaicis et quorumdam Rabbinorum sententiis." 4to. Antverpiæ: Vorstman. 1523.

It is noteworthy that, like his predecessor and successor, he chose the Book of the Preacher for commentary. His work* attained a certain celebrity, so that it merited to be inserted by Pineda in his great "Commentary on Ecclesiastes," published at Seville a century later.

Thus, the close of 1519 saw the new Hebrew Chair vacant yet again, three resignations having taken place in one year! It is also remarkable that the three first Orientalist professors of Louvain were foreigners; on which Nève observes that the circumstance indicates "at least the fraternity and free relations existing between the great European seats of learning in the Middle Ages."

* Dedicated to Abbot John Webb of Coventry.

VIII

OXFORD AND LOUVAIN

On October 9, 1902, the writer had the privilege of attending the special "Congregation" held in the Sheldonian Theatre of Oxford, together with the representative of fifty-six other universities, as delegate of the Catholic University of Louvain. On that historic occasion he had the honour to hand to the Vice-Chancellor of Oxford a Latin letter, engrossed on vellum, of which the following is a translation :*

* The Latin text runs thus :

"Viro Nobilissimo Illustrissimoque David B. Monro, Vice-Cancellario Universitatis Oxoniensis.

"Trecentesimo redeunte nunc anno a condita insigni Bibliotheca Bodleiana, Universitatis Catholicæ Lovaniensis Rector atque Magistri variis de causis muneris sui esse duxerunt perantiquæ et quasi cognatæ Academiæ Oxoniensi laudes et grates exhibere. Intra utramque enim scientiarum et artium scholam, Oxoniensem nempe et Lovaniensem, jam inde a pristinis temporibus, intima viguit mutui officii ac consuetudinis conjunctio. In memoriam quidem revocasse juvabit jam sæculo decimo quinto, Robertum Wilson Oxoniensem ad Universitatem nostram, ante pauca decennia ab Martino Quinto fundatam, se contulisse ibique anno 1472 juris lauream esse nactum. Haud multo post alium ex vestris accepimus, Robertum Shirwood, qui quum linguæ Hebraicæ studium apud nos mirum in modum promovit, litterarum nostram orientalium scholam primus fundasse non immerito reputatur. Quam multi præterea ex alumnis magistrisque vestris, sæculo decimo sexto, exortis in Anglia religionis causa dissidiis, Lovaniensem Academiam adiverint eamque scriptis et doctrina ornaverint illius ætatis testantur annales ; hujusmodi fuere Thomas Harding, Richardus Smith, Nicolaus Saunders, Joannes Storey, Joannes Clemens, Joannes Fowler, aliique plurimi quos longius recensere hic minus est loci.

"On the occasion of the tercentenary of the foundation of the Bodleian Library, the Rector and Professors of the Catholic University of Louvain consider it their duty, for many reasons, to offer their congratulations and thanks to the ancient and, so to speak, sister University of Oxford. For there has existed from early times an interchange of good offices and friendship between the two seats of learning, Oxford and Louvain. It is

---

"Præcipue porro in præsens movet nos singulare nostri grati animi debitum erga ipsius Bibliothecæ Bodleianæ instauratores atque rectores. In hac enim completissima librorum arca anno 1723 repositi fuere primi Avestici in Europam illati codices. Quorum folia nonnulla exscripta et Parisiis servata quum in manus incidissent clarissimi Anquetil Duperron, arduum hic inivit consilium tanti pretii tantæque antiquitatis thesaurum patriæ suæ acquirendi; celebres itaque codices avesticos, summo discrimine et ipse in India consecutus, tandem anno 1771 publici juris fecit atque in vernaculam transtulit linguam. Hinc originem duxerunt quæcunque ab initio sæculi elapsi, præeunte Burnouf, de sacrorum Iraniæ librorum lingua atque doctrina in lucem ediderunt viri rerum orientalium periti. Inter hosce non infimum tenuisse locum clarissimum de Harlez jure merito gloriatur Universitas Lovaniensis.

"At vero arctiori adhuc beneficiorum vinculo se Bodleianæ Bibliothecæ esse adstrictos ex animo recordantur scholæ nostræ orientalis alumni atque magistri quibus inexhausti illius thesauri præpositi summa benignitate liberum aperuerunt aditum ad reconditos ibidem codices visendos atque exscribendos: recordantur clarissimi Abbeloos atque Lamy qui magni Ephraem Edesseni insignia opera primum edenda inde prompserunt; recordatur hodiernus Lovaniensis Academiæ Rector, qui antiquis Coptorum scriptis explorandis operam impensurus, quidquid juvaminis ac benevolentiæ posset avere continue apud vos est consecutus.

"In hujus memori animi documentum, recurrenti anniversaria die instauratæ a Bodleio Bibliothecæ Oxoniensis, simul cum votis et gratulationibus nostris, munusculi gratia, ad vos deferenda curavimus tum opera nonnulla ex codicibus Bodleianis a nostratibus deprompta, tum ipsius nostræ Universitatis annales scriptaque recentiora.

"Faxit Divina Providentia ut quæcumque Academiæ Oxoniensi bona et prospera apprecamur perfecte adimpleantur.

"AD. HEBBELYNCK (*Rector Universitatis*).
"J. VAN BIERVLIET (*Univ. a Secr.*).

"*Kal. Oct.*, 1902."

interesting to recall that in the fifteenth century an Oxford scholar, Robert Wilson, came over to our University, which had been founded but a few decades before by Pope Martin V., and there took his degree in Law in 1472. Not long after this we received another of your men, Robert Sherwood, who, owing to what he did to promote the study of the Hebrew language amongst us, may not unjustly be looked upon as the founder of our school of Oriental studies. Then, again, how many of your scholars and professors in the sixteenth century, owing to the religious dissensions which broke out in England, retired to the Louvain University and adorned it by their writing and teaching as testified by the annals of the times? Among these were Thomas Harding, Richard Smith, Nicholas Saunders, John Storey, John Clements, John Fowler, and many others whom it would be too long to enumerate here.

"But at the present moment we are chiefly moved by a sense of profound gratitude towards the founders and directors of the Bodleian Library. For it was in this splendid collection that, in the year 1723, was deposited the first MS. of the *Avesta* brought to Europe. A few folios of this were copied and taken to Paris, where they fell into the hands of the celebrated Anquetil Duperron, whereupon the latter formed the venturesome resolution of securing for his own country a treasure of such value and so great antiquity. Having himself obtained in India, at the cost of imminent dangers, valuable Avestic Codices, he at length published them, with a French translation, in 1771. This was the very beginning of all that has been published by Orientalists, beginning with Burnouf, during the last century, concerning the language and doctrines of the sacred books of Iran. Among these it is the glory of the University of Louvain that the illustrious de Harlez held a distinguished place.

"Furthermore, the students and teachers of our school of Orientalists are glad to recall that they are bound by a still closer tie of benefits received, to the Bodleian

Library, since the custodians of that inexhaustible treasure-house have, with the greatest kindness, freely granted them facilities for the examining and transcribing of MSS. therein contained. Among these are Abbeloos and Lamy, who copied here the inedited works of the great St. Ephrem of Edessa,* and also the present Rector of the University of Louvain, who, when engaged in copying ancient Coptic MSS., received all possible assistance and courtesy at your hands.

"As a testimony of this gratitude, on the anniversary day of the foundation of the Oxford Library by Bodley, we have caused to be forwarded to you, together with our good wishes and congratulations, a small gift in the shape of a few works edited by some of our men from Bodleian MSS., and also the history and certain more recent publications of our University. We pray that Divine Providence may bestow abundance of all blessings and prosperity on the University of Oxford.

"AD. HEBBELYNCK, *Rector of the University.*

"J. VAN BIERVLIET, *Secretary of the University.*

"*October* 1, 1902."

The historical facts contained in the letter just quoted appear to me to be of sufficient interest, from both the religious and the educational point of view, to deserve a fuller development and exposition, and the present paper must be looked upon as merely a running commentary upon the text of the letter quoted.

I.

The Louvain letter begins by hailing Oxford as both an "ancient" and "sister" institution. Louvain herself is by no means of modern creation: her history goes back as far as the year 1425; but even so, Oxford can claim a far more venerable antiquity. It is true that the myth of her creation by King Alfred the Great has been long

* This statement is not quite accurate; see further on.

since exploded; and all that we can say with certainty is that the University appears to have come into existence by a "secession" of scholars from the already-existing University of Paris early in the thirteenth century, and that, without any regular or definite formal erection, it developed as shown in a preceding article (VI.). In any case, it is possible to obtain a volume, published by the Clarendon Press, containing an alphabetical list of "Oxford Honours" from as early a date as 1220 to our time.* Thus, Oxford is more than two centuries older than her sister University of Louvain.

Early in the fifteenth century the Low Countries, under the enlightened rule of the Dukes of Burgundy or Brabant, felt the pressing need for the intellectual and religious life of their people of a university centre which should play therein the part so long and so successfully played by the universities in surrounding countries—Paris in France, Oxford in England, Cologne in Germany. It would appear that several influential persons had for some time been urging the desirability of the erection of such a *studium generale* for the Flemish country, then flourishing by its trade and commerce, and distinguished by the intelligence of its population. Their representations finally decided Duke John IV. to take in hand the creation of such a centre of learning on the model of those already existing in other countries. Duke John entered into negotiations with Pope Martin V., and the Bull of that Pontiff, dated December 9, 1425, beginning with the words "Sapientiæ immarcessibilis," constitutes the fundamental charter of the new University, thus happily created by a joint action of the ecclesiastical and the civil power. In his Bull, Martin V. describes Louvain as a town "by the grace of God, so well endowed with wealth, excellent climate, accommodation for large multitudes, and well furnished with houses and all other

* "Oxford Honours, 1220-1894: being an Alphabetical Register of Distinctions conferred by the University of Oxford from the Earliest Times" (Oxford: Clarendon Press, 1894).

necessaries, that it seems to be most fitted and suitable for receiving and housing such a university."

The various statutes and regulations for the conduct of the newly-created Alma Mater were undoubtedly drawn up upon the model of those in vogue in the already-existing universities of Europe. In one respect, indeed, Louvain was characterized by a feature which made it very similar to our own Oxford. Unlike many other seats of learning, it was a university of many colleges; in fact, at the date of its temporary suppression by the French revolutionists in 1797, these colleges numbered forty-four, many of which have long ceased to form a part of the University.

As was only to be expected, Louvain, which grew and prospered exceedingly, very soon entered into active intellectual relationship with the other European seats of learning. In those days all universities were more or less international in character. Students of all nations—often poor "wandering scholars"—passed from one country to another, attracted by the fame of some great teacher, and pursued their studies turn by turn at Paris or Oxford, Bologna or Prague, Cologne or Louvain. As indicated in the academic letter read above, the earliest recorded Oxford man to proceed to a Louvain degree was one Robert Wilson, a Bachelor of Laws, who, in 1472, is recorded as having been promoted at Louvain to the degree of LL.D., the *Fasti* of the University adding, with unconscious humour, the characteristic trait that "having received the doctrinal insignia, he gave a grand banquet in the house of his president," one Jean de Grousselt ("solemne epulum exhibuit in ædibus praesidentis sui").*

The next recorded connection of any interest between Oxford and Louvain is alluded to in somewhat too flattering terms in the Rector's letter. "Not long after

* A somewhat later English student, who spent ten years at Louvain, was Nicholas Wootton, afterwards Dean of Canterbury and English Ambassador to Charles V.

this," he writes, "we received another of your men, Robert Shirwood, who, owing to what he did to promote the study of the Hebrew language amongst us, may not unjustly be looked upon as the founder of our school of Oriental studies." This is far too complimentary a reference to the Oxford scholar. I have already told the somewhat curious story of this and another Englishman in anothe rarticle.* I am afraid that the Rector of Louvain was pushing courtesy to a somewhat extreme point in conferring upon Shirwood the title of "founder of our school of Oriental studies."

I have more than once mentioned the name of Erasmus, the great humanist of the Low Countries, that strange and enigmatical character, who played a part so conspicuous, and yet so difficult to understand, in the stirring times of the Renaissance. Erasmus forms the most important connecting-link between Louvain on the one hand and both Oxford and Cambridge on the other during the early sixteenth century. In 1498 the great scholar paid his first visit to Oxford and studied Greek under Linacre, besides forming his long and intimate friendship with Dean Colet and Sir Thomas More. During his third stay in this country, Erasmus resided at Cambridge, where he held for a time both the Margaret Professorship of Divinity and the chair of Greek. It is well known how important an influence he exercised upon the academic history of this country. His influence at Louvain was no less marked. In a letter written in 1521 he declares that Louvain was second to no university in Europe except that of Paris: the number of students was about three thousand, and this number was growing every day. We have already seen him exercising considerable influence in the appointment of members of the university staff. From 1517 to 1521 he lived and taught in Louvain, and it was during this period that many of his most important and most learned

* "Two English Scholars and the Beginnings of Oriental Studies at Louvain," *ante*, p. 195.

works were produced. It was indeed a time of active literary intercourse and correspondence between the leading English and Flemish scholars.*

II.

But a far more and far closer connection between Oxford and Louvain began with the religious troubles in England, as indicated in the letter presented on the occasion of the Bodleian Jubilee. The famous divorce question, under Henry VIII., had its echo in Louvain. Louis de Schore, who obtained his doctorate in Laws in 1531, published, in 1535, an elaborate report upon Henry VIII.'s marriage case,† whilst that case was under trial at Rome, and is said on his tombstone, to have been sent " regem legatus ad Anglum." From this time forward Louvain became a place of refuge for those English scholars, and sometimes their families, who were compelled to fly from England, in many cases at the sacrifice of high and important academic offices, for conscience sake. The first of these was Richard Smith, D.D., Regius Professor of Theology in the University of Oxford, who fled to Louvain in the reign of Edward VI. This distinguished scholar, whom Wood describes as " the greatest pillar for the Roman Catholic cause in his time," was a native of Worcestershire. He was obliged to leave his Oxford professorship under Edward VI. " to make way for Peter Martyr." He arrived in Louvain on April 9, 1549, and was for some time a Professor of Divinity there. On the death of Edward, he was recalled to England, restored to his professorship at Oxford, and made chaplain to Queen Mary. " In Elizabeth's reign," continues the above-quoted historian, " he was

* Of Joannes de Palude, of the Faculty of Arts, it is recorded " vixit familiaris Thomæ Moro," as well as with Erasmus. He wrote an epistle about More's " Utopia."

† " Consilium super viribus Matrimonii inter Henricum VIII. Anglorum Regem et Catherinam Austriacam " (Lovanii, typ. Sessoni, 1535).

committed to custody. Afterwards he went to Douay in Flanders, and was constituted Dean of St. Peter's Church there by Philip, King of Spain, who, erecting an academy there about that time, made him the first King's Professor thereof. He was accounted by his persuasion the best schoolman of his time, and admirably well read in the Fathers and Councils." The University of Douay here mentioned was erected in 1562, and Smith died there in July, 1573.

Another refugee under Edward VI. was the celebrated John Clement, M.A., of Oxford, Professor of Greek and Rhetoric at that University in the time of Wolsey. He was also tutor in the family of Sir Thomas More, and proceeded M.D. Twice did he seek refuge as an exile in Louvain; for, having returned to England under Queen Mary and "practised physick in Esesx," he had to fly again under Elizabeth. In 1570 he married at Mechlin Margaret Giggs, and had one son and four daughters, one of whom, Winifred, married Judge Rastell, to be mentioned further on. Dorothy and Margaret became nuns the latter at St. Ursula's, in Louvain, where, as Sanders quaintly records, she was elected superior over eighty sisters: "A junior over her seniors, an Englishwoman over Germans."*

In 1562 there arrived in Louvain Thomas Harding, D.D., of New College, Regius Professor of Hebrew at Oxford, a native of Beconton, in Devonshire. In Edward VI.'s reign he was a Protestant, but under Mary became a Catholic. On Elizabeth's accession he fled to Louvain, where he remained for the rest of his life. He died there in 1572, and was buried by the altar of the Holy Trinity in St. Gertrude's Church, "where," says Valerius Andreas, "his epitaph, engraved on a brass plate, may still be read as follows:

* This Margaret Clement, together with Dorothy Harris, wife of John Harris, Sir Thomas More's secretary, helped to bury the body of More, "wrapped in a winding-sheet," after his martyrdom. The whole Harris family, like the Clements, took refuge in Louvain.

"Honesto loco natus, in Collegio Wilhelmi de Wyckham educatus, Sacræ Theologiæ Doctor et Hebraicæ Linguæ Professor, ingenio abundans, disertus, acutus, insignis Divini Verbi buccinator, Lovanii multos libros adversus hæreticos nostri temporis conscripsit, quorum adiumento suis multum profuisse certum est. Obiit sexagenarius studio et ægritudine fractus, quum religionis nomine decennale pertulisset exilium, die 16 Septembris, 1572."

Nicholas Harpsfield, student of Winchester School and of New College, Oxford, became fellow of the latter in 1536, B.C.L. in 1544, and two years later Regius Professor of Greek. Under Edward VI. he, like so many others, fled to Louvain; but, returning under Mary, proceeded D.C.L. in 1553, and obtained many important legal preferments in London. Under Elizabeth he was cast into prison, and died there after several years. Harpsfield was a voluminous writer.

A very interesting character among the *émigrés* was "Joannes Ramiger." Under this form the Flemish annalist conceals John Ramridge, D.D. He was of Merton College, Oxford, when he obtained his fellowship in 1528, becoming Doctor of Theology in 1542, and obtained several valuable preferments, including that of Archdeacon of Derby. He was obliged to fly abroad under Elizabeth, and settled in poverty at Louvain.* His fate was a singular and unhappy one. On May 21, 1568, "in his extreme old age." he was going on foot to Mechlin, when, at a place called Heveren, he was set upon by some footpads, who had seen him giving alms to a beggar, and cruelly murdered. His body, we are told, was buried with great reverence by the clergy of Mechlin.

William Rastell, born 1508, was the son of John Rastell, printer and lawyer, and of Elizabeth, sister of Sir Thomas More. In 1525 he went to the University of

* "Desertis bonis et honoribus, exul asperam vitam Lovanii egit" is Molanus' phrase.

Oxford, but left without taking his degree, and set up as a printer, as well as a man of law, in London. On the accession of Edward VI. he retired to the continent and settled in Louvain, where, as above stated, he married Winifred Clement. Under Queen Mary he came back to his native country and was made a puisne judge; but with Elizabeth's accession he had once more to retire to Louvain, where he died. He was a notable printer. His wife had already predeceased him in the reign of Edward VI., and he erected a monument to her in the Collegiate Church of St. Pierre, under the organ loft. His death was a saintly one, and his body was laid to rest by the side of that of his wife.

A much more celebrated *émigré* was Nicholas Saunders, "the most noted defender of the Roman Catholic cause in his time." He was a native of Charlewood in Surrey, and about 1557 was Shagling Lecturer, or, as he himself styles it, "tamquam Regius Professor" of Canon Law at Oxford. About 1560 he retired to the Continent, going first to Rome, where he was made priest and D.D. Somewhat later he distinguished himself at the Council of Trent, and accompanied Cardinal Stanislaus Hosius on his legatine journey through Poland, Prussia, and Lithuania. After this he came to Louvain, where he wrote several important works. Saunders is noted for the extreme bitterness of his attacks on Henry VIII. and Queen Elizabeth, and certain of his statements contained in his work on the Anglican schism have been thought by some to be exaggerated. He has been described as being "to Protestants what Foxe is to Catholics." He lived in Louvain for about thirteen years as Professor of Theology. His end was a strange and tragic one. In 1579 he was sent by Pope Gregory XIII. as legate to Ireland, where, about 1580, he perished of hunger—"wandering in the mountaines," says Lord Burghley, "and raving in a phrensy." Saunders is perhaps the best known, as he was also the keenest, of the polemical controversialists of those times.

In 1586 we find another refugee, one Robert Parkinson, of Lincoln, promoted to the degree of D.D. at Louvain.

Perhaps the most illustrious of all these Oxford refugees was John Storey, the martyr. He was educated in the University of Oxford, chiefly at Henxey Hall; admitted B.C.L. in 1531, and in 1535 appointed to a new chair of law founded by King Henry VIII. In 1537 he was chosen principal of Broadgate's Hall, and the following year created D.C.L. In the beginning of Edward VI.'s reign, owing to his zealous defence of the old religion,* he was obliged to withdraw into Flanders, where he remained until the reign of Mary. He was then recalled, and the patent of his professorship of Oxford was restored to him, though he soon resigned it in order to occupy important legal posts in London. On Elizabeth's accession Dr. Storey was a member of the House of Commons, and spoke so strongly against the Reformation that he was cast into prison, but contrived to escape, and settled for a time in Louvain, where he is quaintly said by Molanus to have spent more time with the Carthusians than at home with his wife. In 1570, being at Antwerp, he was kidnapped on an English vessel belonging to one Parker, brought over to England, committed to the Tower, tried, and eventually hanged, drawn and quartered at Tyburn (June 1, 1571) under circumstances of unusual atrocity, being of the age of seventy years.† His family continued to live in Louvain.

John Fowler, a native of Bristol, was educated at Winchester School and New College, Oxford, becoming a fellow in 1555. Under Elizabeth, he too fled to Belgium, and set up printing presses at Antwerp and Louvain. He

* Dr. Storey is recorded to have exclaimed at a public assembly in the words of the preacher, "Woe to thee, O land, when thy King is a child" (Eccles. x. 16). This exclamation caused such an outburst of indignation that Storey realized that it was no longer safe to remain in England.

† Blessed John Storey is one of the fifty-four English martyrs beatified by Pope Leo XIII. on December 9, 1886. See an excellent life of him by Dom Bede Camm, O.S.B., in his "Lives of the English Martyrs," vol. ii. (1905), pp. 14-110.

is spoken of as a man of learning, well skilled in both Latin and Greek. He married Alice, daughter of John Harris, the secretary of Sir Thomas More and of his wife Dorothy, referred to on the preceding page.*

III.

I must now recall the fact that the occasion which drew so many representatives of universities and learned bodies to Oxford last October was the tercentenary of its famous Bodleian Library. "At the present moment," said the Louvain address, as above quoted, "we are chiefly moved by a sense of profound gratitude to the founders and directors of the Bodleian Library." The history of this famous library, one of the six greatest libraries of the world, forms one of the most interesting chapters of literary history. Without in any way detracting from the undoubted merits of the illustrious and munificent donor whose name it bears, it is only fair

* I have, of course, limited my remarks above to Oxford men at Louvain. Other English exiles, however, likewise sought refuge there. Such were Cuthbert Scott, D.D., Bishop of Chester, a Cambridge man, buried in the church of the Friars Minor, whose epitaph ran:

> "Anglia Cuthbertum peperit nomine Scotum;
> Sed natale solum tribuit Northumbrica tellus.
> Pagina sacra habuit doctorem Cantabrigensem;
> Cestria pontificem, necnon Ecclesia gemmam;
> Integritas vitæ Benardum reddidit orbi;
> Eloquio visus nobis Chrysostomus alter."

Another Cambridge man was Henry Jolliffe, Dean of Bristol and Almoner to Queen Mary, who died in 1573, and lies buried in the Church of St. Michel, Louvain. Of Robert Giles, whose tomb and epitaph are in the same church, "legum Angliæ professor egregius," and who, dying in 1578, in his forty-fourth year, left one daughter, "ex conjuge sua carissima Wenthana, Thomæ Stradlynge, equitis aurati apud Wallos meridionales in majori Brittannia olim strenuissimi, filia," I cannot find whether he was an Oxford or a Cambridge man (perhaps neither). Gillow does not mention him in his Dictionary (but see Catholic Record Society, vol. i., 1905).

Other Louvain refugees, like the Earl of Westmoreland and Lady Jane Dormer, do not belong to my present subject.

to say that Sir Thomas Bodley was the restorer rather than the founder of Oxford's University library. The fact was emphatically acknowledged, both in many of the academical orations made at the centenary and in the handsome record published by the Clarendon Press on that occasion,* that the first creation of a university library or libraries at Oxford goes much further back, to Catholic times and Catholic Churchmen, and that the destruction thereof was owing to Protestant fanaticism at the Reformation.

"Before any actual building had in earlier days been assigned for the purpose, benefactors had made some provision for needy scholars, to whom the purchase of books lay beyond their means, by gifts of MSS., which were preserved in chests within the precincts of St. Mary's Church, and were to be lent out under sufficient pledges for safe return. The earliest name of such a donor which has been handed down is that of Rogerus de Insula, Chancellor of the diocese of Lincoln (in which Oxford then lay) in 1217-20, and afterwards, till his death in 1235, Dean of York. He gave several copies of the Bible. About a hundred years later, Thomas Cobham, Bishop of Worcester, began (some seven years before his death, which occurred in 1327) to make preparation for building a room (now existing on the north of the chancel of St. Mary's Church) over a chapel then used as the meeting-place of the congregation of the University; and, upon his decease, he left money and books towards the carrying out of his purpose."†

The library, thus inaugurated by a Catholic dean and a Catholic bishop, received its most important development under an enlightened Catholic prince and from other Catholic bishops.

"Only a few years elapsed before the library, thus happily begun, outgrew its narrow accommodation. For when the university, upon commencing the erection of the noble Divinity School, sought the aid of Humfrey,

* "Pietas Oxoniensis." † *Ibid.*, p. 8.

Duke of Gloucester, as being the known encourager of learning, he not only contributed money liberally for that purpose, but began also, in 1439, to forward books for the library, in which year his first donation comprised 129 volumes, worth, as Convocation said in a letter of thanks addressed to the Parliament, a thousand pounds and more. And as continuous gifts followed, amounting, before the Duke's death in 1447, to a total of about 600 volumes (besides some received subsequently), the need of a larger room became pressing. To the Duke, therefore, in 1444, Convocation turned again, and prayed for help to erect and furnish, over the Divinity School, a chamber which would be better fitted for the housing and the use of his precious gifts—help which would indeed make him that which he should solemnly be styled, Founder of the Library. It was but slowly after the great patron's death that the work went on, the books in the old library being meanwhile chained in 1454; and at length, after additional gifts had been received (especially from Thomas Kempe, Bishop of London), in 1488 Duke Humfrey's library was opened, and at once received a further considerable gift of books from Archdeacon Richard Lichfield."*

"Kempe gave not only books, but 1,000 marks to complete the school of which the library formed the upper storey; and in 1437 the University, in a letter to him, calls it 'tuam novam librariam' (Anstey, 'Epistolæ Academicæ,' ii., 533). In 1478 the University bound itself to commemorate, by annual Masses, etc., not only Kempe himself after his death, but also his uncle, John Kempe, Archbishop of Canterbury."† I wonder what has become of those Masses now.

It is interesting to remark that the central portion of the Bodleian Library still bears the name of the "good Duke." Only sixty-two years passed when, as the Public Orator, the Rev. Dr. Merry, Rector of Lincoln College, said in his Latin oration: "Sad times fell upon

* *Op. cit.*, p. 6.

† *Ibid.*, n. 1.

the University when superstition and ignorance combined to destroy what learning and munificence had created." The superstition and ignorance were those of the Royal Commissioners of King Edward VI. The precious books and manuscripts that had been collected with such care and at such cost through the munificence of princes and prelates were, in 1550, condemned as Popish by these Commissioners, and either destroyed or sold; many of them, as they were of parchment, were cut up and used as measuring-tapes by tailors. Even the woodwork of the old library was broken up and sold for timber in 1556, so that nothing was left but the four bare walls; and, to quote again the "Pietas Oxoniensis," "the place chosen of old for quietness that fitted it for study remained abnormally quiet for lack of anything to be studied."*

The name of the boy-king, Edward VI., has been handed down in the popular tradition as that of a great patron of learning, owing to a certain number of grammar-schools founded in his reign and under his name. The sad story of the old Oxford library is a striking confirmation of the contention of Catholic (and other) historians that this apparent royal munificence was more than counterbalanced by the fanaticism and rapacity of Edward—or rather of his ministers—which plundered wholesale the goods of the Church. After this we can the better appreciate the bitter exclamation of Dr. John Storey, then Principal of Broadgate's Hall: "Woe to thee, O land, when thy King is a child!" which we quoted just now.

These excesses of Protestant bigotry and fanaticism were very soon after made good by the enlightened generosity and devoted zeal of Sir John Bodley, himself a Protestant of Protestants, who dedicated a considerable portion of his life to the restoration of the library, or, as we may truly say, to the creation of a new one, which now deservedly bears his name, and ranks as one of the

* *Op. cit*, p. 7.

greatest and most precious treasure-houses of books and MSS. in the world. It was opened in 1602, so that in 1902 we were worthily celebrating its third centenary.

The Louvain letter indicates an extremely subtle historical connection between this restored library of Bodley and the modern intellectual development of the Belgian University, and expresses on that account "a sense of profound gratitude towards the founders and directors of the Bodleian Library." As the story here referred to forms one of the most romantic chapters of literary history, I must endeavour, as briefly as I can, to narrate it.

In 1718 one Richard Bourchier, an English merchant in India, purchased from some Parsis a MS. of one of their sacred books, the "Vendidad," in a language and character then unknown in Europe, and sent it by one Mr. Richard Cobbe, in 1723, to the Bodleian Library in Oxford, where it is still preserved. There it lay for several years a mere useless curiosity;* but in 1754, by some means or other, I know not how, a facsimile of four leaves of this MS. found its way to Paris, and was exposed in a glass case in the Bibliothèque du Roi. Here it was seen by an impulsive and enthusiastic young French scholar, Abraham-Hyacinthe Anquetil du Perron, little more than twenty years of age at the time, and enkindled in him a fire of zeal which has had far-reaching consequences in the subsequent history of European learning. He knew, of course, what everybody else knew, that this codex formed a portion of the sacred books of an ancient and once mighty religion of the East, that bore the name of a great prophet and reformer, known to the ancient Greeks as Zoroaster, and who was supposed to have lived at a date of fabulous antiquity—a religion that at one time was the national faith of the

* It is still preserved there. At my visit in 1902, through the kindness of Mr. E. B. Nicholson, Bodley's Librarian, I had the pleasure of handling and examining this historically precious manuscript.

great Persian empire, and about which much had been written from the days of Herodotus, the father of history, down to those of Hyde at the close of the seventeenth century. The early fathers and ecclesiastical writers, too, had preserved the Eastern tradition that the Magi or Wise-Men who came to adore Christ in Bethlehem belonged to this faith. But strange and discordant, often grotesque and exaggerated, were the statements scattered through history about it and its founder. It was known that the Parsis, the so-called Fire Worshippers of India, were the remnants of the adherents of the once Imperial faith, long since crushed and almost exterminated by Mohammedanism, who had found a refuge on Indian shores. They were believed to possess the sacred writings of Zoroaster and his disciples, as well as the knowledge of the long-forgotten languages in which they were preserved. But the Parsi priests jealously guarded their treasures, and even though in one or two rare instances they were persuaded to sell MSS. of their books, nothing had ever induced them to divulge what they knew of their language or contents. Anquetil du Perron was now fired with the ambition to win for his country the glory of wresting from the suspicious priesthood who guarded them the secrets of the old-world faith, and of laying before the learned world a complete account of the Zoroastrian doctrines, based on the actual testimony of the ancient books themselves. So great was his impatience that he enlisted as a common soldier in the French East India Company, quitting Paris with his company (men whom he speaks of as "ces brutaux"), and with no further luggage than a few books, two shirts, two handkerchiefs, and a pair of socks. Reaching l'Orient on November 16, 1754, he was gratified to learn that the King had allowed him a subsidy of 500 livres and a free passage to India. He did not sail, however, till February 7, 1755, nor reach Pondicherry till August 9, after a voyage of six months. Seven long years he spent in India, chiefly in Surat, which he reached in 1758. Facing every kind of difficulty and discouragement, suffering sickness, opposition, perils of war, and even personal violence, never once did he swerve from his self-imposed task. On the part of the dasturs, or Parsi priests, he met with vexatious delays, fraud, extortion, and evasion: still he persevered. His extraordinary courage and industry were rewarded. He learned the Persian language, and, in addition, whatever the Parsis knew of their two ancient sacred languages now known to us as Zend and Pehlevi. He obtained complete copies of all that remained of their sacred books, translated them into French, and collated many MSS. Although England and France were at war at the time, and Surat was captured by the former during his stay there, it is pleasing to record that he received much help and friendly protection from the English, and finally, on April 23, 1761, it was owing to English help that he was able to sail from Bombay with his precious treasures (including 180 MSS.) on board the *Bristol*, arriving at Portsmouth on November 17 of the same year. For a short time, through some misapprehension, he was detained as a prisoner of war, owing to the hostilities proceeding between the two countries, but was soon released. He would not, however, leave England before visiting Oxford to inspect and compare the Avestic MSS. there preserved. After a stay of two days, he returned by Portsmouth and London to Gravesend, whence he embarked for Ostend on February 14, 1762, reaching Paris just a month later. He deposited his MSS. in the Bibliothèque du Roi, and set to work to publish the results of his long years of labour. After nine years' toil, there appeared in 1771 his great work in three volumes, destined to bring about almost a revolution in philological and historical science. It is true the work was full of mistakes and imperfections, not so much through Anquetil du Perron's own fault, as through that of his Parsi teachers, whose knowledge of their own classical languages was singularly imperfect and incorrect. Thus, when his translation of the "Sacred Books of the Avesta" appeared, it met with much scepticism and even ridicule; instead of a work of profound philosophy, it appeared to many of his readers a mere farrago of puerile fables, tedious formulæ, and grotesque prescriptions. A famous young Oxford scholar, Sir William Jones, who later on became the greatest Orientalist of his day, published a letter in exquisite French in which he poured forth with all the wit and bitterness of a Voltaire the vials of almost ferocious ridicule and obloquy upon Anquetil. In fact, he made out that his work was a forgery, and this view was long held by many distinguished scholars. For several years the battle raged over the question of the genuineness or the contrary of the language which Anquetil had thus revealed to the scientific world. Among the scholars who defended Anquetil it is interesting to find the name of the learned Carmelite Father Paulinus di San Bartolommeo,* who, in an essay published in Rome in 1798, not only defended the genuineness of the Avestic language, but even indicated, what was later on to be so abundantly proved, its affinity with the Sanskrit.

Time has abundantly avenged the good faith and substantial accuracy of Anquetil du Perron, and the cruel diatribe of Sir William Jones is now nothing more than a literary curiosity. The rich collections of MSS. deposited in the Paris Library by Anquetil du Perron were studied by one scholar after another, until the great Eugène Burnouf definitely placed Avestic philology on a permanent and certain basis. The language of the Avesta, the so-called Zend, was exhaustively studied, its phonetics and grammatical principles duly recorded and explained, and it took its rightful place by the side of its sister idiom, Sanskrit, the sacred language of ancient India. Thus was Bopp, the father of the modern science of comparative philology, able to

* Author of the first Sanskrit Grammar ever printed (Rome: Propaganda Press, 1790).

utilize it in the compilation of his epoch-making work, "The Comparative Grammar of the Indo-Germanic Languages," and even up to the present day the study of Zend is indispensable for a proper understanding of the history and development of that most important group of languages known to us as the Aryan, or Indo-European family.

No less far-reaching have been the effects of Anquetil du Perron's revelation upon another most important modern branch of learning, the Comparative History of Religions. The sacred books of the Avesta, or, rather, what portions of them have survived the wreck, together with a very considerable proportion of the explanatory, theological, or patristic literature belonging to the after ages of the Zoroastrian faith, and composed in the medieval language known to us as Pehlevi, have, during the course of the nineteenth century, been studied, published, translated, and commented upon by numerous scholars of every nationality. The dogmas and moral precepts, the ceremonial and liturgical prescriptions of the great Zoroastrian creed, are now fully known, and form one of the most valuable as well as most interesting chapters of the history of religions. Now, it is one of the peculiar glories of the modern University of Louvain—resuscitated in 1834 after its temporary suppression by the French Republicans, as recorded earlier on—to have played an important part in the development of Avestic studies, whether from the philological or the theological point of view, through the labours of its most illustrious modern son, the late Charles de Harlez. As a young priest, this gifted scholar, forced, by ill-health and a serious throat affection which never left him, to abandon the work of the parochial ministry, threw himself, with all the ardour of his nature, into those studies which had been inaugurated by Anquetil du Perron, and raised to the highest scientific level by Burnouf, Westergaard, and Spiegel, of whom de Harlez may be considered to have been intellectually, though not actually, the pupil. In 1874 de Harlez joined the staff of the Louvain University and began his great work, the French translation of the Avesta, which, with his many subsequent publications, have exercised a profound influence upon the course of Zend studies in Europe, and upon no man more than upon the famous Darmesteter, though that strange genius would have been the last to acknowledge his indebtedness. But it is chiefly as the reformer of the intellectual life of Louvain that de Harlez comes before us in this paper. With a single exception of the great biologist Carnoy, there is no man whose intellectual power has so remodelled the higher studies in that University as Charles de Harlez. What the one did for the natural sciences, the other did for the philological and historical ones; and it has been said, without much exaggeration, that de Harlez left Louvain on his death in 1899 a hundred years ahead of what he found it on his arrival in 1874. If, then, that illustrious scholar owes his fame and his power to his Avestic studies, it is surely not incorrect, fanciful though the idea may seem, to trace, like an electric current, the intellectual influence which he exercised, back through the school of Burnouf, the labours and genius of Anquetil du Perron, and the now historical "four facsimile leaves," to the Bodleian MS. and its home in that literary treasure-house, erected three hundred years ago by the enlightened munificence of Sir John Bodley. Was it too far-fetched on the part of the Louvain University to express in its letter its "profound gratitude" to the Bodleian for having supplied the tiny seed whence have sprung the rich intellectual gifts which she now enjoys?

IV.

However poetical this idea may seem, there is no doubt about the prosaic reality of the good services acknowledged in the concluding paragraph of the address. It is well known that the Bodleian has become one of the richest storehouses of MSS., particularly of rare and valuable Oriental codices, in the world, with which but three or four of the greatest libraries in Europe can vie. Hence it is that scholars come from all parts to examine, collate, or copy these manuscript treasures. It is true that the Bodleian, by one of the fundamental articles of its constitution, can never lend a single volume of any kind outside of its own walls; and history records the two interesting occasions when, first of all King Charles I. and some years later the mighty Protector Oliver Cromwell, on applying for the loan of a volume, were each in turn stoutly refused, on the strength of this regulation, by the unflinching librarians of their day; and though neither Charles nor Oliver were men to brook lightly a contradiction of their wills, it is to the credit of both that they each gracefully acquiesced and respected the founder's law. On the other hand, scholars, whether English or foreign, wishing to work in the library, are ever received with all kindness and courtesy. Members of the Louvain University, among others, have in our own times, as indicated in the address, availed themselves of this privilege. One or two instances are referred to by name. The distinguished Professor of Holy Scripture and the Semitic Languages, Mgr. T. J. Lamy, during the past few years has published the hitherto inedited hymns and sermons of the greatest of the Syrian Doctors of the Church, St. Ephrem of Edessa. This fine edition, containing the original Syriac texts, with Latin translation, notes, and commentaries, is based upon a number of codices in various European libraries, and among them the Bodleian.* Mgr. A. Hebbelynck, who, as the

* "Sancti Ephraem Syri Hymni et Sermones, quos e codicibus Londiniensibus, Parisiensibus . . . et Oxoniensibus descriptis edidit" Thomas Josephus Lamy (Mechliniæ, Dessain, 4 vols., 1882-1902). There is an inaccuracy in the Louvain address in quoting Mgr. Abbeloos as a collaborator in this important work. It was in the similar edition of the Ecclesiastical Chronicle of Bar-Hebræus, or Abu'l-Faraj, the greatest of the Syrian historians, that Abbeloos, Lamy's most distinguished pupil, co-

present Rector Magnificus, signs the address quoted above, has also been indebted to the courtesy of the authorities of Bodley's Library, whilst copying or collating some of its Coptic MSS., one of which, an exceedingly curious, quasi-gnostic treatise on the "Mysteries of the Greek Alphabet," he published in text and translation in 1902.*

It was as a fitting and graceful acknowledgment of these and other services that the University of Louvain entrusted its delegate, in addition to the Latin address, with a selection of some dozen bound volumes of publications of members of its staff, for presentation to the Bodleian Library, among them being, naturally, the works just described.

What I have written above will, I think, suffice to show the continuous traditions of friendly intercourse and reciprocal services which, for nearly four and a half centuries, have existed between the ancient University of Oxford and her younger, though venerable, sister University of Louvain; and it is possible, perhaps, to trace a long-linked chain of intellectual and moral cause and effect between the going of Robert Lincoln, the Oxford bachelor, to Louvain in 1472, and the sending by Louvain of her delegate to share in the joys of the Oxford celebration of 1902, after an interval of precisely 430 years.

---

operated with the latter thirty years ago ("Gregorii Barhebræi Chronicon Ecclesiasticum" . . . conjuncta opera ediderunt Abbeloos et Lamy," Lovanii, Peeters, 3 vols., 1872-1877), but the text published was that of a British Musuem codex not of a Bodleian MS.

* "Les Mystères des Lettres Grecques d'après un Manuscrit Copte Arabe de la Bibliothèque Bodléienne d'Oxford" (Louvain: Istas, 1902).

BOOKS TO BE CONSULTED.

Pietas Oxoniensis: In Memory of Sir Thomas Bodley, Knt., and the Foundation of the Bodleian Library. Oxford: at the University Press, October, 1902.

MGR. HEBBELYNCK, Recteur Magnifique de l'Université. "Discours prononcé au Grand Auditoire du Collège du Pape Adrien VI., le 15 Octobre, 1902." Louvain: Van Linthout, 1902.

DOM ADAM HAMILTON, O.S.B. "Chronicle of the English Augustinian Canonesses at Louvain." Edinburgh and London: Sands, 1904.

DOM BEDE CAMM, O.S.B. "Lives of the English Martyrs." 2 vols. London: Burns and Oates, 1904-5.

THE CATHOLIC RECORD SOCIETY. "Miscellanea," i. London, 1905.

IX

THE LITANY OF LORETO AND ITS HISTORY

AMONG the most popular devotions of the Catholic Church is unquestionably that form of prayer known to us as the " Litany of Loreto." This favourite prayer in honour of the Mother of God is one of the four litanies which, by recent decrees of the Holy See, are the only ones allowed to be used in public devotions—viz., the ancient Litany of the Saints, the Litany of Jesus, the Litany of the Sacred Heart, and the Litany of Loreto. Of these, of course, only the first is, strictly speaking, of liturgical rank, forming as it does an integral part of many of the liturgical and pontifical offices of the Church. The Litany of the Blessed Virgin, or of Loreto, has, however, come to enjoy a quasi-public, though extra-liturgical, character, owing to the fact that it has become, by popular usage, almost an invariable portion of the service of Benediction of the Blessed Sacrament. Moreover, in late years Pope Leo XIII. officially ordered the recitation of this Litany, together with the Rosary, in all churches during the month of October (Encyclical *Supremi Apostolatus*, September 1, 1883). This is the first occasion upon which the recitation of this litany has been made in any way obligatory. Over and above the official authority which now attaches to the Litany of Loreto, there can be no question of the extreme popularity which it enjoys among Catholics all over the world, largely on account of its own intrinsic beauties and of the thoroughly devotional spirit which pervades it. It is no wonder, therefore, that both the contents and the history of this litany have formed the subject of quite a remarkable number of theological and historical treatises during a space of well-nigh three centuries, from the earliest writer, Pierre Geoffrey, whose meditations on the Litany of Loreto were published at Bordeaux in 1607, and Justinus Michoviensis (1630), down to the modern works of Himmelstein (Würtzburg, 1876) and the more recent and exhaustive essays of Josef Sauren (1895) and of de Santi (1900).* Indeed, the present paper will be little more than a brief summary of the interesting investigations and conclusions so clearly and concisely set forth by the former author, though these have been keenly criticised and frequently corrected by de Santi. It may be of some interest to know that among the earlier writers on this subject was one Dr. William Smith, whose dissertation on four of the petitions of the Litany of Loreto was published at Antwerp in 1767.†

The term "litany," as the name of a form of prayer, goes back to the most ancient times, even to pagan writers before the Christian era. It is a Greek word, used by the historian Dionysius of Halicarnassus, who flourished a few years before Christ—*e.g.*, in narrating the famous history of Lucretia.‡ (Antiq. Rom., lib. iv., cap. 67.) In the early Christian Church the word appears to have been used chiefly, if not exclusively, for processions,§ or else for prayers publicly recited during

* See list at end of article.

† "Dissertatio in hæc quatuor Litaniarum quas vulgo Lauretanas appellamus commata: Vas spirituale, vas honorabile, vas insigne devotionis, rosa mystica" (Antverpiæ, 1767).

‡ *πολλὰς λιτανείας . . . ποιησαμένη.* The word is chiefly used as a plural in Christian usage (Lat. *litaniæ*, It. *litanie*, Fr. *litanies*, in its ecclesiastical sense); also Sp. *litania* and *litanias*. Portuguese is peculiar—*ladainha*.

§ In this sense O. Ital. *letanie*, as in Dante, "Inferno," xx. 9. In a document of A.D. 1092, quoted by Muratori ("Annali d'Italia," v. 222), we read: "Quandocunque *letaniæ* veniebant processions, and naturally consisting chiefly of repetitions of invocations. It is generally believed that the custom of processions with recitations of litanies took its rise at Vienne in France about 450, under St. Mamertus, during the terrible days of earthquakes, pestilence, famine, and fire which struck so much terror throughout Gaul during the fifth century, and again under his successor, St. Avitus, in 519. This was the origin of the Rogation Days, the observance of which is believed to have spread from Gaul to Rome, where Gregory the Great first brought them into general use. There is reason to believe that in the earliest times these liturgical litanies consisted solely of the repetition of the invocations *Kyrie eleison*, *Christe eleison*, and that the names of saints and petitions were added somewhat later. Be this as it may, there can be no doubt that the Greater Litanies, or Litanies of the Saints, though not exactly in the forms we have them now, are the most ancient in the Church.

It is an interesting question to ask what is the antiquity of the Litany of Loreto. My readers will probably be surprised to learn that the difference of opinions which prevails among writers on this subject is extreme. The well-known ecclesiastical writer, Binterim, actually carried the origin of this litany back to Apostolic times. Fr. Hutchison ("Loreto and Nazareth," London, 1863), and Dr. Northcote ("Shrines of the Madonna") both agree upon the beginning of the fifth century. Auguste Nicolas, in his celebrated book on the Blessed Virgin, thinks that they were in use in the sixth century under Gregory the Great, and were sung in procession during a time of pestilence, a clear confusion with the Litany of the Saints above referred to. Scherer, Schneider-Beringer, and Moroni, in his great dictionary, all agree in speaking of its

ad San Donatum . . . audiebant Missam." And l'Imolese, in his note to the above passage of Dante: "Qui vadunt in *letaniis* ambulant lente."

venerable antiquity, and refer to it as belonging to the earliest centuries. Moroni and Glaire further assert that Pope Sergius I., in 637, ordered this litany to be publicly recited on the feast of the Annunciation. Other writers admit that it is doubtful whether the existence of the Litany of Loreto can be traced before the year 1294, the traditional date of the translation of the Holy House to that town. The writer whose essay I am now summarising, Herr Sauren, has undertaken a thorough investigation of these different views, with results that are somewhat surprising. Speaking generally, we may say that his careful investigation of historical sources has led to a conclusion entirely fatal to the supposed great antiquity of the Litany of Loreto, and indeed to what appears to me the unavoidable conclusion that this devotion is not only not very ancient, but that it is, comparatively speaking, modern.

Of course, it must be understood that we are here speaking of the actual Litany of Loreto as an organic whole. Not only is the form of public supplication known as "litanies" of the highest antiquity, but even litanies of Our Lady, remarkably similar to our present ones, are to be found all through ecclesiastical literature. It is very interesting to know that the oldest of all litanies of Our Blessed Lady now extant is an old Irish one, going back to the eighth century, preserved in the "Leabher Breac," in the Royal Library of Dublin, and published in the old Irish text, with English and Latin translations, in 1879. This ancient litany is one of great beauty, containing sixty invocations, some identical with, others very similar to, those in our own form of the Litany. A version of this old Irish litany, together with several others of various dates, is given in the appendix to Sauren's Essay. Among them it may be worth while mentioning a litany contained in the works of St. Bonaventure, another extracted by de Rubeis from an ancient codex of Fréjus, a third contained in an office of Our Lady, printed by Dulcibello in 1503, and others extracted from various similar sources. All these have many points of close analogy with our Litany of Loreto, but all differ considerably, some even very widely from it.

We will now follow our author in endeavouring to ascertain the historical data which are at hand for the certain history of the Litany we now possess. The earliest real historical date for this Litany is a statement by Vicenzo Murri in his Dissertation upon the identity of the Santa Casa (Loreto, 1791), to the effect that in the year 1489 a large silver plate bearing the name of Paolo Savelli, Prince of Albano, was sent as an offering to the shrine, having engraved upon it our present Litany of Loreto.* Martorelli, who wrote in 1743, also states that according to some authorities the Litany was composed in 1493.

On the occasion of the laying of the foundation-stone of the marble building which enshrines the Holy House, in 1531, the Chapter of Loreto, according to the testimony of an eye-witness, Laurentius, "sang the Litany of the Virgin Mary."

In 1547 Giovanni d'Albona, Canon of Loreto, made a foundation with the Augustinians of Recanati to say or sing every Saturday a mass in honour of Our Lady "together with her Litanies." Raffaele Riera, S.J., who from 1554 onwards was penitentiary at Loreto, in his history of the "Santa Casa," mentions a litany of Our Lady which the pilgrims to Loreto were in the habit of singing.

It is certainly remarkable to find that the above quoted dates are the very earliest which can be found connecting a litany of Our Lady with Loreto and the Santa Casa. I say *a* litany because it is not yet quite certain whether each one of the litanies just mentioned was identical with our present Litany or not.

On February 8, 1578, a copy of the Litany of Loreto was sent to Rome accompanied by a letter of Giulio Candiotti, arch-priest of Loreto, petitioning that this Litany might be introduced into the churches of Rome.

* See, however, De Santi, pp. 15-20.

Candiotti writes (Vatican Library, cod. reg. 2,020, p. 363): "I send, with all humility, to your Holiness the new (moderne) lauds or litanies of the Blessed Virgin, taken from Holy Scripture, which are sung to music on Saturday evenings towards the *Ave Maria*, on vigils and feasts of the Madonna, on principal feast days, and on the visit of great princes to this Holy House and Church of Loreto, in order to give your Holiness the opportunity of introducing them on the same days in honour of Our Lady, and having them sung in St. Peter's and elsewhere," etc.

The matter was submitted to examination, and there is preserved in the Vatican Library the manuscript of an official report and *votum*. The anonymous consultant finds the Litany to be devout and edifying, but remarks that several of the titles attributed to Our Lady in this Litany are applied in Holy Scripture in their literal or mystic sense rather to Christ and His Church, though some of them have also been applied by the Church to Our Blessed Lady. At the same time he does not think the new Litany to be of sufficient value to be introduced by an official act into Rome, or extended to the Universal Church.

The Litany here referred to was clearly *not* our Litany of Loreto. The expression "taken from Holy Scripture" (*cavate della sacra scrittura*) applied to the petitions does not strictly fit those of the Litany of Loreto, nor can it be exactly said of any of the latter that they were originally "applied in Holy Scripture rather to Christ and His Church." Further than this, there are to be found in a small book of devotions, published at Ingoldstadt in 1573, and entitled "Thesaurus piarum et christianarum Institutionum," by John Perelli, *two* different litanies with the following titles:

1. "Litany of the Mother of God taken from Holy Scripture and accustomed to be sung in the Holy House of Loreto every Saturday, and on vigils and feasts of Our Blessed Lady."
2. "Another Litany of the Blessed Virgin Mary."

Now, the interesting fact is that the *second* of these two Litanies is identical with our present Litany of Loreto, whilst the first is one whose invocations are all literally taken from Holy Scripture, and is undoubtedly the very litany sent to Rome for approval by Candiotti in 1578, as above narrated.

From these facts follows the conclusion, which Sauren himself finds unexpected and surprising, that up to 1578 our present Litany of Loreto was either unknown at Loreto, or at least not used in public functions, and of quite secondary importance. It is remarkable that so weighty and so recent an authority as Dom Suitbert Baeumer, O.S.B., in his invaluable "History of the Breviary" (Freiburg, 1895), should have been led into the error of stating that the litany sent up to Rome by Candiotti was our present Litany.

Another important date in connection with this subject is afforded by the famous battle of Lepanto, in which the Turks were defeated by the Christian forces, under Don John of Austria, in 1571. As we are told in the lessons of the Roman Breviary (May 24), Pope St. Pius V., in thanksgiving for this glorious victory, added the title "Auxilium Christianorum" to the Litany of Loreto, and as that Pope died in 1572 the addition must have been made immediately after the victory. It is somewhat remarkable that no official decree or other document ordering this addition to the Litany is in existence; no mention is made of it in the Pope's Bull on the victory, so that the statement of the Roman Breviary is our only historical authority for the fact. However, a small book of devotions entitled "Trattato sopra l'historia della S. Chiesa e Casa . . . di Loreto," published at Macerata in 1576, as well as the above-mentioned Ingoldstadt Prayer-Book, contain the invocation "Auxilium Christianorum" inserted in their version of our present Litany of Loreto. From this the consequence must be drawn that as early as 1571 or 1572 our present Litany of Loreto was not only known but officially recognised in Rome—at a time, that is, when quite another litany, the Scriptural, or, as we may conveniently call it, Candiotti's Litany, was the one publicly sung at Loreto. Within a very few years, however, these two litanies must have changed places, for in 1587 the Roman Litany, identical with our present Litany, was not only indulgenced by Sixtus V. in his Bull "Reddituri" of July 11, but also spoken of as the Litany "which is recited in the House of Our Blessed Lady" (*quae in Domo Beatae Mariae Virginis recitantur*). And the following year Rutilio Benzoni, Bishop of Loreto, ordered our present Litany to be solemnly sung during a three days' synod which he held in that city. From this date forward no other Litany is known under the title of Loreto except the one so familiar to us by that name. The former Scriptural Litany of Loreto has passed into practical oblivion. There can be little doubt that Sauren is correct in surmising that the cause of this substitution was the refusal of Rome to approve the Loreto Litany sent by Candiotti in 1578.

Herr Sauren, to whom is due the credit of these interesting discoveries, next discusses the question of the origin of our present Litany. Two theories may be put forward. One theory is that both litanies had their origin in Loreto, were both in use at that shrine, but that the Scriptural Litany enjoyed, up to 1578, higher esteem, and so was sung on Saturdays and feast days. The failure of Candiotti's petition may have brought it into disfavour.

The second, and more probable, theory holds that our present Litany had its origin outside of Loreto, and was brought to the Shrine from elsewhere. This view is supported by the account of the silver tablet sent as an offering to Loreto by Sapelli in 1489, as above related, with our Litany engraved upon it, as well as by the statement of Riera that this Litany was wont to be sung by pilgrims coming to Loreto. And as St. Pius V. added the invocation "Auxilium Christianorum" to a Litany which was not at that date belonging to Loreto, though it has since become so, we may conclude that our present Litany is really one of Roman origin carried to Loreto by pilgrims. Since the silver tablet of 1489 is absolutely the earliest historical datum for the history of our Litany we have therefore no warrant at all for fixing the date of its origin earlier than the late fifteenth century. This is indeed a very far cry from the statements of the numerous writers referred to earlier on in this paper who claim that our Litany goes back to Pope Gregory the Great, to the earliest Christian centuries, or even to Apostolic times.*

A most interesting question now arises as to the *authorship* of our Litany of Loreto. It may be at once said that we have absolutely no information, not even a tradition to go upon, in determining this question. A careful study of the various invocations shows that the author must have been not only a pious, but also a theologically learned man. The titles given to Our Lady are not only skilfully chosen, but are also arranged in an accurate and consequent order. We have already referred to a number of Litanies of our Blessed Lady published in various works of devotion, and reprinted in Sauren's essay. That writer points out that though all these Litanies differ more or less widely from ours, yet that the latter contains many epithets to be found also in the other Litanies, and more especially that an examination of these numbered by him 5, 7, and 8, viz., one published by Dulcibello in 1503, one taken from an old missal in Gothic characters, and published by Cosimo, and a third published at Venice in a small prayer-book in 1561, proves that our present Litany is nothing else than a revised version or redaction of these three Litanies, in any case the work of a learned and

* It may be of some interest to add that our Litany of Loreto was first *printed* in 1576, in the above quoted Italian treatise of the arch-priest Bernardino Cirillo, published at Macerata; and that it was first set to music by Palestrina, and his contemporary, Orlando Lasso, in the second half of the sixteenth century.

skilful editor rather than author. Who this writer may have been it is unfortunately impossible even to surmise.

We may now summarise the net results of this historical investigation as follows:

1. The use of "Litanies," or the recitation of public prayers in the form of strings or series of invocations repeated by the people, goes back to the earliest times of Christianity. Such litanies were at first exclusively used in processions.

2. The earliest form of litanies is that which has come down to us as "the Litanies of the Saints," and which has long enjoyed liturgical rank.

3. There is reason to believe that many forms of litanies in honour of our Blessed Lady were in use in different parts of the Church from fairly early times—at least from the seventh or eighth century, as testified by the old Irish Litany of the "Leabher Breac."

4. These various litanies consisted of series of invocations of the Mother of God, under various symbolical and allegorical titles, taken from the Holy Scripture or the writings of the Fathers of the Church.

5. In the latter part of the sixteenth century *a* litany of the Blessed Virgin, the text of which is still extant, was accustomed to be sung at the sanctuary of Loreto on Saturdays and great Feast Days. Its age is uncertain, but in all probability it was, at that time referred to, only recent. The invocations in this litany are taken exclusively from Holy Scripture.

6. Between 1578 and 1587, probably owing to the refusal of the Holy See to give a solemn approbation to this Scriptural Litany, its use was superseded at Loreto by another litany, said to have been brought thither by pilgrims, in which the titles of Our Lady are taken chiefly from the Fathers and Doctors of the Church. This litany is very probably of Roman origin. It is our present "Litany of Loreto."

7. A comparison of it with other litanies extant shows that it is not an original composition, but a skilful and

learned adaptation of at least three other extant litanies, all printed and published between 1503 and 1561.

8. Its author must, therefore, have been a learned and devout theologian, living probably in Rome, and during the fifteenth century, possibly at its close; his name is entirely lost.

It will now be of some interest briefly to review the various titles of Our Lady as contained in our present Litany of Loreto. This subject has attracted the attention of several pious writers who have commented upon the Litany. Sauren justly remarks that, unlike most of the earlier litanies of Our Lady, wherein the different epithets applied to the Blessed Virgin are thrown together with little or no order, our Litany forms an organic whole, in which every title has its proper place and sequence.

In analysing the invocations, we may properly begin by marking off those four which have an historical origin, and which, not belonging to the original form of our Litany, have been subsequently added to it by Papal authority. These are (1) "Auxilium Christianorum," which, as we have seen, according to the testimony of the Breviary, was added by St. Pius V. in 1571 or 1572, after the battle of Lepanto. (2) "Regina sine labe originali concepta," added by permission of Pius IX. after the definition of the Immaculate Conception in 1854, though strictly speaking no papal document has ever officially extended the use of this invocation to the Universal Church, according to a decree of the Congregation of Rites of April 8, 1865.* (3) "Regina Sacratissimi Rosarii," added by Leo XIII. in his decree of December 24, 1883, ordering this petition to follow immediately the one just mentioned. (4) "Mater Boni Consilii," Leo XIII., by decree April 22, 1903.

* "Meletens . . . *Utrum ex præcepto adjungendum: Regina sine labe originali concepta?* . . . Ad. iii. Negative." It will thus be seen that up to that time the addition of that title was not obligatory. Since the decree of Leo XIII. of December 24, 1883, we may infer that the invocation is now *ex præcepto.*

We may now proceed to analyse the titles of the Litany as a whole. This has been done in different ways by different writers. Justinus Michoviensis, in his already quoted work (vol. i., Discurs. ix., p. 23), points out that there are three motives for which a person merits praise and honour—viz., (1) An illustrious name, (2) virtuous and heroic deeds, (3) high rank and dignity. He finds this order indicated in the Litany, in which we have first the venerable name of Mary. "Sancta Maria," second, her virtues, whether in literal language ("Sancta Dei genitrix" to "Virgo fidelis"), or in metaphorical language ("Speculum justitiæ" to "Stella matutina"), and also her heroic deeds ("Salus infirmorum" to "Auxilium Christianorum"); third, the concluding invocations, all beginning with the title "Queen," to indicate her supereminent rank and dignity.

The analysis of Sauren (following Knoll and Kolb) is more elaborate. He considers the titles of our Lady as falling into two groups—those relating to her own individual personality, and those applying to her in her relation to the Church of Christ. We may express the further analysis in a tabular form:

1. OUR LADY'S PERSONALITY.

As Mother of God.	Sancta Maria to Mater Salvatoris.
As Virgin.	Virgo prudentissima to Virgo fidelis.
As Virgin Mother (by metaphors).	Speculum justitiæ to Vas insigne devotionis.

2. OUR LADY IN RELATION TO THE CHURCH.

Foreshadowed in the Old Testament.	Rosa Mystica to Stella matutina.
Her relation to the Church militant and suffering.	Salus infirmorum to Auxilium Christianorum.
Her relation to the Church triumphant.	Regina angelorum to the end.

Whatever be the value of this somewhat elaborate analysis, it at least serves to show the symmetry and accurate care with which our Litany has been compiled.

But even though such an analysis may bear the appearance of being somewhat fanciful, even a casual examination of the Litany reveals a certain deliberate arrangement of titles, concerning which I may be permitted to quote some words published by me a few years ago: "An analysis of the titles by which Our Lady is addressed in this Litany reveals the fact, which perhaps is rarely adverted to, that after the three introductory titles, if one may so call them, which in a way give the keynote to what follows ('Sancta Maria,' 'Sancta Dei genitrix,' 'Sancta Virgo Virginum'), these titles fall into four distinct groups—viz., (1) One of the ten invocations in which Our Lady is addressed as 'Mother,' and so her Divine Maternity celebrated; (2) one in which, under six invocations, she is styled 'Virgin,' thus proclaiming her Virginity; (3) a longer group of seventeen titles, made up of types and mystic figures, which set her forth as the Mystic Woman, the predestined Woman of the Old Law; and (4) a group of invocations to her as 'Queen,' thus proclaiming her Triumph."*

In accordance with this four-fold division, my friend, Mr. G. A. Oesch, formerly of St. Bede's College, Manchester, at my suggestion composed music to the Litany of Loreto, whose object was "to set forth these four varieties of the titles of Our Lady by four corresponding variations in the music, celebrating respectively her Divine Motherhood, her Virginity, her Mystic Character, and her Queenship, somewhat as in the Litany of the Saints the music varies with the change in the form of invocation" (*loc. cit.*). It will be interesting here to quote the testimony of an eminent Anglican authority: "With regard to the third group, the following remark of Dr. F. G. Lee, the Anglican vicar of Lambeth, in his work, 'The Sinless Conception of the Mother of God' (London, 1892), may be quoted: 'It is both interesting and instructive (eminently calculated to rectify historical errors) to note that the titles

* Preface to "Litany of Loreto for four mixed Voices." Composed by G. A. Oesch. Ratisbon: Pustet, 1892.

and expressions by which the Mother of God is addressed in the Litany of Loreto are almost all found in the writings of the Fathers of the first six centuries. What some persons have been accustomed to regard medieval superstitions are, in truth and reality, patristic facts.' —*Ibid.*, p. 95."

In conclusion, I may remark that, although our Litany cannot, like its predecessor, be called Scriptural, yet a number of the mystic titles quoted from the Fathers are in reality borrowed, or at least adapted by, the latter from one or other passage of Holy Scripture.

The following table, based on and abridged from Sauren, of the titles will show this fact to demonstration :

TITLE.	WRITERS FROM WHOM TAKEN.
Sancta Dei Genitrix.	(*θεοτόκος*, Conc. Eph. 431) SS. Augustine, Ephrem, Basil, Methodius.
S. Virgo Virginum.	Bruno the Carthusian, Petrus Cellensis, Hugh of St. Victor.
Mater Christi.	SS. John Damascene, Augustine, Gregory Nazianzen.
Mater Divinæ Gratiæ.	"M. Gratiæ," Idiota ; "M. Gratiarum," St. Anselm.
Mater purissima.	Johannes Hondemius ; "M. mundissima," St. John Damascene ; "Domina purissima," St. Ephrem.
Mater castissima.	St. Ildephonsus.
Mater inviolata.	St. Ephrem ; "Virgo inviolata," St. Gregory Thaum.
Mater intemerata.	SS. Augustine, Methodius, Jerome.
Mater amabilis.	Gulielmus Parisiensis.
Mater admirablis.	Simeon Metaphrastes, Albert the Great.
Mater Creatoris.	SS. Bonaventure and Anselm, Cæsar Cistariensis.
Mater Salvatoris.	Origen, SS. Epiphanius and Ildephonsus.
Virgo prudentissima.	(*Cf.* Matt. xxv.) Idiota, St. Bonaventure, Albert the Great.
Virgo veneranda.	St. Gregory Nazianzen.
Virgo prædicanda.	"Virgo . . . celebranda," St. John Damascene.
Virgo potens.	(St. Bonaventure, "tu es potentissima.")
Virgo clemens.	Hermannus Contractus.
Virgo fidelis.	Abbot Rupert ; "Virgo fidelissima," Albert the Great.

Title.	Writers from whom Taken.
Speculum justitiæ.	" S. totius justitiæ," Abbot Gueric.
Sedes sapientiæ.	SS. Anselm Bernard, and Laurence Justinian.
Causa nostræ lætitiæ.	"Causa nobis lætitiæ," St. Gregory of Nicomedia " Causa unica lætitiæ," St. Joseph Hymnographus ; " Causa gaudii et lætitiæ," Albert the Great.
Vas spirituale.*	" Vas Spiritus Sancti," Bernardinus de Bustis, Antonius.
Vas honorabile.	' Vas honoratum," Ephiphanius ; "Vas venerabile," St. Bonaventure.
Vas insigne devotionis.	No exact equivalent.
Rosa mystica.	Helinandus (*cf.* Wisdom xxiv. 18 ; xxxix. 17).
Turris Davidica.	Abbot Philippus, Honorius of Autun, Richard of St. Laurence (*cf.* Cant. iv. 4).
Turris eburnea.	Ditto (*cf.* Cant. vii. 4).
Domus aurea.	Isidore of Thessalonia.
Fœderis arca.	Idiota, Petrus Cellensis, Richard of St. Victor.†
Janua Cœli.	St. Peter Damian.
Stella matutina.	St. Peter Damian ; also Idiota and St. Simon Stock.
Salus infirmorum.	" Salus ægrotantium," Johannes Geometra.
Refugium peccatorum.	SS. Ephrem and Bonaventure.
Consolatrix afflictorum.	Bernardinus de Bustis; "Consolatrix mœrentium," Helinandus and Albert the Great.
Auxilium Christianorum.	St. John Damascene.
Regina Angelorum.	St. Josephus Hymnographus.
Regina SS. omnium.	St Anselm.

This brief table will be readily admitted to justify Herr Sauren's conclusion that " the Litany has a dogmatic foundation. It contains nothing inaccurate or exaggerated, but correctly represents the doctrine of the Church concerning the veneration of the Mother of God

* " Vas," as applied to *persons* in both O.T. and N.T.—*e.g.*, St. Paul, styled " vas electionis " by Christ Himself (Acts ix. 15). The Italian (and French) versions *paraphrase*, instead of translating literally, these three invocations: "Dimora dello Spirito sancto—vaso di elezione—modello di vera pietà " (Sauren, p. 41).

† " Arca," applied to Mary by some of the oldest fathers—SS. Methodius, Ephrem, Ambrose.

as resting upon both Scripture and Tradition" (*op. cit.*, p. 50).

It is necessary to add that Sauren's little work attracted very great attention at its appearance, and was discussed by several writers, but by none so fully as by Fr. Angelo de Santi, S.J., who subjected it to an extremely severe and exhaustive criticism, and succeeded in throwing doubt upon, if not in disproving, several statements made by Sauren and the authorities he followed, especially as regards Savelli's silver plate. His pamphlet is a work of great erudition. In its main results—*i.e.*, the *modernity* of our Litany of Loreto and the existence of another, a Scriptural litany, for some time side by side with the former—he practically confirms Sauren's views. The differences in the conclusions he arrives at are these: (1) He considers our present litany to be somewhat older, even at Loreto, than the Scriptural litany, and that it was probably sung in public at Loreto in the first half of the sixteenth century, or perhaps even at the end of the fifteenth, during the Plague. (2) The Scriptural litany was probably composed about 1575, and for a time (say 1578 to 1587) the two litanies existed side by side on almost equal footing, but that after this the Scriptural litany disappeared altogether from use. (3) The present "Loreto" litany was *not* introduced from outside—*e.g.*, from Rome—by pilgrims, but took its rise at Loreto itself, and was not even known in Rome in 1587.

Whatever we may think of these differences of view, Sauren will have always the merit of a pioneer in this interesting subject, and his main thesis may be safely considered as established.

BOOKS TO BE CONSULTED.

JOSEF SAUREN, Rector am St. Marienhospital zu Köln. "Die Lauretanische Litanei nach Ursprung, Geschichte und Inhalt dargestellt." Kempten: Kösel, 1895.

P. ANGELO DE SANTI, S.J.: "Die Lauretanische Litanei: Historisch-kritische Studie." Aus dem Italienischen von Johann Nörpel. Paderborn, Schöningh.

X

A FORGOTTEN CHAPTER OF THE SECOND SPRING

I.

"THE Second Spring!" To which of us is this name not familiar? To what English Catholic is it not the watchword of a glorious past and the harbinger of a still more glorious future? It is a word which, for over half a century, has been sweet upon our lips ever since that July 13, 1852, when the author of the phrase and the great leader of the movement first cried out before the assembled fathers at Oscott, in that most eloquent and impassioned of all his immortal compositions: "The English Church was, and the English Church was not, and the English Church is once again. This is the portent, worthy of a cry. It is the coming in of a Second Spring; it is a restoration in the moral world, such as that which yearly takes place in the physical."

The story is one that has often been told, and will often be told again, because we Catholics cannot easily weary of its repetition. It is one which makes the heart beat quicker with joy and gratitude at the great things which have been done for us by "Him, who is mighty, and blessed is His name."

It is perhaps not too much to say that in the popular mind, and very likely in our own minds, the so-called "Oxford Movement" is more or less identified with that other great spiritual phenomenon just alluded to as the Second Spring—that is to say, the marvellous revival, growth, and development of the Catholic Church in England during the last fifty years of our century. True it is, indeed, that the mighty stirring of the mind and heart of religious England in its old ancestral seat of learning has played an all-important—one is almost tempted to say a preponderating—part in the life of the Catholic Church in this country. It has given to us our greatest leaders in Newman and in Manning; it has given to us many of our chief thinkers and writers in men like Ward and Dalgairns, St. John and Bowden, Ryder and Bellasis, Harper and Coleridge, Allies and Lockhart, and a legion of others; and it is the prestige, both religious, intellectual, and social, of their names that has so greatly elevated our position before the English people. It is, again, the intellectual stimulus which proceeded from this Oxford School that has gone far to vivify the intelligence and to create the literature of modern Catholic England. All this is true, and my summary of the influence of the Oxford Movement upon our Second Spring is, if anything, too weakly expressed.

But I venture to submit, and the object of this paper is to show, that the Oxford Movement was after all but one chapter, however glorious a one, of a complete history. The influence of the Oxford Movement was an influence *external* to the Catholic Church, a movement primarily in the bosom of the Anglican Establishment, working therein with an effect at once elevating and disintegrating, and, as its final result, bringing over to the Catholic Church so much of what was noblest and best of Anglican intellect and heart. But I wish to show that the modern revival of Catholicity has not been the exclusive outcome of this mighty influence from outside. There are other chapters in the history scarcely, if at all, less worthy of record. To take an example which will occur to every mind—a very important share in the resuscitation of Catholic life and practice, and in the multiplication of both clergy and laity, must be attributed to the great stream of immigration from Catholic Ireland, consequent upon the famine and disease which in 1846, 1847, and following years drove so many poor, yet staunch, Catholics to these shores and spread them all over the country.

There is yet another chapter, one less known, or more frequently forgotten, in the history of our Second Spring, and it is the one which I have chosen as the subject of my present paper. It is a revival of Catholic faith and practice in the very midst of the Catholics of this country themselves; itself, the effect of what, to borrow the pet phrase of a late Archbishop of Canterbury, was in very truth literally an "Italian Mission." And it may be doubted whether, without this internal revival, preparing the way for other and more external influences, even such a vital force as that of the Oxford Movement would have been able to produce the far-reaching effects which are attributed to it.

As in all great movements of the human mind, under the providence of God, the history of spiritual phenomena affecting peoples, or even society at large, is generally intimately bound up with the life-history of certain chosen individuals. This has been true on a grand scale in the great internal reformation of the Church in the twelfth century, so intimately connected with the spiritual history of a Francis and a Dominic. This is true, if on a smaller scale, yet with no less intensity, of the Oxford Movement, so inextricably bound up with the intellectual and spiritual development of John Henry Newman. And it is also true, once more, in the history of that other chapter of the Second Spring, with which I am concerned at present. It is for this reason that I must begin my narrative by carrying the reader back to one or two biographical details concerning men whose names are no doubt much less familiar, but scarcely less worthy of our interest.

II.

In the year 1797, four years before the birth of John Henry Newman, there was born in the town of Rovereto, in the Italian Tyrol, the last heir to an ancient and noble family, Antonio Rosmini Serbati, of whom Cardinal Wiseman once predicted that he would one day be ranked with St. Augustine and St. Thomas Aquinas among the most luminous intelligences that this world has produced.* It is, I think, an unfortunate circumstance that the name of this most saintly and most gifted priest is scarcely, if at all, remembered except in connection with certain hotly disputed philosophical tenets and controversies, which too often have been as acrimonious as they are abstruse. Great, however, as was the philosophical acumen of this remarkable man—we have already seen Wiseman's opinion of him—great as has been the part played in the schools by many of his philosophical tenets, high as is the place which he has conquered as a thinker in the estimation even of non-Catholic philosophers of our time—I venture to think that his place in the history of the Catholic Church ought to be marked, not so much by all this, as by his life, which was that of a saint, and by his work, which was that of a founder of a religious society. That society, so true to the spirit of its founder and of its name, so unobtrusive and yet so unfailing in its operations, so justly endeared to those who know it, is the Institute of Charity. It would be impossible here to narrate the history of this foundation, which dates from the years 1827 and 1828. It was a work, not of any sudden precipitation, but rather one which seemed to have been forced upon Rosmini by the over-ruling of Divine Providence. The Institute, as its name indicates, is a society destined to carry out the great work of Divine charity in the

* "Life of Antonio Rosmini Serbati." By William Lockhart. Vol. i., p. 316. London, 1886.

broadest possible manner, and in every way which Providence may open to its members. "The rules and constitutions," says Rosmini's biographer—himself the very first fruit of the Oxford Movement—"of the Institute of Charity as they were formed by the founder and sanctioned by the Church, have this one end in view, to *undertake nothing* beyond the sanctification of our own soul, to *refuse nothing* to which the voice of God's Providence may call us, for this on receiving God's call becomes an element in our own sanctification."* Again Rosmini wrote: "It is necessary to reflect that the Institute is by its nature, as it were, a connecting link between the regular and the secular clergy; hence it requires, on the one part to retain all that forms the essence of the religious state in accordance with the Evangelical and Apostolic teaching, and on the other part to approach to the secular clergy in what is not of the essence of the religious state. Only in this way can it attain its end, which is the exercise of universal charity. By acting in this way I think it will be able to serve God and the Church better, and to render itself a subsidiary body, ready to serve humbly and willingly, as well the regular clergy, with which it has in common the profession of the Evangelical Counsels, as the secular clergy, of which it retains the external form. The Institute desires to be the servant of all, that it may be found of use to all."†

True to the principles here laid down, the Institute of Charity has never ceased to carry out, both in Italy and beyond her borders, works of active charity of every possible kind, at the request of and in co-operation with the Bishops and clergy. Among such works may be enumerated the giving of retreats, the preaching of public missions, the care of parishes, the education of youth, the training of the clergy, the direction of orphanages and industrial schools, the cultivation of

* Lockhart, *ut sup.*, vol. ii., p. 176.
† Lockhart, *ut sup.*, vol. i., pp. 303, 304.

Catholic literature—in a word every form of religious activity demanded by the circumstances of time and place. And it would not be easy to over-estimate the enormous influence in the revival of Catholic life, especially in the North of Italy, which is owing to the action of Rosmini and his Institute. It is now time to say something of the like influence in our own country.

III.

The religious condition of England has never ceased to be a subject of intense interest and sympathy to great and holy souls during the past three centuries. Who does not remember the absorbing devotion of the great St. Paul of the Cross for prayer for the conversion of England, which made him declare that he could never offer up Mass without praying for it, and which was actually one of the determining factors in the establishment of his Congregation of the Passionists? And so Antonio Rosmini was similarly impressed from the beginning with this deep interest in the religious future of the English people. "For the restoration," he writes, "of this, once an island of saints, to the bosom of the Church, I would willingly shed my blood." And though he was never destined to take any personal part in the great work, nor even to touch upon the English shores, Providence so disposed events that, next to Italy, England became the chief scene of the labours of his children. And this leads me to introduce another remarkable character.

On July 14, 1801, and therefore just half a year later than Newman, was born in Rome Aloysius Gentili. Highly gifted by nature, a born poet and an accomplished musician, with a taste for mechanical and electrical science, devoted to the cultivation of modern languages—his was, indeed, an attractive personality. His early life was that of a brilliant young man of the world, full of ambition of a nobler kind, a pet of society, an evident favourite of fortune. His biographer thus describes him at the moment when he seemed to be reaching the zenith of his success: "He was tall and well made in person, without being corpulent, of noble appearance and dignified bearing, his hair was shiningly black, and his complexion fair though somewhat pale, with blue piercing eyes; his voice also was sonorous and agreeable. Besides the advantage of a prepossessing exterior, he was gifted with a retentive memory, a clear understanding, a lively imagination, and a natural eloquence. In addition to his accomplishments in jurisprudence, literature, and other liberal arts and sciences, he was doctor, advocate, professor, and knight. At the same time, he was in good pecuniary circumstances, and in communication with a large circle of aristocratic friends and acquaintances."*

The story of his vocation, and especially of his attraction to the English Mission, is a romantic one. I have above referred to his delight in the study of modern languages, and among these he was especially fond of English. He much frequented English society in Rome, and was a well-known and welcome guest therein. Fr. Lockhart relates how a Protestant relative of his own, years after, on reading the name of Fr. Gentili as a great Catholic preacher in the English newspapers, exclaimed: "Can this be that Luigi Gentili with whom we used to sing duets in Rome?" One of his most esteemed poems was an elegy on the death of a young English lady of high family, Miss Bathurst, who, riding with the French Ambassador along the banks of the Tiber, was thrown by her restive horse into the river and drowned. Gentili's constant intercourse with the English colony in Rome was rudely ended. He formed a romantic attachment for a young English lady of very high rank and great fortune, and the attachment would appear to have been mutual, but his hopes were sternly

* "Life of Aloysius Gentili." By Fr. Pagani, p. 14. London, 1851.

cut short by the lady's parents, who, in order to put an end for ever to his aspirations, immediately sent their daughter back to England. The blow was a severe one to a temperament like Gentili's. It finally shattered the whole fabric of his worldly hopes and ambitions. But, in reality, the disappointment was an act of Divine Providence, which led him to see the vanity of all dreams of earthly happiness. At first he was missed, but very soon forgotten, in English society in Rome. The shock had brought on a severe illness, and his first step on recovery was to seek admission in the Society of Jesus. He would have been accepted, for he was greatly beloved by the fathers of whom he had been a pupil, but his health seemed broken, and the Society did not venture to receive him. All this time he was becoming more and more impressed with the conviction that God called him to the priesthood, and to labour for the conversion of England. And so it was. Providence once more led him to make the acquaintance of Fr. Rosmini, who, at his earnest entreaty, accepted him as a postulant of the newly-founded Institute. He remained in Rome, attending theological lectures, whilst residing at the Irish College, in order, at the same time, to improve his English, and after his ordination to the priesthood in 1830, proceeded to Domodossola to make his noviciate. Whilst Gentili was living at the Irish College, a young English gentleman, who had been converted whilst a student at Cambridge, arrived in Rome. This was Mr. Ambrose Phillips de Lisle, eldest son of the Squire of Garendon and Grace Dieu Manor in Leicestershire. This zealous convert applied to the rector of the Irish College to obtain for him a priest to preach the Catholic faith in the neighbourhood of his ancestral home. The rector, whilst offering Holy Mass, felt inwardly moved to suggest the Abate Gentili as in every way suited to the purpose. This led to a great friendship between the young priest and Mr. de Lisle, the submission of the whole project to Rosmini, and eventually to the coming of the Father to this country in 1835.* A word may here be said of the state of things in England at their arrival, and I will venture to quote a passage of Fr. Lockhart, which sketches the situation better than I can pretend to do: "They came at a very critical time in the religious history of England. Great religious changes have taken place through means of many providential agencies during the fifty years that have passed since their landing. They came just six years after the passing of the Roman Catholic Emancipation Act. This, in granting political freedom and equality with their fellow-subjects to the Catholics, and especially to Catholic Ireland, had practically swept away all that remained on the Statute Book of the Penal Laws against the Catholic religion. The religious persecution had gradually died out; it had long ceased to be exile or death for a priest to minister in England, Scotland, and Ireland. The fines and imprisonment for not attending the services of the Established Church had impoverished the Catholic nobility and gentry, and made the practice of their religion by the poor nearly impossible; but these fines, after two hundred years, had long ceased to be exacted. These changes had resulted from the gradual working of public opinion, and partly from Catholics having become socially insignificant. Before the passing of the Emancipation Act Catholics were excluded by law from all political power; no Catholic Peer could take his seat in the House of Lords; no Catholic could be a member of the House of Commons. For nearly three hundred years the Catholics, even the upper classes, had been almost entirely secluded from general society. They lived in their country seats, almost unknown except to their own tenants and to a few of their more immediate neighbours. The penal laws had been in various ways, of studied purpose, socially degrading. For instance,

* Not without strong opposition in some quarters in England; see "Life and Letters of Ambrose Phillips de Lisle," by Edwin de Lisle, vol. i., pp. 105-110 (London, 1900).

if a Catholic had a horse of more than £5 in value, any Protestant could tender that sum and take the horse.

"The only Catholic places of worship in the country were the domestic chapels attached to Catholic gentlemen's houses, except in some wild parts of Lancashire, Yorkshire, Scotland, and a few other out-of-the-way places, where, as in Ireland, the faith of the people in the Old Religion had never died out. The externals of religion, however, had been reduced to the minimum. In towns the Catholic chapel was always an unpretending building in one of the back streets. In London and other large cities and principal towns some larger Catholic chapels—for they were never then called churches—had been built externally of the style and appearance of Dissenting Meeting Houses, though within exhibiting somewhat of the seemly adornment belonging to Catholic worship.

"The non-Catholic population of England consisted of the members of the Anglican or Established Church, and of the Protestant Dissenters, who were very numerous. The older sects were chiefly the Independents, Baptists, Quakers, and Unitarians. The Established Church had never had much hold on the masses, who would probably have remained Catholics if there had been priests to instruct them, and during the eighteenth century it had fallen into a state of deep religious lethargy. Many of the higher clergy and educated laity were rather mere Socinian Rationalists than Orthodox Christians. About the middle of the eighteenth century a great revival of religious earnestness and belief in the Christian doctrines had begun in the Anglican Church, originated by John Wesley, whose followers, however, withdrew from the Church of England, where they were generally discountenanced and opposed, and formed the large body of modern Dissenters known as Wesleyans or Methodists."*

Such was the England into which Gentili and his companions were sent by Rosmini in 1835.

* "Life of Rosmini," vol. ii., pp. 91-94.

IV.

It may be useful at this point to recall one or two synchronisms between our story, as told so far, and the movement known as the "Oxford Movement," which had been going on meanwhile in the bosom of the Anglican establishment. In 1823 John Henry Newman entered Oriel; the same year Antonio Rosmini first went to Rome; in 1827 Rosmini first received the "Manifestation of Providence," which decided his life-work, the foundation of his Institute; the same year Newman says of himself: "I was rudely awakened from my dream by two great blows—illness and bereavement," and as Tutor of Oriel and Vicar of St. Mary's first "came out of his shell." In 1830 the Institute of Charity began its career at Domodossola, and three years later (in 1833) Newman began his "Tracts for the Times," and ever afterwards looked upon that year as the beginning of the Tractarian Movement.* The year of the coming of the Fathers of Charity, 1835, occurred in the very midst of Newman's Oxford greatness and the busy working out of his theory of the "Via Media." At such a moment the two providential streams of agency, the one from without, the other from within the Church, met on English soil.

It was not merely the invitation of Mr. Phillips de Lisle that brought the Rosminians to England. In the meantime one of the Vicars Apostolic, Bishop Baines, who then ruled over the Western District, having his residence at Bath, had sought to obtain the services of the Fathers for his College of Prior Park. Though Rosmini gave his consent as early as 1831, the period of preparation for the English Mission was a long one; for the little band did not sail from Cività Vecchia till May 22, 1835. They set forth with a more personal blessing and mission from the Holy See than even St. Augustine and his companions received

* Apologia, p. 35.

from St. Gregory the Great, for Pope Gregory XVI. actually came on board the vessel and blessed the three "Italian missioners" just before they sailed—probably a unique event in missionary history!

It is worth while to quote here some of the directions given by Fr. Rosmini to these his first foreign missionaries. Thus he writes to them:

"Do everything in your power to comply with the Bishop's desires, preferring them to charitable works of supererogation.

"You should behave towards the secular clergy in such a way that there may not appear any systematic division between you and them.

"You must be intimately persuaded that the Institute does not seek to aggrandize itself, or to attract public attention; nay, rather let it be obscure, and even cease to exist, if it can thereby contribute to the glory of God. On which account be on your guard against mentioning the Institute without necessity or a reasonable cause, and endeavour to impress this characteristic spirit of lowliness on the minds of your companions.

"I recommend you all three to conform yourselves to the English ways in all things where there is no wrong, putting in practice the words of St. Paul: 'I am made all things to all men.' Do not raise objection to anything in which there is no sin. Each nation has its customs which are good in its own eyes. You should conform yourselves to the customs of those people among whom you are, which should be good in the eyes of your charity. To be too much attached to Italian, Roman, or French customs is no small defect in the servant of God, whose true country is Heaven."*

Golden words, breathing the true Apostolic spirit, and such, it is a pleasure to add, as have always been loyally carried out in all the actions of the Institute of Charity in our midst during the past seventy-five years of its history.

* Pagani, pp. 136-138; Lockhart, vol. ii., p. 90.

We have an amusing record of Gentili's first impressions of London, where they arrived on June 15.

"We seemed," he writes in a letter, "to be really entering the city of Pluto: black houses, a black sky, black shipping, and black-looking sailors—filthy to an extreme degree. The waters of the Thames were tinged with a colour between black and yellow, and emitted a stench highly offensive. On land there prevailed a confused noise, with horses, carriages, and men of every condition, running and crossing each other's path; in fine, to make a long story short, here the devil is seen enthroned, exercising his tyrannical sway over wretched mortals."*

No time was lost in getting to work. A few days later Gentili preached his first sermon in England at Trelawney House, in Cornwall, whither they had been invited by Sir Henry Trelawney, Bart., a zealous convert. He took for his text, "Thou art Peter, and upon this rock I will build My Church," and his discourse made a remarkable impression upon the many Protestants who came to hear it.

Soon after, the missionaries were settled at Prior Park, where early in the following year (1836) Gentili gave a retreat to the whole College; and this was one of the first, if not the first, public retreat according to the method of St. Ignatius, ever given in a secular college in England. For this reason it excited among some good souls no little criticism and opposition as a "novelty!" For two years Gentili was actually made President of Prior Park; but Bishop Baines' plan of combining secular and regular professors in his staff was an ill-advised one, and eventually led to the only possible result—viz., the entire withdrawal of the Fathers from Prior Park College. And this step left them free to devote their energies and their increasing numbers to the real work for which they came—preaching the Faith to the English people.

* Pagani, p. 143.

In 1840 was opened the missionary settlement at Grace Dieu, the seat of Mr. Phillips de Lisle, from which as a centre they evangelized much of the surrounding country, especially Belton, Osgathorpe, and Shepshed,* the total population of which region was reckoned at 6,000, of whom only twenty-seven were Catholics—eight being children, three invalids, and the whole of them poverty-stricken.

Notwithstanding these unpromising surroundings—notwithstanding the bitter hostility of the neighbouring ministers, and Gentili's being publicly burnt in effigy—his ceaseless labours were rewarded in a space of some two years by the reception of sixty-one adult converts, the baptism of sixty-six children under seven, and of twenty other children conditionally, crowned by the conversion of an Anglican clergyman, Rev. Francis Wackerbarth. These consoling fruits were secured by really incessant toil, daily instructions, visits, and religious services of every kind, sometimes in inns, or hired rooms, at others in a poor cottage, or even in the open air. The days of Augustine and his companions had returned amid a Saxon population.

In the meantime the numbers of the Fathers had much grown. Among the Italians are now to be mentioned FF. Pagani, Rinolfi,† and Signini; whilst some Englishmen had joined their ranks, notably the afterwards celebrated Fr. Furlong and Fr. Hutton.

In 1841, the Fathers undertook the important Mission of Loughborough, in Leicestershire, long their chief centre and novitiate.

In 1842 Gentili visited Oxford. It is probable, but

* See "Life and Letters of De Lisle," vol. i., pp. 110, 111.

† Fr. Rinolfi became one of the chief and most famous of the "Itinerant Missioners" after the death of Gentili. For twenty years he was one of the most remarkable English-speaking preachers. His command of the language was perfect; his eloquence, grace of gesture, power of diction, and cogency of argument made him a model of preachers—his zeal made him a perfect Apostle.

not certain, that he met Newman, who by this time had retired to Littlemore, where he was living a kind of monastic life with a few followers. I have met with the statement that Newman's first acquaintance with a Catholic priest was with one of the Fathers of Charity, whom he met on the outside of a stage-coach somewhere about this date, but I cannot, unfortunately, find the reference at present. At any rate, whether Gentili and Newman met at Oxford or not, the visit had important consequences. Gentili *did* meet one of Newman's chief and best beloved followers, William Lockhart, a young Scotch graduate. The result was that in the August of the following year, " Mr. Lockhart, feeling it impossible to resist his conviction that the Anglican Church had fallen into fatal schism in separating from the Holy See, came to visit Fr. Gentili at Loughborough, in whose holiness and learning he had conceived great confidence from the few hours he had spent in his company at Oxford. After making a few days' retreat under him in the chapel-house at Loughborough, he was received into the Catholic Church, and a little later, entered as a postulant of the Order,"*—of which, let me add, he eventually became one of the most distinguished ornaments. This conversion was the very first fruit of the Oxford Movement, preceding as it did the reception of the great leader himself by no less than two years; and it is pleasant to think that it was a Father of Charity, a disciple of Rosmini, who had the great privilege of culling this first ripe fruit of the Second Spring. In Lockhart the two spiritual schools met for the first time, and the favoured disciple of Newman became the favoured disciple of Rosmini.

But this same year—1843—will be for ever memorable in English Church history for the introduction into our spiritual life, by the Fathers of Charity, of four great and potent factors which have done so much to vivify faith and piety. These four works—it may come as

* Lockhart, vol. ii., p. 104.

a surprise to some of my readers to learn—were: (1) The preaching of popular *Missions*; (2) the ceremony of the *Renewal of Baptismal Vows*; (3) the *Quarant' Ore*, or Forty Hours' Exposition of the Blessed Sacrament; and (4) the devotions of the *Month of May*.* Looking back, it appears to us as if religious life must have been almost torpid without these now familiar works of devotion and charity.

The first public Mission was given at Loughborough by FF. Gentili and Furlong, and had an extraordinary success. Sixty-three converts were instructed and received at it.

From this time forward, the work of the Fathers takes a new and far wider development. Great public missions all over the country, whose stirring effects recall the days of SS. Francis and Dominic, alternate with innumerable spiritual retreats to colleges and communities for the next five years. It would be quite impossible to narrate in detail the events of those wonderful five years. It was a stirring up of the mind and heart of the Catholics of England, and a gathering into the net of converts from Protestantism, on a scale which astonishes us as we read of it at this distance of half a century. There is a sameness about these never-ending missions and retreats which will dispense me from doing more than give a mere catalogue, year by year, of the principal ones among them, so that some idea may be gained, however imperfect, of the marvellous "outpouring of Divine grace" that was going on throughout the land during these few years—in the very midst of which period, by the way, John Henry Newman was received into the Catholic Church (October 9, 1845) by the holy Italian Passionist, Fr. Dominic. This same year FF. Gentili and Furlong were, at the request of several Bishops, formally set apart, like Paul and Barnabas, as "Itinerant Missionaries," to be exclusively employed

* A minor innovation, also owing to the Fathers, was the use of the *Roman Collar* by the clergy.

in travelling from place to place, and preaching the Word of God, after the manner of such missionaries in Italy. They were thus the very first Evangelical labourers, whether native or foreign, ever officially deputed to this high office in England since she lost the faith.*

Some idea may be given of their labours and zeal from what has been recorded of various great public missions. They usually gave four or five discourses daily at fixed intervals, taking the sermons alternately, treating both dogmatic and moral Gospel doctrines, especially the Great Truths—the Mystery of the Redemption, the Divine Precepts, the Life of our Lord. And the whole of the time intervening between the discourses was devoted to the arduous work of the confessional. So great usually was the concourse of penitents that the Fathers were kept occupied for eight or ten hours a day. Sometimes they even remained in church all night long hearing confessions, and had absolutely no time either to say Mass or recite the Divine office, much less take any sleep or any nourishment, except in a hasty manner. Such wearisome labours were not interrupted, but only varied, for weeks and even months together. They had to prepare children for their First Communion, instruct converts, restore peace in families, see to the restoration of ill-gotten goods. They also introduced processions, evening benedictions, and other solemn functions at the close of missions.† Fr. Gentili himself, in one of his letters, gives a picture of the scene in certain churches during these missions. He tells us how the secular clergy often organized a sort of "clerical guard," to prevent the too great pressure of the crowd; "for it has often happened to see the church so crammed with people as to make it difficult to effect an entrance. Of those who

* Pagani, p. 217.

† These multifarious labours are all the more astonishing when we reflect that Fr. Gentili always abstained from the use of both flesh-meat and wine.

succeeded, some were kept standing or seated for several hours of the day or night, without being able to move, while waiting their turn to confess. On the day of general Communion, for which preparation was made by appropriate meditation and hymns, the number that presented themselves at the Eucharistic table was so great that it was puzzling to guess from whence they all came."*

V.

I will now give the chronological catalogue I have spoken of above, omitting the missions at less known or unimportant towns:

1844.—Mission at Coventry, at which took place the first public procession with a statue of Our Lady that occurred in England for 300 years. This caused a great sensation; it was specially arranged by way of protest against the "Lady Godiva" procession, which at that time seems to have been carried out in a highly indelicate, if not indecent, manner.

Same year, missions at Whitwick, Liverpool, Banbury, Grantham; retreat for students at Ushaw College.

1845.—Retreat at Old Hall College, Ware. Missions at Hull, Leeds, Sheffield, Leamington, Newport, Huddersfield, Bradford, Coventry; clergy and other retreats at Ware, Oscott, Ushaw, Liverpool. First appearance in Manchester and Dublin (charity sermons). More public missions at Leicester, Worksop, Birmingham, York, Malton, Scarborough, Whitby, Egton Bridge, Newcastle, at which latter place no less than 250 adult Protestants were received into the Church.

1846.—Missions at Sunderland, Durham, Middlesbrough, St. Augustine's (Manchester), Newport, Nottingham, Egton Bridge, London, Dublin, St. Wilfrid's and St. Patrick's (Manchester), Seel Street (Liverpool), London again. Of the Manchester missions I shall give

* Pagani, p. 221.

some details just now. Meanwhile, I am glad to quote a few reminiscences of the Seel Street mission, Liverpool, from a correspondent,* who wrote under date October 17, 1894:

"I cannot give you many particulars, but the mission created a great sensation at the time. Gentili was a spare, mortified-looking man; he spoke broken English, rather difficult to understand till you got accustomed to it. The style of preaching was novel and very impressive. At times there was some humour in it, especially when he spoke of dishonest dealings by tradespeople and various forms of cheating, or pointed to the ladies' grand bonnets as the outcome of some of this dishonesty. The mission was very popular. Even at five o'clock morning service I have seen the church crammed, whilst in the evening the people were actually standing on the broad window-ledges inside the church. I remember, too, we had to fast rigorously for three days, and so much impressed was I by the mission that I really *did* fast in the strictest sense, taking but one meal a day, and made my brother do likewise. At the end of the three days we were both famished, and glad even of a crust of dry bread."

I quote this letter, the writer of which was a young man of about twenty-three at the time, to give some idea of the enormous enthusiasm aroused by Gentili and his co-workers at this period.

1847.—Missions at Cheadle (Staffs.), North Shields, Stockton, Hartlepool, London, Darlington, Preston (where eighty-two Protestants were converted). Another retreat at Ushaw College. Missions in Dublin, St. Chad's, Manchester (sixty-one Protestants converted), Bristol, Huddersfield.

1848.—Mission at Bristol and Bath, the number of Protestants converted at the two being over a hundred; in Dublin, where, in spite of the political excitement of that year, the confessionals were so crowded that the

* My father the late Mr. J. Casartelli.

Fathers often sat there without a break from the last instruction at night till the Mass on the following morning. But a sad and altogether unexpected blow brought to a sudden end the labours of this great mission. Fr. Gentili, the pioneer missioner, was suddenly seized with a fatal fever, and after only a few days' illness passed to his reward on September 26, 1848, amid the lamentations of the whole of that great Catholic city. His mortal remains still repose in Glasnevin Cemetery.

So ended a saintly and brilliant career, one that has left its mark deeply upon the religious life of this country, one to which we all owe much more than we are probably aware of. I cannot leave him without quoting just a few sentences from the splendid panegyric which appeared in the *Tablet* of that time from the pen of Lucas himself. They will give some idea of the impression created by his work upon the most intelligent observers of the time.

"The life of Dr. Gentili, with his brethren, marks an era in the history of this corner of the Church. . . . We think of twelve hundred years ago, when another idolatry profaned this island; when the faith of Christ was not known here; when the spiritual empire of St. Peter included not this island in its embrace. . . . and when from a distant shore 'Augustine and his companions, being as it is reported nearly forty men,' hallowed the Isle of Thanet with their footprints, and planted the Christian mysteries among a barbarous and untaught people. What then took place among us is now beginning to be repeated. . . . The fulness of time has come upon us, and God once more sends us the heralds of His faith from the same land, across the same mountains, from the same city, from the same See, from a Pope bearing the name and swelling with the thoughts of him who twelve hundred years ago laid the first stones of the English Apostolate."

Further on Lucas speaks of the manner and method

of these new Italian missioners as being addressed to the *people* in the literal sense of the term:

"From the beginning the members of his Order have spoken to the people; have endeavoured above all things to reach the heart of the masses; consciously or unconsciously have spoken to the sympathies of the poor, not as absolving them from the law and necessary restraint, but as raising them up to the dignity of law, and freeing them from all other fear." Elsewhere he speaks of Gentili as possessing "an influence such as we remember to have been enjoyed by no preacher in this country, in our time, or as far back as our inquiries extend."

If this language seems exaggerated to us at the present day, we must remember that for many years we have been accustomed by constant experience to great missions preached by Redemptorists, Passionists, Franciscans, Dominicans, Jesuits, members of all religious orders, and of the secular clergy; so that they do not now appear very extraordinary events. The month of May, frequent Benediction of the Blessed Sacrament, the Quarant' Ore, have actually passed into our traditions, and we can scarcely imagine a time when they were not ordinary phenomena of our religious life. It was far different in the early forties: the Fathers of Charity were real pioneers in all these works, and the very novelty of them explains much of the enthusiasm they awakened, and of the profound impression they created in both the Catholic and the Protestant public.

With the death of Gentili I must close this chapter of history. Not that the work of his Institute was at an end. By no means. The work of the itinerant missions was taken up by others, and carried on for years. Chief among these ought to be mentioned his inseparable companion—already often referred to—Fr. Furlong, of whom a few additional words must in justice be said here. Fr. Furlong was born of Irish parents in 1809, and was baptized by the name of

Moses.* From his very childhood he was remarkable for a spirit of piety and prayer. At the age of fifteen he was sent to the Benedictine College of Ampleforth, where his excellent progress in study was surpassed only by that which he made in piety and the love of God. After spending some seven years at Ampleforth, he accompanied Bishop Baines to his newly-established college at Prior Park, where he was in due time ordained priest. Shortly after his ordination he was appointed president of St. Peter's College, and it was during his presidentship that he formed an intimacy with the Fathers of Charity which ultimately led him to join the Institute, as has been already stated.

As a religious Fr. Furlong was conspicuous for his spirit of humility, obedience, and self-sacrifice—virtues which, joined to the great natural gifts of a commanding presence, a clear, musical, and sonorous voice, and a captivating eloquence, eminently qualified him for the office of itinerant missioner, and he was held in such high esteem by the venerated founder of the Institute that, a little before he went to his reward, he wished that Fr. Furlong should be summoned to Italy in order to take an active part in the election of his successor.

One of his brothers in religion, Fr. Caccia, thus wrote of him: "After the death of Fr. Gentili in 1848, Fr. Furlong remained at the head of the itinerant missioners, and was assisted by other fathers of the Institute. He had not the depth of learning that Fr. Gentili had, but the good nature that shone in his countenance, the ardent charity that burned within him, his nationality, common with that of his auditory, had a great influence in Ireland, which was especially the scene of these triumphs of evangelical charity. His gestures, so majestic and spontaneous and yet so natural, the perfect harmony of his voice at all times, whether

* His father wished him to be christened "Mogue," after the patron saint of Wexford, but the priest not understanding, or not recognising the name, called him "Moses."

raised to terrify or lowered to entreat, were so many gifts which were irresistible. Young barristers who were preparing for public law cases at the Assizes, Members of Parliament and of the theatrical profession, flocked to hear and see him, many of whom were drawn to follow the truth which they at first despised, but which the preacher convinced them of by his powerful and captivating eloquence."

Worn out with his great and wonderful labours this zealous missioner and holy religious was called to his reward October 29, 1871. The two last years of his life were passed in retirement at Rugby and Ratcliffe, and he died at the latter house a calm and peaceful death.

Other works that had been begun during Gentili's lifetime by his colleagues still went on, and developed. The Fathers opened permanent missions, and undertook parochial work in several towns, particularly in Rugby, Cardiff, and London. They opened Ratcliffe College, near Leicester, as early as 1846, and it is still flourishing. The Reformatory School at Market Weighton, Yorkshire, and the Industrial Schools at Upton and Clonmel, in Ireland, are other evidences of their zeal and success. Lastly, they established the admirable printing press of St. William's at the Market Weighton Reformatory, which for the excellency and the beauty of the work it produces is almost unrivalled in the kingdom. It is this press which prints most of the publications of the Catholic Truth Society, and it is not by thousands, but by millions, that it reckons its annual output of the pamphlets and leaflets so familiar to us all, and which are doing such incalculable good for religion wherever the English tongue is spoken.

VI.

I cannot, however, conclude this already too lengthy paper without recurring for a moment to the missions of the Fathers of Charity in the city of Manchester in 1845 and 1846. I shall therefore make no apology for transcribing from Pagani's "Life of Father Gentili" those pages which describe these wonderful Manchester Missions, and I believe the information will come as a surprise to many of the local Catholics of the present day. Fr. Pagani writes :

"During the three missions given this year in Manchester there occurred certain events which we think not unworthy of record. With the usual solemnity, on February 15 the mission was first opened in the church of St. Augustine.

"The sermons of the missionaries were well attended, the number of applicants for the Sacrament of Penance increased to such a degree that fifteen confessors, assiduously engaged, scarcely sufficed for the demand. One hundred and twenty-seven Protestants abjured their errors, nearly 9,000 persons communicated, and such was the pious zeal displayed for adorning the altar of the Blessed Sacrament that more than 3,000 wax candles were, for this purpose, offered to the Church.

"The next mission, towards the end of September, was preached at St. Wilfrid's. From the commencement the number of people assembled to hear the Word of God was so great that the missionary was occasionally induced to transfer the pulpit from the church to the public square in order to address a crowd of more than 6,000 persons. The penitents were so numerous that some waited for days in the church until their turn came to enter the confessionals, and seeming, like the Biblical multitude in the wilderness, not to heed the wants of nature. This inconvenience occurred, notwithstanding that several confessors were engaged from six or seven in the morning till twelve at night, if we except the intervals necessary for their refreshment. It even happened that one of the missionaries, on leaving the pulpit in the evening, went direct to his confessional where he remained all night unceasingly occupied till five o'clock in the morning, when he was again called to the plupit to address, as usual, a meditation to the assembly. When Fr. Gentili made his concluding discourse the vast audience was so moved to compunction that the preacher's voice was almost unheard amid the sobs and sighs of the pious multitude. Immediately after the mission at St. Wilfrid's a similar course of instructions was commenced at St. Patrick's Church, situate in the most populous Catholic parish of Manchester. Fr. Gentili, however, found this the most difficult mission he ever had to conduct in his life.

* *

"The memorable mission of St. Patrick's, which began on September 27, was not concluded before November 12, having lasted nearly seven weeks. To the missionaries it proved a task replete with difficulties and trials ; but they were, however, consoled by the happy results of their labours." The number of Protestants received into the Church at this mission was 190, which, adding the 61 received the following year at St. Chad's, makes a total of 398 converts for the three churches of St. Wilfrid, St. Patrick, and St. Chad.

What more than anything else shows the wonderful success which Fr. Gentili and his companions obtained in the mission which they preached at Manchester, and especially at St. Patrick's, is the following memorial which the clergy of Manchester and Salford presented in a body to Fr. Gentili as a public testimony of their respect and gratitude to him and to his fellow labourers.

✠

A MEMORIAL

PRESENTED BY THE CLERGY OF MANCHESTER AND SALFORD

TO

THE VERY REV. DR. GENTILI,

ON OCCASION OF HIS CONCLUDING THE MISSION GIVEN BY HIM, AT ST. PATRICK'S, NOVEMBER 12, 1846.

"VERY REV. FATHER,

"Sensible of the great benefits which have resulted from the missions which you have given in Manchester and other important towns, we cannot suffer you to go from amongst us without endeavouring to acknowledge the favour which you have conferred upon us in devoting so much of your time to the spiritual welfare of the souls committed to our charge. In their names and our own we beg leave to thank you most cordially. The immense multitude of degenerate Catholics who have been reclaimed, and the still more remarkable number of converts which have been received into the Church during the exercises which you have conducted, convince us that the hand of God is with you, and that the practice of giving missions, which you have recently introduced into this country, is one of the greatest blessings which has accrued to religion in modern times.

"When we reflect on the profound learning, the practical skill, the prompt decision, and the invincible courage with which you have encountered and overcome the peculiar difficulties which surrounded the mission of St. Patrick, we feel that a still more ample tribute of admiration and gratitude is due for your charitable and most disinterested exertions.

"We are aware, Rev. Sir, that these difficulties were of no ordinary magnitude, and that consequently a more than ordinary call upon your zeal and charity has been required to overcome them. We know how forbearingly you watched the storm of rebellious opposition with which you were threatened by a party of undutiful children of the Church on the very eve of your departure from St. Wilfrid's, where the seed of the Word of God had happily fructified and brought forth an abundant harvest. We know how, notwithstanding, you repaired to St. Patrick's, and there began the work of peace and reconciliation.

"Though the people are still suffering from the effects of their own folly, yet, we hope, by the judicious counsels which you, Rev. Sir, have suggested, we may be able to complete the work of reconciliation which you have so happily begun, and that in a short time they may all return to the one fold from which they have strayed. Allow us, then, once more to express our grateful sense which we entertain for the services which you have rendered to religion, nor must we forget the brother and companion of your labours, the Rev. Fr. Furlong, who, by his powerful sermons in the various churches of Manchester and Salford and by his prudent, charitable, and patient zeal in the sacred tribunal has entitled himself to the gratitude of many, and to the love and esteem of all. May God, who ever watches over His Church, and who from time to time raises up *light amidst darkness*, still bless your united labours with abundant success. May He bestow upon you long life, that you may continue to labour for His glory, for the propagation of the Faith, the salvation of souls, and for the perfection of that crown of glory which we feel persuaded is laid up for you in His heavenly kingdom.

"In conclusion, reverend Father, we hope that your absence from us will not be long, and that amidst the fields of labour that lie before you, you will occasionally remember us, and pray that we may be strengthened and enabled to water, and to bring to perfection, the precious seed which you have sown.

"Signed,

"W. TURNER,
"JOHN RIMMER,
"THOMAS UNSWORTH, } St. Augustine's.
"ROBERT CROSKELL,
"GEO. GREEN,
"W. J. SHEEHAN. } St. Chad's.
"MATTHIAS FORMBY,
"THOMAS SMITH, } St. Mary's.
"R. B. ROSKELL,
"EDMUND CANTWELL,
"EDWARD UNSWORTH, } St. Patrick's.
"J. F. WHITTAKER,
"JOSEPH MEANEY, } St. Wilfrid's.
"JAMES BOARDMAN, St. John's."

It is interesting to note that of these fourteen signatures, representing as they do the entire Manchester and Salford clergy of sixty years ago, the first (William Turner) became, at the restoration of the hierarchy in 1851, first Bishop of Salford; another (Richard Roskell) became first Provost of Salford, and afterwards, in 1853, second Bishop of Nottingham; John Rimmer, William Sheehan, Matthias Formby, Edmund Cantwell, and James Boardman all became eventually Canons of the Salford Chapter, whilst Robert Croskell, for very many years Provost of the Salford Chapter, survived till the close of 1892.

I am privileged to add here a letter from the Venerable Provost, giving some interesting personal reminiscences of those famous Manchester missions:

"ST. MARY'S, LEVENSHULME,
"*November* 12, 1894.

"In answer to your note received this morning, I hasten to set down the little that I remember of the missionary labours of the Very Rev. Fr. Gentili in Manchester.

"The mission of Fr. Gentili was a revival and extension of the annual courses of instruction given by the Rev. Rowland Broomhead. The homely courses of instruction given for many successive years by the Father of the Mission in Manchester were attended with great fruit; and many exemplary and persevering converts to our holy religion were living when I came from college to St. Augustine's, Manchester, in the year 1835.

"Fr. Gentili was accompanied to Manchester by Fr. Furlong, who accompanied his leader regularly for some years and until his lamented death in Dublin in the full career of his missionary success. I cannot remember the exact date of the first mission given by Dr. Gentili at St. Augustine's, Manchester. Being the first mission given in that town, the excitement was great and the attendance overwhelming. The Doctor's discourses were reasoning and argumentative, and were greatly appreciated by the educated portion of the congregation. But it was not only the intellectual character of his sermons, but his very appearance was a striking sermon.

"A Reverend friend of mine observed to me that when he looked at Dr. Gentili on his presenting himself on the missionary platform, it struck him that he was one who had just come from the immediate presence of God to communicate a heavenly message to the faithful on earth. This view of the able missionary's appearance is confirmed by a circumstance that happened in the course of his first great mission in Manchester. The Doctor had appointed a Sunday afternoon for the Italians residing in Manchester to assemble in St. Augustine's Church that he might address them in their own language. The Italians came in good numbers, but with them a considerable number of English and Irish Catholics, and it was noticed that in certain portions of the Doctor's Italian address numbers of the people who did not understand a word of Italian manifested signs of the deepest emotion, which could be accounted for only by his heavenly appearance, the tones of his voice, and his impressive action.

"As an illustration of the fine thread of argument which the holy missioner pursued, he could not bear any external sounds while he was preaching. When giving a mission at St. Chad's, then recently opened, the masons were engaged in hewing stone in the yard contiguous to the church for the outward wall of the church ground, when the Doctor requested that their work should be discontinued until he had finished his discourse.

"The Doctor and his faithful companion and friend, Fr. Furlong, gave a great and protracted mission at St. Patrick's at the time that the congregation were excited to open rebellion, on account of the removal of Fr. Hearn, against the Bishop, the Right Rev. Dr. Brown, his vicar, and the clergy of Manchester. The holy missionary set himself to work to stem the torrent of violent opposition to authority by powerful preaching, and to give point and efficacy to his sermons; he imitated St. Charles Borromeo by putting on the garb of penance and humiliation to atone for the sins of the people. His zealous efforts produced a salutary effect on many who were reconciled to the Church, and returned in humility and sorrow to the practice of their religious duties.

"The learned, zealous, and most useful career of this saintly missionary was brought to a close in Dublin, to the great sorrow of thousands who held him in the greatest veneration, and his remains were honourably interred in Glasnevin Cemetery, near those of the great patriot, Daniel O'Connell.

"We may confidently trust that he has long since been crowned with unfading glory in heaven, and that his life and example will shed a salubrious influence both in England and Ireland for generations to come.

"Yours faithfully and affectionately in Christ,

"R. PROVOST CROSKELL."

My task is ended. I have tried to show that the Second Spring of the Catholic Church in England, of which we are at this day both the fruits and the witnesses, was the outcome, under God's Providence, not only of the great *external* influence, spiritual and intellectual, which radiated from Oxford, and is inseparably connected with the name and life-history of John Henry Newman, but also of a mighty *internal* operation of a spiritual and intellectual leaven, coming direct from Rome herself, and identified with the life and work of Aloysius Gentili and his brethren of the Institute of Charity.

May their name and fame long be held in affectionate veneration by the Catholics of England!

XI

THE MAKERS OF THE *DUBLIN*

"If the history of the *Dublin Review* could be written in full, we suspect it would be as interesting as the narrative of an eventful human life."

So wrote some years ago the genial and gifted editor of the *Irish Monthly*, Fr. Matthew Russell, S.J.*

"If the secret history of the *Dublin Review* were known to the public, how strange it would appear! So often on the point of sinking, yet always rescued, it looks as if Heaven regarded it propitiously."

So wrote over sixty years ago Bishop (afterwards Cardinal) Wiseman, in a letter to Dr. Charles Russell, dated from Oscott, November 9, 1844.†

Fr. Russell, S.J., above referred to, the nephew of Dr. Charles Russell, who, with Cardinal Wiseman and Daniel O'Connell, ranks as one of the "Makers of the *Dublin*," published during the years 1893-1895 a series of exceedingly interesting bibliographical articles on the history of our Review in the pages of his own excellent periodical.‡ These papers, based upon the invaluable MS. documents of his late uncle, threw a flood of light upon the early history of this Review, and especially upon the identification of a large number of writers, of whom he has been able to compile a list, in parts very complete, derived chiefly from the private memoranda of Mr. Bagshawe, the early editor, and of Mr.

* *Irish Monthly*, vol. xxxiii., p. 54, January, 1895.

† *Ibid.*, p. 56.

‡ *Irish Monthly*, vols. xxi., xxii., xxiii.

Cashel Hoey, sub-editor under Dr. Ward. These interesting and entertaining papers of Fr. Russell are indispensable for anybody wishing to undertake the bibliographical history of our Review. He most kindly allowed his own papers in the *Irish Monthly* to be laid fully under contribution for the compilation of the present article, and, moreover, generously placed at our disposal the MSS. of Cardinal Wiseman and others above referred to.

We have above mentioned the MS. material which the editor of the *Irish Monthly* had at his disposal. The first was a memorandum of Mr. Bagshawe, the early editor, concerning which Fr. Russell writes:

"Through the great kindness of Mrs. Cashel Hoey—herself so distinguished a writer in fiction and in graver departments of literature—the precious little note-book has been placed at last in my hands. It is labelled '*Dublin Review*, 1 to 104,' but, unfortunately, there are gaps in the record. Of the two quarterly parts which form a volume of the Review the first has its writers chronicled on the left-hand page, and the second on the page opposite. Except in one instance towards the end, the articles are specified only by their number, not by subjects."*

For the second series there were available, as we have said, certain memoranda of Mr. Cashel Hoey, the sub-editor. Fr. Russell continues:

"With No. 104 comes to an end the first official record of contributors which Mr. Cashel Hoey inherited from Mr. Bagshawe. As he preserved it carefully and valued it highly, it seems strange that he did not keep a similar record during the many years that he occupied a position similar to Mr. Bagshawe's in the conduct of the Review. Mrs. Cashel Hoey has been kind enough to show the same memorandum books, in which Dr. Ward's most efficient lieutenant took notes concerning the authorship of certain numbers, but apparently with

* *Irish Monthly*, vol. xxi., p. 80.

a view to the carrying out of the principle, 'The labourer is worthy of his hire.' "*

That is to say, these memoranda (very imperfect for the rest) appear to name only, or at least chiefly, those contributors to whom *honoraria* had been paid for their articles, so that gaps are of frequent occurrence in the lists. Notwithstanding their incompleteness, Fr. Russell estimates these editorial records as a "treasure-trove," and their discovery as his "greatest piece of luck" in the department of literary history. Many of the deficiencies he was able to make up from other sources: partly from Fr. Russell's own MSS., consisting, as above remarked, of valuable letters and memoranda, and partly from works since published, in which the contributions of numerous writers to the Review—such as Cardinal Wiseman, Dr. Ward, Mr. Abraham, Mr. Wilberforce, Bishop Grant, Cardinal Manning, and others—have been publicly acknowledged.

In a subsequent letter to the *Tablet* Fr. Russell added the remark: "There are several gaps in the catalogue, which may perhaps be supplied from other sources. For instance, I believe the set of the *Dublin Review* in Oscott College has the writers marked." This was a hint too important to be lost, and the present writer was enabled, through the great kindness of Mgr. Henry Parkinson, D.D., the librarian (now Rector) of Oscott College, to carefully examine the set in the splendid Oscott Library and collate it with the *Irish Monthly* lists. The result is somewhat curious. To a considerable extent the two authorities coincide. But, unfortunately, they agree also in their *lacunæ*. The Oscott volumes, at least in the earlier series, have the names of authors entered in a neat, small handwriting in the table of contents of each. So far, however, from being complete, there are no less than seven quarterly parts† in which the authors' names, though given in

* *Irish Monthly*, vol. xxi., p. 146.

† Viz., vols. xii., No. 24; xxv., No. 50; xxvi., No. 51; xxvii., No. 52; xxix., No. 58; xlii., No. 83; xlvi., No. 91.

Mr. Bagshawe's list in the *Irish Monthly*, are entirely absent in the Oscott volumes. Occasionally one or more articles left anonymous in the *Irish Monthly* are marked in the Oscott one; rarely *vice versâ*. More frequently there is a discrepancy between the two lists, and in most of these cases Fr. Russell, to whom these differences have been submitted, is inclined to consider the Oscott list the more accurate. But in spite of this, it is sufficiently clear that the two lists are *practically identical*. When the *Irish Monthly* list is silent, there the Oscott list fails us too; the volumes indexed at Oscott, with the slight exceptions recorded, just coincide with those indexed in the *Irish Monthly* lists. So that it is evident, either that one of those lists has been copied from the other, or that both are derived from some common original. Whichever be the case, it is to be feared that, unless some other MS. sources exist which have hitherto escaped our notice, data are no longer forthcoming for completing the list of authors of the original series of the Review. With the exception of a few odd articles, forty-one volumes alone of the original series have had the names of the reviewers preserved more or less completely. These names will be found appended in brackets to the table of contents of that series published in the "Jubilee" number of the *Dublin* (April, 1896), the information being derived from the several sources above enumerated. No doubt further research may tend to correct and complete this catalogue.

It had been our intention to treat in a similar manner the contents of the second, or "Ward" series. For this purpose, however, we have been able to obtain but very scanty and unsatisfactory data. Moreover, it has occurred to us that, for other reasons, it might be undesirable to unveil the anonymity of the reviewers of this series. The first series concluded early in 1863. A generation has passed since then, and for the most part the "Old Dublin Reviewers" themselves belong to history. Of the writers of the second series, on the other hand, many are still with us; and literary etiquette might in some cases make it undesirable to publish their names, at least without their own desire. With the opening of the third series the reign of the old-fashioned anonymity came to an end, and subsequently nearly all the articles have, in more modern fashion, boldly borne their authors' signatures.

After these preliminary remarks of a bibliographical nature, we may now turn to consider more strictly the history of the Review itself. In so doing, however, we shall be obliged to disappoint the reader who may expect what Cardinal Wiseman called "the secret history" of the Review. Our object is of a much less ambitious nature, and is limited to a brief sketch of what may more properly be styled "the external history" of the "historic *Dublin*," as it has been so justly called.

I.

The honour of the first inception of the *Dublin Review* is generally attributed, as we have said, to Dr. Wiseman and Daniel O'Connell. Dr. Nicholas Wiseman, at that time (1836) a young man of thirty-four, and rector of the English College in Rome, was just emerging to fame in this country by his literary and scientific attainments. During the preceding year he had read before a select audience in the apartments of Cardinal Weld in Rome his "Lectures on the Connection between Science and Revealed Religion." O'Connell was in the midst of the most exciting period of his stirring career. Strange to say, however, Cardinal Wiseman, in the preface to his "Essays on Various Subjects" (1853), assigns the honour to a third person, the first editor, Mr. Michael J. Quin, writing: "It was in 1836 that the idea of commencing a Catholic quarterly was first conceived by the late learned and excellent Mr. Quin, who applied to the illustrious O'Connell and myself to join in the undertaking."

The first quarterly part of this most important venture, "the Catholic rival to the Whig *Edinburgh*

Review and the Tory *Quarterly*," duly appeared with the date May, 1836, and has continued ever since, in spite of all dangers and difficulties, in unbroken quarterly succession up to the present time. It is curious to remark that for a good many years the appearance of the parts was by no means as regular as we should have expected. The actual month of issue was more or less unsettled; in fact, strange as it may appear, during the first dozen years of its existence there is not a single month of the year whose name does not figure on at least one or two of the quarterly issues.* Complete regularity in this matter does not seem to have been attempted until the opening of the Second Series.

The subsequent history of the Review falls into four periods: The first is that of the original series, which may be fairly styled the "Wiseman-Russell series," from the two eminent *littérateurs* to whom the lion's share of the work and the chief credit of the high literary excellence are undoubtedly due. This series, as already stated, lasted from May, 1836, to April, 1863, filling fifty-two consecutive half-yearly volumes. The "New Series" which followed, from July, 1863, to October, 1878—occupying thirty-one half-yearly volumes, and appearing at the regular quarterly intervals, and in the months (January, April, July, and October) which have now become stereotyped—was pre-eminently the "Ward Series," during which the remarkable personality of that able and trenchant philosopher, Dr. W. G. Ward, who combined in himself the functions of both proprietor and editor, completely predominates the life-history of the *Review*, and gives to this series an individual *cachet* all its own.

The retirement of Dr. Ward, and the passing of the proprietorship into the hands of Bishop (afterwards Cardinal)

* To quote a few examples: January, 1838, 1839, 1847; February, 1840-43; March, 1844-46; April, 1837, 1838; May, 1836-39, 1840-43; June, 1844-46; July, 1836-38; August, 1839-43; September, 1844-46; October, 1837, 1838; November, 1839-42; December, 1836, 1843-45.

Vaughan, and of the editorship into those of the learned Bishop of Newport, Dr. Hedley, mark the opening of the "Third Series," on comparatively novel lines. This series embraced twenty-six half-yearly volumes, lasting from January, 1879, to October, 1891. With the passing of the editorship into the hands of Mgr. Canon James Moyes, the "Fourth Series," began with the January number of 1892, and has occupied twenty-eight half-yearly volumes. Finally, with the January of 1906, the *Dublin* once more begins what may be called a younger "Ward Series," under the editorship of the well-known and talented writer, Mr. Wilfred Ward, son of the former editor, Dr. W. G. Ward.

The choice of the title of the Review was dictated partly, we should imagine, by way of distinctive contrast with the *Edinburgh*,—the name of the Irish capital symbolising a country as essentially Catholic as that of the Scottish capital seemed suggestive of Knox and Calvinism; and partly because it was intended to appeal very largely for its support, both monetary and literary, to the Green Isle of Erin, whose verdant livery has ever been the distinctive colour of the *Dublin*, and whose national arms, with the old motto *Eíre go bráth*, in the proper Erse characters, duly figured on the cover of every number of the original series, and in smaller form in those of the second series. The Review has, indeed, from the beginning always been published in London, but the connection with Ireland was from its earliest days very close. At least one-half, oftentimes much more, of the literary matter of the original series was produced in Ireland; and Irish topics—political, social, educational, or literary—constantly occupied an important share of each quarter's bill of fare. A glance at the table of contents for the earlier years will show this. The first editor, to whom Cardinal Wiseman gives the credit of the original conception of the Review, was Mr. M. J. Quin, a native of Thurles, in Tipperary, a journalist and lawyer of some note in his time (born 1796, died

1843). He, however, edited only the first two quarterly numbers. The third number (December, 1836) was edited by the well-known historical writer, the Rev. M. A. Tierney, and the fourth and fifth (April and July, 1837) by Mr. James Smith of Edinburgh, whose son was the learned Dr. William Smith, afterwards second Archbishop of St. Andrew's and Edinburgh. With the sixth number, the young magazine at last obtained a permanent editor in the person of Mr. H. R. Bagshawe, who retained the editorial chair till the accession of Dr. Ward in 1863. The causes of this uncertainty of tenure in the editorial office were, alas! of the financial kind, which too often dog the steps of an incipient literary venture. Fr. Russell cites a rather pathetic letter of Quin to O'Connell, dated from 25, Southampton Row, Russell Square, January 2, 1837, in which he says:

"In obedience to your opinion, which to me is law, I have surrendered all claim upon the Review funds for any compensation whatever. . . . The question which now remains to be settled is this—In what mode is the Review to be henceforth continued? Its existence is a matter of great importance to religion, to Ireland, to the popular cause. It is impossible that I should edit and write without being paid. A fund should be supplied adequate to pay the editor a reasonable salary, and to remunerate contributors for their articles. Whence is this fund to proceed? This is a question necessary to be answered as soon as possible, in order that preparations should be made forthwith for the fourth number. I have no objection still to continue editor if you wish it, but I cannot give any more of my time to the journal without remuneration. In *writing* and in cash I have already advanced to the Review upwards of £300. Is it reasonable that I alone should be called upon to make such a sacrifice as this?"*

Publishers, too, were doomed to suffer from "that eternal want of pence that vexes public men." The first publisher was "William Spooner, 377, Strand." With

* *Irish Monthly*, vol. xxi., pp. 138, 139.

1838, "Booker and Dolman, 61, New Bond Street," appear on the title-page, changed next year to "C. Dolman (nephew and successor to J. Booker)," the address remaining as before. In 1845 Dolman was succeeded by Richardson and Son, and in 1862 the Richardsons by the firm at first known as "Burns and Lambert," then as "Burns, Lambert, and Oates," and finally by its present style of "Burns and Oates." Of the financial difficulties of the early years we learn a good deal from a long letter of Mr. Charles Dolman to Mr. Daniel O'Connell, M.P., dated February 11, 1839, which is among the MSS. so obligingly placed at our disposal by Fr. Russell. Dolman has most to say of the difficulties and risks of the undertaking, in which Mr. Richards (the printer) and himself "have both lost so much." "I undertook," he says in a subsequent letter (March 29, 1843), "to be responsible for the payments required to carry on the Review under the direction and editorship of Bishop Wiseman* for the period of four years, upon the assurance of support from the guarantee fund which terminated with the last year." He again complains that he has been a severe loser, and then details a new plan proposed by Dr. Wiseman, and which amounts to this—"that the writers of articles shall receive a joint interest in the Review, and will be content to receive the proceeds of the sales, after paying the printing expenses, for the remuneration.'" We also gather from these letters that O'Connell's annual contribution to the guarantee fund was £25. In a letter of December 14, 1843, Dolman, acknowledging a last instalment, thanks the great Irish statesman very warmly for his powerful aid and protection, and for having recommended the Review to the Irish clergy. He thinks that it has hitherto had but slight support from that quarter, but is "but too well aware that there has been on some occasions reasons why perhaps the Review would not (*sic*) and was not well received by them, and

* Dr. Wiseman had meanwhile been nominated Coadjutor Vicar-Apostolic, and consecrated Bishop of Melipotamus in 1840.

justly so; but I trust no such occasion will ever occur again, and that past errors being forgot and forgiven, the Review will reap the benefit of that union and support for want of which it has hitherto languished."

Daniel O'Connell long before this had published under date February 18, 1838, his lithographed letter to the Irish Bishops in favour of the Review, "of which I am one of the proprietors." He says in the document:

"The object with which this publication was instituted was and is to afford the Catholic literature of these countries a fair and legitimate mode of exhibiting itself to the people of the British Empire, and especially to the people of Ireland, in the shape most likely to produce a permanent as well as useful effect. The other quarterly publications are in the hands either of avowed and malignant enemies of Catholicity, or, what is worse, insidious and pretended friends, who affect a false liberality at the expense of Catholic doctrine.

"The *Dublin Review*, though not intended for purely polemical discussion, contains many articles of the deepest interest to the well-informed Catholic disputant. The name of Dr. Wiseman, who is also a proprietor of the work, insures the orthodoxy of the opinions contained in it, and will be admitted to be in itself a pledge of the extent, and depth, and variety of its scientific, as well as theological, information."*

O'Connell's reference to the importance of Wiseman's share in the undertaking was no whit exaggerated. The evidence of this is to be found in his constant contribution of admirable articles to the pages of the Review. These articles, of high literary merit and containing a wealth of erudition, cover a wide field ranging from theology and patristic learning to the fine arts and *belles-lettres*. Many of them are of permanent value. But over and above this, Wiseman was practically the literary editor of the Review, Bagshawe being little more than a business editor. This is abundantly proved by his correspond-

* M. F. Cusack, "The Liberator; his Life and Times," p. 643 (London, 1872).

ence with Dr. Russell, much of which lies before us as we write. He is constantly discussing the articles to be accepted or rejected, suggesting modifications, enumerating the stock in hand for forthcoming numbers, sketching projected series or individual articles, criticising, questioning, exulting, or complaining, as things go satisfactorily or the contrary. The impression left by a perusal of those letters—models, by the way, of neatness and accuracy in penmanship and composition, in spite of the almost crushing stress of official work, especially after the erection of the Hierarchy—is that the Review was Wiseman's pet child. He writes about it with the anxiety of a father for its future, his solicitude for present weakness, his joy and pride at success achieved and commendation won from strangers. We must be allowed to make a few extracts:

"I find everyone pleased with Mr. Marshall's paper ['Developments of Protestantism,' March, 1846], though long. Mr. Newman has spoken to me of it in high admiration" (Letter, April 27, 1846).

And again:

"The other day I was at the British Museum Library, when Panizzi spoke to me with great praise of your article on Hippolytus ['The Newly-found Treatise against All Heresies,' December, 1852]. He told me he had urged several of the very same objections to Mr. Bunsen. But the way he read the article was this: Cureton brought it to him, saying that Bunsen himself had given it him to peruse; he was so much pleased by the gentlemanly and scholarly tone which pervaded it, and the respect with which he was treated, all which presented such a contrast to the manner in which he had been handled in some Protestant reviews.

"From conversation with Panizzi, I am convinced that the *Dublin Review* is much more known, and exercises much more influence, than we think. Panizzi knows the old numbers and articles, and told me how he had read them to friends in the library. Let us have a good number next time" (Letter, January 30 [1853]).

Elsewhere: "I am quite overwhelmed with subjects for the *Review*."

Then comes a list of four important articles he is planning on Scripture and theology, after which he adds: "My light article I find is popular, but I fear people are attributing it to me."

(This was an amusing article in the preceding number —September, 1849—entitled "The Art of Puffing.") The very next sentence is prophetic, and shows what was going on in the minds of Wiseman and others at the time, the very year before the Hierarchy: "I have heard nothing from Rome about the Primacy, but I *fear* much" (Letter, Bexhill, October 17, 1849).

Some time before this, in a letter referring to some necessary alterations in papers contributed by some of the recent Oxford converts—Oakeley, Morris, and others —we meet the gratifying remark: "There was not the slightest difficulty in getting them all modified. Nothing can exceed the docility of our converts" (Letter, December 4, 1846). In a later letter, pleading extra pressure of business, the newly made Cardinal tells his faithful correspondent "we have been talking over plans for improving the Review and combining it with a paper" (London, December 18, 1850). But, fortunately, perhaps, the "combination" never came off. Sometimes we find him criticising the Review, and himself as well. Thus:

"The Review is not deep. It wants some more reasoning and original articles; there seems to me to be too much extract and mere analysis of works. . . . As for my own article ['The Bible in Maynooth,' September, 1852], it was written far too hurriedly, and I ran off the rails, and could not bring out what I wanted. Let us get something good for next time" (Letter, October 2, 1852).

A few months later we have the following interesting comments:

"Do you not think we are getting into too few hands?

Ward, De Morgan, Christie, Newman, Allies, etc., have written for us, and now literally we are alone with Robertson and Dr. Charlton. The rest are chiefly extract papers. Surely the convert element ought to be more cultivated. . . . I see the growing narrowness of our work, and deplore it. Never a paper on Physics, Astronomical Discoveries, Chemistry, Electricity, Steam, Railroads, Physiology, Medicine, Geology, Botany, Law Reform, not even on politics in their wider sense. Never any article on foreign countries, except the bleak North —I mean an original paper. . . . As to myself, besides Lent duties, which increase as the season advances, I am now more and more overpowered by extraneous business, which makes me feel the difference between a Bishop or V.A. and an Archbishop, especially when Cardinal" (Letter, Walthamstow, February 18, 1853).

The ever-growing pressure of business did not, however, prevent the great Cardinal either from continuing to contribute admirable articles of his own to the Review, or from following with undiminished solicitude its career. Three years later—at the very moment he was recovering "from that shabby complaint, influenza, which throws none of the dignity or sympathy of illness around one" —he finds time to indite a long epistle containing somewhat similar criticisms to those above quoted, but also adding a projected programme of topics which he conceives ought to be discussed in the pages of the Review. This syllabus is of sufficient interest to quote almost in full. It runs thus:

"IRELAND.

"1. The State Church.

"2. The Catholic representation: its discharge of its duties, etc.

"3. Education, and the efforts making to thwart and undermine ours.

"4. Proselytism: its history and condition.

"5. Maynooth; Queen's College; Universities.

"6. Land Question, Encumbered Estates Court; results of late changes in the population; emigration, colonization, etc.

"7. Agricultural and commercial industry, flax, fisheries, etc.

"ENGLAND.

"8. Progress of religion, and its wants.
"9. Infidelity: its spread and remedies.
"10. Puseyism; Dennison, etc.
"11. Charitable trusts.
"12. Political position of Catholics.
"13. Education.

"FOREIGN.

"14. English and French alliance, every day becoming a more delicate subject.

"15. Concordats; Austria, Würtenburg (*sic*), Tuscany, and Spain; perhaps Russia. (My lectures on the Concordat having been translated into Italian and German, have gone through several editions. In Austria especially they have been much read. The Pope has read them, and expressed himself much pleased.)

"16. Defence of Catholic powers from the calumnies of the press . . . .

"17. The true character of the Liberal party on the Continent; Mazzini, etc. (It is certain that all written on such subjects is read with great avidity in the clubs. Mr. Bowyer's two articles on Spain and Sardinia, for which I furnished the documents, have done much good.)

"18. The theoretical literature of the Continent. . . .

"It seems to me that such matters as come under these heads should be treated upon clear and definite principles, and every number should bring one or more before the Catholic mind so as to work it up into a clear and consistent view" (Letter, November 7, 1856).

We learn from this same letter that "the root of the evil" is still "the want of adequate means" to attract writers of talent by suitable *honoraria*. "If anything happened to Richardson we should be lost," the writer concludes.

We ought, perhaps, to apologize for these lengthy extracts, but they seem required to do justice to the illustrious prelate who was really the father of the *Dublin Review*, as well as to give an adequate impression of the high ideal, the noble aims, which inspired him during all the more than quarter of a century of his intimate connection with it.

From Wiseman's private letters we may turn to one or two articles published in the Review which convey the same lessons. In one, entitled "The Present Catholic Dangers" (December, 1856), he gives the following summary of the twenty years' life, then just completed, of the periodical:

"During the twenty years' existence of this Review, during vicissitudes and struggles not easily paralleled in the history of such publications, we believe it entitled to one commendation. It was established for an end which it has steadily kept in view. Thoroughly able and willing to sympathise with the difficulties, the traditions, the deep-worn feelings of Catholics, almost before the dawn of the brighter era of conversion, church-building, educational movement, and religious bibliopolism had appeared on the horizon, its conductors endeavoured, gently and gradually, to move forward the Catholic mind without shocking or violently drawing away or aside thoughts familiar to it, and growing side by side with its best inheritance. They avoided all the troubled waters and eddies of domestic contention; nor is it among the least of many praises due to the illustrious O'Connell, who was one of its founders, that, wrapped up as his whole external life was in politics, he consented that the new quarterly should not involve itself in their vortex, even to advocate his own views, but should steer its own course along a calmer stream, and try to bear along with it peaceful and consenting minds.

"Whatever seemed useful to forward the interests of Catholics, just released from the thraldom of ages, to suggest greater boldness, opener confession of faith, better taste, and especially greater familiarity with the resources of Catholic ritual, Catholic devotion, or Catholic feeling, was diligently studied and carried on for years with a steady purpose that did its work."*

And when the original series was just drawing to its close, in the last quarterly issue but one before it passed into other hands, and little more than a couple of years before his death, the great Cardinal, in that noble article, "Our Responsibility," the very last he ever contributed to the pages of the work with which he had so long identified himself, penned a passage of such dignity and beauty that we may well quote it, both as his own literary epitaph and as his last message and testament to those who should come after him in the conduct of his Review. It is as follows:

"From the very first number to this, every article has been written or revised under the sense of the most solemn responsibility to the Church, and to her Lord. If we have been reproached, it has been rather for severity in exclusion than for laxity in admission. Many an article has been ejected rather than rejected, even after being in type, because it was found not to accord with the high and strict principles from which its editorship has never swerved, and which it has never abated. To him who has conducted it for so many years a higher praise could scarcely be given, and by no one, we are sure, has it ever been better deserved. That occasionally an article or a passage may have crept in which did not perfectly come up to the highest standard of ecclesiastical judgment, is not only possible, but probable. Absence, hurry, pressing occupation, ill-

* O.S., vol. xli., pp. 441, 442.

health, or even inadvertence and justifiable confidence, will be sufficient to account for an occasional deviation from rule, should anyone think he detects it. If so, we are certain he will find its corrective or its rectification in some other place.

"For from first to last, as we have said, this Review has been guided by principles fixed and unalterable, and those who have conducted it have done so with the feeling that they must render an account of all that they admitted. However long may be its duration, and under whatever auspices, we are sure that the same deep, earnest, and religious sense will pervade its pages and animate its conductors, that their occupation is a sacred one, a deputation to posterity that our children's children may know how we adhered to the *true faith* of their fathers, how we bore with patience and *gentleness* the persecutions of our enemies, and how we never swerved from *justice* to friend or foe. Our motto may well be PROPTER VERITATEM, ET MANSUETUDINEM ET JUSTITIAM."*

Vast as was the share of Cardinal Wiseman in the life and success of the Review, it may be doubted whether the periodical would ever have survived its early trials but for the co-operation of that other eminent and brilliant scholar, who all through those long years was Wiseman's chief lieutenant and comrade in arms, Dr. Charles Russell, of Maynooth. From the literary point of view Dr. Russell had certainly the lion's share of the actual work. His first article (" Versions of the Scriptures "), contributed when he was a young professor of twenty-four, appeared in the second quarterly issue of the Old Series (July, 1836); his last, "The Critical History of the Sonnet," is to be found in the fifty-fourth and fifty-fifth numbers of the Second Series (October, 1876, and January, 1877). During this space of forty years Dr. Russell was the most constant and most indefatigable of contributors, and the wide range

* O.S., vol. lii., pp. 183, 184.

of the subjects treated, well characterised by the titles of his first and last papers above cited, rivalled that of Wiseman's, and gave evidence of vast erudition—the high literary skill and the versatile culture of one who may perhaps claim to have been the most gifted Catholic scholar of our times. For twenty years he contributed absolutely to every number of the Review, and before 1860 a very large number of issues contain not one, but several, papers from his prolific and graceful pen; in at least one instance he is credited with no less than five articles. His articles were no mere "pot-boilers." Very many of them were of the highest merit. We have seen Bunsen's appreciation of the one concerning himself. Another elaborate study on Lord Rosse's telescopes won him the esteem and lifelong friendship of that distinguished astronomer.

The table of contents published in 1896, imperfect as it is, will show the other eminent Catholic writers of the day who formed part of the brilliant staff gathered round Wiseman and Russell. Dr. Lingard contributed at least three articles—one on "Dodd's Church History of England" (May, 1839), one entitled "Did the Anglican Church Reform Herself?" (May, 1840), and one on "The Ancient Church of England and the Liturgy of the Anglican Church" (August, 1841). Newman, apparently, wrote but a single article for the Review, the one upon Keble's "Lyra Innocentium" in the issue of June, 1846. The learned Drs. Murray and Croly, of Maynooth, were very frequent contributors. So were Dr. Abraham, Professor Robertson, J. F. Palmer, and of course the editor, Mr. Bagshawe, besides others too numerous to cite here. One article, the first in the issue for February, 1843, is assigned in the editorial list to John, Earl of Shrewsbury. To this Fr. Russell appends the remark: "It proves to be an article of sixty-six pages on recent charges delivered by Protestant prelates, among them Henry Edward Manning, Archdeacon of Chichester. If the Earl wrote the learned article he must have been helped by his Chaplain."* The late Lord Chief Justice of England is credited with a single article, in the issue for August, 1860, on "The Civil Correspondence of Wellington." In the Oscott list this is recorded as by "Mr. Chas. A. Russell, Bar., London, nephew of Dr. Russell." The article on "Carlyle's Works," in the issue for September, 1850, which Carlyle, according to Froude, found to be "excellently serious," and conjectured to be from the pen of Dr. Ward, turns out to have been written by John O'Hagan, then a young Newry barrister of twenty-eight, afterwards Mr. Justice O'Hagan, who appears once more in July, 1873, with an article on the O'Keefe case.

A word should be said of the style of these "Old Dublin Reviewers." It partakes of the prevalent "quarterly" style of its time—grave, dignified, erudite—each article commencing with a deliberate "exordium" of more or less rhetorical character, with reflections of a very general nature sometimes *gemino ab ovo*, and occasionally rather remote from the subject in hand. The strict *Review* form is also maintained, and every article "hangs upon its own proper peg" in the form of the titles of a book or books, or even the *Times* newspaper, duly cited at its head. Our more busy times, perhaps, would be impatient of this old-fashioned and stately procedure. Yet it cannot be denied that the old *Dublins* have a charm of erudition and style all their own. "What treasures of orthodox erudition," to quote Fr. Russell once more, "contained in those old volumes . . . what labour, thought, learning, and piety of many hearts and minds are represented in this long series of half-yearly tomes!"†

The list of articles has, too, its historical value. Looked at chronologically, it represents a complete picture of the history of Catholic thought and life for the

* *Irish Monthly*, vol. xxi., p. 85.
† *Ibid.*, vols. xxi., p. 90; xxii., p. 637.

best part of the last century. Beginning almost before the first stirring of the waters of the Oxford Movement, and under the very shadow of penal days, the succeeding volumes gradually introduce us to the full strife of those intellectually stirring times, with Wiseman as the protagonist on the Catholic side. In No. 13 (August, 1839) we come, with almost a shock of glad surprise, upon the now historical article, nay, upon the very page and the very footnote (vol. vii., p. 154) of that article, of which we knew from his own words that it was the "shadow of the hand upon the wall" to John Henry Newman—the protagonist on the Anglican side—and the means in God's Providence which was to decide his future for him. That simple footnote on p. 154 contains "the palmary words of St. Augustine"—*securus judicat orbis terrarum*—which ever afterwards, Newman tells us in his "Apologia," "kept ringing in my ears," and "struck me with a power which I had never felt from words before. . . . By those great words of the ancient Father, the theory of the *Via Media* was absolutely pulverized." And, he adds, "he who has seen a ghost cannot be as if he had never seen it." If the *Dublin Review* had no other title to gratitude it might securely rest its fame on having given to the world that Article VI. of its thirteenth quarterly number, whose effect had been more far-reaching than that of any other magazine article ever written. Gradually the leaders of the Tractarian Movement, from being opponents to be fought with and convinced, come over one by one to us, and in their turn take their places in our ranks as contributors to the Review. Ward, Oakeley, and Marshall simultaneously appear together (as far as our deficient records inform us) in the March issue of 1846; the two first-named become very frequent contributors. Morris, Christie, Formby, Capes, Allies, Anderdon, Manning (December, 1854), Ffoulkes, and other converts of note gradually appear in the list side by side with the members of the older staff. Meanwhile we have come to the epoch of the Hierarchy, and the new Cardinal Archbishop himself in two consecutive numbers (December, 1850, and March, 1851) presents the Catholic view of that burning question. And similarly—space will not allow us to give further examples—all the great contemporary movements in Church and State, in education and literature, in scientific discovery and exploration, are faithfully reflected, as in a mirror, in the *Dublin's* table of contents. One could compile a history of the times from the contemporary pages of the old *Dublin* alone.

Before laying aside for good the volumes of the Original Series we may add one or two little items, rather of interest than of importance, that we have jotted down in the course of our pleasant task of examining these old tomes. Lady writers are by no means the novelty people might imagine them to be in our grave quarterly. The first paper by a lady appears as early as the fourth volume, being on "Irish Novels and Irish Novelists" (April, 1838), attributed to Mrs. Fitzsimons. This lady was a daughter of Daniel O'Connell. It is also somewhat surprising to note that the early Review was not always shy of illustrations. Plates or woodcuts adorn several articles on architecture and archæology,* as well as the one above referred to on Rosse's telescopes.† Wiseman, in his letters to Russell, several times complains of the length of articles. No wonder: in vol. xlvi., No. 92 (June, 1859) an article by Finlayson, on "The Government of the Papal States," actually occupies 125 pages. By way of contrast, the following year, in vol. xlviii., No. 96 (August, 1860), Miss St. John contents herself with a space of a little over five and a half pages for her last article. Editors must have been made of less stern stuff in those days than in ours.

But, lest we should yield to the temptation of becoming

* Vols. ix., No. 18; x., No. 20; xii., No. 23; xix., No. 37.
† Vol. xviii., No. 35.

garrulous, without the excuse of old age, we must regretfully close the venerable tomes of the "Wiseman-Russell" era, and turn our attention, though more briefly, to the series which followed.

II.

A decided alteration, both in outward appearance and in style and tendency, marks the "New Series," which began in July, 1863, with Dr. W. G. Ward as proprietor and editor, and Mr. Cashel Hoey as sub-editor. Dr. Ward's own tastes and talents very naturally impressed themselves strongly upon his Review. Metaphysics now tended to come more and more to the front in the literary menu. Dr. Ward was the chief antagonist of John Stuart Mill, and esteemed by that philosopher as the foeman best worthy of his steel. Hence much of the long metaphysical duel between those two leading minds was fought out in the pages of the *Dublin*. Three other lines of thought were also represented by Dr. Ward's own writings in the Review during this time—one regarding the Papal Infallibility, another touching the "Relations between Religion and Politics," and the third on the burning question of "Catholics and the Higher Education." In a memorial article by Cardinal Manning on the occasion of Ward's death (Third Series, October, 1882), a list is given of all Ward's contributions under these heads (pp. 268-270), to which the reader may be referred. We must remark, however, that he will find some considerable discrepancies between these lists and that compiled from the memoranda of Mr. Cashel Hoey in the *Irish Monthly* (April, 1893). Cardinal Manning, in the article referred to, writes as follows:

"What [the Review] owed to him during the sixteen years in which he was not only editor but chief contributor, and what aid, even after he had ceased to conduct it, he still gave by a constant series of philosophical writings, is well known. And yet the importance of his work is perhaps fully known only to a few who were in immediate contact with him and with the *Dublin Review*. The great success of the First Series of the *Dublin Review*, when it was sustained by the contributions of the illustrious group of men who surrounded the late Cardinal Wiseman in his early career, had, by the same order of time and nature by which we also are now deprived, begun to decline. In the year 1862 Cardinal Wiseman gave to me the legal proprietorship of the *Dublin Review* on the condition that I would insure its continuation. After certain preliminary endeavours, Mr. Ward accepted in full the responsibility of editor. He has stated that all articles passed under the judgment of three censors, who were charged to examine the bearing of them on faith, morals, and ecclesiastical prudence. From the time he undertook the office of editor, he threw himself into it as the work and way in which, as a layman, he was to serve the Church. . . . Perhaps the only other contemporaneous example of the all but identity of an editor with his periodical is *Brownson's Review*. In both cases the power of mind in the editor impressed a dominant character upon the work. This fact may have made the Review less interesting to general readers, but it greatly increased its intrinsic value. . . . The Second Series of the *Dublin Review* did not rank among literary magazines, but it fairly won and kept its place among the weightier and more serious quarterly periodicals."*

Ward himself, in what he justly styles a "personal" article, contributed to vol. viii., No. 15, of his periodical (January, 1867), in the form of a review of his own fourteen preceding numbers, defends the New Series with considerable spirit from two adverse criticisms—the one directed against "what is considered the undue preponderance given by us to theology"; the other, "that our tone is too peremptory and overbearing, that we erect our own private opinion into a kind of a shibboleth (as it has been expressed to us), and that we speak of

* N. S., vol. viii., pp. 265, 266.

those who oppose our own private views just as though they opposed the Church's authoritative teaching."* Those were, indeed, the days of hot controversy and hard hitting all round. Very warm waxed the warfare round dogmatic questions like the Vatican Council, the Papal Infallibility and its extent, the Syllabus, and religious "liberalism," and the vexed questions of Catholic colleges and the national universities. The atmosphere in which the "Ward Series" lived was therefore essentially polemical, both with regard to external foes and to internal disputants. In the concluding number of the series (October, 1878) Cardinal Manning, in a "letter" which forms the first article, gives a general approval to the line taken up by Ward in the course of these controversies. His Eminence also adds:

"In the course of this period three special subjects of great moment have been forced both by events and by anti-Catholic public opinion upon our attention—I mean the Temporal Power of the Holy See, the relations of the Spiritual and Civil Powers, and the Infallibility of the Head of the Church. In all these your vigilant and powerful writings have signally contributed to produce the unity of mind which exists among us, and a more considerate and respectful tone even in our antagonists."†

As we have said, we are not writing the "Secret History" of the *Dublin*; that is a matter to be left to a future and a more remote generation. The very wide difference of opinion, and the almost acrimonious tone of discussion which they engendered among men of the highest intellectual and spiritual excellence, have left traces both in published articles and in private correspondence. We can now afford to look back calmly on the burning domestic questions of thirty years ago, and to recognise the earnestness of purpose and conviction of the disputants on both sides.

* N. S., vol. viii., pp. 164, 167.
† N. S., vol. xxxi., pp. 275, 276.

In his reply to Cardinal Manning's gracious message, Ward, in the same number, pays a handsome tribute to his faithful lieutenant:

"It has been the chief felicity" (he says) "of my editorial lot that I have obtained the co-operation of one so eminently qualified to supply these deficiencies as Mr. Cashel Hoey. It was once said to me most truly that he has rather been joint-editor than sub-editor. One-half of the Review has been in some sense under his supreme control; and it is a matter of extreme gratification to look back at the entire harmony which has prevailed from the first between him and myself. In the various anxieties which inevitably beset me from time to time, he has invariably shown himself, not only to be a calm and sagacious adviser, but even more, to be the most cordial and sympathetic of friends."*

The staff of writers gathered around Ward and Cashel Hoey was also a very brilliant one. Dr. Russell, indeed, as we have seen, continued his active co-operation up to the beginning of 1877, as also did Dr. Murray. The latter's article—"The Vatican Council: its Authority and Work"—in the issue for January, 1873, was considered by Dr. Ward, we are told,† the best paper he had ever sent to him" during the same series. Professor St. George Mivart commenced his long critical "Examination of Herbert Spencer's Psychology," which continued its career right into the Third Series. Other writers who contributed to the series were Mr. Edward Healy Thompson, Fr. Anderdon, S.J., Fr. Coleridge, S.J., Mr. J. C. Earle, Mr. W. H. Wilberforce, Canon Oakeley, Canon (afterwards Bishop) Hedley, Fr. Roger Bede Vaughan, O.S.B. (afterwards Archbishop of Sydney), Fr. Herbert Vaughan, D.D. (the late Cardinal Archbishop), Mr. Allies, Dr. Ives (the converted Bishop of the Episcopal Church of America), Mr. David Lewis, Mr. Marshall, and, of course,

* N. S., vol. xxxi., pp. 277, 278.
† *Irish Monthly*, vol. xxi., p. 209.

both Mr. and Mrs. Cashel Hoey. These names, at least, besides a few others, have been preserved for us in the sub-editor's memoranda, which are, unfortunately, very incomplete. Fr. Russell opines that the touching "filial memorial" on the death of Cardinal Wiseman, which opens the April issue for 1865, was penned by Dr. Manning, so soon to succeed to the vacant archiepiscopal throne. That "memorial" contains Cardinal Wiseman's own memorandum, dated Easter, 1853, narrating the origin and early history of the *Dublin*, which appeared as preface to his volume of "Essays" issued in that year, and from which we have already quoted. It also records the fact that:

"In the last two years since it passed into other hands the declining health of our lamented Cardinal compelled him to postpone again and again the kind and encouraging promises he made to us of contributions from his pen. No line written by him has therefore appeared in it."*

The following well-merited panegyric of Wiseman's work in the Old Series is added:

"If at the end of our labours the Second Series of the *Dublin Review* should yield from all the hands which may contribute to it three volumes of essays worthy to stand afar off by those of Cardinal Wiseman, for beauty, variety, learning, freshness, originality—above all, for pure, solid Catholic doctrine and high filial devotion to Rome—we shall hope that we have not failed in the trust which he has bequeathed to us."

III.

The final number of the Second or "Ward Series" of the Review (October, 1878), concluding its thirty-first volume, contained a fly-leaf with the following announcement:

"The historic *Dublin*, now in the forty-second year

* N. S., vol. iv., p. 270.

of its existence, has been made over by Mr. W. G. Ward to his lordship the Bishop of Salford. On the first of January, the first number of a new, or Third Series, will appear, under the editorship of the Right Rev. Bishop Hedley.

"While faithfully adhering to the great Catholic principles for the maintenance of which it came into existence, and which have been its *raison d'être* and its very life for over forty years, the *Dublin Review* will now undergo certain modifications, calculated to render it more widely popular and more acceptable to a larger number of tastes and interests.

"The Review, in its Third Series, will aim at maintaining its traditional high standard of theological and metaphysical science; in its historical, literary, and political articles it will endeavour to combine solidity and usefulness with brilliancy of treatment; and each number will contain a summary of the contents of foreign Catholic contemporary periodicals, short notices of all new Catholic works, and a quarterly review of science.

"The work of the *Dublin Review* will be, as heretofore, to deepen Catholic intellectual life; to promote Catholic interests; to enlighten and assist those who are seeking for Catholic truth; to utter warnings against dangers to faith and practice; and to diminish as far as possible that friction arising from national, local, or personal narrowness which retards the onward march of Catholic principle. Its motto, as that of all Catholic journals, must be—Truth, Culture, and Conciliation.

"In order to render the Review the more interesting, all the articles will be signed with the names of the writers."

The strict rule of anonymity had already been partially relaxed in the Second Series. The "Historical Notes of the Tractarian Movement," which appeared in its earlier issues, were signed by their author, Canon Oakeley. Initials, like "M. D. T.," "T. F. M." (*i.e.*, Mathew), and "R. E. G.," were occasionally allowed to appear.

Papers by Mr. St. G. Mivart (October, 1876), Fr. H. Formby (January, 1877), and the Hon. W. (afterwards Lord) Petre (July, 1878), were published over their authors' full names, the object of Dr. Ward being to allow certain of his contributors liberty to express views with which he did not desire the Review or its editor to be identified. In the Third Series the signing of articles was carried out as a principle, though by no means uniformly observed; in No. 9 (January, 1881) only a single article, by Bishop Spalding, is signed or acknowledged! By degrees, however, the custom became practically universal. Librarians will do well to note that for the first four volumes of the Third Series the numeration of the second was continued—xxxii. to xxxv.; with the next volume the New Series began an independent numbering of its own, and the first half-yearly volume of 1881 is marked vol. v. This was carried on up to the close of the series, the last volume of it being xxvi., which ended 1891.

As announced in the circular quoted, the Third Series opened under the editorship of the Right Rev. John Cuthbert Hedley, O.S.B., the learned Bishop of Newport, who himself contributed to the first number the admirable article on "Catholicism and Culture," which opens the series. This first issue (January, 1879) had also the fortune to secure an article on "The Work and Wants of the Church in England," from the pen of Cardinal Manning, and one on "The Evangelization of Africa," from that of his destined successor, Bishop (afterwards Cardinal) Vaughan. The series thus began under very bright auspices, and a number of very distinguished names appear in the table of contents of subsequent numbers. Cardinal Manning is credited with at least five subsequent articles, of which the last (July, 1891) was entitled "Leo XIII. on the Condition of Labour," but half a year before the great Cardinal's death. We learn from some editorial correspondence that His Eminence had also planned a paper upon General

Gordon early in 1885, but unfortunately "gives it up—has not time." The article on the subject which did appear in April ("The Destiny of Khartoum") was, though not signed, from the indefatigable pen of Miss E. M. Clarke, whose industry as a *Dublin* reviewer during this series rivals that of Dr. Russell himself; and we gather that Gordon's sister "wrote to the writer to thank her for it, as expressive of her own feelings in the portion where Gordon's desertion is described." Another future Cardinal, Dr. Moran, at that time Bishop of Ossory, contributed an interesting paper on "The Birthplace of St. Patrick" to the issue of April, 1880, and one on "The Condition of Catholics in Ireland a Hundred Years Ago" to that of January, 1882. The late Bishop Clifford, of Clifton, brought out in those of April and October, 1881, his novel theory concerning the "Days of the Week and the Works of Creation," which excited no little interest and controversy at the time. Among other episcopal contributors to the series will be noticed the erudite Bishop Healy, Bishop Ullathorne, and, of course, the episcopal editor. This Third Series also secured a large share of foreign contributors—a very rare feature in the earlier series. Among these we meet with Professors de Harlez, Lamy, Alberdingk Thijm, and Colinet of Louvain, the Abbé Motais, Bishop Spalding of Peoria, and Senator Power of Ottawa.

Other novelties announced in the programme were duly introduced, and have since remained marked features of the *Dublin*, differentiating it to some extent from other old quarterlies. The department of book notices received a very considerable extension. In the earliest issues of the Original Series, no notices of the kind appear, but only an occasional "summary" of foreign literature, though, strange to say, for several years a short appendix of "Miscellaneous Intelligence," political as well as religious, was added to each issue. The notices of books appear to have commenced with the May number of 1840, in vol. viii., Original Series, but, even to the end of the series, never exceeded very modest proportions. Dr. Ward's series gave a much greater development to these short reviews; but in the Third and Fourth Series they have assumed still larger importance. Other new and useful departments now added were the "Science Notes" and "Notes on Travel and Exploration" still regularly continued.

Bishop Hedley was ably assisted in his editorial duties by an excellent sub-editor, the Rev. W. E. Driffield, whose name deserves to be recorded with due honour side by side with those of Bagshawe and Cashel Hoey. At the close of 1884 Dr. Hedley resigned the editorial chair which was then assumed by the Right Rev. Herbert Vaughan, then Bishop of Salford, who thus again, like Dr. Ward, combined the functions of proprietor and editor, which he retained till the close of 1891. The multifarious duties and occupations of the editor's busy episcopal life very naturally threw an ever-increasing share of labour upon the devoted sub-editor, and to a very considerable extent Father Driffield may be said to have been rather the acting editor during the last few years of the series.

With the beginning of 1892 the editorship was conferred upon the Right Rev. James Moyes, D.D., since Canon Theologian of Westminster, and with the change commenced also the Fourth Series of the *Dublin Review*. There was somewhat of an alteration in outward appearance, and in one respect at least a reversion to the memories of the Original "Wiseman" Series. The new first volume of the series was numbered vol. cx., the numeration thus going right back to the beginning, and the first issue bore number "220," by a curious miscalculation, which will puzzle some future librarian, for it should have been "219." This first quarterly issue was scarcely in the hands of its readers when the whole country was shocked by the news of the death of the venerable Cardinal Archbishop of Westminster, who himself twenty-seven years before had consecrated in the pages of the Review a "Memorial" to his predecessor, Cardinal Wiseman. A graceful and pathetic memorial article from the pen of the lamented Fr. Lockhart appeared in the subsequent issue (April, 1892). It is interesting also to note that the opening article of this Fourth Series was that on "England's Devotion to St. Peter," by the then Bishop of Salford, who, at the very moment the second part of the article was issuing from the press in the April number, had succeeded Manning and Wiseman on the metropolitan throne of Westminster, as he had succeeded them in the proprietorship of the "historic *Dublin*." The intimate connection between the three successive Cardinal Archbishops of Westminster and the great Catholic quarterly, of which this coincidence is but the outward symbol, is not a little remarkable, and confirms the impression of the very large part played by the Review in the history of Catholic thought and life during sixty years.

It will be unnecessary to say more about the Review, now in its seventieth year of existence, and with the whole twentieth century, as we may hope, before it. If the past be any augury of the future, the omens are certainly propitious. We can heartily wish it God-speed in its career.

Certain writers have sometimes speculated, in idle mood, what work they would choose if condemned for years to solitary imprisonment, or to banishment on a desert isle, with no other companion than one single set of volumes. Was it not Matthew Arnold who thought he would select Migne's edition of the Fathers ?* The present writer is not at all sure whether, if he were in the predicament, he would not take for his choice the volumes of the *Dublin Review* from 1836 to 1906.

* And, strangely enough, in a paper concerning an article in the *Dublin Review* itself !

XII

THE CATHOLIC CHURCH IN JAPAN

I.—The Ancient Church of Japan.

THE war of 1894–95 between the nations of the extreme East, the collapse of the Chinese Goliath and the unvarying success of the Japanese David, and the still more astonishing Titanic contest between Russia and Japan of 1904–5, have excited a widespread and intense interest in all that relates to Japan and the Japanese.

But the Japanese have an attractiveness all their own, and quite independent of any temporary political circumstances. The race is an extremely interesting one in itself. This has been well expressed not long ago by a competent observer. M. Ribaud, a Catholic missionary of Hakodate, writes thus in the *Missions Catholiques* of Lyons for February 22, 1895:

"The beauty of this province of Miyagi, which we are now traversing, is suggestive of thought. We seem to have before us some beautiful scene in Greece. Greece? Yes, for Japan is not a little like to Greece. Has not Japan landscapes as lovely as those of Athens, Corinth, or Ionia? Does the pellucid atmosphere of Miyagi or Iwate yield in delicacy to that of Attica? And if the physical features and climate of Japan are like to those of Greece in so many ways, are they not likely to impress upon the Japanese character some traits of the Hellenic type? The vivacity of wit, the facility and abundance of speech, which have rendered the Athenian name famous, are to be found to a striking degree among the Japanese. The *τί καινόν*, which paints so well the insatiable curiosity of the Greek, is at every instant on the lips of the Japanese.* What shall I say of the passion for independence, fostered in Greece by the very nature of the soil? It is found, for the same reason, in Japan, carried to its highest pitch, and with it the love of country. If we peruse the annals, without pushing our researches into ancient times—that nebulous period wherein we see the Empress Jingo marching to the conquest of Corea—nor even to the sanguinary struggles of the fourteenth century, in which the celebrated Ieyasu, breaking through all the obstacles with his puissant hand, succeeded in snatching the sceptre from the Mikado—but simply glancing at the recent revolutions which have restored to the Emperor the authority of which he had been despoiled, how many traits of valour, energy, and ardent patriotism do we not discover which need not pale side by side with the noblest deeds of patriotism of the heroes of Thermopylæ and Mantinaea!"

But the history, present condition, and prospects of Christianity in Japan is a subject which scarcely needs these considerations to render it one of surpassing interest. The contact between a race so highly endowed by nature as that of the Japanese and the powerful leaven of Christianity, must of necessity produce reactions and results destined to be little less momentous than similar contacts in the past between Christianity and, let us say, the Keltic and Anglo-Saxon races. To the student of philosophy, as well as to the historian, it must be interesting in the highest degree to watch such processes of spiritual chemistry.

The ancient island-empire of Nippon was first made

* "The Japanese are very curious by nature," wrote St. Francis Xavier in 1551, "and as desirous of learning as ever any people were. . . . They desire very much to hear novelties, especially about religion" (Letter lxxxiv., Coleridge, vol. ii., p. 300).

known to the Western world under the name of "Cipangu" in 1295 by Marco Polo, the famous Venetian traveller, and from that time forward appeared on maps, its discovery being among the objects which Columbus set before him in his memorable voyages to the West. The first Europeans to reach the archipelago, however, were three Portuguese fugitives, who were driven upon the southern islands in 1542—the very same year, by the way, in which St. Francis Xavier landed at Goa. But much more important events were the two visits of Mendez Pinto in 1545 and 1547, of which he himself has left a detailed account, published in English by Mr. H. Cogan in 1891. In the second of these visits Pinto received on board a Japanese fugitive named Anjiro (or Han-Siro) and his servant. Taken to Malacca, the two Japanese there made the acquaintance of St. Francis Xavier, who was intensely interested in the two fugitives and in what they had to tell him of their country. He took them with him to Goa, where both were instructed and became Christians, Anjiro being baptized under the name of Paul of the Holy Faith.

Those acquainted with the life of the Apostle of the Indies, and more especially readers of Fr. Coleridge's admirable "Life and Letters of St. Francis Xavier," will scarce need reminding how deep an impression was made on the saint's mind by what he heard from these Japanese converts, and how Japan became to him truly a land of predilection. From the moment of his meeting with Anjiro the idea of a missionary expedition to Japan took hold of his soul.

It was not until 1549 that Francis was able to undertake his great task—the evangelization of the island-empire. On April 25 he embarked at Cochin for Malacca, whence, on the Nativity of St. John Baptist, he sailed for Japan "on board the ship of a heathen merchant, a Chinaman." The voyage lasted seven weeks, and a most interesting account of it is given by Francis himself in his first letter from the place of his arrival. He had with him the two Japanese, Anjiro (otherwise "Paul of the Holy Faith") and the latter's servant, Fr. Cosmo de Torres, and a lay-brother, João Fernandez.

"So by the guidance of God," he writes, "we came at last to this country, which we had so much longed for, on the very day of the Feast of Our Blessed Lady's Assumption, 1549. We could not make another port, and so we put into Cagoxima, which is the native place of Paul of the Holy Faith. We were most kindly received there both by Paul's relations and connections and also by the rest of the people of the place."*

The port of Cagoxima—*i.e.*, Kagoshima†—lies upon the deep inlet which indents the southern extremity of Kyushu, the southernmost island of the archipelago. It was at the time the capital of the principality of Satsuma. The first successes of the saint and his companions were truly gratifying. We have his own words for it. He writes:

"The prince of this place was six leagues away from Cagoxima, and when Paul went to pay his respects to him he was very glad of his return, and showed him much honour, asking him also a great many things about the manners, the power, and the resources of the Portuguese. When Paul told him all about them, he seemed to be very highly delighted with what he had heard. Paul had taken with him a very fine picture of Our Blessed Lady with the Child Jesus sitting in her lap, which we had brought from India. When the prince saw the picture which Paul had brought he was quite struck with wonder; he at once fell on his knees and venerated it in the most pious manner, and ordered all who were present to do the same. After this his mother saw it and gazed upon it, and was filled with wonderful admira-

* Coleridge, vol. ii., p. 232.

† We shall adopt in this paper the spelling of modern Orientalists for Japanese names and words. It must be remembered that the early Jesuit missioners spelled according to the Portuguese sounds. The Portuguese *x* is pronounced as *sh*.

tion and delight; and a few days after, when Paul had returned to Cagoxima, she sent a man—and a very good person he was—to see about getting a copy of it taken somehow or other. However, there were no means of doing the thing at Cagoxima, and so the matter went no further. The same lady sent us a request by the same hand that we would give her in writing the chief points of the Christian religion. So Paul devoted some days to this work, and wrote out in his own native language a great many things concerning Christian mysteries and laws. You may take my word for it, and also give God great thanks, that a very wide field is here opened to you for your well-roused piety to spend its energies in."

In this same very long letter, addressed to the Society at Goa, Francis, besides a very full account of the Japanese manners and customs, gives us his opinion of the Japanese people, of whom he speaks with something like enthusiasm. "The nation with which we have had to do here," he declares, "surpasses in goodness any of the nations lately discovered. I really think that among barbarous nations there can be none that has more natural goodness than the Japanese."

St. Francis Xavier stayed little more than two years in Japan. He and his companions laboured successively at Hirado, Hakata, Yamaguchi, Kyoto,* and Bungo, though with very varying success. The Prince of Satsuma himself became hostile, influenced by the jealousy of the Buddhist bonzes. At Yamaguchi the mean and forlorn appearance of Francis caused him to be driven out of the city with obloquy. Yet his two years' stay in Japan produced an indelible impression. The Church of Japan was securely founded, and from the sweat and tears of its first great apostle there sprang that glorious harvest which was destined to ripen in an incredibly short space of time.

St. Francis Xavier left Japan in the November of 1551.

* Called by St. Francis "Myako"—*i.e.*, the capital, for such it was in his time.

His intention was to visit the vast empire of China, and then begin to sow the seeds of Christianity as he had done in Nippon. He had heard much about China whilst in the neighbouring kingdom, and had met Chinamen there. "The Chinese whom I have seen," he says, "are acute and eager to learn. Their intellect is superior even to the Japanese." And again: "China is that sort of kingdom that, if the seed of the Gospel is once sown, it may be propagated far and wide."* But it was not merely the desire to carry the truth to China that moved Francis to this new expedition. He saw in it a means of reacting upon his beloved Japan. For, as he remarks in one of his letters, the Japanese used to especially urge against the Christian teaching "that if things were as we preached, how was it that the Chinese knew nothing about them?" This was only natural, since Japan had derived her civilization, her letters, her religion from China, and consequently "the Japanese have a very high idea of the wisdom of the Chinese, whether as to the mysteries of religion, or as to manners and civil institutions."† And, writing to his great superior, St. Ignatius, just after leaving Japan, he says explicitly: "As soon as the Japanese learn that the Chinese have embraced the faith of Jesus Christ, there is reason to hope that the obstinacy with which they are attached to their own false sects will be lessened."‡ This same letter to St. Ignatius betrays the depth of the affection which attached St. Francis to this people, for he exclaims therein: "No words can express all that I owe to the Japanese." And how wonderful in the light of subsequent history is the prophecy contained in another part of this letter, where he writes: "As far as I know, the Japanese nation is the single and only nation of them all which seems likely to preserve unshaken and for ever the profession of Christian holiness if once it embrace

* Letter lxxxvi., Coleridge, p. 348.
† Letter lxxxiv., Coleridge, pp. 300, 301.
‡ Letter lxxxviii., Coleridge, p. 373.

it." These words will surely recur to our memory later on in reading of the event of March 17, 1865!

Everyone knows that St. Francis Xavier was never destined to reach the shores of China, and that he died an outcast on the little island of San Chan, at the mouth of the Canton river, on December 2, 1552, like Moses in sight of the Promised Land.

The following half-century marks an epoch of marvellous prosperity in the Japanese missions. Numerous Jesuit Fathers and lay-brothers were sent over, as Francis had desired, to carry on the work so auspiciously begun. Within thirty years it is calculated that over 200,000 Japanese, including several bonzes, had been converted, and the Princes of Omura, Bungo, and Arima were among these neophytes. Nagasaki was the chief focus of Christian life. By 1567 it was said that the population of that city was almost entirely Catholic. The virtual ruler of Japan at this time was Nobunaga, the celebrated Minister and commandant of the forces. This able Minister was distinctly favourable to the Christians during all his administration of nine years (1573–1582). All this time the Jesuit Fathers had been pushing forward their apostolic work, and had met with marvellous success. In Kyoto and Yamaguchi, in Osaka and Sakai, as well as in Kyushu, they had founded flourishing churches, established colleges for the formation of a native clergy, opened hospitals and asylums, and extended their influence far and wide. The latter part of Nobunaga's supremacy was perhaps the era of their greatest prosperity. At this time Chamberlain estimates the number of Japanese Christians at not less than 600,000. Nobunaga's patronage of the Christians was largely inspired by political motives. His strong Government had made him hated by the Buddhist bonzes, whose overwhelming power he effectually held in check, and who looked upon him as a usurper, as he technically was. It was this disaffection of the bonzes that led him to support the Christian missionaries.

They seem to have attributed his patronage to higher motives, and to have looked forward to his conversion. But though churches were built under his patronage at Kyoto and at Azuchi, on Lake Biwa, near his own beautiful residence, he never seems to have seriously intended to become a Christian. For some time after Nobunaga's death nothing occurred to interfere with the development of the Church; indeed, that date (1582) coincides with the mission of Fr. Valignani from Gregory XIII., now to be mentioned.

The fervour, zeal, and devotion of these new Christians were worthy of the early days of Christianity. The Holy See was very soon able to rejoice in the addition to the fold of legions of devoted children. Gregory XIII. deputed Fr. Alessandro Valignani, S.J., with gifts to the converted Japanese princes, and they in their turn in 1582 despatched a solemn embassy to Rome, consisting of two young princes and two counsellors, who were accompanied by Fr. Valignani and another Jesuit. This embassy was received with all state and splendour both by Gregory XIII., who died during their stay in Rome (1585), and by his successor, Sixtus V. But on their return to their native country the Japanese delegates found that troubles had already broken out.*

It was in 1587 that the first anti-Christian edict was issued by the celebrated Taiko-Sama, one of the greatest rulers Japan has ever known; and the years from that date till 1650 may be fairly designated the era of the

* This was not the only Japanese embassy to the Holy See at that time. At the Tenth International Congress of Orientalists, held at Geneva in September, 1894, the eminent Sinologue, Professor Valenziani, of Rome, read a paper on two passages of the "Nippon hyak' kets' den," a kind of biographical encyclopædia, by which he established the fact that during the last years of the sixteenth century Gamau Udji-sato, daimyo of Aidzou, sent no less than four different embassies to the reigning Pontiff, with the purely political object of detaching him from the Spaniards, against whom the Japanese were contending in the Philippines. As the President of the section, Professor Schlegel, remarked, these facts were entirely new and hitherto unknown to European scholars.

persecutions, the special and abiding glory of the Japanese Church.

Before, however, we enter upon the history of these persecutions, the mention of Taiko-Sama's name calls for a brief explanation of the state of Japanese government at that time. In our ecclesiastical histories this first persecutor is always spoken of as "the Emperor Taico-sama." The title is entirely erroneous. To explain how the early missionaries fell into this error, it will be necessary to refer to a much earlier period of Japanese history. The series of the Emperors (or "Mikados") of Japan go back in an unbroken line from our own day to the founder of the dynasty, Jimmu, who appears to have reigned from 660 to 585 B.C. But at the close of the twelfth century of our era the all-powerful Minister Yoritomo succeeded in establishing the curious system of government known as the *Shogunate*, which endured till so recent a date as 1868. This system resembles nothing so much as that of "the mayors of the palace" under the later Merovingian kings. The "Shogun"* was Commander-in-Chief of the forces, and also Viceregent of the Empire. And though for long periods he was actually the *de facto* ruler, still, during the whole eight centuries of the Shogunate this potentate always scrupulously observed the outward show of reverence for, and absolute dependence upon, the Emperor, whose humble servant he professed to be, and whose commission he always received for the performance of his duties. This curious form of government is described with fair accuracy in the memoir on Japan drawn up by Paul Anjiro, with the peculiarity that he styles the Emperor "Voo" and the Shogun "Goxo"—words of which we have not seen an explanation anywhere.† Yet the early Jesuit mission-

* The name was long known in Europe under the quasi-Chinese form, "Tycoon."

† Perhaps "Voo" may be meant for the Japanese word "Wau," ruler or sovereign, and "Ten-wau," heavenly King, is actually a title of the Mikado. But "Gossiyo" (literally, exalted place) is also one of the titles of the Emperor himself.

aries seem to be quite oblivious of the existence of the Mikados, or Emperors, whose names never appear in the acts of the ancient Church of Japan.

The famous Taiko-Sama (literally, "Lord Taiko") was in reality the Prime Minister, Commander-in-Chief, and Viceregent, known in Japanese history as Hideyoshi. He was not Emperor, and never obtained even the exalted title of Shogun, but was content with the lower one of "Kwambaku," though his power was none the less absolute. His predecessor in power, of whom we have spoken above, the scarcely less celebrated Nobunaga, like himself, held the authority without enjoying the title of Shogun.

In 1585 Hideyoshi, after a brief period of confusion, became the virtual ruler of Japan. At first he does not seem to have been hostile to the Christians, but his sentiments gradually underwent a change. Various reasons have been assigned for his development into a persecutor. Prominent among these must have been the influence of the bonzes, who doubtless did their best to arouse his suspicions against the foreigners. He was, indeed, already inclined to look upon the Jesuits as secret envoys of the King of Portugal. But whatever dislike to Christianity had been growing up in his mind was fanned to a flame by the firmness and constancy of certain Christian maidens who refused to yield to his lustful passions, and preferred death to sin. The first step towards persecution was Taiko-Sama's edict of 1587. All "foreign religious teachers" were commanded to quit Japan within twenty days under pain of death. The Jesuit Fathers thereupon withdrew to Nagasaki, where it would appear they were allowed to devote themselves to the spiritual wants of the Europeans. Yet so far from these measures checking the growth of Christianity, not only did the Japanese converts remain staunch in their faith, but it is calculated that during the next few years over 60,000 more were added to the fold. Meanwhile new elements were introduced.

Much has been made by Protestant writers of the mutual jealousies of the Jesuits and the other Orders. A word must therefore be here said upon this subject.

It appears that in 1485 Pope Gregory XIII. issued a brief giving to the Society of Jesus the exclusive charge of the Japanese missions, as, indeed, it had well merited by its extraordinary successes. The Spanish Government viewed with a jealous eye whatever secured the monopoly of the Portuguese in the country; and the governor of the Philippines soon after despatched an embassy to Hideyoshi, seeking to obtain permission to trade at some of the Japanese ports, and with the embassy he sent four Franciscans, who were thus indirectly permitted to establish themselves in Kyoto and Nagasaki (1593). Taiko-Sama at first seemed favourably disposed to these Franciscans, and they soon took the opportunity of publicly preaching the Gospel, which they did with great success. This activity, combined with the mischievous gossip of a Portuguese (or Spanish*) sea-captain, seems to have roused Taiko-Sama to fury. The imprudent fellow boasted that the King of Spain had sent his own missionaries into Japan in order to pave the way to a future conquest of the islands. Nothing more was required to give the signal for a cruel persecution. The death-penalty was decreed against all the Christian preachers. The first fruits of the glorious Japanese army of martyrs were the twenty-six who were crucified at Nagasaki on February 5, 1597. They numbered six Franciscan Fathers, including the superior, Fr. Peter Baptist, fifteen Japanese tertiaries of the same Order, three Japanese Jesuits, and two servants. At the thrilling scene of this martyrdom, which has been too

* The accounts are contradictory, as is also the chronology of these events. I have followed the valuable "Compendium Historiæ Ecclesiasticæ," published at Pulo-Pinang (Straits Settlements), 1885, which differs considerably in the order of its narrative from Mr. D. Murray ("Japan," in "The Story of the Nations" series; London: Fisher Unwin, 1894), whose dates appear to me to be hopelessly confused.

often told to allow of repetition here, was present the first Bishop who had yet set foot on Japanese soil. This was Pedro Martinez, S.J., appointed Bishop of Japan by Sixtus V., whose singular privilege it was to transmit to Rome the acts of the Proto-martyrs, of which he himself had been an eye-witness.

It is only fair to remark here that some of the responsibility for the persecution appears to be due to the action of the converted Japanese princes, who, not content with embracing the Catholic faith, seem to have been only too ready to force it upon their subjects, and to pose as regular persecutors of Buddhism. Those were not days when "toleration" was understood in any country; but it would really appear that this untimely zeal of some of these princes reacted disastrously upon the pagan rulers.

Taiko-Sama, or Hideyoshi, died in 1598. After some years of civil war, the power passed into the hands of a man scarcely less able than himself, Ieyasu, in whom the office of Shogun (in abeyance since 1573) was restored, and who founded the Tokugawa dynasty, or Shogunate. A period of comparative peace and prosperity for the Japanese Church now ensued. Bishop Luiz Serqueyra, S.J., was able greatly to console and confirm his flock, which he ruled peacefully till 1614. Ieyasu even received the Bishop with a certain degree of favour in 1606 at Kyoto, and the following year the Provincial of the Jesuits. About the same time Dominican and Augustinian Fathers began to arrive and swell the ranks of the missioners. At the beginning of the seventeenth century the number of Japanese Christians is said to have risen to 1,800,000. But the peace was to be of short duration; it was but the prelude to one of the most awful persecutions ever recorded in the history of the Church.

Even during the period just referred to a certain amount of local persecution of the Christians was going on, especially in the principality of Fingo (Higo), where several martyrs suffered. But in 1617 the persecution became general, and for twenty years it endured with a violence surpassing that of Nero. It is a lamentable fact that much of the responsibility of this terrible persecution must be laid at the door of the Dutch Protestants, who, as well as the English, at this time began to trade largely with Japan. National jealousy of the Portuguese and Spanish, as well as religious hatred, were rife at the time, and there is only too strong evidence to believe that the new-comers did much to poison the mind of the Shogun against the Catholics. Mr. Murray thinks that Ieyasu had also been enraged by the solemn celebration of the beatification of Ignatius Loyola (1609) by public processions of the Bishop and all the religious orders through Nagasaki, in spite of a "warning proclamation" issued in 1606. But this was long years before the outburst of the persecution; the actual edict for the extirpation of Christianity to secure the safety of the empire was issued in 1614. All members of religious orders, whether native or European, were to be expelled the country, the churches which had been erected were to be pulled down, and Japanese converts were to be compelled to renounce their faith. Some 300 persons were shipped from Japan on October 25, but eighteen Jesuit Fathers and nine lay-brothers escaped and lay concealed. Among other exiles was the powerful noble Takeyama, known in the Christian annals as Justus Ucondono. He was one of those converted princes, and is accused of having carried out a system of persecution against the Buddhists in his territory of Akashi. But whatever misguided zeal he may have shown in that matter, he certainly set a bright example of personal heroism in the hour of trial. He stimulated his fellow-Christians by his constancy in the Faith, and his readiness to forego all honours and dignities in its defence. Already banished, in Taiko-Sama's reign, he was now deported to the Philippines, where he died of a painful sickness in 1615.

The new edict was carried out with ruthless severity. A special department, entitled "The Christian Inquiry," was instituted for the purpose of searching out Christians and forcing them to apostasy. Priests and laity were hunted down; large rewards were offered for information against Christians in every rank of life; a special scale was published for the betrayal of parents by their children, and of children by their parents. Ieyasu died in 1616, just at the beginning of the persecution, but it was continued with relentless fury by his son and successor. History has but one verdict upon the diabolic atrocity of the persecution. "One may search the grim history of early Christian martyrology," writes the author of "The Conquests of the Cross," published by Messrs. Cassell, "without finding anything to surpass the heroism of the Roman Catholic martyrs of Japan. Burnt on stakes made of crosses, torn limb from limb, buried alive, they yet refused to recant." "It has never been surpassed," says Mr. D. Murray of this persecution, "for cruelty and brutality on the part of the persecutors, or for courage and constancy on the part of those who suffered."* Mr. Gubbins, in the Japanese Asiatic Society's *Transactions*, after detailing some of the more barbarous tortures inflicted, adds: "Let it not be supposed that we have drawn on the Jesuit accounts solely for this information. An examination of the Japanese records will show that the case is not overstated."

Painful as is the subject, some record must be made of what these heroic confessors of the faith had to undergo. "We read," says the last-quoted writer, "of their being hurled from the tops of precipices, of their being buried alive, of their being torn asunder by oxen, of their being tied up in rice-bags, which were heaped up together, and of the pile thus formed being set on fire. Others were tortured before death by the insertion of sharp spikes under the nails of their hands and feet, while some poor wretches, by a refinement of horrid cruelty, were shut up in cages and there left to starve with food before their eyes."

* "Japan."

Specially awful were the torments inflicted in the caves of Un-gen (or On-sen) between Nagasaki and Shimabara. Here some were plunged into the boiling sulphur-springs, others suffocated by the fumes, some forced to drink enormous quantities of water, and then, like Margaret Clitheroe, pressed to death beneath crushing weights. But of all the tortures the most terrible was that known as " the Fosse," or suspension head downwards into a pit, the martyr hanging by a rope fastened to the feet and attached to a projecting post. The suffering was excruciating, blood exuding from the mouth and nostrils, and the pressure on the brain being almost unendurable. Yet the victim usually survived eight or nine days ! We can hardly be surprised that many succumbed under the trial, and that a number fell away into apostasy. Yet what were they compared with the glorious army of martyrs, including women and children, mostly natives, who triumphed and won their crown ? Statistics alone are capable of giving an idea of the terrible character of the persecution. It is reckoned that over 1,000 religious of the four orders—Jesuits, Franciscans, Dominicans, and Augustinians—shed their blood for the faith during its course, whilst the number of native Japanese lay-folk who perished exceeded 200,000 ! " Since the Apostolic times no grander spectacle has been exhibited to the Christian world ; it embraced episodes beautiful enough to delight the angels, and refinements of wickedness sufficient to excite the jealousy of demons."*

Everybody has heard of the trampling on the cross which Europeans were required to perform to save their lives. This test was known to the Japanese as *e-fumi*, and was carried out under the direction of an officer, styled *Kirishitan Bugyo*, or " Christian Inquisitor." Specimens of the metal trampling-plates upon which the crucifix was engraved—made, too, from the metal obtained from the Christian altars—are still to be seen in

* Louvet, "Les Missions Catholiques au XIXme Siècle," Paris, 1895, p. 235.

the Uyeno Museum in Tokyo. The Dutch made no difficulty in submitting to the test, and for the sake of trade privileges were content several times a year to trample upon the figure of Him whom they professed to worship as their Saviour.

The last scene in this terrible tragedy was the revolt in the principality of Arima in 1638. One can hardly wonder, perhaps, at the Christians being driven to desperation by their twenty years' persecution. Yet Mr. Murray points out that it is but justice to remember that this rebellion was not due exclusively to the Christians, but that it was probably originated by other causes—namely, the misgovernment and senseless cruelty of two successive daimyos of Arima, whose tyranny drove the farmers of Arima and Amakusa to open revolt.* Then it was that the Christians rose *en masse* in the province to swell the ranks of the insurgents, the total number amounting, it is said, to 40,000. Then came the long siege of the strong position of Shimabara. It will be remembered that the Dutch under Koeckebacker, on this occasion, acceded to the request of the Government, and lent their powder and cannon to the besiegers. Dr. Geerts has written a defence of Koeckebacker's action in the Japan Asiatic Society's *Transactions*, and thinks he could not help doing what he did, and that any European would have done the same in the same position. Finally, Shimabara was carried by assault after a siege of 102 days, and a general massacre ensued. We have Koeckebacker's own authority that of the 40,000, young and old, all, except one, were slaughtered. From that moment Christianity appeared to be extinct in Japan. The last Bishop of the ancient Church of Japan, Luis Sotelo, O.S.F., had perished, having been burnt alive in 1624. A few scattered remnants yet remained. Edicts continued to be issued against the pestilent sect of the Christians.

"For more than two hundred years notice-boards

* "Japan," pp. 257-260.

stood beside highways, ferries, and mountain passes, containing among other prohibitions the following : ' So long as the sun shall warm the earth, let no Christian be so bold as to come to Japan ; and let all know that the King of Spain himself, or the Christian's God, or the Great God of all, if He violate this commandment, shall pay for it with His head.' "*

So the Church, which at the beginning of the century counted 1,800,000 souls, appeared by its close to be absolutely extinct. A silence of death settled down upon it. We hear, indeed, of an Italian Jesuit, Fr. John Baptist Sidotti, reaching the shores of Japan in 1709 ; but he was immediately captured and thrust into prison, where he soon perished. He was the last Jesuit who has ever trodden the Japanese soil. After his death darkness, black as night, spread over the scene, for it must be remembered that not only was Christianity (apparently) exterminated, but all intercourse with foreigners, even for trade, was abruptly broken off, the only partial exception being in favour of the Chinese and Dutch.

Before leaving the subject of the ancient Church of Japan, it would seem but justice to record one more of its titles to glory, though, indeed, a minor one. We refer to the labours of the early missioners in behalf of philology and literature. Protestant writers have recorded with astonishment the fact that, whilst the Dutch, favoured as they were by the Japanese Government, did nothing in the cause of science, it is to the Catholic missioners, in spite of the terrible times of persecution, that Europe owes the earliest works relating to the Japanese language and literature. Thus the Dutch Orientalist Hoffmann, writing in the *Journal* of the German Oriental Society (vol. xii., pp. 443 *et seq.*), says :

" It cannot but excite just surprise, as Adelung has already remarked with disapprobation, that the Dutch, whether merely from lack of interest or from petty

* See Cobbold, " Religion in Japan," p. 94 (London: S.P.C.K., 1894).

motives of selfishness, have waited until the most recent times before publishing anything of value concerning the language and literature of Japan. And yet they had every opportunity to do so. . . . Holland cannot easily allege any serious excuse for not taking the task earlier in hand. They had only to continue building upon a ground already prepared for them by the Portuguese in a highly commendable manner, as was always the case, and bequeathed by them to their successors in Japan, who were the Dutch themselves. . . . To whom, then, are we indebted for the first scientific knowledge of the Japanese language? To the Dutch? Oh no! To Portuguese missioners like Alvarez, Rodriguez, and Collado, who had already published their Japanese grammars and dictionaries at the close of the sixteenth and beginning of the seventeenth centuries."*

The above-mentioned João Rodriguez, S.J., arrived in Japan in 1583, and under his directions a series of important publications appeared between 1590 and 1610. In 1595 there was printed in the Jesuit College at Amakusa the now rare Portuguese-Latin-Japanese Dictionary, occupying 906 quarto pages, and of remarkable completeness. In 1603 followed a Japanese-Portuguese Dictionary. In 1604 Fr. Rodriguez's Japanese Grammar was printed at Nagasaki. The Dominicans rivalled the Jesuits in their literary zeal. The above-named Diego Collado was a Dominican, whose Dictionary and Grammar of the Japanese language appeared in Rome in 1632. Three years before, the Dominicans of Manila had printed a Spanish translation of the Jesuit Dictionary. After Rodriguez, who died in 1633, other missioners, such as Lopez and Sylva, worked in the same field. For two centuries, moreover, the reports of the Catholic missioners were the best and almost the only sources of a knowledge of Japan and the Japanese people. Fr. Froës, S.J., in the second

* See Jos. Dahlmann, S.J., "Die Sprachkunde und die Missionen," pp. 57, 58 (Freiburg: Herder, 1891).

half of the sixteenth century, deserves special mention in this respect. According to Anushin, he was the first European to speak of the curious primeval race of the Ainos.

A number of religious works in the Japanese language for the use of native Christians were compiled and published by the Catholic missioners. Bishop Serqueyra, whom we have spoken of above, composed a work on moral theology. One of the Franciscan Fathers, known as Diego de las Llagas, was a native Japanese, who, besides translating the "Flos Sanctorum" into his mother tongue, published also a Japanese Grammar and a Spanish-Latin-Japanese Dictionary.

Special mention must also be made of the efforts of the early missioners to accommodate the Japanese language to the Roman alphabet—a work which has been taken up earnestly in our own time by the Romaji-Kai, and which occupied a considerable share of the attention of the Geneva International Congress of Orientalists in 1894. In 1590 the Jesuit missioners began to cast European type in Japan, and they elaborated a complete system of transcription in Roman characters. Mr. Ernest Satow, the eminent Japanese scholar, has published an interesting monograph, "The Jesuit Mission Press in Japan, 1590-1610" (London, 1888), in which a full account is given of the literary labours of our missioners in this regard. Numerous Japanese works, printed according to this system, exist in the libraries of Europe.

II. The "Second Spring" in Japan.

Though Catholicity in Japan was to all intents and purposes extinct, the blood of so many martyrs was not destined to be shed in vain. During the death-silence of well-nigh two centuries, the Holy See did not altogether forget this once so hopeful field of spiritual harvest. Almost contemporaneously with the final struggles of the Church of Japan, an entirely new movement was taking shape in Europe, leading eventually, under the marvellous guidance of Providence, to the erection of the Seminary of the Foreign Missions in Paris, and the formation of the greatest foreign missionary agency which the Church has ever seen, the illustrious Société des Missions Étrangères. In so far as the society can be said to have had "founders"—for in the literal sense of the word it had really no founder* —it is the two first Vicars Apostolic for the Far East—Mgr. Pallu and Mgr. de la Motte Lambert, appointed in 1658 by Pope Alexander VII.—who have the nearest claim to that title. The primary end of the new society was the creation of a native clergy in the foreign missionary countries confided to its charge; the second one, the preaching of the Gospel to the heathen. The first centre of its work was in the kingdom of Siam, where a general seminary for the training of native clergy was erected in the old capital, Ayuthia. The earliest countries of the Far East evangelized by the members of the society were Annam (Cochin China), Tonkin, Siam, and parts of China. Yet even at that early date the eyes of the society seem to have been turned towards the Forbidden Land, for two of its very first missionary Bishops—Mgr. Laneau and Mgr. Cicé—received in turn the barren title of Vicars Apostolic of Japan.† Nothing at all practical, however, was attempted till early on in the last century.‡ Curiosity was awakened in 1831 by the shipwreck of a Japanese vessel on the shores of the Philippines. Some twenty shipwrecked sailors were

* See on this subject Ad. Launay, "Histoire Générale de la Société des Missions Étrangères," tom. i. (Paris, 1894).

† Ad. Launay, p. 202.

‡ It is recorded in the Pulo-Pinang "Compendium Historiæ Ecclesiasticæ," (1885), that at the close of the eighteenth century a few men arrived in Cochin China saying they were Japanese missionaries, and begging for some sacred vestments from the Vicar Apostolic, to whom they made themselves known under the greatest secrecy. The sequel does not appear (p. 127).

kindly received by the Spaniards, who were surprised to find them wearing Christian medals, which they appeared to reverence with superstitious veneration. On inquiry, they said they had descended to them from their ancestors. These descendants of the ancient Christians were all instructed and baptized. Already the Anglican Bible Society had been making efforts to introduce their Bibles into Japan, but had met with little success, and even been forced to fly.

To Gregory XVI. was reserved the glory of reopening the sealed book of the history of the Japanese Church. In 1832 he erected the Vicariate Apostolic of Korea, attaching to it the Liu-Kiu (Ryu-Kyu, or Loo-Choo) Islands, dependencies of Japan, in the hope that they might become a gate opening into the Island Kingdom, as indeed they proved to be. Some attempts—not altogether unsuccessful—seem to have been made at this time by the Société des Missions Étrangères to send a few Catechists into Japan, with what fruit we know not. In 1838 we find Mgr. Imbert writing home, under date November 22: "Souvent il m'arrive de tourner des regards et presque d'espérance vers les rives du Japon." It was the two hundredth anniversary of the massacre of Shimabara.

A new factor was about this time introduced into the Japanese problem. The various governments of Europe and the United States were making more and more energetic efforts to bring about an opening-up of Japan for commercial purposes. In the constant negotiations for this end the various navies necessarily played a leading part; the real diplomatists were the admirals and commodores, French or English, American or Russian, who carried on the only possible communications with the coy government of the Shoguns. The French authorities were willing to associate their efforts with those of the great French missionary society to gain a footing in the Land of Promise. In 1844 the French squadron was under the command of Rear-

Admiral Cécile. He consented to despatch the *Alcmène*, under command of Fornier-Duplon, to the Liu-Kiu Islands, having on board M. Forcade, a priest of the Missions Étrangères, and Augustine Ko, a native catechist, who had already suffered as a confessor of the faith, and subsequently became a priest. On the Feast of the Patronage of St. Joseph, April 28, the capital of the group, Nafa, was reached, and negotiations were at once opened with the government of the petty king. The end was that the two missioners were allowed to remain. They soon found, however, that their condition was little better than an honourable durance. They were installed in a Buddhist monastery, but subjected to a constant and harassing surveillance.

"I was barely allowed," wrote M. Forcade, "to take a little exercise on the sand or mud by the seashore, and even then I might not go out alone. I was surrounded by the inevitable mandarins, preceded by satellites armed with bamboos to strike the poor people and drive off any passers-by, which was naturally calculated to render me an object of odium."

The Japanese Government having got wind of these proceedings, promptly demanded the missionary's head; but the Dutch resident at Deshimo, to his credit be it said, interposed his good services, and perhaps respect for the French squadron had its influence; the danger passed over. So two years went by, without any possibility of communicating with the natives even of Nafa. In 1846 Pope Gregory XVI., to show his interest in the work, nominated M. Forcade, Bishop of Samos and Vicar Apostolic of Japan. The same year Admiral Cécile called at Nafa with his squadron and endeavoured to negotiate a treaty. The missioners were now allowed to remain in the Tu-mai lamassery and to procure books for the study of the language, and were relieved from the vexatious surveillance they had hitherto endured. Two new missionary priests, MM. Adnet and Leturdu, arrived at the Liu-Kiu Islands, whilst Mgr. Forcade went to France in the interests of his vicariate.

A gap of eight years now occurs in the progress of our history. In 1854, under the pontificate of Pius IX., M. Collin, a missionary of Manchuria, was nominated Prefect Apostolic of Japan, but died immediately after his nomination. M. Libois, the new superior, sent out three new missioners to the Liu-Kiu Islands under M. Girard; but their position was a very painful one, and, like their predecessors, they were subjected to incessant and vexatious surveillance. Once more the French naval commandant, Admiral Guérin, interposed his good offices, and a new treaty was made with the king. The missioners were now allowed to buy some land and build a house in the centre of the town. But as regards evangelical work, all they could possibly achieve was to baptize a few babies at the point of death, and also a few old people.

In 1856 Admiral Laguerre, taking a missionary on board, visited Nagasaki; but all his efforts at friendly negotiation were in vain. Other European nations had in the interval been more successful. The real opening-up of Japan is to be credited to the United States, for it was Commodore Perry who, in 1853, conducted the first successful negotiation with the Shogun's Government, not without a very considerable and perhaps necessary display of force, and the American treaty was ratified in 1854. Treaties followed with Great Britain in the same year, Russia in 1855, and Holland in 1856, each providing for the admission of traders to two Japanese ports. France was still knocking at the door. In 1857 two frigates, having two missionaries on board, touched at Nagasaki, and one of the priests actually landed, but was quickly obliged to beat a retreat.

At last, in 1858, Japan was finally opened to the French, and as a consequence to the missioners of the French Society. To Baron Gros belongs the credit of negotiating the treaty at Yeddo (now called Tokyo), signed on October 9. The ports of Yokohama, Nagasaki, and Hakodate were opened by this diplomatic key. Religious liberty was allowed to foreigners, not yet to natives. On November 28 M. Girard, now Pro-Vicar Apostolic of Japan, writes in exulting strains to the Central Council of the Society of the Propagation of the Faith:

"After ten years of waiting and painful uncertainty, about the future of a mission always so dear to us, to behold the gates at length opened is an event in which we cannot fail to see the direct intervention of Almighty God. The treaty awards to the Minister Plenipotentiary the right of travelling all over the empire. We hope that one of us may be able to accompany him and seek out the remnants of the ancient Christian settlements said still to exist in Japan."*

Very little, however, could be done at first. Prudence made caution absolutely necessary. Missionaries were placed in each of the three treaty ports to attend to the spiritual wants of European Catholics, and chapels were erected at Yokohama and Nagasaki. That of the former town was dedicated with considerable pomp on January 12, 1861, and many Japanese, undeterred by severe Government edicts, daily visited it out of curiosity.

We must now turn our eyes for a moment to Rome. Already, as early as 1627, Pope Urban VIII. had permitted the Franciscans and Jesuits to celebrate yearly an Office and Mass in honour of the martyrs of their respective congregations who, as above narrated, had been crucified at Nagasaki under Taiko-Sama in 1597. Their cause pursued its course in Rome, and finally, on Whit Sunday, 1862, Pius IX., surrounded by an extraordinary gathering of Catholic Bishops from all parts of the world, had the consolation of solemnly proclaiming the canonisation of these twenty-six first martyrs of Japan.

What followed in Japan seemed like a visible answer

* Ad. Launay, p. 365.

to the honours thus so splendidly rendered to these heroes of the faith. On February 19, 1865, the fine Catholic church dedicated to the twenty-six martyrs was opened at Nagasaki, the scene of their martyrdom. This church had been built by M. Bernard Petitjean, a native of the diocese of Autun, who, having joined the Société des Missions Étrangères, had been sent out to Japan in 1860. We must let this illustrious missionary, whose name will be for ever indissolubly bound up with the history of the Japanese Church, narrate the wondrous sequel in his own oft-quoted words:

"Scarce a month had elapsed since the benediction of the church at Nagasaki. On March 17, 1865, about half-past twelve, some fifteen persons were standing at the church door. Urged, no doubt, by my Angel Guardian, I went up and opened the door. I had scarce time to say a *Pater* when three women, between fifty and sixty years of age, knelt down beside me, and said in a low voice, placing their hand upon their heart:

"'The hearts of all of us here do not differ from yours.'

"'Indeed!' I exclaimed. 'Whence do you come?'

"They mentioned their village, adding: 'At home everybody is the same as we are!'

"Blessed be Thou, O my God! for all the happiness which filled my soul. What a compensation for five years of barren ministry! Scarce had our dear Japanese opened their hearts to us than they displayed an amount of trustfulness which contrasts strangely with the behaviour of their pagan brethren. I was obliged to answer all their questions, and to talk to them of *O Deous Sama*, *O Yaso Sama*, and *Santa Maria Sama*, by which names they designate God, Jesus Christ, and the Blessed Virgin. The view of the statue of the Madonna and Child recalled Christmas to them, which they said they had celebrated in the eleventh month.* They

* According to the old Japanese calendar, the year began with our February.

asked me if we were not at the seventeenth day of the Time of Sadness (*i.e.*, Lent); nor was St. Joseph unknown to them; they call him *O Yaso Samana yo fu*, 'the adoptive father of our Lord.' In the midst of this volley of questions footsteps were heard; immediately all dispersed. But as soon as the new-comers were recognised all returned, laughing at their fright.

"'They are people of our village,' they said. 'They have the same hearts as we have.'

"However, we had to separate for fear of awakening the suspicions of the officials, whose visit I feared. On Maunday Thursday and Good Friday, April 13 and 14, 1,500 people visited the church of Nagasaki. The presbytery was invaded; the faithful took the opportunity to satisfy their devotion before the crucifix and the statues of Our Lady. During the early days of May the missioners learnt of the existence of 2,500 Christians scattered in the neighbourhood of the city. On May 15 there arrived delegates from an island not very far from here. After a short interview we dismissed them, detaining only the catechist and the leader of the pilgrimage. The catechist, named Peter, gave us the most valuable information. Let me first say that his formula for baptism does not differ at all from ours, and that he pronounces it very distinctly. He declares that there are many Christians left up and down all over Japan. He cited in particular one place where there are over 1,000 Christian families. He then asked us about the Great Chief of the Kingdom of Rome, whose name he desired to know. When I told him that the Vicar of Christ, the saintly Pope Pius IX., would be very happy to learn the consoling news given us by himself and his fellow-countrymen, he gave full expression to his joy. Nevertheless, before leaving he wished to make quite sure that we were the true successors of the ancient missioners. 'Have you no children?' he asked timidly.

"'You and all your brethren, Christian and heathens of Japan, are all the children whom God has given us.

Other children we cannot have. The priest must, like your first Apostles, remain all his life unmarried.'

"At this reply Peter and his companion bent their heads down to the ground and cried out: 'They are celibate. Thank God!' "*

Next day an entire Christian village invited a visit from the missioners. Two days later 600 more Christians sent a deputation to Nagasaki. By June 8 the missioners had learnt the existence of twenty-five "Christianities," and seven "baptizers" were put into direct relation with them.

"Thus (to quote M. Launay's admirable résumé of this marvellous episode), in spite of the absence of all exterior help, without any sacraments—except baptism—by the action of God in the first place, and in the next by the faithful transmission in families of the teaching and example of the Japanese Christians and martyrs of the sixteenth and seventeenth centuries, the sacred fire of the True Faith, or at least a still burning spark of this fire, had remained concealed in a country tyrannized over by a government the most despotic and the most hostile to the Christian religion. All that was required was to blow upon this spark and to rekindle its flame in order to realise once more the wish expressed by our Saviour: 'I am come to cast fire upon the earth, and what do I desire but that it be enkindled?' "

Such was the almost miraculous event of March 17, 1865, in honour of which Pius IX. established a feast, with the rank of a greater double, to be celebrated for ever in Japan under the title of "The Finding of the Christians."

It was a graceful recognition of the part played by Fr. Petitjean in this resurrection of the Japanese Church that further prompted Pius IX. to nominate him the following year (1866) Bishop of Myrophitus and Vicar Apostolic of Japan.

* Ad. Launay, pp. 457-459.

One of the first acts of the new Bishop was to erect a statue to "Our Lady of Japan" in 1867, and the same year Pius IX. pronounced the beatification of 205 more of the early Japanese martyrs, including both men and women.

We cannot be astonished that, in spite of all precautions, the secret soon leaked out in Japan. Christianity was still a proscribed religion, forbidden under pain of death. No wonder the year 1867 saw the commencement of fresh attempts at persecution. In 1868 a fresh edict was issued and displayed on the public notice-boards, declaring: "The evil sect called Christian is strictly prohibited. Suspicious persons should be reported to the proper officers, and rewards will be given." One of the missioners, M. Laucaigne (afterwards Vicar Apostolic), had a narrow escape of being arrested. Sixty-five Christians of Urakami were actually seized.

This same year (1868) saw the great national revolution, which entirely altered the system of government. This is not the place to narrate this, the most important political event which has occurred for seven centuries in Japan. Suffice it to say that the upshot of the struggle was the abolition of the Shogunate, established by Yoritomo as far back as 1192, and the resumption of supreme and undivided power by the real Emperor, the Mikado, whose supremacy had been practically dormant during all those long centuries. It was the still reigning Mikado, Mutsuhito, then only sixteen years of age, under whom this great revolution was effected. Strange to say, this restoration of the Imperial power was coincident with a recrudescence of persecution. Fresh imperial edicts against Christians were published. Between October, 1869, and January, 1870, 4,500 Christians were deported from Urakami and the Goto Islands, the chief centres of Catholicity. Pius IX. addressed to these confessors a letter of encouragement. In reply to remonstrances from the Powers, the Government of Tokyo in a memorandum accused the missioners of fomenting disorder. And it was a considerable time before the Consuls could induce the Government to recall the exiles, and withdraw the measures decreed against the Christians.

The next few years are designated in the annual reports of the missioners as a time of mingled persecution and liberty. For, in spite of the expiring efforts of hostility and repression, the growth of Catholicity and the expansion of Catholic works went on very rapidly. It was not until 1873 that all religious persecution ceased. It is calculated that between 1868 and 1873 from 6,000 to 8,000 Christians were torn from their families, deported, and subjected to cruel tortures, so that nearly 2,000 died in prison.* On March 14, 1873, all the Christian prisoners were set at liberty, though the missioners were not yet allowed to penetrate into the interior.

From this time forward the history of Catholicity in Japan has been one of most gratifying progress. The number of missionary priests sent out by the society largely increased, rising from 3 in 1860 to 28 in 1880, and to 98 in 1895. Nuns were introduced, belonging to the two Societies of St. Paul of Chartres and of the Child Jesus. The first religious women entered Japan in 1872, and soon had several native postulants. The first native nun (at least, in modern times), and also the first to die, was Agatha Kataoka Fūkū, in religion Sister Margaret, the sister and daughter of martyrs, who herself died quite young from the effects of the ill-usage she had endured as a child in gaol, where she saw her father perish under the blows of the executioner. In 1882 Sister Julia (Maria Fūyū), and in 1885 Sister Mary (Melania Kustugi Totu) were professed. These were the firstfruits of the religious life in the new Church of Japan. There are now a good number of native nuns, both professed and postulants. A native clergy, too, has been created, the first Japanese priest having been ordained in September,

* Louvet, p. 238.

1883, and some thirty native priests are already at work. "If," says Louvet, "in the hour of trial this heroic Church, which was able with mere catechists to preserve the faith, had had a native clergy, it is probable that Japan would at the present day be wellnigh Christian."*

The ecclesiastical government of Japan has necessarily developed to keep pace with this religious growth. In 1876 (June 3) Pope Pius IX. divided the vicariate of Japan into two—a north and a south vicariate. His successor, Leo XIII., in 1888 (March 16), created a third vicariate—Central Japan—out of that of South Japan; and in 1891 (April 17) divided that of North Japan, erecting the new vicariate of Hakodate. The preceding year, on the twenty-fifth anniversary of the "Discovery of the Christian," the First Provincial Synod of Japan was held at Nagasaki, close to the tomb of Bishop Petitjean (who had died October 7, 1884), and in the very church where the wonderful event of March 17, 1865, had taken place.

"Who could then have told Fr. Petitjean," wrote his successor, Mgr. Jules Cousin, "that twenty-five years later there would be assembled at the foot of the same altar four Bishops, with over thirty missioners and native priests, and that his first meeting with a few poor women who were praying to *Santa Maria* would have had such rapid and consoling results?"†

At this synod was first announced the great and crowning act long contemplated by Leo XIII.—the formal creation of the Japanese hierarchy. This was effected by the Apostolic Letter "Non maius Nobis," dated June 15, 1891. In this interesting document the Holy Father, after a brief but succinct summary of the history of Catholicity in Japan from the time of St. Francis Xavier down to our own day, refers in graceful terms to the "courtesy of justice" of the present Japanese Government towards Catholic missioners, and

* Louvet, p. 239.

† *Illustrated Catholic Missions*, vol. iv., p. 63.

especially to the interchange of amenities between the Holy See and the Mikado. The latter had solemnly received Mgr. Osouf in 1885 with an autograph letter from Leo XIII., expressing the Pontiff's gratitude at the benevolent disposition of the Japanese Government; and in his turn had deputed a diplomatist to Rome to offer his Imperial congratulations on the Pope's sacerdotal jubilee.*

The Pontiff then proceeds to create and delimit the four sees. The Metropolitan See is fixed at Tokyo, "the illustrious city which is the capital of the Empire and the residence of the most serene Emperor," and is bounded on the north by the provinces of Ichigo, Iwashiro and Iwaki; in the south it embraces the provinces of Iechizen and Owari, and extends to the shores of Lake Biwa. It is thus a continuation of the old vicariate of North Japan, minus that of Hakodate, which had been detached only in the April of the same year.

Of the suffragan sees, that of Hakodate, like the vicariate of the same name, embraces the whole of Japan north of the archdiocese, with Yezo, the island of the Ainus, and the Kurile Islands. The see of Nagasaki occupies South Japan, in continuation of the old vicariate, embracing the islands of Kyu-Shu, Hirado, Goto, Chushima, the Liu-Kiu Isles, and several smaller ones. All the rest, the former vicariate of Central Japan, from Lake Biwa to the south of the main island of Nippon, and including the island of Shikoku, forms the diocese of Osaka. The former Vicars Apostolic now became Bishops with territorial titles: Mgr. Osouf being first Archbishop of Tokyo, and Metropolitan; Mgr. Cousin, Bishop of Nagasaki; Mgr. Midon, Bishop of Osaka; and Mgr. Berlioz, Bishop of Hakodate.

* Two other indications of the changed dispositions of the Mikado's Government deserve to be quoted here. In 1877, when a fresh persecution threatened in Korea, and Mgr. Ridel, V.A., was arrested, the Japanese Government intervened in his favour. On August 11, 1884, an Imperial Decree disestablished Buddhism and Shintoism, the State religions, and declared the bonzes to be no longer State officials.

With the creation of the hierarchy, the Church of Japan enters upon an entirely new era of her history.*

The following table gives a summary view of the growth of the Japanese Church in this century:

Year.	Superiors.	Missioners.	Native Clergy.	Churches and Chapels.	Schools.	Number of Catholics.
1860	1 Prefect Apostolic	2	0	0	0	(none known)
1870	1 Vicar Apostolic -	13	0	4	0	10,000
1880	2 Vicars Apostolic	28	0	80	60	23,989
1891	{1 Archbishop, 3 Bishops} -	82	15	164	64	44,505
1904	{1 Archbishop, 4 Bishops} -	119	29	165	84	68,336

* We append in this footnote a "series episcoporum" of Japan, taken from the Pulo-Pinang "Compendium," and not easy to find elsewhere, and brought up to the present day:

I. Antonio Oviedo, S.J., Patriarch of Ethiopia; appointed "Bishop of Japan" by St. Pius V., but declined to accept.
II. Melchior Carnero, S.J., Bishop of Nicæa; Coadjutor to above, but died at Macao.
III. Sebastian Morales, S.J., Bishop of Japan under Sixtus V.; died at Mozambique on his way out.
IV. Pedro Martinez, S.J., Bishop of Japan, the first to land; was present at the sufferings of the twenty-six martyrs.
V. Luiz Serqueyra, S.J., Coadjutor; ruled till 1614.
VI. Didaco Valens, S.J., died at Macao on his way out.
VII. Luis Sotelo, O.S.F., Bishop of East and North Japan; reached Nagasaki 1622, arrested and burnt alive 1624.
VIII. Auguste Forcade, S.M.E., Bishop of Samos, and V.A. of Japan. (After his death FF. Collin, Libois, and Girard, Superiors.)
IX. Bernard Petitjean, S.M.E., Bishop of Myrophitus and V.A. of Japan, 1866; V.A. of South Japan, 1876; died 1884.
X. Joseph Laucaigne, S.M.E., Bishop of Apollonia, and Auxiliary to preceding, 1873; died 1885.
XI. Pierre M. Osouf, S.M.E., Bishop of Arsinoe, and V.A. of North Japan, 1877; Archbishop of Tokyo, 1891.
XII. Jules A. Cousin, S.M.E., Bishop of Acmonia, and V.A. of South Japan, 1885; Bishop of Nagasaki, 1891.
XIII. Felix M. Midon, S.M.E., Bishop of Cæsaropolis, and V.A. of Central Japan, 1888; Bishop of Osaka, 1891; died 1893.
XIV. Alexandre Berlioz, S.M.E., Bishop of Kalinsda, V.A., and then Bishop of Hakodate, 1891.
XV. Henri Vasselon, S.M.E., second Bishop of Osaka, 1894.
XVI. Jules Chatron, S.M.E., third Bishop of Osaka, 1896.
XVII. Pierre Mugabure, S.M.E., Bishop of Sagalasso and Coadjutor of Tokyo, 1901.

III. The Future of the Church in Japan.

And the future? The establishment of the Japanese hierarchy may be very correctly regarded as the close of one epoch and the opening of another. What are the prospects of the Catholic Church in the Japan of the twentieth century?

To guide us in forming a probable estimate of the outlook, we have the best possible sources of information: the views of the experienced missionary Bishops who constitute the Japanese hierarchy, as contained in their annual reports to the society which has sent them forth to their evangelical labours. Let us then consult the *Compte Rendu des Travaux*, published in 1894 and since.

These reports have undoubtedly their consoling side. The number of Catholics in 1904 was 68,336—a growth of 23,831 since 1891 (see preceding table). During the twelve months the number of adult pagans converted and baptized had been 2,105; the number of children of Christian parents baptized (representing the *natural* growth of the Church), 1,747. Works of education and charity show a gratifying increase. Special mention is made of the two excellent leper asylums of Gotemba and Kumamoto. Leprosy is still a terrible scourge of the Japanese Archipelago, and very heartrending are the accounts published from time to time by our Catholic missioners, especially FF. Vigroux and Corre, in the pages of *Illustrated Catholic Missions*,* of the wretched and abandoned victims of this fell disorder. The work among the lepers will doubtless bring with it many spiritual blessings on our missionary work, and must produce a great effect on the native mind. It is consoling, again, to read of the primitive fervour which still characterizes the Christians of the Goto Islands, "the heritage of the ancient Church of Japan"; of the living

* See especially vol. iv., p. 176; vol. vi., p. 48; vol. vii., p. 103; vol. ix., pp. 70, 135.

zeal and self-denying labours of the catechists of Oshima; and of the great hopes entertained of the future conversion of the Ainus, whom Fr. Rousseau finds "docile, sympathetic, and humble," their chief defects being excessive timidity, and, alas! the love of intoxicating drink.

It is a gratifying fact that the patriotic, and often heroic, conduct of Catholic sailors, soldiers and officers during the great Chinese and Russian wars of the past ten years has largely increased the credit of, and the respect for, Catholicity in the Japanese mind.

But it is useless to deny that there are many dark clouds looming over the future of Japanese Catholicity. The era of actual persecution is over,* but it may well be doubted whether the dangers that seem to threaten are not more formidable than the sword and fire of the persecutor. The Bishops' reports are full of these perils. The Archbishop of Tokyo enumerates four agencies at work which impede the advance of Catholicity; these are, the active hostility of the bonzes, the antagonism of the sects, political agitation and the growing dislike of foreigners, and chiefly the anti-Catholic press. Two of these agencies deserve a word of fuller explanation. Since Japan was opened to foreign intercourse, a very large number of missions have been founded by various European and American sects. The best account of these will be found in Mr. Cobbold's extremely interesting little book, "Religion in Japan," which deserves commendation for its general fairness and for the appreciative manner in which it treats our Catholic missions, both ancient and modern. The Russian Church pursues an active propaganda, has a fine Cathedral at Tokyo, and claims a total membership of over 20,000, divided into 219 congregations. The number of adult baptisms

* Strangely enough, however, even at the present day, "our missionaries are allowed to reside in the interior of Japan only on sufferance and as travellers. The passports issued for this purpose have to be renewed half-yearly" ("Compte Rendu des Travaux," p. 94).

for 1892 is given as 952; and the proximity of Russian Asia to Japan is highly favourable to this mission. The various Protestant missions are so numerous as to be confusing. The Americans were first in the field, having begun work in 1859. Three of these missions—viz., those of the American Episcopal Church, the Church of England, and the English Church in Canada, have formed a kind of alliance, holding biennial synods, under the general title of "Nippon Sei Kokwai," or "Church of Japan." The total membership of this group is stated to be 4,300, of whom 3,000 belong to the Anglican Church (represented by both the Church Missionary Society and the Society for the Promotion of the Gospel). There are three or four American and English Bishops. Another amalgamation of religious bodies is that entitled "The Church of Christ in Japan," made up of several American sects and the United Presbyterians of Scotland, claiming a membership of 11,190. Then there are the "Kumi-ai Churches"—*i.e.*, the Congregationalists —with a total of 10,700. Lastly, there are a number of *disjecta membra*, such as American and Canadian Methodists, Baptists, Swiss Protestants, American Friends, Scandinavian Church, and Unitarians, totalling about 8,640. The sum total of members of the Greek Church and Protestant sects of all denominations is now reckoned at over 66,000.

Now, even if all these discordant sects displayed no hostility to the work of the Catholic Church, it cannot be doubted that the spectacle of the disintegration of the Christian name and the contradictory nature of their respective teachings must produce the worst possible effect upon the keen and intelligent mind of the Japanese, and must afford a powerful argument to the bonzes in comparing Christianity unfavourably with Buddhism; nor are they slow to avail themselves of so formidable a weapon. Miss Bickersteth (daughter of an Anglican Bishop), in her book "Japan as we saw It" (1893), quoted by Mr. Cobbold, does not fail to remark this:

"It was impossible not to be struck," she says, "with the present complication of religious matters in the country as compared with the days of Xavier. . . . The divisions of Christendom are nowhere more evident than in its foreign missions to an intellectual people like the Japanese. The Greek, the Roman, the Anglican Churches, the endless 'splits' of Nonconformity, must and do present to the Japanese mind a bewildering selection of possibilities in religious truth."

In connection with this, Mr. Cobbold comments strongly on the disastrous "trimming" in formulæ, chiefly with reference to the Divinity of Christ, practised by some of the Nonconformist sects, and which he calls "full of painful significance."* The same writer perceives that the married missionary of the sects is specially unsuited to Japan, as to other Eastern fields,† and certainly cannot tend to their Christianisation. It will be evident, therefore, that the advent of all these sects has rendered the work of the Catholic missionaries far more arduous and precarious.

An anti-Catholic press is quite a new element of difficulty to cope with:

"The great means," writes M. Ligneul—"the principal means—employed by the sectaries and by enemies of all kinds and all shades against the propagation of Christianity is the press. The press is nowadays, at least as much as in Europe, the real power. Everybody reads, and each one, especially since the establishment of constitutional government, pretends more than ever before to judge of everything for himself."‡

Some remarkable statistics regarding the Japanese press are given by Archbishop Osouf. In 1892 the number of books published in Japan was 20,647, of which 7,334 were new works, and the rest translations or re-editions. Of newspapers there were 792, and of these 69 were religious, issuing a total of 1,837,000

* Cobbold, p. 106. † *Ibid.*, p. 111

‡ *Compte Rendu*, p. 38.

numbers. In 1902 the numbers of publications on religious subjects had risen to 1,134. The largest proportion of these works and papers were Buddhist. The Protestants have 22 papers or other periodicals, and large numbers of books; the catalogues of two Tokyo booksellers mention 600 of all sizes and prices. The Russians issue a fortnightly periodical of 32 pages. And the Catholics? For some time they issued a small Catholic paper of only 18 pages; this failed, but at present there are two Catholic monthly periodicals, one of 50 pages edited by Fr. Maeda, a native Japanese, the other by Fr. Lemoine. It appears to us that what is most urgently needed is a Japanese Catholic Truth Society!

The great event of 1893 was the issue of an anti-Christian work by one Inoue Tetsujiro, a professor of the Imperial University, who had studied at the University of Berlin, whence he returned with the degree of Ph.D. and a knowledge of three European languages. It has been his endeavour to rehabilitate Buddhist pantheism by clothing it in the garb of German rationalistic philosophy. The book is written in a very attractive, almost irresistible, style; the high reputation of its author for learning secured him at once a hearing, and in a few weeks the book had an immense success. Its main thesis is that Christianity is contrary to the welfare of the Japanese State and family. The true religion of Japan is patriotism. Christianity is anti-Japanese. The writer dishes up all kinds of old arguments: the decadence of Catholic nations in Europe, and the contempt of the educated classes for Catholicism; the alleged incompatibility of its teaching, with the results of experimental science; the intellectual inferiority of the clergy; the moral corruption of Europe, in spite of its profession of Christianity; the absence of patriotic teaching in the Gospel, the apparent opposition of some of its doctrines to family duties; even the Inquisition and Galileo find their place among the two hundred objections piled up together with little or no attempt at proof, but in eloquent language, and all leading to the same conclusion—" Christianity is contrary to the welfare of country and home." In the present disposition of the Japanese mind one can easily understand the phenomenal success of this book, which was soon followed by two others of a like nature, and doubtless others will yet appear. The missioner quoted above—M. Ligneul—did not delay in producing a reply to this pernicious work, the refutation of which is by no means difficult. The first volume of this reply was already printed, and great good was anticipated from its appearance. According to Japanese law, however, before a book can be issued from the press, two copies must be deposited at the Ministry of the Interior. This was done by M. Ligneul, and the very day before his book was to be published a Ministerial decree prohibited its issue on the ground that " it menaced the public peace !" The impression produced was extremely painful. " On the one hand," writes the Archbishop, " we see Christianity publicly and very violently attacked, on the other we are placed in the impossibility of publishing a reply. It is very hard ! However," his Grace adds, " there is hope that some good may yet result." Nearly all the newspapers published the official censure. The book of M. Ligneul has thereby already gained a certain notoriety, and is being widely asked for.

In his report for 1903, the Archbishop has some further information on this subject. He writes :

" It would be impossible to give an idea of the deluge of books, newspapers, reviews, and publications of all sorts which inundate Japan. To continue the struggle in this field without losing courage one must have an invincible confidence in the power of truth. Fr. Drouart, who carries on with equal zeal the care of his district and the composition of controversial works, has solved, in an excellent book, thirty of the most serious objections against God, Jesus Christ, and the Church. Fr. Steichen has issued an important work (in both French and

English)—'The Christian Daimyos: a Century of Religious and Political History in Japan (1549–1650).' His work is a source of light for Japanese history itself, as well as for that of the Church in Japan. M. Ligneul, the indefatigable apostle of religious controversy, and his skilful collaborator, Fr. Maeda, have published, sometimes separately, sometimes in conjunction, about a pamphlet a month on different subjects, generally on burning questions of the day. An influential Tokyo newspaper lately tendered well-deserved homage to M. Ligneul. After mentioning several of his publications, the writer of the article added: 'As a controversialist, M. Ligneul has probably never had his equal in the Christian Church in Japan. Among the objections urged against Christianity there are very few indeed which he has not answered with great competence.' "

But there is a factor in the life and development of the Japanese nation deeper than any of those yet referred to, and which in the long-run threatens to be more dangerous to the Church than any other. This is the ever-growing spirit of materialism and indifferentism, lamented by almost every one of the missioners.

Our readers will scarce need to be reminded of the extraordinary and probably unprecedented change which has come over the political and social life of Japan during the reign of the present Mikado. That change can best be expressed as the "Europeanization" of Japan. Western civilization has been taken over *en bloc*, and, without any transition, the quaint Japan of the Shoguns and the daimyos, with their strange costumes, grotesque armour, and half-barbarous system of feudal aristocracy, has been transformed into a modern constitutional kingdom, with its Houses of Parliament and responsible Ministry, its latest Parisian or London fashions, its railways, telegraphs, bicycles, machinery, universities, learned societies, newspapers, and all the other paraphernalia of our so-called "civilization." The late war has shown how in the matter of armaments and military organization, in ironclads, torpedo-boats, and the whole equipment of army and navy, Japan can now claim to rank among the Great Powers of the day. Unfortunately, this civilization thus suddenly thrust upon the Japanese people is of a purely materialistic nature. As is the case in India, European education, the spirit of "corrosive criticism," has shattered the belief in the ancient religions of the country, whose puerilities and superstitions have become only too apparent to more enlightened minds, and have substituted no form of religious belief in their place. The result is a blank scepticism, a purely negative rationalism. This result is well expressed in a passage quoted by Mr. Cobbold:

"A dull apathy as regards religion has settled down upon the educated classes of Japan. The gods of heathenism have crumbled to nothing before modern science and civilization, and the glimmer of light and truth to which they pointed has gone as well."*

This is the cry of all the missioners, as the following extracts from the *Compte Rendu* will show:

"The characteristic note of the period we are passing through," writes M. Bulet, "is, if I am not mistaken, a real religious indifference, which is more difficult to overcome than the ancient hostility which made martyrs."

The Bishop of Nagasaki, Mgr. Cousin, enumerates as the chief obstacle to be encountered "the ever-growing indifference of the population in regard to religious matters. This indifference is produced by books, newspapers, the official education, the thirst for material well-being, for which the extension of commerce and relations with the outer world have opened up new resources."

The Bishop of Osaka enumerates the difficulties of his ministry, and among them "the general spirit of the people—a spirit which is intelligent, open, supple, but completely absorbed by politics and the fever of material

* "Religion in Japan," p. 109.

progress." At Miyazu, we read, "the opening of a commercial port and that of a naval port at Maizuru have so preoccupied men's minds that they can find neither time nor disposition to study a foreign religion."

The sad results of this state of things are visible on every page of the reports. There is an actual slackening in the tide of conversions, and a falling off among the Christians themselves. "Nearly all the missionaries," reports Archbishop Osouf, "complain of a want in their Christians, the absence of zeal to propagate their religion around them." M. Steichen, writing of his district of Shizuoka, declares:

"This year has been the most painful of my life. To judge by the number of baptisms I have to report, one might doubt of the zeal of my five catechists. Nothing could be more unjust. . . . St. Paul (2 Tim. iv.) has well described the state of my district: 'There shall be a time when they will not endure sound doctrine, but will turn away their hearing from the truth, and will be turned into fables.'"

At Matsumoto M. Drouart deplores the stationary state of Christianity, in spite of the labours of his predecessors and himself. In the archdiocese, the boarding-school for girls, in spite of the unbounded devotedness of the nuns, does not increase; the number of elementary schools and pupils has slightly decreased. With the consoling exception of Oshima, the Bishop of Nagasaki does not foresee anywhere in his diocese any considerable movement of conversions.

"If we look" (writes F. Claudius Ferrand) "at the Japan of to-day, really, does it not seem that she goes farther away from the Catholic truth, as she grows in power and advances in the road of progress? The high classes of Japanese society, both those which govern and those which teach, do they not openly profess the most absolute rationalism? Whoever elevates himself above the vulgar herd, whether by fame or science, whether by social position or by riches, does he not make it a title of glory to publicly parade his contempt of all religion. Is not atheism officially taught in the schools, patronized by the press, preached by the so-called scholars and philosophers who keep schools? Does it not seem that it is the fashion and forms an essential part of the programme followed by those who direct New Japan? Yes, certainly, we must admit that it is outside of all Christian thought, not to say against Him who effects this progress which astonishes the world."

It will be interesting, before concluding, to cite the views, no longer of a European observer, but of a native Catholic Japanese. Writing to Father Claudius Ferrand, the founder of the "Geshikuya," a Catholic hostel for Japanese students frequenting the university and professional schools in the capital, this native priest, Father Maeda Chōto, says:

"I am a Catholic priest and Japanese. I cannot be indifferent, I must not be, in regard to all that concerns our religion and my country. . . .

"Leibnitz has said: 'I have always thought that we could reform mankind if we reformed the education of youths.' In fact the young men of to-day are the men of to-morrow; good or bad they will mostly be what their education has made them. Also everyone says and repeats it: Youth, here is the future, here is the hope. It is true, but perhaps also ruin in preparation. This is why for thirty years the activity of the Japanese has turned specially towards education. It is by education that all the changes of this country have been brought about. All who have been able to profit of this means have done so to instil into the new generation the spirit and the ideas that they wished to give them. The Protestants in particular have used it more than any of the others. By teaching under all its forms, all its degrees, they have exercised over all the country an influence hard to believe. Among the men of the press, before the public eye, in public schools, in politics, the first and the most remarkable have come from their schools or at least have been brought up after their principles. By the men that Protestantism has formed it is nearly in a position to govern all intellects.

"And in our Catholic Church? There have been for a long time works of faith and of charity of all kinds. For orphans, boys and girls, for young women, for the sick, for the poor leper, great efforts have been made and not without success. For the purchase of property, for installations of churches and suitable houses, the Mission has exhausted all its resources. Devoted auxiliaries also have brought to the missionaries for the education of youths an extremely precious help. But this special work 'for youths' which every man anxious for the future waited, asked for, of which the necessity imposed itself and imposes itself stronger to-day than ever, you are the first that undertook it, and thanks to your zeal, your industry, your inventive spirit, we now see it in the way of producing happy results. Once more, my reverend father, receive our gratitude.

"To this work is attached another, no less important than the first, and which cannot be developed without it. Will you allow me to speak of it? It is the press. Until the present day to speak of books, newspapers, reviews 'in a country of missions' has always seemed a dream. In the minds of the Catholics of Europe, Japan is still a savage country; the Catechism, Prayer-Book, and the beads were enough. With but few exceptions the appeals made to charity for 'the work of the press' have always remained without response. This time perhaps the Russo-Japanese War will have shown that the Japanese are not in such a profound ignorance, and that they have already made some progress. The truth is that there is not a country in the world, even the United States of America, which has more intellectual life than Japan. All ideas in circulation in other countries immediately appear in Japan. By the reviews, the newspapers, and books they are published right away and known. Religion, politics, moral systems, science, arts, industries, commerce, the latest in literature, impious, immoral, everything is announced, published, translated, and read. The worst novels are known and vulgarized. The press flood the country every day with productions from all sources and of all sorts. Revolution, socialism, even anarchy, everything is there.

"And in all this confusion of all opinions and also of all errors, Catholic truth until the present is hardly represented. Notwithstanding great personal sacrifices, and a zeal worthy of all praise, the part which the missionaries have been able to take in the movement of the Press in Japan is far from being in proportion to the importance of the Catholic religion, with the utility that it could have for the good of the country, with the rôle to which victorious Japan henceforth aspires in the Extreme Orient. To light to-day the torch of truth in Japan is to enlighten quite a large portion of the world.

"For this, Reverend Father, you know what is missing—men practised in wielding the pen, and resources to maintain them. Men you prepare in your family home, 'your nursery of men,' and you will find the necessary funds.

"The American and English people are better prepared than any other for understanding such a situation, and for helping practically by their sympathy and their generosity. Among the numerous friends and acquaintances that you now have beyond the great ocean, I pray you, Reverend Father, plead once more the cause of our Church and our Japan. 'For the Catholic Press,' *the principal organ of our Christian life*, your appeal will certainly be heard."

But we have quoted enough to convince our readers of the great dangers which threaten the future of the Church in Japan, all the more alarming because far more subtle and insidious than all the ferocious cruelties of Hideyoshi and Ieyasu, and their successors. The devoted pastors of the Church are, thank God, fully alive to the signs of the times, as their own words prove. Dark as the outlook may be in many respects, terrible as is the struggle before them—for they may truly say "our wrestling is not with flesh and blood," but with the spirit of worldliness and infidelity—we still feel encouraged to hope of ultimate triumph. All the roseate expectations of 1865, and still more of 1891, are probably not to be realised so soon; but it seems almost a want of faith to doubt that the prayers and groans of St. Francis Xavier, and the blood of so many martyrs, known and unknown, poured forth like water during the sixteenth and seventeenth centuries, will, in God's own good time, bear a glorious harvest in the century which is beginning. *Fiat, fiat!*

BOOKS TO BE CONSULTED.

LOUIS EUG. LOUVET. "Les Missions Catholiques au XIXe Siècle." Lille-Paris: Société de St. Augustin, 1891.

AD. LAUNAY. "Histoire Générale de la Société des Missions Etrangères," t. iii. Paris: Téqui, 1894.

"Société des Missions Etrangères." *Compte Rendu des Travaux* (annual).

M. STEICHEN. "The Christian Daimyos; a Century of Religious and Political History in Japan (1549-1640)." Tokyo: Rikkyo Gakuin Press (1904).

MARNAS. "La Religion de Jésus résusscitée au Japan," two vols. Paris, 1894.

"Supplementum ad Compendium Historiæ Ecclestiasicæ." Pulo-Pinang: Collegium Generale, 1895.

DAVID MURRAY. "Japan" ("Story of the Nations"). London: Fisher Unwin, 1894.

GEORGE A. COBBOLD. "Religion in Japan—Shintoism, Buddhism, Christianity." London: S.P.C.K., 1894.

XIII

THE DANCING PROCESSION AT ECHTERNACH

It is a curious fact, and perhaps a providential one, that the only two striking survivals of curious medieval celebrations testifying to the vitality of the faith in the Christian masses are to be found amongst those Teutonic nations with whom began the great revolt against the Faith in the sixteenth century. Not the hot-blooded and imaginative sons of Italy or Spain, but the phlegmatic, hard-headed, and intellectual children of Germany—South and North—have preserved intact to our days those two strange fragments of the ages of faith whose origins are lost in the twilight of the Middle Ages—the *Passionspiel* of Ober-Ammergau and the *Springprozession* of Echternach. Having had the good fortune in 1880 to assist at the decennial performance of the Bavarian Passion Play, I was only too glad of the opportunity in 1884 of seeing also the annual " Dancing Procession " of this extremely ancient town. A spell of delightful weather enabled me to combine a large amount of pleasure with the mingled curiosity and devotion that led me thither. I have not space here to introduce to the notice of my readers the natural beauties of the charming little Grand Duchy of Luxemburg, above all, to describe in detail the wondrous scenery of the Mühlerthal. I was fortunate enough to fall in with a large and agreeable party bent on a foot tour through this delightful valley *en route* for Echternach. Let me here open a brief parenthesis to recommend any of my readers who are within convenient distance, and who are not afraid to face a good mountain scramble and a six or seven hours' walk, not to miss the chance of a really pleasant day's out, crowned by a visit to a shrine that ought to interest all Englishmen—that of St. Willibrord, one of the greatest men that England ever produced, the Apostle of Northern Germany and of the Netherlands. We took train from the city of Luxemburg to the small station of Gründhof, whence we set off on foot through a beautiful country to gain the entrance to the romantic valley, with its wild rocks, its fantastic caverns, and its luxuriant vegetation, which goes winding through the heart of the land until it opens out into the lovely valley of the Sauer. Half-way on our long walk we came to the village Berdorf, where the tourist ought not to fail to visit the village church, and see the curious old Roman pagan altar, which was consecrated for Christian use by St. Willibrord himself, and is still used as the high-altar of the church. The massive square block is well preserved, with the figures at each of the four sides of Hercules, Juno, Apollo, and Minerva. Beyond Berdorf, the Mühlerthal assumes a more peaceful and less wild aspect, and reminds one of nothing so much as the "fairy glen" of Bettws-y-Coed, only prolonged for many and many a mile. The shades of evening were already falling when we emerged at last from the narrow fastnesses of the "Wolf's Glen," and saw lying at our feet the fruitful valley embosoming the old abbey town of Echternach, whose origin dates back to pre-Roman times—as attested by its Keltic name* and the abundant Keltic remains found in its vicinity. Needless to say, we found the little town of barely 4,000 inhabitants densely crowded, and it was no easy matter to procure a night's lodging for all our party.

Historians are at a loss to give an account of the origin of the strange "Dancing Procession" in honour of St. Willibrord, which is held here every Whit Tuesday; for, strange to say, the earlier chronicles maintain a

* Lat. Epternacum.

strict silence on the subject. It is not till 1553 that we find any definite indication of the dance, but a picture painted in that year represents St. Willibrord blessing the dancers. A decree of the local magistrates about the same date also speaks of the "Springh heiligenn . . . uff Pofingst dinstag." The historian Brouwer, who was born in 1559, often describes this curious ceremony, and declares that as a child he had heard the procession spoken of by very old people as a tradition of great antiquity. A petition of the parish priests of the Eifel in 1770 to the Archbishop of Trier states that their ancestors had established this painful act of penance by vow in times of great necessity 300 years before. But although the actual dancing is not traceable by documents to a higher antiquity, yet the pilgrimages and processions of the neighbouring parts of Germany to the tomb of St. Willibrord are traceable back to the very death of the saint himself. For this we have the explicit testimony of another great Anglo-Saxon of the next generation, Alcuin, the friend of Charlemagne, who, both in his prose and poetical Life of St. Willibrord, describes the crowds of pilgrims who flocked to the shrine at Echternach and the numerous miracles wrought there.

> "Vincula rumpuntur per se properantibus illuc
> Qui sua cum lacrymis veniunt mala crimina flere,
> Et toti redeunt, Christo donante, soluti."

Still more distinctly does Abbot Thiofred (died 1110) describe in considerable detail the great procession held in Whit Week, according to immemorial right ("ritu perpetuo et quasi a progenie in progenies transmissa"); but does not seem to mention the dancing, unless the word *tripudium*, frequently used by him, refers to the custom. Certainly the meaning of dancing is attributed to it in Ducange. A number of antiquarians, and among them Cardinal Pitra, attribute a still greater antiquity to the dancing procession, for they consider it likely that it is nothing else than some old heathen dance or triumphal march, which St. Willibrord may have found in use among the wild populations whom he converted to Christianity, and which he may have changed into a Christian celebration, just as the Church did so often and so prudently during the conversion of the European tribes, and as Pope Gregory the Great actually allowed and advised in the case of various pilgrimages and other usages of heathen nations. This would be all the more natural in the case of St. Willibrord, who, as we have seen, consecrated the pagan altar for Christian use at Berdorf, and I believe at one or two other places in Belgium. "We should not be astonished," says Cardinal Pitra, "if an inquiry into the origin of the procession should lead us to some military and national march of the ancient Frisians or Saxons, whom St. Willibrord had permitted to preserve as they followed him, even up to the doors of his monastery, their patriarchal dance." One of the main arguments in favour of this theory is the extremely ancient traditional melody of the procession, which seems to bear rather a joyful than a penitential character. Other writers have come to the conclusion that the traditional religious processions to the tomb of St. Willibrord, which have been going on since his death, were, during the fourteenth century, purposely altered into a penitential exercise by means of the fatiguing and painful kind of dance which now distinguishes it. That was the century of terrible epidemics, especially of epilepsy and the so-called "St. Vitus's dance." As the old chronicler writes:

> "L'an trieze cens soixante et quatorze
> A Metz advint piteuse chose,
> Qu'en la cité ville et champs
> Gens danssoient du bien sainct Jean.
> Le prestre en faisant son office,
> Les seigneurs séans en justice,
> Le laboureur en son labour,
> Sur qui que tombait la douleur,
> Et danssiaent neuf ou dix jours,
> Sans avoir repos ny séjour."

As a matter of fact, it is known for certain that this was the origin of the spring procession at Prüm, founded about 1340, but long since extinct. Again, it is certain that the object of the dancing processions now, and for the last few centuries, has been penitential, and especially for the averting of St. Vitus's dance and epilepsy. Lastly, the popular legend, which may be read in Collin de Plancy's "Fiddler of Echternach," connects the dance with Vitus himself, who appears as a wondrous fiddler, and whose adventures are strangely like those of the Pied Piper of Hamelin. Whichever of these two theories we accept, it is clear that in the dancing procession we have a curious custom of very great antiquity, preserving not merely its vitality, but actually, after its brief interruption during the days of Joseph II. and the French Revolution, yearly increasing in size and popularity, as the following numbers of those who take part in it will show: 1831, 4,500; 1841, 8,887; 1861, 10,991; 1872, 12,272; 1881, 15,541. The whole ceremony and its surroundings impress the spectator mostly by the wonderful faith and devotion of the thousands of pilgrims who flock to it. Not without difficulty were the numerous priests able to say Mass in the ancient parish church where the shrine of St. Willibrord is exposed to the veneration of the faithful under the high-altar. From early daybreak long processions of peasantry, headed by their clergy, and with cross and banners, are seen wending their way down the fruitful hillsides towards the banks of the Sauer. They are all singing and praying aloud, and have come journeys of six, eight, or ten hours on foot—men, women, and children. The famous Gross-Prüm pilgrimage, indeed, comes a journey of three days. Each procession pours into the parish church, and makes the tour of the high-altar, singing or reciting the Litany of St. Willibrord at the very top of their voices; and, as many of the pilgrimages are in the edifice at the same time, the effect is rather impressive than harmonious. Indeed, I can assure the reader that a priest has some difficulty in saying Mass amidst the surging sea of voices which fill the church, or, indeed, of making his way to the altar through the dense mass of human beings which fill the place.

At nine o'clock the great " Maxglocke," the big bell given by Emperor Maximilian, the " last of the Knights," and the last of the numerous Imperial pilgrims, in 1512, rang out the opening of the ceremony. The *Veni Creator* having been intoned by the clergy in front of the tomb of St. Willibrord, the great procession moved across the ancient pre-Roman bridge to the Prussian side of the Sauer, where, on the bank of that river, a short sermon was delivered. I regret to say that the crowd was so dense that I was unable to approach the bridge, much less pass it, and so am unable to describe this part of the day's proceedings. The sermon ended, the town bands struck up the peculiar old traditional melody, and, as if by magic, as when the legendary Vitus drew the first notes across his magic violin, the thousands assembled in their ranks for the procession began their curious hop or dance, and the entire body slowly started their toil-some march through the old town. I was fortunate in being accommodated at a window of the pro-Gymnasium, whose courteous rector also afforded me hospitality on the preceding night. Looking down from this point of vantage, the sight was indeed a memorable one. First came the clergy in surplice, with a choir of singers, cross, and banners ; then the band playing the often-mentioned *melopeon* of the dance.

The melody is scarcely a melancholy one, but rather suggestive of a joyful origin. It has something quaint about it, and when it has been heard for some three hours, repeated over and over again on every kind of instru-ment of the most atrocious character, suggestive of pain-fully asthmatic German bands, it haunts the memory, and is not easily forgotten. I had been told by every-body that the impression produced by the procession was not, as might be expected, ludicrous or grotesque, but rather weird and painful. Let me hasten to say that my own experience fully confirms this judgment. Immediately after the band the hundreds of school-children, the boys all in their shirt-sleeves, hopping merrily and evidently enjoying the exercise, form rather an amusing and pleasing picture. Many of these children are hired to dance for people who are unable to take part in the procession themselves. On our arrival at Echternach the night before, we were met by a decent-looking lad, who politely doffed his cap, and asked if we required any-one to dance for us on the morrow. They receive a small gratuity for thus acting as proxies. But when you see between ten and twelve thousand grown-up men and women, hardy, sunburnt sons of toil, some of great age, others afflicted with various bodily infirmities, their faces marked by the deepest seriousness and earnestness, painfully springing the curious steps—two steps forward and one obliquely backwards—laughter dies away from your lips ; you are moved rather to sadness—sometimes to tears. It must be remembered that all these people are going through the exercise as a penitential work, either to obtain delivery for themselves or some member of their family from the terrible visitation of epilepsy or kindred diseases, or in thanksgiving for cures obtained, or else to avert the same from their families, or, lastly, in fulfilment of some vow of themselves or their ancestors. This accounts for the great earnestness displayed on their features and in their movements. Many of the men dance in their shirt-sleeves. I noticed that nearly all the women, young and old, carried ample baskets on their left arm, no doubt containing the day's provisions. The ranks vary from four to six persons in breadth. As a rule, the dancers seem to go by families, though in some parts the men and women are grouped separately. The so-called dance is executed with precision only by a few, who really take the steps with considerable accuracy ; in most cases it resolves itself into a kind of hop or skip forward and backward, to the cadence of the music. It is extremely curious to look down from a window upon the surging mass of people swaying alternately backwards and forwards, with a slow onward movement, exactly like the waves of the sea at the edge of the coast. Now and again there are pauses for much-needed rest, and then after a few minutes the quaint movement is resumed. Here and there comes a band, or a small knot of amateur musicians, perhaps a fiddle and a couple of flutes, or a flute and a kettle-drum, or an accordion with a triangle, all repeating the melody, and nearly all of the very vilest description. About three hours are consumed in the entire course of the 1,225 steps. The procession winds through the town up the sixty-two steep steps of the Petersberg, into the church, round the shrine of St. Willibrord, out into the churchyard, and finally thrice round the wooden cross in the same. Generally the weather at this time is intensely hot, and then the "springing" under the blazing rays of an almost tropical sun is a terrible work of mortification indeed. Fortunately, the weather at my visit was overcast and cool. But even so, all along the course charitable people were to be seen running out of their houses and offering glasses of wine or sugared water, or even vinegar and water, to the exhausted dancers. Let me here note as a pleasing feature that every person in the streets, whether among dancers or spectators remained bareheaded during the whole time of the procession. Nothing could exceed the respect and reverence shown on all sides. Among the persons particularly noticed in the procession, I must mention an old woman, who carried astride on her shoulders a girl of some ten or twelve years, afflicted with epilepsy, clinging to her neck. The old dame danced with painful earnestness, and the sight of her struggling beneath the weight of her unfortunate burthen was really pitiful to behold. Another woman carried her afflicted child in her arms, and evidently must have suffered much under the weight of it during the three mortal hours of the procession. Two well-dressed girls, holding their afflicted brother between them, were springing with an energy that was actually painful to witness. Several blind persons were among the "springers." I also noticed a curious little dwarf of minute proportions, who danced with great zeal and devotion. The lines of dancers generally held together, either hand in hand, or by means of umbrellas or even pocket-handkerchiefs stretched from one to the other to facilitate their movement. At the end of the dancers came the dense body of "prayers" (*Beter*), perhaps two or three thousand in number, not dancing, but praying aloud with wondrous fervour. In an Englishman the constant refrain, "Heiliger Willibrordus, bitt für uns!" borne in upon thousands of voices, cannot but produce a thrill of patriotic gratification, but at the same time a feeling of regret that this great Saxon Apostle is so little known in his native land.

It is calculated that 10,000 or 15,000 spectators thronged the little town. Among them were the newly-consecrated Bishop of Luxemburg, Mgr. Koppes, and his Excellency the Papal Internuncio at the Hague, Mgr. Spolverini. The number of ecclesiastics—German, Belgian, and French—was enormous. I also noticed two curious hermits in a kind of monastic dress; for in the rocks which border the valley of the Sauer there is still to be found here and there an odd cavern or grotto which houses a solitary hermit as in days of yore.

About one o'clock the famous procession and the whole of the religious proceedings were over, and the rest of the day was given up to more worldly affairs in the shape of a kind of *Kermess*, or great fair. The market-place is crowded with booths of all kinds of wonders and monstrosities, shooting-galleries, wax-works, merry-go-rounds, and all the varied paraphernalia of village wakes, while the streets are lined with stalls for the sale of every conceivable article, from sugar saints to boots and shoes.

I had intended to say something of the superb old

Benedictine Abbey, once one of the most famous in all Europe, and the "flos regulæ" of St. Benedict, and of the splendid basilica, now so happily restored; but I fear that I have already too long trespassed on the patience of my readers. I feel, however, bound to say that I saw nothing degrading, repulsive, or ludicrous in the curious sight I was privileged to witness. Quaint, strange, weird, even somewhat painful, it all is; but the main impression left on the mind is that of the marvellous spirit of faith, of devotion, and of penance, rooted so firmly in the very nature of this hardy German peasantry, as testified by the more than 20,000 pilgrims, whether springers or spectators, who crowded into the little and ancient town of St. Willibrord, the Northumbrian Saint and Apostle of Lower Germany.

ADDENDA.

To p. 341. The little volume "Le Catholicisme au Japon," by Albert Vogt (Paris, Librairie Bloud), did not fall into my hands until the present book was completed. I should also add "Les Missions Catholiques Françaises au XIXe Siècle," by Fr. Piolet, t. iii. (Paris).

To p. 353. An account of the "Dancing Procession" this year (1905) by an eye-witness ("M. R.") appears in *The Harvest* for October, 1905.

INDEX

Abbeloos, Monsignor, 200, 219 *note*
Abbots Langley, village of, 55
Abelard, 78
Abraham, Mr., 271, 286
Achaemenid Kings of Persia, 13
Adelaide, divorced wife of Frederick Barbarossa, 85
Adelperga, 31
Adelung, 316
Adelwald, 41
Adnacul or *Adhnachd* (a burial-place), 9
Adnet, Abbé, 321
Adrian I., Pope, 152 *note*
Adrian II., Pope, 152 *note*
Adrian III., Pope, 152 *note*
Adrian IV. (Nicholas Breakspeare) and Ireland, 53; and Henry II., 53; birthplace, 55; boyhood, 56; studies at Paris and Arles, 57; connection with Order of the Norbertines, 57 *et seq.;* enters the Abbey of St. Rufus at Avignon, 59-60; elected abbot, 60 *et seq.;* appeals to Rome against his monks, 61; retained by Eugenius III. and created cardinal, 62; appointed Apostolic Legate to Scandinavia, 63; visits England, 63; his work in Norway, 63 *et seq.;* his work in Sweden, 65; his mission to Denmark, 65; tries to avert a dispute between Sweden and Denmark, 65; his linguistic attainments, 65-66; elected Pope, 66; struggle with the Roman republicans, 67-68, 70 *et seq.;* places Rome under an interdict, 68; dealings with Frederick Barbarossa, 69 *et seq.;* the question of homage, 71 *et seq.;* crowns Frederick at Rome, 74; quarrel with William II., Norman King of Sicily, 75 *et seq.;* relations with the Eastern Churches, 76; relations with England, 77 *et seq.;* alleged grant of Ireland to Henry II., 79 *et seq.;* renewal of struggle with Frederick Barbarossa, 84 *et seq.;* the champion of Italian liberty, 86 *et seq.;* his death, 87; personal character, 88; works, 88; policy, 88; bibliography, 89; other references, 105, 106, 152 *note*, 153
Adrian V., Pope, 152 *note*
Adrian VI. (Adrian of Utrecht) and Princess Margaret of York, 104-105, 111; birth and parentage, 105; educated by the Brothers of the Common Life, 106; goes to Louvain University, 108; gains the title of "Primus," 109; studies theology at the Collège du Saint-Esprit, 109; professor of philosophy and theology, 110; Canon of St. Pierre, 110; Curé of the Béguinage, 110; Doctor of Divinity, 110 *et seq.;* receives many benefices, 111; professor at University of Louvain, 112; publishes his "Quæstiones in Quartum Sententiarum Librum" and "Questiones Quodlibeticæ," 112; elected Chancellor of University, 113; twice chosen Rector Magnificus, 113; personal appearance and character, 113 *et seq.;* erects college at Louvain, 114, 150;

23—2

comes under the notice of Pope Julius II., 114; tutor to Prince Charles and his sisters, 116 *et seq.;* nominated by Charles to a seat on the council of the Low Countries, 117; sent on embassies, 117-118; nominated Regent of Castile, 118; made Bishop of Tortosa, 119; resigns his benefices in Low Countries, 119; nominated Grand Inquisitor of Arragon and Navarre, 119 *et seq.;* created Cardinal by Leo X., 120; made Viceroy of Castile, 122; elected Pope, 123 *et seq.;* election not due to the influence of Charles V., 131 *et seq.;* retains his baptismal name, 132; refuses to become the tool of Charles V., 134-135; the journey from Spain to Rome, 135 *et seq.;* reforms Papal Court, 139 *et seq.;* relations with humanism, 142 *et seq.;* aims similar to those of Pope Pius II., 143 *note;* efforts to beat back the Turk, 143 *et seq.*, 149; and Lutheranism, 145 *et seq.;* desires to convoke an Œcumenical Council, 147; canonizes St. Antoninus and St. Benno, 148; forms international league to defend Italy against Francis I., 149; illness and death, 149 *et seq.;* estimate of his work, 152 *et seq.;* bibliography, 153; further reference, 192
Adrian Florisze, Master, 105
Ælian on inhumation, 12
Africa, funeral customs of, 21-22
Agelmund, first King of the Lombards, 34, 41
Agilulf, King, 30, 41
Aguilera, monastery of, 121
Ahuïtzoll, slaughter of, 21
Ahura-Mazda, 13
Aio (or Agio), 33, 34
Aix-la-Chapelle, 121
Aken, near Paderborn, 191 *note*
Alaric, 16
Albano, Nicholas Breakspeare created Bishop of, 62
Albert the Great, Blessed, 235, 236
Alboin, King, 38, 40, 41, 42, 44, 46
Alcalá, University of, 119, 192
Alcuin, 31, 155 *note*, 346
Aldrich, 163
Alexander of Hales, 159,
Alexander II., Pope, 83
Alexander III., Pope, 78 *note*, 83
Alexander VI., Pope, 162
Alfred, King, 48; and the foundation of Oxford, 200, 201
Aligherius (Dante), etymology of name, 48, 49
All Souls College, Oxford, 160
Allen, Dr. William (afterwards Cardinal), 180, 181, 182, 185
Allies, Mr. T. W., 239, 281, 288, 293
Alvarez, Father, S.J., 317
Alzog, Dr., 75
Ambri, 33
American Episcopal Church in Japan, 334
Ampleforth College, 259
Ampolla, 136
Anagni, 68
"Analecta Juris Pontificii," 81
Anastasius IV., Pope, 66
Anderdon, Father, S.J., 288, 293
Andrew, 175
Angles, 43
"Anglicanism" and scientific theology, 180
Anglo-Saxons and Lombards, points of contact as regards dress, 44, 47; language, 45-47; political institutions, 47-48; love of liberty, 48; temperament and character, 48-50
Angro-Mainyus, 13
Animism, 187
Anjiro (Han-Siro), afterwards Paul of the Holy Faith, 302, 303, 308
"Annals of the Four Masters" on the state of Ireland about the time of Pope Adrian IV., 84
Anstey, "Epistolæ Academicæ" quoted, 211
Anthaib, 34
Antibes, 136
Antonius, 236
Antwerp, 196, 208
Anushin, 318
Apollodorus of Rhodes on building of funeral pyre, 11
Apostolic origin of Litany of Loreto, alleged, 224, 230
Areson, Bishop John, 99
Arianism, Lombards and, 41
Arichis II., 31

Arima, revolt of Christians in principality of, 315
Arles, Nicholas Breakspeare studies at, 57, 59
Armstrong, Mr. T., 55
Arnaldo da Brescia, 67, 68, 70, 71
Arnold, Sir Edwin, 186
Arnold of Gheilhoven, 96
Arnold, Matthew, 299
Arthur, Prince (brother of Henry VIII.), 169
Arthur, fellow of St. John's College, Cambridge, 165, 166
Articles in *Dublin Review*, suggestions by Cardinal Wiseman for, 281, 282
Aryans and neolithic age, 7; cradle-land of, 9; originators of cremation, 8, 9, 22, 24; funeral customs of, 15, 16
Ascham, Roger, 173, 177
Assi, 33
Assipitti (probably the Usipetes of Cæsar and Tacitus), 33
Assyrian Empire, burial customs of 16
Assyriology, 186
Astodâns (bone receptacles), 14
Athelstan, 48
Audoin, 38, 44
Augsburg, printing press at, 92, 96
Augustinians at Oxford, 166, 173; of Recanati, 226; arrive in Japan, 311; martyrs in Japan, 314
Australia, funeral customs of, 22
Authari, King, 41, 42
"Auxilium Christianorum," origin of the invocation, 228, 229, 232
"Avesta," 9, 14; Louvain and the, 187; first manuscript of the, 199, 216
Ayuthia, ancient capital of Siam, 319
Aztecs, 21, 22

Babylonian Empire, burial customs of, 16
Babylonian and Oriental Record, 14
Bacon, Lord, 106 *note*, 159 *note*, 184
Bacon, Robert, 158
Bacon, Roger, 155 *note*, 158, 159 *and note*, 185
Baeumer, Dom Suitbert, O.S.B., slight error in his "History of the Breviary," 228
Bagshawe, Mr. H. R., editor of *Dublin Review*, 269, 270, 272, 278, 286, 298
Bainab, 34
Baines, Bishop, Vicar Apostolic of the Western District, 248, 250, 259
Bamberg, Abbey of St. Michael at, 98
Baptism retained by the "rediscovered" Christians of Japan, 325, 326
Baptismal vows, renewal of, 253
Baptists in Japan, 334
Barcelona, 136; Cucufatis Monastery at, 98; priest-printers at, 99
Bardenea, 37
Bardengau, 35
Bardowyk, 35
Bari, 76
Barnabites, 139
Barnes, Robert, Augustinian Prior, 166, 167
Baronius, Annals of, 80
Bartolemeo, "priest-printer" of Florence, 99
Basel, printing press at, 92, 99; John Wesel at, 190
Basil, Bishop of Thessalonica, 76
Bathhurst, Miss, 244
Bauwens, Dr. Isidore, on funeral and mourning customs, 2 *et seq.*, 7, 8, 18, 25
Baxter, Mr. Dudley, 62 *note*
Beardeneu, 37
Beardincgford, 37
Beatrice, heiress of Burgundy, 85
Beconton, Devonshire, 206
Bedmond, hamlet of, 55
Beelen, 190
Belgium, Royal Academy of, 188
Bellasis, Mr. Sergeant, 239
Bellesheim, 81
Bellintonus, Mattheus, 151 *note*
Benedictines at Oxford, 159, 173
Benevento, dukedom of, 31, 40, 76
Benson, Dr., Archbishop of Canterbury, 240
Benzoni, Rutilio, Bishop of Loreto, 229
Berdorf, altar in church at, 345, 347
Bergamo, 50; its "priest-printer," 99
Berlioz, Mgr., Bishop of Hakodate, 330, 331 *note*

Bernard a Sancto Leone, 58
Bernardinus de Bustis, 236
Berners, Dame Juliana, Prioress of Sopewell, 96
Berni, 143
Berthier, Père, O.P., 157 *note*
Berthold, Archbishop of Mainz, 93
Besançon, Diet of, 85
Bettws-y-Coed and the Mühlerthal, 345
Bible and inhumation among the Jews, 17, 18
Bible, Antwerp Polyglot, 189
Bible, editions of, in fifteenth and sixteenth centuries, 100-102
Bible in early University library at Oxford, 211
Bible Society and Japan, 320
Bibliothèque du Roi, Paris, 213, 215, 216
Bickersteth, Miss, on the rivalry of the Christian sects in Japan, 334-335
Biella, 50
Binterim on the antiquity of the Litany of Loreto, 224
Bishops, list of Japanese, 331 *note*
Blanche Nef, wreck of the, 56
Bluime, 36
Boardman, Rev. James, 265
Boat burial. *See* Water burial
Bocher, Joan, 177 *note*
Bodleian Library, Oxford, 198 *et seq.*; 210 *et seq.*
Bodley, Sir Thomas, 210, 212, 218, 221 *note*
"Bokys of Hawking and Hunting," by Dame Juliana Berners, Prioress of Sopewell, 96
Bologna, Diet of, 86; University of, 156, 157 *note*, 177, 201, 202
Bonanni, 59
Boneto Locatello, 99
Bonnani, 151 *note*
Bono, Giovanni, 151 *note*
"Bonus Joannes," Monk of Savona, 97
Bonzes, influence of the, 306, 309, 330 *note*, 333, 334
Booker and Dolman, publishers, 277
Bopp, philologist, 216
Bourchier, Richard, merchant, 213
Bowden, Father of the Oratory, 239
Bowyer, Mr. (afterwards Sir George), 282
Bozidar, Duke of Servia, 97
Brabant, Counts of, 104 *note*, 105, 201
Bradley on spelling of "Scandinavia," 35 *note*
Brahmanism and cremation, 24
Breakspeare, Nicholas. *See* Adrian IV.
Breakspeare, Boso, 78 *and note*
Breakspeare, Robert, 56
Breslau, "priest printers" at, 99
Breviary, Roman, on the origin of the title "Auxilium Christianum," 228
Brewer, Professor, 155, 167 *note*
Bridgett, Father, C.SS.R., 155
Brindisi, 76
British Museum Library, 220 *note*
Brixen, "priest-printers" at, 99
Broadgate's Hall, Oxford, 208
Broomhead, Father Rowland, 266
Brothers of the Common Life, 95, 106, 190
Brower on the dancing procession, 346
Brown, Dr., Vicar Apostolic (afterwards first Bishop of Liverpool), 267
Browne, 180
Brownson's Review, 291
Bruckner on the Lombards. *See* chap. ii. *passim*
Brün, "priest-printers" at, 99
Bruno the Carthusian, 235
Brussels, press at Convent of Nazareth at, 95
Bryan, 163
Bucer, Martin, 174, 175
Buda-Pesth, printing press at, 92
Buddhism and cremation, 14, 24; disestablished in Japan, 330 *note*
Bulet, Abbé, on religious indifference in Japan, 339
"Bullarium," Roman, 80
Bullock, 163, 174
Bullock, Dr., 91
Bunsen, Chevalier, 279, 286
Burghley, Lord, 177-179, 207
Burgundaib, 34
Burgundians, 34, 39
Burgundy, Dukes of, 201
Burial, art of, 1; general conclusions, 24-25; bibliography, 25. *See* also Cremation, Inhumation,

Exposition, Water-burial, Embalming, Tree-burial, Platform-burial, Funeral customs
Burnouf, Eugène, 199, 217, 218
Burns and Lambert, publishers, 277
Burns and Oates, publishers, 277
Busleiden, Giles (Ægidius Buslidius), 142, 191, 194
Busleiden, Jerome, 191 *et seq.*
Bustum (a tomb), 9

Caccia, Father, on Father Furlong, 259-260
Cæsar Cistariensis, 235
Cæsarism, 89
Caius College, Cambridge, 177, 179
Caius, Dr., 177, 179
Calvinists, at Cambridge, 169
"Cambridge Modern History" on the conclave which elected Adrian VI., 127; and relations between Leo X. and Raffaele, 143 *note;* and Luther, 146
Cambridge, University of, chapter vi., *passim;* work of Blessed John Fisher at, 162 *et seq.*, 170 *et seq.;* Lutheranism at, 165 *et seq.;* Royal divorce and, 168 *et seq.*; Reformation changes at, 176; foundation of Queen Mary's reign, 177
Camden, 183
Camm, Dom Bede, 208 *note*
Campeggio, Cardinal Lorenzo, 120, 138
Campion, Blessed Edmund, S.J., 180
Candia, 145
Candiotti, Giulio, Arch-priest of Loreto, 22[illegible]-229
Cannibalism in Australia and Africa, 22
Canstadt race, 3
Cantwell, Rev. Edmund, 265
Capes, Mr. J. M., 288
Caraffa, Cardinal (afterwards Paul IV.), 99
Cardinal College, Oxford, 163, 170
Carfax, the, Oxford, 168
Carnero, Melchior, S.J., Bishop of Nicæa, 33 *note*
Carnoy, Professor, biologist, 218
Carriers, curious Indian custom, 21 and *note*
Carthusians, 108
Cartwright, 180, 181
Carvajal, Bernardino, Cardinal di Santa Croce, 114, 125, 137
Casaroto, Giampietro, 98
Casartelli, Mr. J., and the great mission in Liverpool, 256
Cashel Hoey, Mr., and the *Dublin Review*, 270, 290, 293, 294, 298
Cashel Hoey, Mrs., and the *Dublin Review*, 270, 294
Cassell's "Conquests of the Cross" quoted, 313
Catherine Hall, Cambridge, 160
Catherine, Queen of Henry VIII., 168 *et seq.*
Catholic Record Society "Miscellanea," 221
Catholic Truth Society and the printing press, 103
Cattle, slaughtering of black, in Greek and Roman funeral rites, 11
Cecil, William, Baron Burghley, Chancellor of University of Cambridge, 177-179, 207
Cécile, Rear-Admiral, assists missioners to reach the Liu Kiu Islands, 321
Celibacy, idea of, preserved among the survivors of early Japanese Christianity, 325-326
Cenna (or Zinna), monastery at, 98
"Centum Gravimina," 147
Cerberus, 11
Cesarini, Cardinal, 136
Cettinje, monastery press at, 97
Chaldean burial-places, 17
Chamberlain, 306
Chancellor, office of, at University of Oxford, 157
Charlemagne visited by Paul the Deacon, 31; deposes Desiderius, 40
Charles the Bold, Duke of Burgundy, 104, 114, 116
Charles V., Emperor, 114 *et seq.*
Charles I., King, and the Bodleian Library, 219
Charlton, Dr., 281
Charnock, 162
Châtron, Jules, S.M.E., Bishop of Osaka, 331 *note*, 339
Chedsey, 174, 175
Cheke, John, 173, 177
Cheregato, Francesco, Papal Legate, 147

Chevillard, Abbé, "Siam et les Siamois," 23-24
Chinese favour inhumation, 14; influence on Japanese, 305
Chorten (cenotaph), 15
Chōto, Father Maeda, on the needs of the Church in Japan, 336, 338, 341-343
Christi, Father, S.J., 281, 288
Christina, Prioress of Markgate, 77
Christmas kept by the survivors of early Japanese Christianity, 324
"Chronicon Monast. S. Albani," 77 and *note*
Church and printing press: authorities, 90 *note*; printing, in its origin and early history, essentially a Catholic art, 90-93; grants indulgences for sale and dissemination of printed books, 93; the Religious Orders set up presses, 94 *et seq.*; the secular "priest-printers" develop the art, 98 *et seq.*; the clergy patronize lay printers, 99; the Luther legend, 100-102
Church Missionary Society in Japan, 334
Cicé, Monsignor, 319
Cicero, 12
Cirillo, Bernardino, author of the Macerata Prayer-Book, 230 *note*
Cistercians at Oxford, 173
Cività Vecchia, 124, 137, 145
Clarendon Press, Oxford, 201, 210
Clarke, Miss E. M., 297
Clarke, John, 167
Clement, Dorothy, 205
Clement, John, Professor of Greek at Oxford, 199, 206
Clement, Margaret, 205 and *note*
Clement of Padua, 98
Clement VII., Pope, 145, 152 *note*, 164
Clement, Winifred, 205, 207
Clerk, English Ambassador in Rome, 128
Clifford, Dr., Bishop of Clifton, 297
Clitheroe, Venerable Margaret, 314
Cluny, Abbey of, 98
Cobbe, Richard, 213
Cobbold, Mr. G. A., on religion in Japan, 315-316, 333, 339, 343
Cobham, Thomas, Bishop of Worcester, 210
Codes, Lombard, 48
Codex Gothanus, 30
Cogan, Mr. H., 302
Coleridge, Father, S.J., 239, 293, 301 *note*, 302, 303, 305
Colet, Dean, 161, 203
Colinet, Professor, 297
Collado, Father, O.P., 317
Collège du Pape Adrien VI., Louvain, 114 and *note*
Collin, Abbé, nominated Prefect Apostolic of Japan, 322
Collin de Plancy's "Fiddler of Echternach," 348
Cologne, printing press at, 92; Carthusians, 97; Bible of, 101; University of, 201, 202
Columbus, 302
Commission, Special, for the Royal Divorce, 168 *et seq.*
Commissioners of King Edward VI. at Oxford, 212
Como, province of, 49, 50
"Comparative History of Religions," 186, 187
"Comparative Mythology," 186
"Compendium Historiæ Ecclesiasticæ," 310 *note*, 319 *note*, 331 *note*, 343
Compte Rendu des Travaux de la "Société des Missions Etrangères," 332, 333 *note*, 335, 339, 343
Comuneros, Civil War of the, 122
Conclave on death of Leo X., 127 *et seq.*
Concordat, Cardinal Wiseman's lectures on, 282
Congregation of Rites, decree respecting the invocation "Regina sine labe originali concepta," 232 and *note*
Congregationalists in Japan, 334
"Consolations" of Boethius, 97
Constantinople, art of printing in, 92
Cooper, 155
Copenhagen, "priest-printers" at, 99
Corpus Christi College, Oxford, 163, 180, 192 and *note*
Corre, Abbé, 332
Cortes of Valencia presided over by Adrian VI., 121 *et seq.*
Cosmio, publisher, 230
Cottisford, Dr., University Commissioner, 167
Cousin, Mgr., Bishop of Nagasaki, 329-331 *note*, 339, 34

Coventry, 195, 255
Cox, Dr., 175
Cranmer, Thomas, 168, 174
Creighton, Mandell, Dr., Bishop of London, 53, 81, 88; and chap. v. *passim*
Cremation not found among Palæolithic races, 4; first traces in Neolithic Age, 5; first appears in Spain with introduction of bronze, 6; disappears from Spain in the "Silver Age," 6; general conclusions of Dr. Bauwens, 7; Aryans originated cremation, 7, 8, 24; practised by only a few non-Aryan races, 8; evidence of its prevalence before Aryan separation, 8, 9; Eranians abandon cremation, 8, 9, 13; cremation in Vedic times, 10, 11-12; in Homer and Virgil, 11, 12; Apollodorus of Rhodes, 11; among the Greeks, 12; among the Romans, 12, 13, 18; among Buddhists, 14; in Tibet, 15; among Gauls, Germans, and Scandinavians. 16; traces found in Tunis, 18; in America (island of St. Catherine), 20; among the American Indians, 21; East Indian Archipelago, 22; general conclusions, 24, 25
Croatia, 149
Croly, Dr., 286
Crô-Magnon race, 3
Cromwell, Oliver, and the Bodleian Library, 219
Crook, Mr. T. Mewburn, 55
Croskell, Rev. Robert (afterwards Provost of Salford), 265; account of Dr. Gentilli's mission in Manchester, 265-268
Cross, trampling on the, in Japanese persecutions, 314-315
Crumwell, Thomas, 164, 172, 173
Cunimund, 38, 42
Cunningham, General, 15
Cureton, Dr., 279
Curia, Adrian VI. and, 140
Cusack, M. F., 278 *note*
Cusanus, Cardinal Nicholas, 94
Cyrus, 13

Dahlmann, Father, Joseph, S.J., 317 *note*
Dakhma (a burning place), 9, 13, 14
Dalaber, 167
Dalgairns, Father, of the Oratory, 239
Dalmatia, 149
Da Lucca, Francesco, 99
Damberger, 81
Dancing procession at Echternach, the two great survivals of ages of faith, 344; the road to Echternach, 344-345; no definite indication of the dance until 1553, 346; theory of its pagan origin, 346-347; theory of its Christian origin, 347-348; scene in the parish church, 348-349; the procession itself, 349-352; the spectators, 352; the *Kermess* or fair, 352; the main impression, 353
Dante, 92, 158, 223-224 *note*
Darmesteter, Professor James, Orientalist, 218
D'Assoneville, Jacques, professor of the Sorbonne, 112
De Bonaccursi, Francesco, 99
De Bossi, Andrea, Bishop of Alaria, 93-94
De Foix, André, 123
De Grousselt, Jean, 202
De Gubernatis, 186
De Harlez, Monsignor, Orientalist, 190, 199, 217, 218, 297
De Morgan, Professor, 281
De Morgianis, Lorenzo, 99
De la Chaulx, Ambassador of Charles V., 133, 134
De la Motte Lambert, Monsignor, 319
De Langobardorum gestis, 30
Delft, 106, 107
De Lisle, Mr. Ambrose Phillips, meets Dr. Gentili in Rome, 245; invites him to England, 245, 248; makes his house "Grace Dieu" centre of missionary activity, 251
De Lisle, Mr. Edwin, 246 *note*
Denifle, Father, O.P., 157
Denmark, Cardinal Nicholas Breakspeare's mission to, 65; art of printing in, 92
De Palude, Joannes, 204 *note*
De Quincey, Thomas, 1
De Rubeis, 225
De Rycke, Louise, 109
De Santi, Father Angelo, S.J., 223, 226 *note*, 237
De Schore, Louis, 204

Deshimo, Dutch resident at, protects missioner, 321
Desiderius, thirtieth and last Lombard king, 31, 40
D'Estienne, 7
De Torres, Father Cosmo, S.J., 303
Dêvadâru (deodar or divine tree), 10
Deventer, 107
Deza, Grand Inquisitor of Arragon and Navarre, 120
"Dictionary of National Biography" on Adrian IV., 53, 81, 88
Diego de las Llagas, Father, O.S.F., 318
Dietsche Warande, articles in, on "The Church and the Printing-press," 90 *note*
Dio Cassius, 30
Dionysius of Halicarnassus, historian, 223
Disabilities of English Catholics before Emancipation Act, 246-247
Di San Bartolommeo, Father Paul, Carmelite and Orientalist, 217 and *note*
"Divina Commedia," one of the earliest printed books, 92 *note*
Divorce Question of Henry VIII., English Universities and the, 168 *et seq.*, 182 *note;* supported by Robert Wakefield, 195; University of Louvain and the, 204
Dolman, C., publisher, 277
Domenico da Pistoja, 97
Dominicans, Adrian VI. and, 150; at Oxford, 158, 173, 180; in Japan, 311; martyrs, 314; literary activity, 317
Dominic, Father, Passionist, 253
Domodossola, novitiate of the Institute of Charity, 245, 248
"Donation of Constantine," 80, 82, 84
Dormer, Lady Jane, 209 *note*
Dorpius, Martin, 112
Douay, 182, 205
Drane, Mother Augusta Theodosia, 158 *note*
Dress, Lombard and Anglo-Saxon, 44, 47
Driffield, Rev. W. E., 298
Drouart, Abbé, 337, 340
Dublin [*Review*], Makers of the; Bibliographical details, 269-273; Wiseman attributes first inception to Mr. Michael Quin, 273; irregularity of issue, 274 and *note;* four periods in its history, 274-275; choice of the title, 275; editors of first series, 275-276; financial difficulties, 276-277; O'Connell recommends it to Irish clergy and Bishops, 277-278; Wiseman practically literary editor, 278-279; reference to *Review* in his letters and articles, 279-284; Wiseman on the spirit of the *Review*, 284-285; Dr. Russell's work, 285-286; other contributors, 286-287; style of the articles, 287; the *Review* and the Oxford Movement, 288; lady contributors, 289; illustrations, 289; length of articles, 289; characteristics of the second series under Dr. Ward, 290-292; work of Mr. Cashel Hoey, 293; the chief contributors, 293-294; the spirit of the third series under Bishop Hedley, 294-295; all the articles must be signed, 296; chief contributors, 296-297; new features, 297-298; editor and subeditor, 298; the fourth series under Canon Moyes, 298-299
Dublin Review on Nicholas Breakspeare, 60 *note*
Ducange, 346
Du Chaillu, Mr. Paul, on "The Viking Age," 16
Dugdale, 155
Dulcibello, printer, 225, 230
Duns Scotus, 159, 172, 185
Du Perron, Abraham - Hyacinthe Anquetil, 199, 213 *et seq.*
Durazzo, Archbishop of, 151
Dutch attempt to revive the University of Louvain, 187 *et seq.*
Dutch Pope, the. *See* Adrian VI., chap. v.
Dutch Protestants partly responsible for persecution of Japanese Catholics, 312; trample on the Cross, 315; give help against Christians in Shimabara, 315

Ealhilda, Queen of Myrgingi, 44
Earle, Mr. J. C., 293
Eastern Church, Adrian VI. and, 150
East Indian Archipelago, favours cremation, 22
Eber's "Aegypten," 19

Ecclesiastes, book of, 187, 195, 196
Echternach. *See* Dancing procession at.
Education, Catholic higher, and *Dublin Review*, 290
Edward the Confessor, 48
Edward III., King, 104 *note*
Edward IV., King, 104, 114
Edward VI., King, 174, 176, 177
Egidio, Cardinal of Viterbo, 140, 189
Egyptians, burial customs of, 19
Egyptology, 186
Eïfel, petition of the parish priests of the, 346
Εκλαυσαν, 18
Elend monk of Füssen, 96
Elgin, Friars Preachers established at, by Adrian VI., 150
Elias Levita, 189
Elizabeth, Queen, 174, 178 *et seq.*
Ellenbog, Prior of Ottobeuren, 96
Emancipation, act of Catholic, 246
Embalming in Egypt, 19; in America, 20
Embassy from Japanese princes to the Holy See, 307 and *note*, 330
English Historical Review on the alleged Papal gift of Ireland to Henry II., 81 *et seq.*
English Orientalists at Louvain: Thomas Wakefield, 194-195; Robert Sherwood, 195-196
English Pope. (*See* Adrian IV.)
Ephesus, council of, 235
"Epistola Apologetica Magistri Pauli de Middleburgo ad Doctores Lovanienses," 190
Eranians and cremation, 8, 9, 13-14
Erasmus, 107, 108, 110, 142, 143, 161, 162 *et seq.*, 191-194, 204 *note*
Erfurt, monastery of St. Peter at, 96; university at, 90, 100, 101, 102
Eskil, Archbishop of Lund, 65, 84
Eton College, 161
Eucharist, Holy, English Lutherans and the, 166; English Zwinglians and the, 175
Eugenius III., 61 *et seq.*, 87
"Europeanization" of Japan, 338-339
Exposition of bodies among Eranians and Turanians, 13, 14; in Greater Tibet, 15; in America, 21
Exquiros, Battle of, 123
Eyestein, Prince of Norway, 64

Fagius, 174
Falk, 90 *note*, 98
Faröe Islands under Metropolitan See of Nidaros, 64
Feast of the "Finding of the Christians" established by Pope Pius IX., 326, 329
Felitzin quoted, 7
Felten, Dr. J., 155 *note*
Ferdinand, Archduke of Austria, 149
Ferdinand the Catholic, 117
Ferdinand, Duke of Wirtemberg, 194
Fergusson, 7
Fernandez, João, 303
Ferrand, Father Claudius, on irreligion in Japan, 340-341
Fetish worship, 187
Feyerabend, Maurus, 96
Ffoulkes, E. S., 288
Finlayson, Mr., 289
Fishacre, Richard, 158
Fisher, Blessed John, 162 *et seq.*, 165, 170-171
Fitzsimons, Mrs., 289
Fleming, Robert, 161
Flesh-stripping, 5, 14, 20, 23, 24
Florence, Dominican press at, 97; "priest-printers" of, 99; republic of, 149
Folklore, 187
Fonte Buono, monastery at, 98
Forcade Abbé (afterwards Bishop of Samos and Vicar Apostolic of Japan), 321, 322, 331 *note*
Forman, 165
Formby, Father H., 288, 296
Formby, Rev. Matthias, 265
Fornier-Duplon, M., 321
"Fosse," Japanese method of torture, 314
Fowler, John, 199, 208
Fox, Edward, Bishop of Hereford, 168
Foxe's "Book of Martyrs, 168, 207
Fox, Richard, Bishop of Winchester, 163, 192
Franciscans, Adrian VI. and, 150; at Oxford, 158 *et seq.*, 173, 180; in Japan, 310; martyrs in Japan, 310, 314, 323

Francis I., King of France, 123, 125, 127, 130, 134, 139, 148, 192
Frank, 191 *note*
Franks, 39, 46
Frederick Barbarossa invades Italy, 69 *et seq.;* struggle with Adrian IV. as regards homage, 71 *et seq.;* crowned at Rome by Pope, 74; quells a riot at Rome, 74; renews his quarrel with Pope, 84 *et seq.;* second invasion of Italy, 86 *et seq.;* 134
Frederick, Elector of Saxony, 146
Free, John, 161
Fréjus, ancient codex of, 225
French Revolution and Louvain, 187
Freya, 33, 41, 43
Friars and the English Universities, 158
Friars Minor, Church at Louvain, 209 *note.*
Fribourg University, 154
Frisians, 43
Froës, Father, S.J., 317
Froude, J. A., 169, 170
Fūkū, Agatha Kataoka (Sister Margaret), 328
Funeral customs:
  Bodies buried in sitting or crouching position, 5, 6, 15,
  Burial of animals (favourite horse, etc.) with bodies, 23
  Burial of objects (weapons, food, etc.) with bodies, 5, 6, 10, 11, 16, 23
  Cannibalism, 22, 23
  Flesh stripping, 5, 14, 20, 23, 24
  Interments beneath the house floor, 6, 12
  of Africa, 22
  of America, 20, 21
  of Australia, 22
  of early Aryan conquerors of India, 10
  of East India Archipelago, 22, 23
  of Egyptians, 19
  of Eranians, 13-14
  of Gauls, Germans, Scandinavians, and Visigoths, 16
  of Greece and Rome, 11-12
  of Israelites, 17-18
  of Little Tibet, 15
Funeral customs *continued:*
  of Phœnicians, 18
  Slaughter of attendants (slaves, etc.), 21, 22, 23
  Widow-burning, 10-11, 23
Funeral pyre, building of described by Apollodorus of Rhodes, Homer and Virgil, 11 and *note*
Funus, 9
Furfooz race, 4
Furlong, Father, 251, 253, 258-259, 264, 266, 267
Future life, various burial rites and the, 24
Fūyū, Maria (Sister Julia), 328
Fylde, 36

Galileo in Japanese controversy, 336
Gamau Udji-sato, daimyo of Aidzou, 307 *note*
Gambara, priestess of the earth, 33, 41
Gamut, origin of names for the notes of the, 32 *note*
Gardiner, Mr. S. R., 177 *note*, 178 *note*
Gardiner, Stephen, Bishop of Winchester, 168, 173, 177
Garibald, Duke of Bavaria, 41, 42, 48
Garibaldi, etymology of name, 48
Garrett, Thomas, of Magdalen College, Oxford, 167
Gasquet, Abbot, O.S.B., 81, 109 *note*, 155, 164 *note*
Gauls, ancient, practise both cremation and inhumation, 16
Geerts, Dr., and the siege of Shima-bara, 315
Genealogical table of royal personages mentioned in connection with Pope Adrian VI., 115 *note*
Genoa, 136, 144, 149
Gentili, Dr. Aloysius, sketch of his career, 243-246; first impressions of London, 250; first work in England, 250-251; visits Oxford, 251-252; vegetarian and total abstainer, 254 *note*; sudden death of, 257; tribute by Frederick Lucas, 257-258; great mission at Manchester, 261-268; testimonial from Manchester clergy, 263-265
Geoffrey, Pierre, 223
George, Duke of Montenegro, 97
George, Duke of Saxony, 146

Gepidæ, 38, 39
Gerard, Cardinal, attack on, 68
Germaine, wife of Ferdinand the Catholic, 119
Germans use cremation, inhumation, and water burial, 16
Gertrude, mother of Adrian VI., 105, 106
Gesenius, 189 *note*
"Geshikuya," Catholic hostel for university students at Tokio, 341
Geudens, Right Rev. Abbot, 57, 58 *note*
Ghibellines, 145
Giggs, Margaret, 205
Giles, Robert, 209 *note*
Giles, Wenthana, 209 *note*
Gillow, Mr. Joseph, 209 *note*
Ginnell, L., 81
Giovanni d'Albona, Canon of Loreto, 226
Giraldus Cambrensis, 80
Girard, Abbé, 322, 323
Girona, Bishop of, 124, 125
Gladstone, Mr. W. E., on the "Medieval Universities," chap. vi. *passim;* 186
Glaire, 225
Godiva, Lady, procession at Coventry, 255
Godocus Badius, 112
Goerzee, Adrian VI. receives benefice of, 111
Golanda, 34 and *note*
Gonell, 163
Gonville Hall, Cambridge, 177
Gordon, General, Cardinal Manning and, article on, 296-297
Goths, 39
Goto Islands, 327, 332
Gradenigo, Luigi, Venetian ambassador, 141
Grammar schools founded in reign of Edward VI., 212
Grant, Dr., Bishop of Southwark, 271
Greece and Japan, parallels between, 300-301
Greek studies neglected at Universities after Reformation, 182
Green, Rev. George, 265
Green, J. R., 38 *note*, 157 and *note*
Greenland under Metropolitan See of Nidaros, 64
Gregory the Great, Pope, and conversion of the Lombards, 40-41; and Lombard language, 46; and Rogation days, 224; and Litany of Loreto, 230; and heathen usages, 347
Gregory VII., Pope, 88
Gregory XIII., Pope, and Nicholas Saunders, 208; receives Japanese embassy, 307; gives Jesuits charge of Japanese missions, 310
Gregory, XVI., Pope, and the "Italian missioners," 248-249; erects vicariates in Korea and Japan, 320, 321
Grey, William, 161
Grimm, J., 8, 11, 42
Grocyn, 161
Groote, Gerard, 106
Gros, Baron, 322
Grosseteste, Robert, Bishop of Lincoln, 155 *note*
Gross-Prüm pilgrimage to Echternach, 348
"Groto solitos sive Speculum Conscientiæ" of Arnold of Gheilhoven, 95-96
Gründhof, 345
Gryphius, 194
Gubbins, Mr., on the persecution of Japanese Christians, 313
Gudeoc, 34
Guelphs, 145
Gueric, Abbot, 236
Guérin, Admiral, 322
Guido d'Arezzo and the names for the notes of the gamut, 32 *note*
Gulielmus Parisiensis, 235
Gunther, Abbot of St. Peter's, Erfurt, 96
Gunthorp, John, 161
Guttenberg, John, 91

Hakodate, Vicariate of, 329, 330
Hall's "Society in the Elizabethan Age," 183 *note*
Hamard, 7
Hamburg, Metropolitan See of, 63
Hamilton, Dom Adam, O.S.B., 221
Hammer, Adrian IV. and the building of the cathedral of, 64-65
Hanlon, Bishop, on the funeral customs of Little Tibet, 15
Hanmer collection of medals at St. Bede's College, Manchester, 151 *note*
Harald, King of Norway, 64
Harding, Thomas, Regius Professor of Hebrew at Oxford, 199, 205-206

Harper, Father, S.J., 239
Harpsfield, Nicholas, Regius Professor of Greek, 206
Harris, Alice, 209
Harris, Dorothy, 205 *note*, 209
Harris, John, secretary to Sir Thomas More, 205 *note*, 209
Hartmann, L. M., 36, 42, 51
Harvest, article in the, on the "Dancing Procession," 354
Healy, Dr., Archbishop of Tuam, 297
Hearne, Father Daniel, of St. Patrick's, Manchester, 267
Hebbelynck, Mgr. Ad., Rector Magnificus of the University of Louvain, 200, 219-220 and *notes*, 221
Hebrew studies in the Middle Ages, 182, 188 *et seq.*
Hedley, Dr., Bishop of Newport, and the *Dublin Review*, 275, 293, 295-298
Hefele, Bishop, 85 *note*
Heidelberg, 190, 191
Helinandus, 236
Helmechis, 38
Hélyot, 59
Hem, convent at, 96
Hengist and Horsa, 33 *note*
Henry I., King of England, 54
Henry II. and Adrian IV., 53; sends gifts to Adrian on his election, 77; controversy respecting gift of Ireland to, 79 *et seq.*
Henry VI., King, 160
Henry VIII., King, and Adrian VI., 126, 127, 128, 130, 148; and English Universities, 165, 168 *et seq.*
Henxey Hall, Oxford, 208
Heraklês, 12, 187
Hermann of Nassau, 191
Hermanus Contractus, 235
Hermolaus Barbarus, Venetian Ambassador, 108
Herodotus, 214
Herschel, Sir John, 159 *note*
Hertha, Teutonic goddess worshipped by Lombards, 30
Heruli, 35, 36
Hetzel, 190 *note*
Hetzius, Dietrich, Flemish Secretary to Adrian VI., 152 *note*
Heveren (Flanders), 206
Hideyoshi (or Taiko-Sama) issues Edict against Christians, 307, 309, 343
Hierarchy, creation of Japanese, 329
Higdon, Dr., Dean of Cardinal College, Oxford, 167
"High Church" system, origin of, 181
Himmelstein, ecclesiastical writer, 223
Hodgkin, T., "Italy and her Invaders" quoted, 26-27, 30 *note*, 51; on legends Lombard migrations, 35, 36; rejects the story of Rosamund, 38 *note;* on the Germanic origin of Langobards, 42 *et seq.*
Hoffmann, Professor, on the work of Portuguese missions in Japan, 316-317
Hofler on Pope Adrian VI., 120 *note*, 130 *note*, 150 *note*, 153
Holstein, 36
Holy House of Loreto, 225-227
Holy See allows English Catholics to attend the Universities, 154; letter of Leo XIII., "Ad Anglos," 154
Homage, Papal right to, recognised by German law, 72; submitted to by Frederick Barbarossa, 72 *et seq.*
Homer on building of funeral pyre, 11
Hondemius, Johannes, 235
Honorius of Autun, 236
Honours, list of Oxford, 201 and *note*
Horse or hounds, burying favourite, 23
Hosius, Cardinal Stanislaus (Papal Legate at Council of Trent), 207
Huber, 176
Hugh of St. Victor, 235
Hugo, Abbot Charles Louis, 57 and *note*, 58 and *note*, 59
"Humanism," 161, 164
Humphrey, Duke of Gloucester, gifts to Oxford University Library, 211-212
"Hundred Years' War" between Empire and Papacy, 74-75
Huns, 26
Hutchison, Father, on the antiquity of the Litany of Loreto, 224
Hutton, Father, 251
Huxley, Professor, 186
Hyde, Thomas, Orientalist, 214

Ibor, 33 and *note*, 34
Iceland under Metropolitan See of Nidaros, 64; first printing-press in, 99
Idiota, 235, 236
Ieyasu, founder of the Tokugawa Dynasty, 301, 311, 313, 343
Illustrated Catholic Missions, 15, 329, 332
Imbert, Mgr., 320
Immaculate Conception, Adrian IV. and the, 88
Incas of ancient Peru, 20
Indifference, religious, in Japan, 339-340
Indulgences denounced at Cambridge, 165
Inge, Prince of Norway, 64
Ingoldstadt Prayer-Book and the invocation "Auxilium Christianorum," 228
Ingvaeones, 45
Inhumation practised universally by Palæolithic races, 4; prevalent among Neolithic races, 5; the only method employed during the "Silver Age" in Spain, 6; abandoned by Eranians, 9; prior to cremation among Greeks, 12; practised in Rome, 12; employed by Chinese, 14; practised by Greeks, Germans, Scandinavians, and Visigoths, 16; Semites essentially a burying race, 16 *et seq.*; the Jews bury their dead, 17, 18; the exclusive funeral rite of the Egyptians, 19; in America, 20; practically universal in Africa, 21, 22; general conclusions, 24, 25
Innocent II., Pope, 72
Inquisition, 189, 190 *note*; in Japanese controversy, 336
Institute of Charity: foundation and constitutions, 241-243; and Prior Park College, 248, 250; Pope Gregory XVI. blesses the English missioners, 248-249; instructions of Rosmini to English missioners, 249; first work in England, 250-252; four great spiritual works, 252-253; the work of the "Itinerant Missionaries," 253-255; chronological catalogue of missions, 255-256, death of Dr. Gentili, 257-258; sketch of career of Father Furlong, 258-260; further developments, 260
Interdict, Rome placed under, by Adrian IV., 68
Ireland: alleged grant to Henry II., 53; statement of the controversy, 79 *et seq.*; state of Ireland in Adrian IV.'s time, 82 *et seq.*; Cardinal Wiseman, suggestions for articles in *Dublin Review* on, 281-282
Ireland, quoted on, Richard Fishacre, 158
Irish College, Rome, Dr. Gentili and the, 245
Irish Immigration and the "Second Spring," 240
Irish Monthly. *See* Russell, Father Matthew, S.J.
Iron Crown, Frederick Barbarossa receives, 69
Irreligion in Japan, 336-341
Isabella, Infanta, 116
Isidore of Thessalonia, 236
Islam, 89
Isle of Man transferred from province of York to that of Nidaros, 64
Israelites and inhumation, 17, 18
"Italian," meaning of the term, 27
Ives, Dr. (converted Bishop of the Episcopal Church of America), 293

Janssen, 90 *note*, 100, 102
Japan: the Catholic Church in—
I. The ancient Church, 300-318; interest of the subject, 300-301; discovery of Japan, 302; work of St. Francis Xavier, 302-304; why St. Francis Xavier left Japan, 305; success of Jesuit missions, 306-307; Japanese Embassy to Pope Gregory XIII., 307; sketch of Japanese Government, 308; Hideyoshi persecutes the Christians, 309; various religious orders in Japan, 310; first martyrs, 310-311; mistaken zeal of native Christian princes, 311; peace under Ieyasu, 311; cause of the great persecution, 312; sufferings of the Christians, 312-315; massacre of Shimabara, 315; extinction of Christianity in Japan, 315, 316; labours of

early missioners in behalf of philology and literature, 316-318
II. The Second Spring, 318-331; "Société des Missions Étrangères," 319; Japanese wrecked off Philippines, 319-320; Missioners get to Liu Kiu Islands, 320-322; United States get admission to Japanese ports, 322; Missions opened at Yokohama and Nagasaki, 323; canonization of twenty-six Japanese martyrs, 323; "the finding of the Christians," 323-326; overthrow of the Shogunate, 327; fresh persecution, 327-328; introduction of nuns, 328; native priests and nuns, 328-329; development of ecclesiastical government, 329; erection of Heirarchy, 329, 330; amenities between Mikado and Holy See, 330; list of bishops, 331
III. Future of the Church, 332-343; recent returns, 332, 333; four hindrances, 333; rivalry of the sects, 333-335; the anti-Catholic press, 335-337; materialism and indifferentism, 338-341; hope for the future, 341-343
Japanese practise cremation, 8
Jars, funeral, 6, 17, 18
Jealousies of religious orders in the East, 310
Jehu, 69
Jenks, Rowland, 180
Jeremiah, 17
Jesuits, 180; in Japan, chap. xii. *passim*
Jesus College, Cambridge, 160
Jevons, Mr. F. B., 25
Jevons, Professor W. S., on Roger Bacon, 159 *note*
Jewell, Bishop, 177
Jimmu, founder of the present Japanese dynasty, 308
Jingo, Empress, 301
Joannes de Westphalia (John Wessel of Gröningen), 190 and *note*
Johan, son of King Sverker of Sweden, 65
Johannes, Geometra, 236
John of Austria, 228
John IV., Duke of Brabant, 187, 201
John of Salisbury, 67, 78, 79, 80, 81
John of St. Giles, 158
John XII., Pope, 133
John XXII, Pope, 80
Jolliffe, Henry, Dean of Bristol, 209 *note*
Jones, Sir William, Orientalist, 216
Jordan, Blessed, General of the Dominicans, 158
Joseph II., 348
Journal of the German Oriental Society quoted, 316-317
Julius II., Pope, 114
Jungmann, Professor B., 81
Justinus Michoviensis on the Litany of Loreto, 223, 233

Kagoshima, 303
Karlby, great burial ground at, 5
Kelly, 81
Kempe, John, Archbishop of Canterbury, 211
Kempe, Thomas, Bishop of London, 211
Kilwardby, Cardinal Robert, Archbishop of Canterbury, 158, 185
King's College, Cambridge, 160
Kingship among Lombards and Anglo-Saxons elective, 47-48
Kirishitan Bugyo or Japanese Christian inquisitor, 314
Kissinger, Sixtus, first introduced printing into Naples, 98
Knights Hospitallers of St. John, 76, 144 *et seq.*
Knoll on the Litany of Loreto, 233
Ko, Augustine, 321
Koburger's press, 100
Koeckebacker, 315
Koegel, 37
Koelhoff, chronicle of, 92
Kolb on the Litany of Loreto, 233
Koppes, Mgr., Bishop of Luxemburg, 352
Kraus, Professor, 143 *note*
Kuenen, 186
Kumbha (funeral urn), 11

Ladak (Little Tibet), Bishop Hanlon on the funeral customs of, 15

Lady Margaret Chair of Divinity at Cambridge, 162
Laguerre, Admiral, 322
Lake Dwellers, 4, 5, 7
Lambeth, 166
Lamissio, legend of, 34, 41
Lamy, Professor, T. J., 110 *note*, 193, 200, 219-220 and *note*, 297
Laneau, Monsignor, 319
Lanfranc, 49
Langius, 193
Langton Stephen, Archbishop of Canterbury, 155 *note*
Language of Lombards, 45 *et seq.;* Japanese, 318
Lanigan, 81
"Lankosargi," 29
Lantenai, Abbey of, 97
Latham, Dr., 37, 45
Latimer, Hugh, Bishop of Worcester, 166, 176
Latimer, William, 161
Laucaigne, Abbé, 327, 331 *note*
Laud, Archbishop, 181
Laudabiliter, so-called Bull, 79, 81, 82 *note*, 83 *note*
Launay, Abbé, 319 *notes:* 324-326, 343
Laurentius, 226
Laurentius Holbeccius, Hebrew dictionary of, 195
Laws of the Twelve Tables, 12
Layton Dr., 172
"Leabher Breac," 8th century litany of Our Lady, 225, 231
Lee, Dr. F. G., and the invocations of the Litany of Loreto, 234-235
Legh, Dr., 172
Legnano, Battle of, 87
Leibnitz, 341
Leicester, Robert Dudley, Earl of, Chancellor of Oxford, 180, 181
Leipsic, "priest-printers" at, 99
Leland, 183
Lent (the time of sadness), kept by the survivors of early Japanese Christianity, 325
Leonhard, Abbot, of Ottobeuren, 96
Leonora, Infanta, 116
Leo X., Pope, 120, 124, 140, 142, 143 and *note*, 189
Leo XIII., 55, 76, 143, 208 *note*, 222, 232 and *note*, 233, 329
Lepanto, Battle of, 228, 232
Lepitre, Abbé A., on Adrian VI., 112 *note*, 120 *note*, 153
Leprosy in Japan, 332
Lerinda, "priest-printers" at, 99
Leturdu, Abbé, 321
Lever, 176
Lewis, Mr. David, 293
Lewis, Mr., estimate of Roger Bacon, 159 *note*
Libois, Abbé, 322
Lichfield, Archdeacon Richard, 211
Liège, 152 *note*
Lienhardt, Abbot, 57
Ligneul, Abbé, on the anti-Catholic press of Japan, 335; replies to Professor Tetsujiro, 337; his work prohibited, 337; value of his work, 338
L'Imolese, 224 *note*
Linacre, Thomas, 161, 203
Lincoln, Bishop of, and the Chancellorship of Oxford University, 157
Lincoln College, Oxford, 160
Lincoln, Robert, 220
Lingard, Dr., 81, 286
Linköping, Synod of, 65
Litanies, four allowed for public recitations, 222; the term "litany," 223, 231
"Little Bilney," 165-166
Liu-Kiu Islands attached to Vicariate of Korea, 320-321; attempts to open them up for commerce, 320; Abbé Forcade reaches Nafa, 321; terrible sufferings of missionaries, 322-323
Liutprand, 32, 40, 43, 48
Lochorst, 151
Lockhart, Father, 239, 241 *note*, 242 and *note*, 244, 246, 247, 249, 252, 299
Logroño, 124
Lollards, 166
Lombards or Langobards, a savage horde from Pannonia, 26; name Germanic, 28; closely connected with Anglo-Saxons, 28; Roman civilization and culture have prevailed among them, 28-29; classical Roman writers and early history of, 29-30; native legends and early history of, 30, 32 *et seq.;* Paul, the deacon's "History of the Lombards," 31, 32; origin of name *Langobardi*, 33; had serf population, 33, 34; often known as "Bardi," 36; meaning of word

"Langobard," 37; all Germanic traces in Italy not Lombardic, 39; Lombard influence not limited to modern Lombardy, 40; two centuries of Lombard supremacy, 40; conversion of the Lombards, 40-41; wealth of folk legends, 41-42; probably of Low German origin, 42 *et seq.*; the Lombard language, 45 *et seq.*; the political institutions, 47 *et seq.*; dress of, 44, 47; influence on architecture, commerce, and science, 49-50; modern Lombardy, 50; bibliography of, 51
Lombard Street, 27, 49
London, first printing-press in, 92
Longland, Bishop of Lincoln, 168
Lope de Vega, 92
Lopez, Father, S.J., 317
Lorenz, Bishop of Würzburg, 93
Lorenzo d'Aquila, 98
Loreto, History of the Litany of, its unique position among Catholic devotions, 222-223; meaning and history of the word "litany," 223-224; opinions as to the age of the litany of Loreto, 224-225, 237; ancient litanies to Our Lady, 225-226; uncertainty as to the existence of our present litany before the latter half of sixteenth century, 226-228; probably officially recognised in Rome after the Battle of Lepanto, 228-229; two theories as to the origin of our present litany, 229-230; authorship of the existing litany, 230-231; summary of the investigation, 231-232; history of certain additions to the litany, 232; analysis of the invocations in our litany, 233-235; table showing patristic and Scriptural sources of the invocations, 235-236; opinion of Fr. De Santi, S.J., 237; books to be consulted, 237
Lorraine, Duke of, 58 *note*
Lothair, Emperor, 72
Loudon, Dr., 167, 172
Loughborough, Leicestershire, 251, 253
Louis, King of Hungary, 149
Louis VII., King of France, 62, 87
Louis XI., King of France, 107
Louvain and Oxford. *See* Oxford and Louvain.
Louvain, two English scholars and the beginning of Oriental studies in. *See* "Oriental Studies in Louvain."
Louvain, University of, 104, 105, 107; discipline, 107; faculties, 108; and Renascence, 108; other references, 150, 154, 166, 182 *note*. *See* also chaps. vii. and viii. *passim*.
Louvet quoted on persecution in Japan, 314, 328, 329, 343
Low German character of the Lombards proved, 43-44
Lübeck, "priest-printers" at, 99
Luca di Penna, 86
Lucas, Claudius, 58 *note*
Lucas, Mr. Frederick, on Dr. Gentili, 257-258
Lucca, Republic of, 149
Lucius II., Pope, 62 *note*
Lucretia, 223
Lund, Metropolitan See of, 63
Luther, 127, 139, 145, 165, 166, 168, 189, 190
Lutheranism at the Universities, 165 *et seq.*
Luther legend, 90, 100 *et seq.*
Luxemburg, Grand Duchy of, 344
Lycurgus condemns cremation, 12
Lyly, William, 161
Lynch, Archdeacon, 80
Lyons, Carthusian Monastery at, 98

Macarius, monk of Cettinje, 97
Macerata Prayer-Book and invocation, "Auxilium Christianorum," 228, 230 *note*
MacGeoghegan, 81
MacMurrough, King of Leinster, 83
Maeda, Father, on the needs of the Church in Japan, 336, 338, 341-343
Magdalen College, Oxford, 160, 161, 174, 175
Magdeburg, Premonstratensian convent at, 98
"Magistri Comacini," 49
Magi, tradition respecting, 214; bodies transferred from Milan, 85 *note*
Mainz, 92, 99, 146
Makpelah, burying-place of the kings, 18
Mallet, 174

Malone, Father Sylvester, 81, 83, 89
Malta, 145
Manchester Guardian quoted, 52, 156
Manning, Cardinal, 239, 271, 286, 288, 290, 294, 296
Manuel, Don Juan, Imperial Ambassador at Rome, 132, 133
Marathon, 12
Marco Polo, 302
Marforio, statute of, 142
Margaret, Countess of Richmond, 162
Margaret of Austria, 115
Margaret, Princess of York, 104, 105, 111
Maria, Infanta, 116
Marienthal, 96 *note*
Marius, 13
Market Weighton Reformatory, work of printing-press at, 260
Marmery, J. Vellin, 159 *note*
Marnas on religion in Japan, 343
Marseilles, 136
Marsh, Adam, O.S.F., 159
Marshall, Mr. T. W., 279, 288, 293
Martin, Abbé, 155 *note*
Martinez, Pedro, S.J., first resident Bishop of Japan, 311, 331 *note*
Martin V., Pope, 187, 199, 201
Martorelli on the date of the Litany of Loreto, 226
Martyrs, Japanese, number of, 314, 315; canonization of, 323, 327
Mary, Queen, 174, 176 *et seq.*
"Mater Boni Consilii," origin of invocation, 232
Materialism in Japan, 338-341
Matthæus Hadrianus, 191, 193 *et seq.*
Matthew Paris, 80, 158
Mauringa, 33, 34, 36, 41
Maximilian, Emperor, 115, 349
May devotions introduced by Fathers of Charity, 253, 258
McCarthy, Mr. James, on funeral jars in Siam, 6 *note*
Meaney, Rev. Joseph, 265
Mechlin, 115, 116, 188, 206
Medals of Adrian VI., 151 *note*
Medici, Cardinal, 129
Melanchthon, 168, 172, 174, 193
Melchior, Abbot, 96
Mendez Pinto, 302
Merry, Dr., Rector of Lincoln College, Oxford, 211
Merton College, Oxford, 159, 180, 206
"Metalogicus" of John of Salisbury, 78, 79, 81
Methodists in Japan, 334
Metz, "priest-printers" at, 99
Mey, Vice-Chancellor of Cambridge University, 181
Mexicans practise cremation, 8
Midon, Mgr., Bishop of Osaka, 330, 331 *note*
Migne, Abbé, 299
Milan, Duke of, 149
Milan stands out against Frederick Barbarossa, 86; monastic presses near, 97; the secular "priest-printers" of, 99
Mill, John Stuart, and the *Dublin Review*, 290
Mirama, convent at, 98
Mirandola, Pico della, 189
Missions Catholiques of Lyons quoted, 300-301
Missions, preaching of popular, in England, 253
Missions, remarkable, given by Fathers of Charity (1844), Coventry, 255; (1846), Seel Street, Liverpool, 255-256; (1845-1846), Manchester, 261-268
Mivart, Mr. St. George, and the *Dublin Review*, 293, 296
Modrone, 50
Molanus, 104 *note*, 206 *note*, 208
Möller, 42
Monasteries, suppression of the, its effects on the Universities, 172 *et seq.*
Mongolians, 14
Monro, Professsor D. B., Vice-Chancellor of University of Oxford, 197
Mont-César, castle on, 104, 116 *note*
Monte Cassino, Abbey of, 31, 32
Montpellier, University of, 177
Montserrat, monastic press at, 98
Monza, 40
Morales, Sebastian, S.J., Bishop of Japan, 331 *note*
Moran, Cardinal, 81, 297
Moravia, 36
More, Sir Thomas, 161, 162, 192

note, 203, 204 *note*, 205 and *note*, 206, 209
Morice, Father, O.M.I., on "Carrier Sociology and Mythology," 21 *note*
Moringus, 104 *note*, 109
Moroni, 224, 225
Morris, Father John, S.J., 280, 288
Morris, Father W. B., of the Oratory, 81
Motais, Abbé, 297
"Mounds" of America, 4, 19-20
Moyes, James, Canon, and the *Dublin Review*, 275, 298-299
Much on origin of Langobards, 42, 43
Mugheir, burial-ground at, 16
Mühlerthal, the, 344, 345
Müller, Professor Max, 9, 186
Müller, Sophus, 25
Mullinger, 155, 163, 171, 177, 182
Muratori, 78, 223 *note*
"Murder as a Fine Art," 1
Murray, Dr., 286, 293
Murray, Mr. D., 310 *note*, 312, 313, 315, 343
Murri, Vicenzo, on the date of the Litany of Loreto, 226
Mutsuhito, Mikado, 327, 330

Naçus, 13
Nafa, capital of Liu-Kiu Islands, 321
Nagasaki, 306, 309, 312, 322-326, 329-331
Namur, monastery at, 98
Naples, first introduction of printing into, 99
Napoleon I., 85, 145
Narses, 38
Navarre, attempted conquest by Francis I. of France, 123
Neanderthal race, 3
Nego, Girolamo, 142
Neolithic Age, 4, 5, 7
Nepi, 71, 73
Nepotism, suppressed by Adrian VI., 140
Nève, Professor Félix, 182 *note*, 188, 190, 192 *note*, 195, 196
New College Oxford, 206, 208
Newman, Cardinal, 238-241, 248, 252, 253, 268, 279, 281, 286, 288
Nice, 124, 136
Nicholas, Auguste, on the antiquity of the Litany of Loreto, 224
Nicholas, Cardinal of Aragon, 78 *note*
Nicholson, Mr. E. B., 213 *note*
Nicolaus de Lyra, 189
Nidaros, erection of Metropolitan See of, 64
Nobunaga and Christianity, 306, 307, 309
Nonconformists in England before Catholic revival, 247
Norgate, Miss Kate, 81, 83 and *note*
Northcote, Dr., on the antiquity of the Litany of Loreto, 224
Norway, Cardinal Nicholas Breakspeare's mission to, 63 *et seq.*
Notre Dame, Church of (Antwerp), Adrian VI., Dean of, 111
Nuns sent to Japan, 328
Nüremberg, printing-press at, 92; Diet of, 147

Oakeley, Canon, 280, 288, 293, 295
Obatala, 187
Ober Ammergau, Passion Play at, 344
Occo, Adolf, 93
O'Connell, Daniel, 267; and the *Dublin Review*, 269, 273, 276-278, 283, 289
Oem, Dr. Florencius, Syndic of Utrecht, 126
Oesch, G. A., and musical setting of Litany of Loreto, 234 and *note*
O'Hagan, Mr. John (afterwards Mr. Justice), 287
Order of the Child Jesus send nuns to Japan, 328
Orientalism among Catholic scholars before the Reformation, 188 *et seq.*
Orientalists, International Congress of, at Geneva, 307 *note*, 318
Oriental studies in Europe, what they owe to Du Perron, 213 *et seq.*
Oriental studies in Louvain: Orientalism and theology, 186 *et seq.*; Oriental studies always held a high place at Louvain, 187; Orientalism among Catholic scholars before Reformation, 188-189; began in the printer's office, 189 *et seq.*: earliest work in the lecture-room: Matthæus Hadrianus, 191

et seq.; foundation of the Trilingual College, 191 *et seq.;* first teaching under the auspices of the Faculty of Arts, 193; two Englishmen hold chair of Hebrew, 194-196; Robert Wakefield, 194-195; Robert Sherwood, 195-196
Origen, 235
Origo gentis Langobardorum, 30
Orkneys transferred from province of York to that of Nidaros, 64
Orlando di Lasso and the Litany of Loreto, 230 *note*
O'Rourke, King of Breiffny, 83
Ortiz, provisor of the Bishop of Calahora, 124
Oscott College, 238, 271
Osouf, Mgr., received by Mikado, 330, 331 *note;* on Japanese press, 335-338; on religious indifference in Japan, 340
Ostia, 137
Ostrogoths, 26
Ottobeuren, Abbey of, 96
Oviedo, Antonio, S.J., Bishop of Japan, 331 *note*
Oxford and Louvain: address of the University of Louvain at tercentenary of Bodleian Library, 197 *et seq.;* Oxford two centuries older than Louvain, 200-201; the influence of the Church on the development of both Universities, 201-202; like Oxford, Louvain was a University of many colleges, 202; connections between them, 203 *et seq.;* Erasmus closely connected with both, 203; Oxford men who found refuge at Louvain at the Reformation, 204 *et seq.;* history of the Bodleian, 209-213; Avestic studies at Louvain owe much to the Bodleian Library, 213 *et seq.;* the labours of Du Perron, 213-218; kindness of the Bodleian librarians to Louvain scholars, 220-221
Oxford, first printing-press at, 92; Dr. Gentili at, 251-252
Oxford, University of, 107, 156, 157 and *note*, 158; the "New Learning" and, 161; work of Churchmen at Oxford, 163; epidemics at, 164; Lutheranism and, 167 *et seq.;* Royal divorce and, 168 *et seq.;* effect of the suppression of the monasteries on the, 172 *et seq.;* Chancellorship of Bishop Gardiner, 173; Peter Martyr lectures at, 175; Catholic party during Elizabeth's reign at, 178 *et seq.*

Pace, Richard, sent by Henry VIII. on mission to Rome, 132
Pacheco, Doña Maria, 122
Pacomius, 97
Padua, University of, 177, 191
Pagani, Father, Rosminian, 244, 249-251, 254, 255, 261
Pagi, 66
Palæolithic races, 3-5, 19
Palermo, 75
Palestrina and the Litany of Loreto, 230 *note*
Pallu, Mgr., 319
Palmer, J. F., 286
Pampeluna, siege of, 123
Panizzi praises article on *Dublin Review*, 279
Pannartz, Arnald, 94
Papal infallibility and *Dublin Review*, 290, 292
Paquot, 193
Paris, University of, 57, 107, 157 *note*, 158, 170 *et seq.*, 177, 190, 192, 201-203
Parker, shipowner, 208
Parkinson, Mgr. Henry, Rector of Oscott College, 271
Parkinson, Dr. Robert, 208
Parma, Carthusian press at, 97
Parsis of Bombay, 13, 215
Paschal II., Pope, 63
Pasquino, statue of, 129, 142
Passionists, congregation of the, 243, 253, 258
Pastor, Dr. Ludwig, 128 *note*, 143 *note*, 164 *note*
Patras, 59
Paul II., Pope, 93
Paul the Deacon quotes *De Langobardorum gestis*, 30; sketch of his life, 31; connection with St. Bede, 31-32; and origin of names of the notes of the gamut, 32 *note;* preserves the old saga of Lombard migrations, 32, *et seq.*, 42 *note;* on similarity of Lombard and Anglo-Saxon dress, 44, 47; and Lombard songs, 46

Paulsen, 157 *note*
Pavia, 40
Peacham, 183
Peckham, Archbishop, 159
Perelli, John, gives titles of two different litanies of Our Lady, 227
Perne, 177
Perry, Commodore, 322
Persecutions in Japan, first persecution probably due to Spaniards, 310; second due in great part to English and Dutch, 311-316; third (1868), 327-328
Peter Baptist, Father, O.S.F., 310
Peter de Valence, 165
Peterhouse, Cambridge, 159
Peter Lombard, 27, 49, 112 *note*, 172
Peter Martyr, 121, 174, 175, 177, 204
Peter of Blois, 77
Peter, Prefect of Rome, and Arnaldo da Brescia, 70
Peter's pence first raised in Norway by Nicholas Breakspeare, 64; Henry II. promises an annual tribute of, 82
Peter the Patrician, 30
Petitjean, Abbé Bernard, 324-326; (afterwards Bishop of Myrophitus and Vicar Apostolic of Japan), 329, 331 *note*
Petre, Hon. and Rev. W. (afterwards Lord), 296
Petrus Cellensis, 235, 236
Pfulf, Father, S.J., 81
Philip II., 189, 205
Philippus, Abbot, 236
Phœnicians, burial customs of, 18
Phos-spun (hereditary undertaker), 15
Pictet, Adolphe, "Origines Indo-Européennes" cited, 8; on burial rites in pre-Vedic times, 11-12
Pied Piper of Hamelin, 348
"Pietas Oxoniensis" quoted, 210, 211, 212, 221
Pietro da Pisa, 97
Pilkington, Bishop of Durham, 179
Pineda, 196
Pirckheimer, 191
Pitra, Cardinal, 346, 347
Pitts, 196
Pius V., Pope, and the title, "Auxilium Christianorum," 228, 229, 232
Pius IX., Pope, 232, 323, 325, 326, 327, 329
Pius X., Pope, and Adrian VI., 153
Place names, note on spelling of Japanese, 303 *note*
Plague in Rome (1523), 138, 149
Plantin, 189
Platæa, 12
Platform burial among the Sioux Indians, 21
Pliny, 12, 35 *note*
Plochmann and Irischer edition of Luther's works quoted, 102
Pluralities, Adrian VI. and, 111 *et seq.*
Plutarch on inhumation, 12
Pole, Cardinal, 178
Political institutions of Lombards, 47 *et seq.*
Pollard, Professor, 146
"Polycraticus" of John of Salisbury, 67, 78, 79
Pondicherry, 214
Poor scholars at English Universities, 160, 161, 173, 183 *et seq.*; at Louvain, 202
Pope, the survivors of early Japanese Christianity inquire after, 325
Pope, Sir Thomas, 177
Porto Marino, 136
"Postillæ," 102
Potken, Adam, priest of Xanten, 101
Power, Senator (of Ottawa), 297
Prague, University of, 107, 202
Prâsavya rite, 10
Predil Pass, Lombard trek across the, 40
Premonstratensians, connection of Nicholas Breakspeare with, 57 *et seq.*
Press, anti-Catholic, in Japan, 335-338
Press, Oriental, at Louvain, 190
Printing-press. *See* "The Church and the Printing-press": in the fifteenth century, 92-93, 94; much used by religious orders, 94 *et seq.*
Prior Park College, the Fathers of Charity and, 248, 250, 259
Processions with litanies, rise of, 224
Procopius, 35
Protestantism and the Universities, 165 *et seq.*
Protestant missions in Japan, 334-335
Prüm, procession at, 348
Ptolemy, 30, 43
Public schools and Universities, 161

Pulleyn, Robert, Archdeacon of Rochester and the first English Cardinal, 62 *note*
Puritanism, 178, 180 *et seq.*
Pusztas of Hungary, 36
Pyramids, 19
Pythagoreans bury their dead, 12

Quakers (American) in Japan, 334
Quarant' Ore introduced into England, 253, 258
Queen's College, Cambridge, 160
Quin, Mr. Michael J., first editor of the *Dublin Review*, 273, 275, 276
Quirino, Vincenzo, 116

Raby, Mr. Richard, on Adrian IV., 53, 67, 89
"Race chemistry," 27
"Race philosophy," 27
Raffaele and Leo X., 143 *note*
Ralph de Diceto, 80
Ramridge, Dr. John (Joannes Ramiger), 206
Ramsgate, plundering of monastic library at, 195
Rastell, Elizabeth, sister of Sir Thomas More, 206
Rastell, John, printer and lawyer, 206
Rastell, Judge William, 205-207
Ratchis, King of the Lombards, 31, 38 *note*
Ratcliffe College, Leicester, 260
Ravenna, Adrian IV. and Frederick II. quarrel about the archbishopric of, 86
Reform, Adrian VI. and, 139 *et seq.*
Reformation and English Universities, *vide* Universities, English, and the Reformation, chap. vi., 154-185
Reform, University, in modern times a reversion to pre-Reformation ideals, 184-185
Regesta of Adrian VI., loss of, 152 *note*
Regina Cœli, Abbey of, Louvain, 104
"Regina Sacratissimi Rosarii," origin of invocation, 232
"Regini sine labe originali concepta," origin of the invocation, 232
Reinhold von Tassel (Chancellor of Frederick Barbarossa), 85 and *note*
Religion and politics, relation of, *Dublin Review* and, 290
Religious orders and printing-press, 94 *et seq.*
Renan, 186
Renascence, Adrian VI. and, 142 *et seq.*
Rendal, Professor, 9
Renzano, 151 *note*
Republican party at Rome struggle with Adrian IV., 67-68; invite Frederick Barbarossa to Rome, 69
Retreats in colleges according to method of St. Ignatius, 250
Reubner, Ernestus, 57
Reuchlin, 189, 191, 194
Reusens, Professor E. H. J., 112-113 *note*, 116 *note*, 153
Revolution and Louvain University, 202
Rheims, English scholars at, 181
Rhodes, Island of, invested by Turks, 144; capitulation, 145
Ribaud, Abbé, on parallels between Japan and Greece, 300-301
Richard, Abbot of St. Alban's, 56
Richard of St. Lawrence, 236
Richard of St. Victor, 236
Richards, Mr., printer, 277
Richardson and Son, publishers, 277, 283
Ridel, Mgr., Vicar Apostolic of Korea, 330 *note*
Riera, Father Raffaele, S.J., 226, 229
Riesi, 153
Rig Veda, on funeral ritual of early Aryan conquerors of India, 10-11; rite for inhumation and cremation, 11-12
Rimmer, Rev. John, 265
Rinolfi, Father, 251 and *note*
Robertson, Canon James Craigie, historian, 121
Robertson, Professor J. B, 281, 286
Rodgers, John, 177 *note*
Rodriguez, Father João, S.J., 317
Rogation Days, origin of, 224
Rogerus de Insula, Chancellor of Diocese of Lincoln, 210
Roger Wendover, 80
Roland, Cardinal (afterwards Pope Alexander III.), 85
Roman collar introduced into England by Fathers of Charity, 253 *note*

Romanes Lecture, 1892: Mr. W. E. Gladstone on the History of Universities, chap. vi. *passim*
Rome, introduction of printing, 94; convent of Sant' Eusebio, 98; progress of printing at Rome during fifteenth century, 99; "priest-printers" at, 99
Roncaglia, Diet of, 69, 86
Rosamund, story of, 38 and *notes*, 39 and *notes*, 42
Roskell, Rev. Richard B. (afterwards second Bishop of Nottingham), 265
Rosmini-Serbati, Antonio, founds Institute of Charity, 241-243; interested in conversion of England, 243; accepts Aloysius Gentili, 245; instructions to Fathers going to England, 249
Rosse, Lord, telescope of, 286
Rostock, 95
Rota, supreme tribunal of Rome, 138
Rothari, laws of King, 30, 40, 43, 48
Rousseau, Abbé, on conversion of the Ainus, 333
Royal Library of Dublin, 225
Rudolf, Bishop of Scherenberg, 93
Rugians, 39
Rugiland, 34, 36
Rupert, Abbot, 235
Russell, Dr. Charles (President of Maynooth College) and the *Dublin Review*, 285-286, 293
Russell, Father Matthew, S.J., on the history of the *Dublin Review*. *See* chap. xi. *passim*
Russell of Killowen, Lord, 287
Russian Church, Orthodox, 89; in Japan, 333-334
Ryder, Father, of the Oratory, 239

Salerno, University of, 156
San Paolo fuori le Mura, 137
"Santa Casa," 226
Santa Maria dell' Anima, Church of, at Rome, 151
Sanuto, Marino, Venetian historian, 151
Sapareu (professional corpse-butcher), 24
Saragossa, 136
Saraph, note on its meaning in 1 Kings xxxi., vv. 12, 13, and Jer. xxxiv., v. 5, 17
Satow, Mr. Ernest, 318
Saul, 17
Saunders, Nicholas, Regius Professor of Canon Law at Oxford, 199, 207
Sauren, Herr Josef, on the Litany of Loreto, chap. ix. *passim*
Savelli, Paolo, Prince of Albano, 226, 229, 236
Savona, Augustinian convent at, 97
Adrian VI. at, 136
Saxons, 39, 43
Sayce, Rev. Professor, 9
Scandanan, Isle of, 32, 35
Scandinavia, 35 and *note*, 40, 51
Scandinavian Church and Cardinal Nicholas Breakspeare, 52, 62-66; in Japan, 334
Scandinavians use cremation, inhumation, and water burial, 16
Sceafa, Anglo-Saxon hero, 44
Schafarik, 97
Schenkbecker, 99
Scherer, 224
Schiner, Cardinal, 130
Schlegel, Professor, 307 *note*
Schmidt, Lud., 36
Schmitt Leonhard, 37, 42
Schneider-Beringer, 224
Schrader, O., "Prehistoric Antiquities of the Aryan Peoples," 7, 25; on the Lake Dwellers, 7; on cremation and inhumation in Vedic times, 11-12
Schussenried, monastic press at, 98
Scipios, 12
Scoringa, 33, 35
Scott, Dr. Cuthbert, Bishop of Chester, 209 *note*
Second Spring: A Forgotten Chapter of the: origin of the phrase, 238; influence of Oxford movement on, 238-239; influence of Irish immigration on, 240; influence of the "Italian Mission," 240; Rosmini's "Institute of Charity" (foundation and constitutions of), 241-243; continental interest in the conversion of England, 243; the career of Dr. Gentili, 243-246; state of Catholics in England previous to 1835, 246-247; synchronisms between the work of Newman and Rosmini, 248; the coming of the "Italian mission," 248-250; first work of the Rosminians, 250-255; chronological catalogue of mis-

sions given by Fathers of Charity, 255-256; death of Dr. Gentili, 257-258; career of Father Furlong, 258-260; account of the great mission in Manchester (1845-1846), 261-268
Sects in Japan, 333 *et seq.*
Secular "priest-printers," 98 *et seq*
Secundus, Abbot of Trent, 30
Sedgwick, 175
Seebohm, 155
Σῆμα (a mound), 10
Semitic races, burial customs of, 16
Senates of Universities and Reformation, 182
Septuagint, 18
Sergius I., Pope, 225
Serqueyra, Bishop Luiz, S.J., 311, 318, 331 *note*
Sessa, Duke of, 150 *note*
Seville, 196
Sheehan, Rev. W. J., 265
Sheldonian Theatre, Oxford, 197
Shetlands transferred from province of York to that of Nidaros, 64
Shimabara, siege of and massacre at, 315, 320
Shintoism disestablished in Japan, 330 *note*
Shirwood, Robert, 195-196, 199, 203
Shogunate system of government, 308; overthrow of, 327
Shrewsbury, John, Earl of, 286-287
Siam burial customs, 6 *note*, 24
Sidotti, Father John Baptist, S.J., 316
Siena, Republic of, 149
Signini, Father, 251
Sigurd, Prince of Norway, 64
"Silver Age" in Spain, 6, 12
Simeon Metaphrastes, 235
Siret, MM. Henri and Louis, their discoveries in Spain, 5, 6
Sixtus IV., Pope, 128 *note*
Sixtus V., Pope, and the Litany of Loreto, 229; receives Japanese embassy, 307
Slav, printed books, 97
Smith, Doctor of Canon Law at Cambridge, 165
Smith, Mr. James, 276
Smith, Dr. Richard, 174, 175, 199, 204-205
Smith, Dr. William, second Archbishop of St. Andrews and Edinburgh, 276
Smith, Dr. William, 223
Smith, Rev. Fr. Thomas, 265
Smith, Sir Thomas, 183
Snelling, Fr. William, O.S.B., 161
Snorro, 64
"Société des Missions Étrangères" and missions to Japan, 319-341, *passim*
"Society for the Propagation of the Gospel" in Japan, 334
Solon, 12
Somaschi, Order of the, Clerks Regular of, 139
Somerset, Duke of, Protector, 174, 175
Sontheim, convent of discalced Franciscans at, 98
Sopewell, convent of, 96
Sorbonne at Paris visited by Adrian VI., 117
Sotelo, Bishop Luis, O.S.F., 315, 331 *note*
Spalding, Dr. Bishop, of Peoria, 296, 297
Speakman, Miss, M.A., and Abbey of St. Rufus, 60 *note*
Spedding, James, 184 *note*
Spelman, 155, 163
Spiegel, Orientalist, 217
Spoleto, dukedom of, 40
Spolverini, Mgr., Papal Internuncio at the Hague, 352
Spooner, William, publisher, 276
"Spy race," 3
S'rēphah, note on its meaning in 2 Chron. xvi., v. 14, 17
St. Albans, Abbey of, 55, 56, 96
St. Ambrose, 236 *note*
St. Anselm, 49, 235, 236
St. Augustine, 60, 61, 235
St. Avitus, 224
St. Basil, 235
St. Bede, 31, 32, 155 *note*
St. Bernard, 236
St. Bonaventure, 225, 235, 236
St. Catherine, island of, contains traces of cremated remains, 20
St. Charles Borromeo, 267
St. Dominic, 158, 240, 253
St. Edmund Rich, Archbishop of Canterbury, 157, 185
St. Ephrem of Edessa, 200, 219 and *note*, 235, 236 and *note*
St. Epiphanius, 235, 236

St. Francis of Assisi, 240, 253
St. Francis Borgia "coaches" Emperor Charles V. in mathematics, 115
St. Francis Xavier on the curiosity of the Japanese, 301 *note;* lands at Goa, 302; meets two Japanese at Malacca, 302; lands at Kagoshima, 303; the Prince is favourable to Christianity, 303-304; speaks highly of Japanese character, 304; work during his two years stay, 304; death, 306
St. Frideswide's Church, Oxford, 168
St. Gaetano, 139
St. Gertrude's Church, Louvain, 205
St. Gregory Nazianzen, 235
St. Gregory of Nicomedia, 236
St. Gregory Thaumaturgus, 235
St. Gregory the Great and pagan practices, 347. *See* also Gregory the Great
Ste. Gudule, Church of, at Brussels, 130
St. Ignatius Loyola, 123, 139, 150, 312
St. Ildephonsus, 235
St. Isidore of Seville, 37
St. Jerome, 186, 235
St. Jerome Emilian, 139
St. John Damascene, 235, 236
St. John, Father, of the Oratory, 239
St. John, Miss, 289
St. John's College, Cambridge, 171 *et seq.*
St. John's College, Oxford, 177, 179
St. Joseph, devotion of the survivors of early Japanese Christianity to, 325
St. Joseph Hymnographus, 236
St. Laurence Justinian, 236
St. Mamertus, 224
St. Mary's Church, Oxford, 168, 210
St. Mary's Church, Utrecht, Adrian VI., canon and treasurer of, 111
St. Mary Major, Church of, Rome, 149
St. Methodius, 235, 236 *note*
St. Michael, church of, at Louvain, 209 *note*
St. Norbert, 59 *note*
St. Olaf, King, 64
St. Paul of Chartres, nuns of go to Japan, 328
St. Paul of the Cross, 243
St. Peter Damian, 236
St. Peter's, Anderlecht (Brussels), Adrian VI., Canon of, 111
St. Peter's, Douay, 205
St. Peter's, collegiate church at Louvain, 207
St. Pius V., Pope, 152
St. Quentin (Maubeuge), Adrian VI., Provost of, 111
St. Rufus, monastery of, at Avignon, 58, 59, 60, 79
St. Simon Stock, 236
St. Stephen Harding, 155 *note*
St. Thomas Aquinas, 112
St. Thomas of Canterbury, 78
St. Ursula's Convent, Louvain, 205
"St. Vitus's dance" and the Dancing Procession of Echternach, 347-348
St. Willibrord, 155 *note;* chap. xiii., *passim*
St. Yrier de la Perche, monastery of, near Limoges, 98
Stapleton, Dr. Thomas, 180, 185
Statue of our Lady, first carried in public procession at Coventry, 255
Stavenger, John, Bishop of, created Metropolitan, 64; extent of his jurisdiction, 64
Steichen Abbé, 337, 340, 343
Stockholm, art of printing in, 92
Storey, John, Blessed, 199, 208, 212,
Strabo, 29
Stradlynge, Thomas, 209 *note*
Strasburg, Carthusian press at, 97
Strauss, 186
Strongbow, Earl of Striguil, 83
Subiaco, Abbey of, 94
Suliman II., 127, 144-145
Sulla, 13
Suppression of the monasteries, 172 *et seq*, 195
Surat, 214-215
Sûs, discovery of cremated remains at, 18
Sutri, 71
"Suttee" or widow-burning not practised in Vedic times, 10-11
Swabians, 39, 43
Sweden, Cardinal Nicholas Breakspeare's mission to, 65
Sweynheym, Konrad, 94
Swinburne, Mr., and the story of Rosamund, 39 and *note*

Swiss Protestants in Japan, 334
Sylva, Father, S.J., 317
Synod, First Provincial of Japan, 329
Syriac version of New Testament, 189

Tablet, 154 *note*, 257-258, 271
Tacitus, 29, 43
Taiko-Sama. *See* Hideyoshi
Takeyama (Justus Ucondono) exiled to Philippines, 312
Tarleton, A. H., on Adrian IV., chap. iii. *passim*
Tarragona, 136
Tato, 35
Taylor, Dr. Isaac, 9
Temporal power of the Pope, 84
Tetsujiro, Professor Inoue, attack on Christianity, 336
Thatcher, Professor, O.J., 81, 82 *note*, 89
Theatines, congregation of the, 139
Theodolinda, Queen, and conversion of Lombards, 41, 42
Theodoricus Martinus Alostensis (Thierry Martens of Alost), 191
Theophilus, schismatic Patriarch of Alexandria, 150
Thijm, Professor Alberdingk, 155 *note*, 297
Thinx (an assembly), 48
Thiofred, Abbot, 347
Thomas à Kempis, 95, 106, 107, 190
Thompson, Mr. Edward Healy, 293
Thoth, 187
Thsathsa (small image), 15
Thucydides, 12
Θύμβος, 10
Tiara in Adrian IV.'s time, 52 *note*
Tiberius, 29
Tiele, 186
Tierney, Rev. M. A., historian, 276
Times, the, and the only English Pope, 60 *note*
Tiptoft, Earl of Worcester, 161
Tivoli, 74
Toledo holds out against Charles V., 122
Tortona, 69
Totu, Melania Kustugi (Sister Mary), 328
Towers of Silence, 14
Tractarian movement and the *Dublin Review*, 288
Transactions of the Japan Asiatic Society, 313, 315
Transactions of the Royal Society of Canada on "Carrier Sociology and Mythology," 21 *note*
"Traveller's Song," 44
Travers, "Ecclesiasticæ Disciplinæ Explicatio," 181
Treaties with Japan, 322
Tree-burial of America, 21
Trelawney, Sir Henry, Bart., 250
Trent, "priest-printers" at, 99; Council of, 111, 148, 207
Tresham, 175
Trilingual College at Louvain, 191 *et seq.*
Trinity College, Cambridge, 171, 174, 176
Trinity College, Oxford, 177
Trollope, "Memoir of the Life of Adrian IV.," 53
Trondhjem (formerly Nidaros), 64
Tübingen, 194
Turanians, 14
Turks and Adrian VI., 143 *et seq.*, 149
Turner, Rev. William (afterwards first Bishop of Salford), 265
Turrecremata, Cardinal, 99
Tuscany, 40
Tyburn, 208
Tyler, Professor E. B., 4
Tynwald, etymology of word, 48 *note*

Uberto, Archbishop of Milan, 86
Ullathorne, Dr., Bishop of Birmingham, 297
Ulm, printing-press at, 92
Umbria, 40
Un-gen (or On-sen), Christians tortured in the caves of, 314
Unitarians in Japan, 334
United Presbyterians of Scotland in Japan, 334
United States first opens up Japan, 322
Universities, English, and the Reformation: greatness of their loss to Catholicism, 154-155; for the most part ecclesiastical in foundation and development, 156 *et seq.*; the work of the friars, 157 *et seq.*; character and discipline, 160;

foundations of the fifteenth century, 160-161; "Humanism" at Oxford and Cambridge, 161 *et seq.*; Lutheranism at, 165 *et seq.*; the question of the royal divorce, 168 *et seq.*; the plundering and enslaving of the, 171 *et seq.*; the Commission of Visitation, 174 *et seq.*; the effect of Queen Mary's reign on, 176 *et seq.*; Elizabeth and the, 178 *et seq.*; struggle between Anglicanism and Puritanism at, 180 *et seq.*; summary of the results of the Reformation in the, 181 *et seq.*; on the studies, 182-183; on college life and discipline, 183; on the class of students, 183; the trend of modern reform, 184-185; bibliography, 185
Unsworth, Rev. Edward, 265
Unsworth, Rev. Thomas, 265
Urakami Islands, 327
Urban VIII., Pope, and Japanese martyrs, 323
"Utopia," Sir Thomas More's, 204 *note*
Utrecht, 105, 109, 150, 153
Uyeno museum in Tokyo, 314-315

Valens, Didaco, S.J., Bishop of Japan, 331 *note*
Valenziani, Professor, on Japanese embassies to the Holy See, 307 *note*
Valerius, Andreas, 104 *note*, 188, 191, 192, 195, 205
Valignani, Father Alessandro, S.J., 307
Valladolid, monastic press at, 98
Vandals, 26, 33, 41
Van den Gheyn, Père, S.J., on cradle land of Aryans, 9 *note*
Van de Steere, Chrysostom, 58
Van Enkenvoert, Cardinal William, 131, 150, 151
Van Even, Ed., 190 *note*
Varuna, 187
Vasselon, Henri, S.M.E., Bishop of Osaka, 331 *note*
Vatican Library, 227
Vaughan, Cardinal, 62 *note*, 95, 274-275, 293, 295, 296, 298, 299
Vaughan, Dom Roger Bede (afterwards Archbishop of Sydney), 293
"Vedas," Louvain and the, 187
Velleius, Paterculus, 26, 29
"Vendidad," MSS. of the, 213
Venice, Minorite press at, 97 liturgical works printed at, 97; monastic press at, 98; "priest-printers" at, 98; Adrian VI. and, 135, 144, 149
Venturinus, Prior of Savona, 96
Vermigli (Peter Martyr), 121, 174, 175, 177, 204
Vernulæus, 104 *note*
Vespucci, Provost of the Duomo at Florence, 98
Via Appia, 12
Vienne, 224
Vigroux, Abbé, 332
Villaler, Battle of, 122
Villefranche, 136
Villiers de l'Île-Adam, Grand-Master of Knights Hospitallers of St. John, 144, 145
Vincenza, "priest-printers" at, 99
Virgil on building of funeral pyre, 11
Visconti, 50
Visigoths, 16, 26
Vitelli, Cornelio, 161
Viterbo, Adrian IV. at, 76
Vitoria, 123-125, 137
Vives, Louis, 131, 147, 163, 164
Vogt, Albert, on Catholicism in Japan, 354
Von der Linde, 90 *note*, 94
Von Pflugck-Harttung, 81
Von Stolzenberg-Luttmersen, 36
Vorstman, 196

Wackerbarth, Rev. Francis, 251
Wadstena, convent of St. Bridget at, 98
Waghenare, Petrus, 57, 58
Wakefield, Robert, Orientalist, 182 and *note*, 194, 195
Wakefield, Thomas, Professor of Hebrew at Cambridge, 183, 195
Ward, Dr. William George, 239 connection with *Dublin Review*, 270-272, 274, 281, 288, 290-294, 295, 298
Ward, Mrs. Humphrey, 186
Ward, Mr. Wilfred, 275
Warham, Archbishop of Canterbury, 163, 170
Warka, burial-ground at, 16
Warwick, Duke of Northumberland, 174, 175
Washington University, 154

Waston, 163
Water burial among Germans and Scandinavians, 16; among American Indians, 21
Watford, 55
Weapons, utensils, food, etc., buried with bodies, 23
Webb, Abbot John, of Coventry, 196 *note*
Werner, Dr. K., 155 *note*
Werner, Rolewinck, the Carthusian, 91
Wesley, John, 247
Wessel, John, of Gröningen, 190
Wessel, John, of Oberwesel, 190 *note*
West, Bishop of Ely, 166
Westergaard, Orientalist, 217
Westmoreland, Earl of, 209 *note*
Westrum, 36
White, Father, S.J., and so-called Bull "Laudabiliter," 80
White, Sir Thomas, 177
Whitgift, Dr. (Archbishop of Canterbury), 179, 181
Whittaker, Rev. J. F., 265
Widsith, "Traveller's Song" attributed to, 44, 46
Wilberforce, Mr. W. H., 271, 293
William of Croÿ, Marquis of Chièvres, 117, 121
William II., Abbot of St. Rufus, 60
William II., King of Sicily, quarrels with Adrian IV., 75
William of Ockham, 159
William the Conqueror, 83
Wilson, Robert, 199, 202
Wimbledon, Battle of, 38 *note*
Wimpheling, Jacob, 91-92
Winchester, archives of, 82 - 83; School, 161, 206, 208
Winnili, 32, 33, 35-37, 41, 42, 51
Wiseman, Cardinal, 241; connection with *Dublin Review*, chap. xi., *passim*
Witte, Bernhard, 91
Wittemberg, 193
Wives, slaves, buried with husband and master, 23
Wodan (or Godan), 33, 37, 41, 43
Wolgemuth, engravings of, 100
Wolsey, Cardinal, 126, 128, 130, 131, 138, 148, 163, 167, 170, 205
Wood, Antony, historian, 155, 204
Wootton, Nicholas, Dean of Canterbury, 202 *note*
Worms, Diet of, 146
Wycliffism, 165

Ximenes (Jimenes), Cardinal, 118 *et seq.*, 152, 189, 192

"Yih-King," Louvain and the, 187
Yokohama, dedication of chapel at, 323
Yoritomo and *Shogunate* system of government, 308, 327
York, See of, loses jurisdiction over Orkneys, Shetlands, and Isle of Man, 64
Young, 174, 175

Zarathushtra or Zoroaster, 13, 214 *et seq.*
Zedekiah, 17
Zeuss, 36, 42
Zimmer on cremation and inhumation in Vedic times, 11
Zimmermann, Father A., S.J., on the English Universities and the Reformation, chap. vi. *passim*, 192 *note*, 195
Zinna (or Cenna), monastery at, 98
Zoroaster, 13, 214 *et seq.*
Zwinglians, 169, 175
Zwolle, 107, 190

R. AND T. WASHBOURNE, PATERNOSTER ROW, LONDON.

Lightning Source UK Ltd.
Milton Keynes UK
UKHW012356140119
335568UK00012B/1230/P